The Descendants of Hugh Howell

Janel Marie Howell & Jeannette Phethean

HERITAGE BOOKS
2006

HERITAGE BOOKS
AN IMPRINT OF HERITAGE BOOKS, INC.

Books, CDs, and more—Worldwide

For our listing of thousands of titles see our website
at
www.HeritageBooks.com

Published 2006 by
HERITAGE BOOKS, INC.
Publishing Division
65 East Main Street
Westminster, Maryland 21157-5026

International Standard Book Number: 978-0-7884-1459-3

TABLE OF CONTENTS

FOREWORD

In 1996, when I first ventured into the maze of the Internet, I hoped to be able to find some Howell cousins who might have information to help me learn more about my elusive great grandfather. For months, I struggled, but found little help, until one night, just before Christmas, I received an email from someone who wrote: " I am related to Hugh and Samson Howell of the Hope area, Warren County, New Jersey. Are you related? Hopefully we can exchange information. Janel Howell." My shouts of excitement may have been heard a mile away. I quickly wrote back, sending what little information I had.

Within a short time, we had become email junkies, seldom letting a day go by without writing a few words of encouragement to each other. I'd met Blanche Donovan, who was searching for this family, right in my area, but she and her husband had recently left Florida for Arizona. Now the circle had widened to three, and in a short time, others were found, and the information flew back and forth across this country and Canada.

A year later, when we began to sort it all out, Janel and I discussed the possibility of putting together a book about our family. The idea grew, and the book in your hands is the result. Without the help and sharing of a lot of dedicated Howell researchers , we could never have done it. All of us have worked on this research for several years, and I hope you will be pleased with this effort to put it all together.

These people have been generous with their time and research, and we'd like to thank each one of them: Kathy Armstrong, John Buchanan, John Butler, Albert M. Compton, Barbara Crane, Bette Glenn Cunningham, Blanche Thompson Donovan, Jeanne Laundrie Fugina, Marfy Goodspeed, Carl Howell, Evan Howell, Robert Howell, Phyllis Troyer Hunt, Mildred law, Albert E. Lee, Nancy Shaver Lytle, Douglas A. Mitchell, Robert G. Moore, Louise Ponce, Denise Prince, Debbie Reynen, Jane Ellen Rich and Jackie Rudolph. You will find their addresses throughout the book.

We know that the material we've included may be incomplete, and possibly inaccurate, but we didn't want to delay publishing it, since we feel that delay may prevent its ever being published. Who among us is getting any younger? If you find errors or omissions, please let us know about them. If you find misspelled words or names, we'd like to know about them, too. We've tried, with many proof readings and many corrections, to be correct, but fingers don't always follow thoughts.

I'd like to add a few words of tribute to Janel Howell, who has so inspired me with her dedication to this project. I admire her, and love her as I would a daughter. She has encouraged me to continue with this, though there were many times I was ready to quit. It was she who walked the cemeteries in Warren County, New Jersey, photographing grave markers of our people, and she who read miles of microfilm, copying Howell information. She was the one who collected the birth, marriage and death certificates and the obituaries from the New Jersey newspapers. Most importantly, though, it was she who found and brought together all the people named above, and asked them to share their knowledge of this family. We both hope this book will be helpful to all Howell family members.

Janel Howell

Jeannette Phethean

FIRST GENERATION

1. **Hugh HOWELL** was born on 17 April 1659 in Wales. Little is known about him, except for a few family stories, which must be accepted as mostly imaginary. The story of the capture of Hugh and a brother by Captain Kidd and his pirate crew has been accepted by other family members through the years, but a brief study of history shows the impossibility of its being true. Since the Howell name is essentially Welsh, Hugh's birth in Wales can be believed, but Captain Kidd didn't go into the pirate business until about 1696, while he was on a privateering expedition off the Barbary Coast. (Kidd was well-known in New York as a wealthy shipping owner.) By that date, Hugh was a man, and probably well-established in New Jersey.

Additionally, the whereabouts of the unnamed brother have never been found, and so we think that Hugh Howell came to this country by some other means, possibly as a soldier in the British army. Although there were several Howell families in New Jersey, none of them seems to be linked to Hugh Howell.

Another source claims relationship to Edward Howell, one of the early settlers of Long Island. The problem with this idea is that Hugh is said to have been born in Wales, and Edward and his sons were all in Boston, Massachusetts by 1639, having come there from England some time before that. These accounts say Hugh's mother was probably a Sayre, the first wife of **Edmund Howell**, the youngest son of **Edward Howell**. Miss Sayre reportedly was born in the colonies, died soon after her marriage to **Edmund Howell,** and is not known to have had any children at all.[1] **Edmund Howell** married a second time, to **Sarah Judson** in 1664, and had two daughters and a son. In addition to these facts, the name Sampson does not appear in any generation, to the present time, of the **Edward Howell** family.

Primary sources which mention Hugh Howell are few, the first being a deed given to **John Holcombe**, dated 1705, for land on the Delaware in the present city of Lambertville, New Jersey. Holcombe's tract included a tract formerly belonging to **Richard Bull** which was bounded on the south "by lands formerly belonging to **Hugh Howell**, now owned by **Robert Eaton**." Though no trace of Eaton's transfer of this property can be found, this, and other deeds related to it, places **Hugh Howell** on the shore of the Delaware River prior to 1703.

In 1732, Hugh was listed among the debtors to the estate of **John Severns** of Trenton, New Jersey. [2](It is interesting to note that this same document names four other Howell men, any one of whom could have been the "unnamed brother"

---

[1]George Rogers Howell, The Early History of Southampton, L.I., New York, (1887; reprint, Bowie, MD: Heritage Books, Inc., 1989) 319.
[2]William Nelson & A. Van Doren Honeyman, New Jersey Archives, Documents Relating to the History of the State of New Jersey, (1918; reprint, Bowie, MD: Heritage Books, Inc., 1992) 424 - 426.

mentioned above. All were debtors to the same estate. They were **David Howell, Daniel** and **Thomas Howell** of Amwell, and **Christopher Howell**, the latter probably a descendant of the above **Edward Howell** of Long Island. There was also a **John Howel** named.)

An inventory of the estate of **John Holcombe**, of Amwell, Hunterdon County, New Jersey, dated September 24, 1743, names **Hugh Howell** and his son Sampson among the estate's debtors. [3]If we assume that Hugh and his son Sampson lived in Amwell, too, there may well have been a connection to those other Howells, named in the 1732 Severns estate.

On November 30, 1745, Hugh's name appeared on the Public Auction list of **John Runyon** of Rock Hill, Somerset County.[4] This may represent the settling of his estate, as he had died on 14 September, 1745.[5]

Hugh may have had other children, and at least one New Jersey history indicates Sampson was his second son. We have found nothing to substantiate this claim. A recent book, "The Howells of New Jersey, Virginia, Ohio and Points West" by Richard E. Wallace, Robert W. Cameron and Carmen J. Finley, traces the descendants of a **Hugh Howell**, probably born in New Jersey in 1720, and, while they found papers claiming a relationship between their Hugh and the Hugh who fathered Sampson, they were not able to prove that claim. [6] We offer no evidence in support of or against a possible sibling for our Sampson.

The question of Hugh's wife remains a mystery. Some sources say there is a marriage on record for a **Hugh Howell** and **Marie Ton**, in England, but this marriage appears to have taken place many years prior to the birth of the **Hugh Howell** who is Sampson's parent. So we have left that open for discussion, and further research.

Though the name of his wife is not known, **Hugh Howell** had one known son:

+2 i. **Sampson HOWELL.**

---

[3]ibid., 241.
[4]ibid., 409 - 410.
[5]Tombstone in Baptistown, New Jersey Cemetery, still readable, with birth and death dates.
[6]Richard E. Wallace et al, The Howells of New Jersey, Virginia, Ohio and Points West, (Bowie, MD: Heritage Books, Inc., 1994) 3 - 4.

SECOND GENERATION

2. **Sampson HOWELL** was born on 17 December 1718 in Hunterdon County, New Jersey. He was a farmer, said to have been the first of the Howells to settle in Hope, Sussex County, New Jersey. (Sussex County was divided into two counties on 20 November 1824; the southern part is now Warren, while the north retained the name Sussex.) [7]

Sampson Howell had a reputation as a hunter in the region of the Jenny Jump Mountain, where he built and operated a sawmill. He was also well-known as a preacher, and maintainted excellent relationships with the Indians in the area, who would frequently come to visit, and stay until they had been fed.

Sampson was a preacher of some standing, and a member of the Church of England. This may explain his apparent lack of involvement in the Revolution, since none of his sons seems to have served in the Army. It may also explain why two sons moved their families to Canada about 1801. A contributing factor in this reluctance to take up arms may also have been Sampson's loyalty to King George, the titular head of the Church of England.

Sampson didn't leave a will, so far as is known, but he did sell much of his property to his sons Levi, Sampson and Jonah. Presumably the two sons in Canada received their inheritances in the form of cash.

Sampson Howell may have come to Sussex County with Samuel Green and his family. They settled in Hope Township, as did Sampson. He supplied lumber for the Moravians who were building a settlement in the county, and operated a large farm there. His first log cabin was built on Jenny Jump Mountain, about 1758, and a later home was built farther east in 1760. About 1778, he built a large two-story stone home, which is still being used.

Most of the books which mention Sampson at all also refer to the pirate story in connection with his father, Hugh. We found, too, that these books, give incomplete lists of his children and their spouses. One of our correspondents is descended from a **Mary Lavinia HOWELL**, born about 1752, and died in 1831, who was buried in the Dark Moon Cemetery in Marksboro, New Jersey. This lady was married to **Isaac Lanning**, who was born in 1748 and died on 30 August 1811. Since the couple had a son whose middle name was Howell, perhaps there was a daughter. We cannot prove otherwise at this time.

Sampson HOWELL was married to **Jane VANDERBILT** about 1745 in Sussex County, New Jersey. Jane VANDERBILT was born in 1722, possibly in New Jersey. She died on 14 August 1805 in Hope, Sussex County, and was buried in

---

[7]George Wyckoff Cummins, History of Warren County, New Jersey, (New York: Lewis Historical Publishing Co., 1911), 25.

Union Cemetery, Hope, Warren County, New Jersey Sampson HOWELL and Jane VANDERBILT had the following children:

+3	i.	**Levi HOWELL.**
+4	ii.	**Samson HOWELL.**
+5	iii.	**Jonah HOWELL.**
+6	iv.	**William HOWELL.**
+7	v.	**Garret HOWELL.**

Sampson HOWELL died on 3 February 1803 in Hope, and was buried in the Union Cemetery there.

Some researchers have added a daughter, Elizabeth, to the family, with a birth date about 1768, and a death date of 1 July 1842. We have found no proof of this child's existence. One person thought she had married **Abraham NEWMAN**, but Abraham NEWMAN married **Elizabeth BURGE**, as proved by a deed of Abraham NEWMAN to Joseph NEWMAN for "two plots of land descended to Elizabeth NEWMAN, one of the heirs of **Peter BURGE**."[8]

---

[8]Sussex County Courthouse, Newton, NJ. Deed Book CA, p. 513, Recorded 13 August 1814.

THIRD GENERATION

3. **Levi HOWELL** was born in 1746 in Hunterdon County, New Jersey. Levi lived all his life in Warren and Sussex counties, a farmer, and a very religious man from the tone of his letters to his son, Sampson, and to his brothers, William and Garret, in Canada. In one of these letters, he wrote that his sons, Levi, Jr. and George, had begun "drinking spirits" which was a source of great distress to him. (Oddly enough, later on, some of the Howell men operated a distillery on their property.) This was probably a close-knit family, since his letters indicate that he made the long journey to Canada, on horseback, to visit his brothers more than once.

Levi purchased his property from his father, and sold it some of it to his son Levi in 1810, as is confirmed by deeds recorded in Warren County. Some of this property later was sold to Levi Junior's children.[9] Levi sold 150 acres, part of the 400 acres his wife inherited from her father, Samuel Green, to Nicholas Albertson, his son-in-law.

The land for the Union Church Cemetery was donated by Levi Howell and John Albertson. The earliest services were held in Albertson's barn, near where the old church stood. Later they worshipped in John Howell's home. Levi was an early member of the Methodist Episcopal Church, appearing in 1810 church records.

Levi Howell was a Freeholder of Hardwick Township 1796-1798, 1799-1800, and 1802-1803, was on the Town Committee 1811-1813, and was collector of Hardwick in 1796.

Levi was married to **Mary GREEN** (daughter of **Samuel GREEN** and **Hannah WRIGHT**) about 1767 in Sussex County, New Jersey. No proof of the date of their marriage exists, but, because of his strict religious leanings, it is doubtful that a child would have been conceived before marriage. We have assumed a date of 1770 for the marriage. Mary was born in January 1749 in Greenwich, Sussex County; she died on 20 January 1836 in Hope, and was buried in Union Cemetery, Hope, Warren County, New Jersey. Mary is also called Maria in some source materials. Her father, Samuel GREEN, was a surveyor, one of the first white settlers in Sussex County. Levi HOWELL and Mary GREEN had these children:

+8	i.	**Jane HOWELL.**
+9	ii.	**John HOWELL.**
+10	iii.	**Samson HOWELL.**
+11	iv.	**Levi HOWELL.**
+12	v.	**Levina HOWELL.**
+13	vi.	**Jonah HOWELL.**

---

[9]Deed from Levi Howell, Jr. to George W. Howell and John S. Howell, 3 September 1847, (recorded 25 October 1847), Deed Book 28, p. 325, Recorder's Office, Warren County Courthouse, Belvidere, NJ.

+14	vii.	**William Green HOWELL.**
+15	viii.	**Mary HOWELL.**
+16	ix.	**George Green HOWELL.**
+17	x.	**Rebecca HOWELL.**
+18	xi.	**Samuel Green HOWELL.**

Levi HOWELL, Sr. died on 1 August 1825 in Hardwick Twp., Warren County. He was buried in Union Cemetery, Hope, Warren County.

4. **Samson HOWELL** was born on 1 May 1752 in Hunterdon County, New Jersey. Sampson and his family lived in Hardwick, Sussex (now Warren) County. He was married to **Elizabeth RICHARDS** (daughter of **James RICHARDS** and **Agnes NEWMAN**) in 1776 in Sussex County. Elizabeth RICHARDS was born on 3 March 1759 in Sussex County. Samson and Elizabeth had these children:

+19	i.	**Isaac HOWELL.**
+20	ii.	**James HOWELL.**
+21	iii.	**Levina HOWELL.**
+22	iv.	**Levi HOWELL.**
+23	v.	**Nathan HOWELL.**
+24	vi.	**Garret HOWELL.**
+25	vii.	**John Richards HOWELL.**
+26	viii.	**Aaron HOWELL.**
27	ix.	**Achsah HOWELL** was born on 29 November 1792, in Hardwick Township. She married **David KINNEY**. They lived in Livonia, Livingston County, NY.
28	x.	**Letitia HOWELL** was born on 8 May 1795 in Hardwick Township. She married **James BUCKLEY** on 4 May 1814, and they moved to Alton, Illinois.
+29	xi.	**Uzal Ogden HOWELL.**

Samson HOWELL died on 20 December 1810 in Hope, Sussex County, New Jersey, and was buried in the Union Cemetery in Hope. Elizabeth RICHARDS died on 18 April 1818 in Sussex County, and was buried beside her husband.

In his will, Samson left his wife, Elizabeth, two rooms in his home, two feather beds and furnishings, and left the "remainder of my lands and premises" to his youngest son, Uzal Ogden HOWELL, on the condition that he maintain his mother "in a decent and commendable manner, both in health and sickness, not letting her want for anything, during her natural life, as long as she remains a widow". This will was drawn in 1802, when Uzal Ogden was just five years old. [10]

5. **Jonah HOWELL** was born on 7 September 1756 in Hunterdon County, New Jersey. He died on 26 January 1849 in Hardwick Twp., and was buried in Union

---

[10]New Jersey Archives, Vol. XII Calendar of Wills, p. 193.

Cemetery, Hope, Warren County, New Jersey. Jonah's will was probated 10 February 1849 in Belvidere, New Jersey.

Jonah married (1) **Sarah CORWIN**, who was born in 1756 in New Jersey. She died on 11 February 1819, and was buried in Union Cemetery. Jonah HOWELL and Sarah CORWIN had the following children:

+30 i. **Mary HOWELL.**
+31 ii. **Asa E. HOWELL.**
+32 iii. **Caleb HOWELL.**
33 iv. **Levinah HOWELL** was born in 1799 in Sussex County. She died on 4 May 1818 in Sussex County, and was buried in the Union Cemetery.

Jonah was married (2) to **Mary COOL** about 1825. Mary COOL was born in 1781 in New Jersey. She died on 27 August 1848.

6. **William HOWELL** was born on 2 May 1760 in Hardwick Twp., Sussex County, New Jersey. About 1802, William and his family moved to Upper Canada, settling first in Jerseyville, and later moving to Dumfries Township. He died on 28 May 1843 in Jerseyville, Ancaster Twp., Wentworth County, Ontario. He was buried in St. George United Cemetery, S. Dumfries, Brant County, Ontario. William married **Hannah DAVIS**, who was born in 1760 in New Jersey. She died in 1804 in West Flamboro, Wentworth County, Ontario, and was buried in Christie Burying Ground, Brant County, Ontario. William and Hannah had the following children:

+34 i. **James HOWELL.**
+35 ii. **John HOWELL.**
+36 iii. **Sampson HOWELL.**
+37 iv. **Jane HOWELL.**
+38 v. **Isaac Lanning HOWELL.**
39 vi. **Lavinia HOWELL** was born on 27 August 1791 in New Jersey. She married **Done (Doan) GRIFFITH** in 1808, and died on 19 September 1868 in Augusta, MI.
+40 vii. **Jonah HOWELL.**
+41 viii. **Abraham HOWELL.**
+42 ix. **Samuel HOWELL.**
+43 x. **William HOWELL Jr.**
44 xi. **Firman HOWELL** was born in 1804 in Ontario. He died young, and was buried in the Christie Burying Ground, in Brant County.

After Hannah's death in 1804, William is believed to have married again, but his wife's name is not known.

7. **Garret HOWELL** was born on 25 February 1762 in Hope, Sussex County, New Jersey. He died on 25 May 1833 in Ancaster Twp., Wentworth County, Ontario, and was buried in Jerseyville Cemetery.. Garret was married (1) to **Elizabeth PEERSLEY** in 1780 in Sussex County, New Jersey. Elizabeth PEERSLEY was born in 1760 in Sussex County, where she died on 14 January 1788. Garret HOWELL and Elizabeth PEERSLEY had these children:

45	i.	**Samson HOWELL** was born on 30 January 1781 in Sussex County, and died on 28 March 1782. He was buried in Union Cemetery, where his tombstone may still be seen.
+46	ii.	**Daniel Peersley HOWELL.**
+47	iii.	**Ruth HOWELL.**
+48	iv.	**Levi HOWELL.**
+49	v.	**Garret HOWELL.**

Garret married (2) **Sarah THATCHER** on 15 January 1789 in Sussex County. Sarah THATCHER was born on 13 April 1767 in New Jersey, died on 1 June 1837, and was buried in Ancaster Township, Wentworth County, Ontario. About 1802, the family emigrated to Upper Canada, where they settled in Jerseyville, so called because of the number of former New Jersey residents living there. Garret is said to have built the first brick house in that town. He was also a licensed exhorter in the Methodist church. His obituary called him "the father of Methodism in the area of Jerseyville."[11] Garret and Sarah had these children:

+50	i.	**Sampson HOWELL.**
51	ii.	**Thomas HOWELL** was born on 14 August 1791 and died on 1 October 1791, in Sussex County.
+52	iii.	**Peter HOWELL.**
53	iv.	An unnamed son was born on 4 June 1794 in Sussex County, and died soon after.
54	v.	An unnamed girl, a twin to the above, was born and died on 4 June 1794.
55	vi.	**Elizabeth F. HOWELL** was born on 1 October 1795 in Hope. She married **William SHACKLETON** on 3 January 1814. They moved to Grand Rapids, Michigan, where she died on 30 January 1879.
56	vii.	**Samuel T. HOWELL** was born on 25 July 1797 in Hope, and died there on 19 May 1801.
+57	viii.	**Moses Hazen HOWELL.**
+58	ix.	**Isaac Lanning HOWELL.**
59	x.	**Lydia HOWELL** was born on 4 August 1803 in Ancaster Township. She married **John COPE** on 11 May 1820. He was born about 1803. Lydia died on 29 December 1873.

---

[11]Hilda Grimwood, Zion Hill's Heritage, (publisher unknown, 1975) 4.

60 xi. **Gideon HOWELL** was born on 7 October 1805 in Ancaster Township. He married **Margaret CASCARONE** on 16 February 1825 in Wentworth County. Gideon died there on 14 September 1827.

+61 xii. **Enoch HOWELL.**

+62 xiii. **Margaret HOWELL.**

+63 xiv. **William HOWELL.**

+64 xv. **Esther Anne HOWELL.**

ABRAHAM S. HOWELL
Born about 1811.

JOHN H. HOWELL
1835 - 1921

FOURTH GENERATION

8. **Jane HOWELL** was born on 26 December 1768 in Sussex County. She died on 22 May 1843, and was buried in Union Cemetery, Hope, Warren County, New Jersey. She married **Rev. Nicholas ALBERTSON** (son of **Garret ALBERTSON** and **Elizabeth REYNOLDS**) on 14 June 1789 in Sussex County. Rev. Nicholas ALBERTSON was born on 11 October 1764 in Sussex County. He died in 1853 in Hope, Warren County, and was buried in Union Cemetery. Jane and Nicholas ALBERTSON had the following children:[12]

+65	i.	**Lavinah ALBERTSON.**
66	ii.	**Levi ALBERTSON** was born in 1790 in Frelinghuysen, and died there on 18 August 1826.
67	iii.	**Garret ALBERTSON** was born on 6 June 1791, and died in 1875 in Frelinghuysen.
+68	iv.	**Samson ALBERTSON.**
69	v.	**Mary ALBERTSON** was born in 1803 in Frelinghuysen. She was unmarried.
70	vi.	**Margaret ALBERTSON** was born in 1805, died on 14 September 1855, in Frelinghuysen, and was buried in Union Cemetery. She was unmarried.
71	vii.	**Sally Ann ALBERTSON** was born in 1807 in Frelinghuysen, died there on 3 November 1823, and was buried in Union Cemetery. She was unmarried.
+72	viii.	**Isaac Read ALBERTSON.**
+73	ix.	**Samuel ALBERTSON.**
74	x.	**George ALBERTSON** was born in Frelinghuysen.
75	xi.	**Elizabeth ALBERTSON** married **Unknown COOK.**

9. **John HOWELL** was born in 1770. He died on 2 November 1843, and was buried in Union Cemetery. John Howell's house was used as a church before the Methodist Episcopal Church was built. John HOWELL was married to **Lydia WHITESELL** (daughter of **Andrew WHITESELL** and **Margaretha GREEN**) who was born in 1774 in New Jersey. She died on 17 February 1843, and was buried in Union Cemetery. John HOWELL and Lydia WHITESELL had the following children:

+76	i.	**Margaret HOWELL.**
+77	ii.	**Mary G. HOWELL.**
+78	iii.	**Charles Wesley HOWELL.**
+79	iv.	**Levi HOWELL.**
80	v.	**Charity A. HOWELL** was born on 10 February 1807, died on 27 January 1891, and was buried in Union Cemetery.

---

[12]1850 U.S. Census (population) New Jersey, Warren Co., Frelinghuysen, p. 487, nos. 154/165, National Archives Microfilm Publication, M432, roll 465.

+81 vi. **Abraham S. HOWELL.**
+82 vii. **Asa Jacob HOWELL.**
+83 viii. **John H. HOWELL.**
84 ix. **Isaac HOWELL** was named in John's will, but nothing is known about him.

10. **Samson HOWELL** was born on 11 August 1772 in Hardwick Twp., Sussex County, NJ. He died on 17 March 1851 in Trafalgar, Halton County, Ontario, and was buried in Palermo United Church Cemetery, Trafalgar. His obituary says that he and Mary came to Canada in 1806, and settled in Dundas, Trafalgar Township. He had served with the British Army in the War of 1812.

He was married to **Mary Charity TRILLER** (daughter of **Philip TRILLER** and **Mary Catherine YOUNG**) in September 1800 in Sussex County. Mary, usually called Charity, was born on 24 February 1776 in New Jersey. She died on 13 May 1854 in Ontario, and was buried in Palermo United Church Cemetery. Samson and Mary had the following children:

85 i. **Philip Young HOWELL** was born in Sussex County, died on 7 October 1804, and was buried in Union Cemetery.
+86 ii. **John Triller HOWELL.**
87 iii. **William Boyd HOWELL** was born about 1803. He married **Keturah LANNING** on 2 October 1827 in Warren County.[13] She was born on 21 July 1809 in Sussex County, and died on 27 June 1828 in Trafalgar, Ontario. He married (2) **Harriet Louisa DELAMOUR**, (born 1814, died 1900 in Ontario), on 28 August 1848 in Trafalgar.
88 iv. **Sarah Catherine BARNS** was born on 27 April 1845. She died in 1864 in Trafalgar.Samson and Charity adopted her after her parents, **Elisha** and **Mary BARNS**, died.

11. **Levi HOWELL Jr**. was born on 20 June 1776 in Hardwick Twp., Sussex County. He died on 22 July 1850, and was buried in Free Union Cemetery, Mountain Lake, Warren County. Levi Jr. had a large farm in Hope Township, and in 1847, he sold land to his sons John S. and George W. HOWELL.[14]
Levi Jr. married **Phebe SMITH** (daughter of **John SMITH** and **Phebe VAN DOREN**) on 28 July 1796 in Sussex County.[15] Phebe SMITH was born on 27 October 1778 in New Jersey. She died on 2 April 1854 in Hope, Warren County,

---

[13]Warren County, NJ. Marriage Records, LDS Microfilm #0960890, Vol. 1, p. 25
[14]Deed from Levi Howell to George W. and John S. Howell, Warren County, NJ Deed Book 28:325.
[15]Sussex County, New Jersey Marriage Book A, page 96.

and was buried in Free Union Cemetery, Mountain Lake. Levi and Phebe had the following children:[16]

+89 i. **Phebe HOWELL**. Although the 1850 census for Hope doesn't list Phebe, her children are listed with the household. We believe they were there because Levi, Sr., had died shortly before the enumerator visited. Phebe could possibly have been at another relative's home, or with her husband's family. We were not able to locate her in the census.

90 ii. **Jefferson HOWELL** was born in 1810 in Hope.

91 iii. **Sampson J. HOWELL** was born in 1811 in Hope. He married **Ann SAVACOOL** (the Sussex County Marriage records spell her name SAVERCOOL) on 30 December 1834 in Sussex County. Sampson was a farmer; he died in October 1854, and Ann died on 7 October 1869. Both were buried in Old Newton Cemetery, Sussex County.

+92 iv. **George W. HOWELL.**

+93 v. **John Stinson HOWELL.**

12. **Levina HOWELL** was born on 24 October 1778 in Hardwick Twp., Sussex County, where she died on 18 December 1824. Letters her father wrote to her brother in Canada said Levinah had borne at least 15 children, but few of them survived. Levinah HOWELL married **Abram SMITH**. Their children were:

94 i. **George Washington SMITH.**

95 ii. **John SMITH** was born on 8 April 1786 in Sussex County, and died there on 30 August 1801.

96 iii. **Mary Ann SMITH** was born on 12 August 1804, and died on 18 April 1814 in Sussex County.

13. **Jonah HOWELL** was born on 3 November 1781 in Hardwick Twp., Sussex County. He died on 18 October 1855 in Pinckneyville, Andover Twp., Sussex County, and was buried in the Howell Family Cemetery in Andover. He married **Mary PIERSON** on 15 May 1804 in Hardwick Twp. Jonah and Mary lived in the German Flats area of Pinckneyville, in 1828. Jonah owned a farm, and a blacksmith shop as well as a grist mill. Mary PIERSON was born on 2 March 1777 in Hardwick Twp. She died on 18 December 1852 in Andover Twp.m, and was buried in the Howell Family Cemetery. Their children were:[17]

---

[16]1850 U.S. Census (population) New Jersey, Warren Co., Hope Twp., p. 421, nos. 487/508, National Archives Microfilm Publication, M432, roll 465. Note that the addition of the daughter, Phebe, is presumed, to account for the two young Price children in this home. The 1850 census was taken within days of the father's death. Her existence was confirmed later, by a descendant.

[17]1850 U.S. Census (population) New Jersey, Sussex Co., Newton Twp., p. 168,

97 i. **Elizabeth HOWELL** was born on 10 March 1805 in Sussex County, and died about 1853.
98 ii. **Rebecca Maria HOWELL** was born on 27 November 1806, died on 26 November 1886 in Newton, and was buried in Newton Cemetery.
+99 iii. **Levi HOWELL.**
100 iv. **Sarah Ann HOWELL** was born on 28 October 1811 in Sussex County.
101 v. **Susan HOWELL** was born on 29 November 1815 in Sussex County.
+102 vi. **Daniel P. HOWELL.**
+103 vii. **Samuel Green HOWELL.**

14. **William Green HOWELL** was born on 26 October 1783 in Sussex County, New Jersey. He died on 14 July 1835 in Frelinghuysen, Warren County, and was buried in Union Cemetery. In 1802, William sold land in Sussex county to his brother Jonah and to his father. William was married to **Lavinia MIDDLESWORTH** (daughter of **Abe MIDDLESWORTH**) about 1806. Lavinia MIDDLESWORTH was born on 23 July 1789. She died on 27 July 1833, and was buried in Union Cemetery. William and Lavinia had these children:

104 i. **Samuel HOWELL** was born in December 1807, died on 1 May 1808 in Sussex County, and was buried in Union Cemetery.
105 ii. **Levi M. HOWELL** was born in 1813 in Johnsonburg, Sussex County, where he died on 19 December 1869, from severe burns. He was buried in Union Cemetery. Levi was a farmer. [18]
+106 iii. **Lavinia HOWELL.**
+107 iv. **William F. B. HOWELL.**
+108 v. **Mary HOWELL.**
+109 vi. **A. J. HOWELL.**

William and Lavinia were also the parents of two daughters who died soon after birth; both are buried in Union Cemetery.

15. **Mary HOWELL** was born on 14 September 1785 in Sussex County. She died on 25 May 1859 in Frelinghuysen, Warren County, and was buried in Union Cemetery. Her husband, **John HARRIS** was born on 16 September 1780 in New Jersey. He died on 27 April 1854, and was buried in Union Cemetery. Mary HOWELL and John HARRIS had one child:[19]

---

nos. 109/ 112, National Archives Microfilm Publication, M432, roll 464.
[18]Death Return, Levi M. Howell, New Jersey State Archives, Volume AP, p. 319.
[19]1850 U.S. Census (population) New Jersey, Warren Co., Frelinghuysen, p. 488, nos. 172/184 , National Archives Microfilm Publication, M432, roll 465.

110 i. **Levinah J. HARRIS**, listed in the marriage records as Lavinia Jane,[20] was born in 1820 in Hardwick, Warren County. She married **George Warren HAWKE** on 11 December 1847 in Warren County. He was born in 1818 in New Jersey.

16. **George Green HOWELL** was born on 17 June 1787 in Hope, Sussex County. He died on 14 November 1858 in Frelinghuysen, Warren County, and was buried in Union Cemetery. He was a farmer. He married **Lydia JOHNSON** (daughter of **Andrew JOHNSON**) on 28 September 1808 in Sussex County. Lydia JOHNSON was born in 1793 in Knowlton, Sussex County. She died on 16 January 1847 in Hardwick Twp., and was buried in Union Cemetery. They had these children:

+111 i. **Anthony Johnson HOWELL.**

+112 ii. **Levi HOWELL.**

+113 iii. **Samuel G. HOWELL Jr.**

114 iv. **Johanna HOWELL** was born on 6 May 1820 in Hardwick Twp. She married **Henry LEFFLER**, and they moved to Illinois.

+115 v. **Euphemia Osborne HOWELL.**

116 vi. **Mary Ann HOWELL** was born on 9 January 1824 in Hardwick Twp. She married **William Heitsman** on 4 September 1845 in Sussex County. [21]He was born on 26 December 1818 and died on 2 April 1896 in Luzerne County, PA, where they farmed. She died there on 28 December 1906, and both are buried in Centremoreland Cemetery, Wyoming County, PA.

+117 vii. **William HOWELL.**

+118 viii. **James HOWELL.**

+119 ix. **Ziba O. HOWELL.**

+120 x. **George S. HOWELL.**

By 1850, Lydia had died, and Euphemia, her two small daughters, and his sons, Ziba and George S., were back home with George. Sarah, born 1839, possibly a daughter of their widowed son, Levi, was also living in the home. George was a farmer, with real estate valued at $9,000 in that census.[22]

17. **Rebecca HOWELL** was born in 1791 in Sussex County. She died on 18 June 1864 in Hardwick Twp., and was buried in Union Brick Cemetery, Blairstown, Warren County. Her husband, **Richard READ** was born on 24 October 1783, and died on 3 March 1867 in New Jersey. Their children were:[23]

---

[20]Warren County, NJ Marriage records, LDS Microfilm #0960890.

[21]Warren County, NJ Marriage records, LDS Microfilm #0960890.

[22]1850 U.S. Census (population) New Jersey, Warren Co., Hardwick Twp., p. 487, nos.155/167, National Archives Microfilm Publication, M432, roll 465.

[23]1850 U.S. Census (population) New Jersey, Warren Co., Frelinghuysen, p. 483,

121	i.	**Sarah Ann READ** was born in 1825 in Frelinghuysen, Warren County, NJ.
122	ii.	**Levinah J. READ** was born in 1827 in Frelinghuysen.
+123	iii.	**Ira K. READ.**
124	iv.	**Azubah READ** was born in 1829 in Frelinghuysen.
125	v.	**Rebecca M. READ** was born in 1831 in Frelinghuysen.
126	vi.	**Jonah H. READ** was born in 1836 in Frelinghuysen.

18. **Samuel Green HOWELL** was born on 14 July 1797 in Sussex County, New Jersey. He died on 5 March 1866, and was buried in Union Cemetery. He was married to **Eleanor FREESE** on 7 November 1822 in Sussex County.[24] Eleanor FREESE was born on 24 June 1800 in New Jersey. She died on 16 November 1884, and was buried in Union Cemetery. Samuel was a foundryman whose real estate was valued at $450 in the 1850 census. By the time of the 1860 census, the other children had moved out, but son Levi, his wife and child were living with Samuel and Eleanor. Samuel Green HOWELL and Eleanor FREESE had these children: [25]

127	i.	**Maria Jane HOWELL** was born in 1824 in Frelinghuysen, Warren County.
+128	ii.	**Levi J. HOWELL.**
+129	iii.	**Lucinda Ann HOWELL.**
+130	iv.	**Charles Marshall HOWELL.**
131	v.	**George G. HOWELL** was born on 25 February 1839, died on 22 June 1859 in Frelinghuysen, and was buried in Union Cemetery.
132	vi.	**Eleanor (Ellen) M. HOWELL** was born in 1841 in Frelinghuysen.

19. **Isaac HOWELL** was born on 26 April 1777 in Hardwick Township, Sussex County, New Jersey. He died on 8 April 1835 in Warren County, and was buried in Union Cemetery. He was married to **Sophia SHAVER** (daughter of **Frederick SHAVER** and **Elizabeth TRILLER**) on 9 March 1802 in Sussex County. Sophia SHAVER was born in 1778 in Hardwick Township. She died on 18 September 1831 in Warren County, and was buried in Union Cemetery. Isaac HOWELL and Sophia SHAVER had these children:

+133	i.	**Philip Shaver HOWELL.**
+134	ii.	**Elizabeth HOWELL.**
+135	iii.	**Susan Ann HOWELL.**
+136	iv.	**David K. HOWELL.**

---

nos. 99 /110, National Archives Microfilm Publication, M432, roll 465.
[24]Sussex County Marriage Book A, page 97.
[25]1850 U.S. Census (population) New Jersey, Warren Co., Frelinghuysen, p. 488, nos. 168/180, National Archives Microfilm Publication, M432, roll 465.

20. **James HOWELL** was born on 27 November 1778 in Hardwick Towship. He died on 23 December 1837 in Nichols, Tioga County, New York. He married **Amelia LANNING** (daughter of **Robert LANNING** and **Sarah CORYELL**) on 6 March 1798 in Independence, Warren County, New Jersey. Amelia LANNING was born on 1 October 1781 in Independence Towship, Sussex County, New Jersey. The couple moved to Nichols, New York about 1806. She died on 30 March 1823 in Nichols. Both James and Amelia were buried in Asbury Cemetery in Nichols. Their children were:

137	i	**William P. HOWELL** was born on 25 October 1803 in Nichols. He died on 15 September 1830, and was buried in Asbury Cemetery.
+138	ii.	**Frances HOWELL.**
+139	iii.	**John L. HOWELL.**
+140	i.	**Mary Ann HOWELL.**
+141	v.	**Elizabeth HOWELL** was born in Nichols.
142	vi.	**Robert HOWELL.**

21. **Levina HOWELL** was born in 1780 in Hardwick Twp. She died on 20 October 1851 in Frelinghuysen, and was buried in Johnsonburg Cemetery, Johnsonburg, NJ. She married **George VAN HORN** on 24 August 1811 in Sussex County. George VAN HORN was born on 14 October 1771 in Frelinghuysen, Sussex County. He died on 20 January 1848 in Warren County, and was buried in Johnsonburg Cemetery. They had the following children:[26]

+143	i.	**William S. VAN HORN.**
+144	ii.	**Isaac H. VAN HORN.**
+145	iii.	**David Green VAN HORN.**
+146	iv.	**Abraham Shaver VAN HORN.**
+147	v.	**George VAN HORN.**

22. **Levi HOWELL** was born in 1782 in Hardwick Twp. He died on 20 September 1860, and was buried in Johnsonburg Cemetery, Johnsonburg, NJ. His wife, **Margaret HAMILTON** (daughter of **Aaron HAMILTON**) was born in 1791. She died on 22 December 1867, and was buried in Johnsonburg Cemetery. Levi was a farmer. Levi and Margaret had these children:[27]

+148	i.	**Aaron Benjamin HOWELL.**
149	ii.	**Nelson HOWELL** was born on 17 July 1815 in Independence. He died on 6 September 1888, and was buried in Johnsonburg Cemetery. In 1880, he lived with his nephew, **Benjamin HOWELL.**
+150	iii.	**Susan HOWELL.**

---

[26]1850 U.S. Census (population) New Jersey, Warren Co., Frelinghuysen, p. 488, 173/185, National Archives Microfilm Publication, M432, roll 465.
[27]ibid., Independence Twp., p. 520, nos. 260/271.

+151 iv. **Garret K. HOWELL.**
152 v. **William Hamilton HOWELL** is named in a family Bible record. We have no other information.

23. **Nathan HOWELL** was born on 11 November 1784 in Hardwick Township, Sussex County, New Jersey. He died in 1851 in Ancaster Township, Wentworth County, Ontario, and was buried in St. George United Cemetery, S. Dumfries, Brant County, Ontario. Nathan was a farmer, and a member of the Methodist church. On 2 November 1844, Nathan received a grant of 202 acres of land from the British Crown, having sworn allegiance to the Crown, and been loyal to the British cause. He sold 85 acres of this land to Elam BONHAM, who later sold sections of it.

Nathan was married (1) to **Susannah BIRD** on 21 November 1806 in Sussex County, New Jersey. Nathan and his family emigrated to Canada about 1817, and remained there. Nathan HOWELL and Susannah BIRD had one known child:

+153 i. **Uzal Ogden HOWELL.**

We do not know what happened to Susannah BIRD, but later Nathan HOWELL married (2) **Dorothea WAUGH**, who was born in 1793 in Brant County, Ontario. She died on 3 November 1883 in Colborne, Huron County, Ontario.Nathan HOWELL and Dorothea WAUGH had these children:[28]

154 i. **Harriet HOWELL** was born in November 1829, and died on 1 March 1832 in S. Dumfries.
+155 ii. **Samson Waugh HOWELL.**
+156 iii. **Harvey Clinton HOWELL.**

24. **Garret HOWELL** was born on 28 September 1786 in Hardwick Township, Sussex County, New Jersey. He died on 12 January 1837, and was buried in Union Cemetery. Garret married **Christina RICE** (daughter of **Andrew RICE** and **Catherine UNKNOWN**), who was born on 22 January 1787 in New Jersey. She died on 22 November 1864, and was buried in Union Cemetery. Garret HOWELL and Christina RICE had these children:[29]

+157 i. **Samson G. HOWELL.**
158 ii. **Euphemia HOWELL** was born on 2 April 1811 in Frelinghuysen, Sussex County, New Jersey. She died on 10 April 1887 in Hope, and was buried in

---

[28]Family information contributed by: Jeanne Laundrie Fugina, 934 Fountain St., Fountain City, WI 54629, and by Phyllis Troyer Hunt, 2310 Terness, Waterford, MI 48329.

[29]1850 U.S. Census (population) New Jersey, Warren Co., Hope Twp., p. 434, nos. 720/735, National Archives Microfilm Publication, M432, roll 465.

Union Cemetery.[30]

+159 iii. **Letitia HOWELL.**

+160 iv. **Gideon Leeds HOWELL.**

161 v. **Isaac HOWELL** was born in Sussex County. He was named in Garret's will, but we have no further information on him.

+162 vi. **Elizabeth HOWELL.**

+163 vii. **Susan A. HOWELL.**

+164 viii. **Jonah HOWELL.**

+165 ix. **Jonathan Thompson HOWELL.**

166 x. **Lavina HOWELL** was born on 29 January 1832. She married **John CUMMINS** in January 1856 in Hope Township. She died on 25 October 1888.

25. **John Richards HOWELL** was born on 26 June 1788 in Hardwick Township. He died on 9 October 1826, and was buried in Yellow Frame Cemetery, Frelinghuysen, Warren County, New Jersey. John served on the Town Committee of Hardwick in 1814. He was married to **Sarah ARMSTRONG** on 18 January 1814. Sarah ARMSTRONG was born in 1794 in New Jersey. She died on 12 October 1849, and was buried in Yellow Frame Cemetery. John Richards HOWELL and Sarah ARMSTRONG had these children:

+167 i. **Alice HOWELL.**

+168 ii. **Elizabeth S. HOWELL.**

169 iii. **Eleanor HOWELL** was born in October 1822 in Sussex County. She died in 1902, and was buried in Cedar Ridge Cemetery, Blairstown, NJ. She was a milliner.

+170 iv. **Ann L. HOWELL.**

171 v. **Margaretta A. HOWELL** was born on 12 April 1826 in Warren County. She died in 1920, of a cerebral hemorrhage, and was buried in Cedar Ridge Cemetery. The 1887 Blairstown Directory listed her as a milliner.

26. **Aaron HOWELL** was born on 3 October 1790 in Hardwick Township. He died on 5 March 1857 in Egg Harbor, Burlington County, New Jersey. Aaron was a farmer in Little Egg Harbor, Burlington County, at the time of the 1850 census.[31] He married **Mary DILDINE** (daughter of **Samuel DILDINE** and **Rhoda OGDEN**) on 30 September 1815 in Sussex County. Mary DILDINE was born on 13 January 1786 in New Jersey. They had these children:[32]

---

[30]Obituary, Washington (NJ) Star, 14 April 1887.

[31]1850 U.S. Census (population) New Jersey, Burlington Co., Little Egg Harbor, p.376, nos.128/131, National Archives Microfilm Publication, M432, roll 443.

[32]Francis Bazley Lee, Genealogical and Memorial History of the State of New Jersey, (New York: Lewis Historical Publications Co., 1910) pp. 348-349.

172 i. **Dr. Aaron HOWELL.**
173 ii. **Ada HOWELL** married **Sexton HOWELL.**
174 iii. **Caroline HOWELL** married **Godfrey NOLAN** in Little Egg Harbor.
175 iv. **Elizabeth HOWELL** married **Joseph HEADLEY** on 17 September 1848 in Little Egg Harbor.
176 v. **Ella HOWELL** married Jeremiah **COLKITT.**
177 vi. **John R. HOWELL.**
+178 vii. **Laban HOWELL.**
+179 viii. **Thaddeus HOWELL.**
180 ix. **Thomas HOWELL** was born in 1830 in Little Egg Harbor, and in 1850, was living at home, working as an oysterman.
181 x. **George HOWELL** was born in 1834 in Little Egg Harbor. He married **Mary NUGENT** on 6 June 1857 in Little Egg Harbor.
182 xi. **William HOWELL** was born in 1836 in Little Egg Harbor.

29. **Uzal Ogden HOWELL** was born on 16 December 1797 in Hardwick Twp. He died on 7 April 1834 in Warren County, and was buried in Union Cemetery, Hackettstown, Warren County. Uzal built a saw mill on the Vasbinder property at the outlet of Glover's Creek. Farther down the creek were the sawmill, bending shop and distillery of the Howell brothers.

Uzal was on the first board of Chosen Freeholders of Warren County, which met 11 May 1825, at the home of James MCMURTRIE, in Belvidere. He was elected Coroner 18 October 1825, and again on 25 October 1828. He was married to **Mariah Matilda CUMMINS** (daughter of **Christian CUMMINS** and **Elizabeth WHITESELL**) on 21 November 1818 in Sussex County. Mariah Matilda CUMMINS was born on 16 September 1801, and died on 23 April 1889. Uzal Ogden HOWELL and Mariah Matilda CUMMINS had these children:

+183 i. **Alexander Cummins HOWELL.**
+184 ii. **Christeon Goodrech HOWELL.**
+185 iii. **Uzal Hampton HOWELL.**
+186 iv. **Isaac Byington HOWELL.**
187 v. **Lydia Ann HOWELL** was born on 23 July 1829, and died on 7 December 1839 in Warren County.
+188 vi. **Sampson Ogden HOWELL.**

Mariah married (2) **Barnabas BIGLER**, on 24 May 1845. Barnabas was born about 1780. In 1850, they lived in Mansfield, and her son, Sampson, was living with them.

30. **Mary HOWELL** was born on 17 September 1791 in Sussex County. She died on 19 November 1866, and was buried in Rockport Presbyterian Cemetery, Port Murray, New Jersey. She married **Elisha OSMUN** on 20 February 1810 in Sussex

County.[33] Elisha OSMUN was born about 1786, died on 22 February 1868, and was buried in Rockport Presbyterian Cemetery. Their children were:

189	i.	**John OSMUN** was born in 1820 in Mansfield Twp., Sussex County.
190	ii.	**Caleb OSMUN** was born in 1823 in Mansfield Twp.
191	iii.	**Joseph OSMUN** was born in 1825 in Mansfield Twp.
192	iv.	**Joanna OSMUN** was born in 1832 in Belvidere, Warren County.
193	v.	**Elizabeth OSMUN** was born in 1833 in Belvidere.
194	vi.	**James OSMUN** was born in 1835 in Belvidere.

31. **Asa E. HOWELL** was born in 1794 in Hardwick Twp. He died on 25 March 1860 in Warren County, and was buried in Union Cemetery. Asa was a farmer. He was married (1) to **Mrs. Charlotte ALLEN** on 20 October 1814. Charlotte ALLEN was born in 1795 in NJ. She died on 31 January 1828, and was buried in Union Cemetery. Asa and Charlotte had these children:

+195	i.	**Eden S. HOWELL.**
196	ii.	**Ann Marll HOWELL** was born in 1826, and died on 8 January 1827; she was buried in Union Cemetery.
197	iii.	**Anna Maria HOWELL** was born on 6 September 1827, and died on 8 January 1828; she also was buried in Union Cemetery.

Asa was married (2) to **Mrs. Elsey TREAT** on 30 July 1829 in Sussex County, New Jersey.[34] Elsey TREAT was born on 8 January 1801. She died on 17 December 1867. Asa E. HOWELL and Elsey TREAT had one child:[35]

198	i.	**Caleb Corwine HOWELL** was born on 31 August 1830. He died on 16 December 1852, and was buried in Union Cemetery.

By 1860, Elsey was living in Hope Twp., with Isaiah TREAT, probably a son by her first husband.[36]

32. **Caleb HOWELL** was born on 24 October 1796 in Hardwick Twp. He died on 19 August 1866, and was buried in Union Cemetery. Caleb was a farmer, with real estate valued at $12,040 in the 1850 census for Frelinghuysen, Warren County, NJ. Caleb married **Sarah M. CUMMINS** (daughter of **Christian**

---

[33] Warren County, NJ Marriage records, LDS Microfilm #0960890, Vol. 1, p. 256.
[34] Warren County, NJ Marriage records, LDS Microfilm #0960890. Vol. 1, p.66.
[35] 1850 U.S. Census (population) New Jersey, Warren Co., Hope Twp, p. 436 , nos.716/748, National Archives Microfilm Publication, M432, roll 465.
[36] 1860 U.S. Census (population) New Jersey, Warren County, Hope Twp., p. 15, nos. 95/95, National Archives Microfilm Publication M653, roll 711.

CUMMINS and **Elizabeth WHITESELL**), who was born on 16 July 1798 in New Jersey. She died on 21 February 1878, and was buried in Union Cemetery. Their children were:

+199	i.	**Margaret C. HOWELL.**
+200	ii.	**Sarah Mariah HOWELL.**
201	iii.	**Unknown female HOWELL** was born and died in Warren County, and was buried in Union Cemetery.
202	iv.	**Maria Matilda HOWELL** was born on 18 June 1826 in Warren County, died on 9 June 1860, and was buried in Union Cemetery.
203	v.	**Gideon L. HOWELL** was born on 21 December 1828 and died on 19 March 1829 in Warren County; he was buried in Union Cemetery.
+204	vi.	**Perninah B. HOWELL.**
205	vii.	**Jonah HOWELL** was born on 15 December 1833 in Warren County. He died on 15 November 1902 in Warren County, and was buried in Union Cemetery.
206	viii.	**Electa Ann HOWELL** was born on 23 March 1836 in Warren County, where she died on 17 June 1839, and was buried in Union Cemetery.
+207	ix.	**Savilla J. HOWELL.**
+208	x.	**Hester Anne HOWELL.**

34. **James HOWELL** was born on 3 November 1782 in Sussex County. He died on 2 July 1860 in Ontario, and was buried in Zion Hill Cemetery, Ancaster, Wentworth County, Ontario. He married **Hannah TEMPLER,** who was born in 1792. She died on 5 November 1854, and was buried in Zion Hill Cemetery. James HOWELL and Hannah TEMPLER had the following children:

209	i.	**Lavinia HOWELL** married **Joseph DRAKE.**
210	ii.	**Peter Templer HOWELL** was born in 1816 in Ontario. He died on 14 October 1892. His wife, **Catherine ELLIOTT**, was born in 1824 and died in 1911. Both were buried in Bethel United Church Cemetery, WilmotTwp.,Waterloo County, Ontario
+211	iii.	**Jonah T. HOWELL.**
212	iv.	**Samuel HOWELL** was born on 31 January 1821 in Ontario. He died on 24 August 1853, and was buried in Zion Hill Cemetery.
+213	v.	**Mercy HOWELL.**
214	vi.	**Joseph HOWELL** was born on 16 April 1826 in Ontario. He died on 19 October 1828, and was buried in Zion Hill Cemetery.
+215	vii.	**Sarah HOWELL.**
+216	viii.	**Mary Jane HOWELL.**

35. **John HOWELL** was born on 18 April 1785 in Sussex County. John settled in Wentworth County, Ontario. He died on 25 October 1849, and was buried in Zion Hill Cemetery. He married **Rachel KITCHEN**, who was born on 1 December 1790. She died on 12 February 1850, and was buried in Zion Hill Cemetery. John HOWELL and Rachel KITCHEN had the following children:

217	i.	**Unidentified male HOWELL**, born in 1811 in Ontario, died while helping to shear sheep.
+218	ii.	**Isaac Reid HOWELL.**
219	iii.	**Sarah HOWELL** was born on 1 September 1813 in Ontario.
220	iv.	**Rachel Kitchen HOWELL** was born in 1815 in Wentworth County, Ontario.
221	v..	**Hannah HOWELL** was born in 1815, a twin to Rachel
+222	vi.	**Levi D. HOWELL.**
+223	vii.	**John HOWELL.**
224	viii.	**Mary HOWELL** was born in 1820 in Ontario.
+225	ix.	**William HOWELL.**
226	x.	**Lewis HOWELL** was born in 1825 in Wentworth County, Ontario.

36. **Sampson HOWELL** was born on 12 August 1786 in Hope, Sussex County, NJ. Sampson went to Canada, where he died on 1 May 1869. He was buried in S. Dumfries Baptist Cemetery, Brant County, Ontario. He was a farmer. He married (1) **Marcia GREEN** who was born in NJ. After her death Sampson married (2) **Eliza HILTON** who was born on 30 September 1797 in England. She died on 14 March 1871 in Ancaster Twp., Wentworth County, Ontario. She was buried in S. Dumfries Baptist Cemetery. Sampson and Eliza had one child:

+227	i.	**Mary Eliza FARR.**

37. **Jane HOWELL** was born in 1787 in Sussex County. She died in 1870. She married **Joseph KITCHEN** (son of **John KITCHEN** and **Susanna BIRD**), who was born on 29 October 1786 in Alexandria Twp., NJ. He died on 31 December 1868 in Vittoria, Winham Twp., Norfolk County. Jane HOWELL and Joseph KITCHEN had one child:

228	i.	**George Green KITCHEN.**

38. **Isaac Lanning HOWELL** was born on 5 December 1788 in Hope, Sussex County, NJ. He died on 5 March 1860 in S. Dumfries, Brant County, Ontario, and was buried in Hunter Hoodless Cemetery, S. Dumfries. A two-part newspaper article[37], based on interviews with present-day descendants, gives much information on this man. He is said to have been a "one-eyed" sharpshooter, a son of a United Empire Loyalist, who fought in the battles of Queenstown Heights and

---

[37]Brant News, Brantford, Ontario, 20 January and 27 January 1982.

Lundy's Lane in the War of 1812. For his service, he was granted land at the head of the Hamilton Bay, which he traded for a pump. In 1820, he settled on and cleared a parcel of land in the North part of Lot 10, Concession 3, and Lot 10 Concession 4, about 213 acres in all. In 1982, this land was still being farmed by some of his descendants. Isaac married **Mary "Polly" KITCHEN**, who was born on 24 October 1794 in Greenwich Township, Sussex County, New Jersey. She died on 21 November 1841, and was buried in Hunter Hoodless Cemetery. Their children were:

+229 i. **Jane HOWELL.**
+230 ii. **Rachel HOWELL.**
+231 iii. **Sarah "Sally" HOWELL.**
232 iv. **Harriet HOWELL** was born on 2 November 1823 in S. Dumfries. She died on 7 February 1835, and was buried in Hunter Hoodless Cemetery.
+233 v. **Firman Aikman HOWELL.**
+234 vi. **Lemuel HOWELL.**
235 vii. **Margaret HOWELL** was born in 1832. She died in 1851, of a fever.

40. **Jonah HOWELL** was born on 27 June 1793 in Sussex County, New Jersey. He died on 24 September 1861 in S. Dumfries, and was buried in St. George United Cemetery. He was a farmer. Jonah married **Mary WAUGH**, who was born in 1796. She died on 2 June 1870, and was buried in St. George United Cemetery. Jonah HOWELL and Mary WAUGH had the following children:

+236 i. **Thomas Waugh HOWELL.**
+237 ii. **Hannah HOWELL.**
+238 iii. **James HOWELL.**
+239 iv. **Margaret HOWELL.**
+240 v. **Henry HOWELL.**
241 vi. **William HOWELL** was born in Ontario.

41. **Abraham HOWELL** was born on 15 May 1797, died on 3 February 1882, and was buried in Zion Hill Cemetery, Ancaster, Wentworth County, Ontario. He married **Achsah WILSON**. Their children were:

+242 i. **Hannah HOWELL.**
+243 ii. **Peter M. HOWELL.**
244 iii. **Isaac HOWELL**, born about 1841 in S. Dumfries, was a farmer. He married **Sarah BOOTTY** on 18 January 1865 in Ontario. Sarah, daughter of **Isaac H. BOOTTY** and **Margaret UNKNOWN**, was born about 1839.

42. **Samuel HOWELL** was born on 1 January 1801. He married **Margaret FORTNER**. They had one child:

245 i. **James HOWELL** was born about 1833 in S. Dumfries. He married **Rachel PEMBLETON**(daughter of **Amos PEMBLETON** and **Clarinda UNKNOWN**) on 5 December 1860 in Ontario.

43. **William HOWELL Jr.** was born on 15 January 1803 in Ontario, Canada. He was living in Trafalgar, Ontario in 1871. He died on 31 January 1892, and was buried in Zion Hill Cemetery. He was a carpenter. He married (1) **Nancy LOCKMAN**, and, later, (2) **Mary LITTLE** about 1839 in S. Dumfries, Brant County, Ontario. Mary LITTLE was born on 29 September 1820 in USA. She died on 19 October 1895, and was buried in Zion Hill Cemetery. William and Mary had these children:

246 i. **Fanny HOWELL** was born about 1841 in S. Dumfries.
+247 ii. **William HOWELL.**
+248 iii. **Jane A. HOWELL.**
249 iv. **Matilda HOWELL** was born and died in Ontario. She was buried in Burford Cemetery.
250 v. **Hanna HOWELL** was born about 1848 in S. Dumfries. She married **Wellington MOORE.**
251 vi. **Caroline M. HOWELL** was born on 28 December 1852 in S. Dumfries. She died on 15 May 1925, and was buried in Zion Hill Cemetery.
252 vii. **Mary HOWELL** was born in 1856 in Burford Township, Brant County.
+253 viii. **Sadie HOWELL.**
254 ix. **Ellen "Nellie" HOWELL** was born in 1865 in Ontario, and died in 1929. She was buried in Holy Trinity Anglican Cemetery, Burford, Brant County. She married **Robert BALKWELL.**
255 x. **Edward HOWELL** was born in 1866 in Burford Township, Brant County.
256 xi. **Israel HOWELL** was born in 1868 in Burford Township.
257 xii. **Susan HOWELL** was born in 1870 in Burford Township, Brant County.

46. **Daniel Peersley HOWELL** was born on 28 June 1782 in Sussex County, New Jersey. He died on 29 March 1869 in Jerseyville, Ontario, and was buried in Jerseyville Cemetery. He was married to **Mary SHACKLETON** on 5 December 1806 in Sussex County, New Jersey.[44] Mary SHACKLETON was born on 6 May 1784 in New Jersey. Mary and Daniel moved to Canada in 1806 or 1807. She died on 26 October 1854 in Jersey Settlement, Ontario. They had these children:

258 i. **Infant Son HOWELL,** died at birth.

---

[44]Sussex County Marriage Book A, page 97.

259 ii. **Garret HOWELL** was born about 1810. He died, unmarried, in England, in 1874.
260 iii. **Elizabeth "Betsy" HOWELL** was born on 21 December 1812, and died on 26 May 1832. She married **William SMITH** on 14 October 1830 in Wentworth County, Ontario.
261 iv. **Levi HOWELL** was born on 12 April 1815, died on 24 May 1904, and was buried in Jerseyville Cemetery. He married **Elizabeth BRAY** in 1834.
+262 v. **Isaac Reid HOWELL.**
263 vi. **David M. HOWELL** was born in 1818, and died on 27 April 1887 in Brantford.
+264 vii. **George Ferguson HOWELL.**
+265 viii. **Daniel HOWELL.**

47. **Ruth HOWELL** was born on 27 July 1784 in Sussex County, New Jersey. She died on 20 February 1869 in Wentworth County, Ontario. She was married to **Samuel DEAN** on 18 January 1802 in Grimsby, Lincoln County, Ontario. Samuel DEAN was born about 1778 in Sussex County, New Jersey. Ruth and Samuel DEAN had the following children:

+266 i. **James DEAN.**
267 ii. **Samuel DEAN** was born about 1807, and died in 1878. He was buried in Fruitland, Wentworth County. He married **Caroline SINGER** on 20 December 1833. Caroline was born in 1833 and died in 1870.
268 iii. **Garret DEAN** was born about 1809, died in 1877, and was buried in Fruitland. He married **Hannah SINGER**, who was born in 1807 and died in 1885.
269 iv. **David DEAN** was born in 1810, died in 1831, and was buried in Stoney Creek, Wentworth County.
270 v. **Martha DEAN** was born about 1813.
+271 vi. **Levi DEAN.**
272 vii. **Ruth DEAN** was born in 1817. She married **Levi NEIL.**
273 viii. **Abraham DEAN** was born in 1822. He died and was buried in Fruitland.
+274 ix. **Ann DEAN.**

48. **Levi HOWELL** was born on 2 May 1786 in Sussex County, New Jersey. He died on 24 November 1845 in Ontario, and was buried in St. George United Cemetery. Levi went to Canada about 1810. He was married to **Margaret Ann STENABAUGH** (daughter of **John STENABAUGH** and **Mary UNKNOWN**) on 13 October 1818 in Ancaster Twp., Wentworth County, Ontario. Margaret Ann STENABAUGH was born on 10 February 1797 in Sussex County, New Jersey. She died on 2 March 1876 in Ontario, and was buried in St. George United Cemetery. They had these children:

+275	i.	**Mary HOWELL.**
+276	ii.	**Daniel HOWELL.**
+277	iii.	**Philip Stenabaugh HOWELL.**
+278	iv.	**Peter HOWELL.**
+279	v.	**Lydia HOWELL.**
+280	vi.	**George M. HOWELL.**
+281	vii.	**Margaret Ann HOWELL.**

49. **Garret HOWELL** was born on 3 January 1788 in Sussex County, New Jersey. He died on 2 October 1874 in Ancaster Twp., Wentworth County, Ontario. He was a farmer. Garret followed his father to Canada about 1809, settling in Ancaster. He was married (1) to **Mary OGDEN** (daughter of **Benjamin OGDEN** and **Hannah READ**) in 1809 in Sussex County, New Jersey. Mary OGDEN was born on 26 January 1788 in Sussex County. She died on 3 January 1852 in Ontario, and was buried in Jerseyville Cemetery. Their children were:

+282	i.	**David HOWELL.**
283	ii.	**Elizabeth HOWELL** was born on 5 January 1810 in Ancaster Twp. She married **John VANSICKLE** in 1830 in Beverly Twp., Wentworth County.
284	iii.	**Matilda HOWELL** was born on 24 July 1811 in Ancaster Twp. She married **Charles HAMMILL**, about 1830.
285	iv.	**Sarah HOWELL** was born on 1 September 1813 in Ancaster Twp.
+286	v.	**Benjamin Ogden HOWELL.**
+287	vi.	**Isaac Lanning HOWELL.**
288	vii.	**Ruth HOWELL** was born on 5 January 1821 in Ancaster Twp.
289	viii.	**Mary HOWELL** was bon on 8 November 1822 in Ancaster Twp. She married **William SHAVER** on 30 April 1844.
+290	ix.	**Levi C. HOWELL.**
291	x.	**Phoebe Jane HOWELL** was born on 5 July 1831 in Ancaster Twp.
292	xi.	**Jane HOWELL** was born in 1834 in Ancaster Twp. She was unmarried.

Garret was married (2) to **Sarah CORNELL** on 3 April 1855 in Ontario, Canada. Sarah CORNELL was born in Wentworth County, Ontario. After their marriage, Garret moved to her home, and sold his neighboring 100 acre lot to his son, Levi C. on 27 February 1854, who later sold to James Harrington.

50. **Sampson HOWELL** was born on 3 February 1790 in Sussex County, NJ. He died on 2 August 1841, of small pox. He was married to **Jane MORDEN** on 19 November 1815 in Canada. Jane MORDEN was born about 1794 in Ontario. Sampson HOWELL and Jane MORDEN had one child:

293 i. **D. M. HOWELL** was born in 1816 in Ontario.

52. **Peter HOWELL** was born on 11 August 1792 in Hope, Sussex County, New Jersey. He died on 26 February 1868 in Jerseyville. Peter was in the War of 1812, served with the militia during the 1837 Rebellion and later became Justice of the Peace. He was married to **Elizabeth MILLER** (daughter of **George MILLER**) on 11 August 1814. Elizabeth was born on 10 December 1798 in Hackettstown, Sussex County, New Jersey. She died on 22 February 1886. Peter and Elizabeth had these children:

+294 i. **George Miller HOWELL.**
+295 ii. **Sarah HOWELL.**
+296 iii. **Jane HOWELL.**
297 iv. **Margaret HOWELL** was born in 1823. She married **Aaron NASH** in 1853. Aaron was a merchant in Dundas, and Mary was a teacher. They moved to Paris, Ontario in 1860, where they were active in the Methodist Church. Aaron died in 1893, and Mary died on 7 May, year not known.
+298 v. **Catharine HOWELL.**
299 vi. **Mary S. HOWELL** was born in 1827 in Jerseyville. She married **William W. GALLOWAY** on 18 February 1858 in Jerseyville.
300 vii. **Matilda HOWELL** was born on 6 December 1829 in Jerseyville, died there on 11 June 1857, and was buried in Jerseyville Cemetery. She married **Darius C. RICHMOND** on 18 April 1854. He died in 1908 in Woodstock, Oxford County, Ontario.
+301 viii. **Harriet HOWELL.**
302 ix. **Elizabeth Ann HOWELL** was born in 1836. She married **George R. DAVIDSON.**

57. **Moses Hazen HOWELL** was born on 23 September 1799 in Hope, Sussex County, New Jersey. He died on 6 February 1879 in Jerseyville. He was buried in Jerseyville Cemetery. Moses moved to Niagara in 1799 and to Ancaster in 1802. He was a blacksmith and a farmer. In the 1851 Census he owned 5 shops and a 12 horsepower steam sawmill which had cost $500.00. He was one of the members elected to the first Municipal Council of the Township of Ancaster on 21 January 1850. He was married to **Deborah WILSON** (daughter of **Obed WILSON**) on 4 December 1821. Deborah WILSON was born on 8 November 1801 in Welland County, Ontario. She died on 27 December 1870 in Ancaster Twp., and was buried in Jerseyville Cemetery. Moses Hazen HOWELL and Deborah WILSON had these children:

+303 i. **Sophia HOWELL.**
+304 ii. **Wesley HOWELL.**
+305 iii. **Nelson HOWELL.**

+306 iv. **Morris HOWELL.**
+307 v. **Ruth HOWELL.**
308 vi. **George HOWELL** was born on 25 November 1832 in Jerseyville, died on 20 July 1835, and was buried in Jerseyville Cemetery.
+309 vii. **Obed HOWELL.**
310 viii. **Hannah HOWELL** was born on 19 June 1835 in Jerseyville. She died on 17 February 1863, and was buried in Woodstock, Oxford County, Ontario. She married **Darius C. RICHMOND** on 31 March 1858 in Jerseyville. He died in July 1908 in Woodstock.
+311 ix. **Clark HOWELL.**
+312 x. **Lydia HOWELL.**
313 xi. **Sarah HOWELL** was born on 31 August 1844 in Jerseyville, and died in Grand Rapids, Michigan. She married **John HALL** on 18 August 1874.

58. **Isaac Lanning HOWELL** was born on 6 May 1801 in Hope, Sussex County, New Jersey. He died on 28 September 1846 in Jerseyville, and was buried in Jerseyville Cemetery. He was a local preacher. He was married to **Rachel UNKNOWN** on 12 March 1822 in Ontario. Their children were:

314 i. **Unnamed male HOWELL** was born on 25 May 1823.
315 ii. **Peter HOWELL** was born on 17 July 1824, died on 9 February 1844 in Ancaster Twp., and was buried in Jerseyville Cemetery.
316 iii. **Edmond HOWELL** was born on 24 May 1828. He died on 3 September 1848, and was buried in Jerseyville Cemetery.
317 iv. **Mary HOWELL** was born on 22 February 1830. She died on 7 November 1884 in Mt. Brydges, Caradoc Twp., Middlesex Co., Ontario.
+318 v. **Nancy HOWELL.**
+319 vi. **Elizabeth HOWELL.**
+320 vii. **Lois Ann HOWELL.**
321 viii. **Sarah Ann HOWELL.**
322 ix. **Daniel T. HOWELL.**

61. **Enoch HOWELL** was born on 27 August 1807 in Ancaster Twp., Wentworth County, Ontario. He died on 29 July 1889 in Brant County, and was buried in Princeton Cemetery, Blenheim Twp., Oxford County, Ontario. He was in the militia in 1828. He was married to **Drusella DRAKE** on 8 March 1825 in Ontario. Drusella DRAKE died on 9 March 1883, and was buried in Princeton Cemetery. Enoch HOWELL and Drusella DRAKE had the following children:

323 i. **Elizabeth HOWELL** was born on 8 December 1845 in Ancaster Twp. She died on 1 November 1861 in

Burford Township, Brant County, Ontario, and was buried in Fairfield Cemetery, Burford Twp.

324 ii. **Hamilton Wesley HOWELL** was born on 22 April 1853 in Onondaga Twp., Brant County, Ontario.

325 iii. **Reuben D. HOWELL** was married to **R. PAGE**, daughter of **James PAGE** in 1864.

62. **Margaret HOWELL** was born on 17 July 1809 in Ancaster Twp. She died on 17 February 1901 in Montrose, Genesee County, Michigan. She married **Isaac HORNING** on 18 September 1828 in Ancaster Twp. Isaac HORNING was born on 27 August 1801, died on 6 March 1867 in Ancaster Twp. and was buried in Zion Hill Cemetery. Isaac was said to be German, and was an artist, according to the 1871 census. Margaret HOWELL and Isaac HORNING had the following children:

326 i. **Gideon HORNING** was living in Taymouth in 1901, when his mother died.

327 ii. **James HORNING** was in Richmond in 1901.

328 iii. **John HORNING** lived in Buffalo, NY in 1901.

329 iv. **Oliver HORNING** was living in Keamore, NY, in 1901.

330 v. **Abram HORNING** was in Montrose, Michigan when his mother died.

331 vi. **Sarah HORNING** married **Unknown HOWELL** and lived in Carlton, Michigan in 1901.

332 vii. **Lavilla HORNING** lived in Sage, Michigan in 1901, having married **Unknown WEIR.**

333 viii. **Catherine HORNING** was born on 9 August 1833, died on 13 September 1833, and was buried in Zion Hill Cemetery.

334 ix. **Lorenzo HORNING** was born on 6 September 1836. He died on 26 June 1847, and was buried in Zion Hill Cemetery.

63. **William HOWELL** was born on 18 November 1811 in Ancaster Twp., Wentworth County, Ontario. He died on 13 August 1845 in Onondaga Twp., Brant County, Ontario. He was buried in Brant Cemetery, Brantford Twp., Brant County, Ontario. He was married to **Elizabeth DAY** (daughter of **Solomon DAY** and **Sarah UNKNOWN**) on 5 October 1831 in Onondaga Twp. Elizabeth DAY was born in 1810 in Wentworth County, Ontario. She died on 14 March 1890 in Onondaga Twp. and was buried in Brant Cemetery. William HOWELL and Elizabeth DAY had the following children:

335 i. **George Whitfield HOWELL** was born in October 1833, in Onandaga Twp. He married **Elizabeth POPPLEWELL** (daughter of **John POPPLEWELL** and **Sarah SPENCER**) on 14 March 1861 in Brant County.

336 ii. **Jane A. HOWELL** was born in 1835 in Onondaga Twp. She married **Simon OLMSTEAD**, and they lived in Townsend.

+337 iii. **Alexander James HOWELL**.

+338 iv. **Isaac HOWELL.**

339 v. **John W. HOWELL** was born in 1841 in Onondaga Twp., and died in 1920. He married **Hester SHAVER** (daughter **of Frederick SHAVER** and **Margaret MCKEE**). She was born in 1841 and died in 1924.

+340 vi. **William Hamilton HOWELL.**

64. **Esther Anne HOWELL** was born on 30 November 1813 in Ancaster Twp., Wentworth County, Ontario. She died on 28 September 1857 in Beverly Township, Wentworth County, and was buried in Jerseyville Cemetery. She was married to **John BENNETT** on 17 March 1842 in Ontario. He was born on 28 June 1813, and died on 11 March 1896. Esther Anne and John BENNETT had the following children:

341 i. **Eliza Augusta BENNETT** was born in June 1843, died on 2 September 1843, and was buried in Jerseyville Cemetery.

342 ii. **Calista Adelaide BENNETT** was born on 4 July 1846, died on 16 September 1858, and was buried in Jerseyville Cemetery.

GEORGE W. HOWELL, his wife, RACHEL HARRIET STACKHOUSE HOWELL, their daughter, HELEN ELIZABETH HOWELL and an unidentified little boy, about 1879.

FIFTH GENERATION

65. **Lavinah ALBERTSON** was born on 11 October 1795 in Frelinghuysen, Warren County, NJ. She died on 9 February 1868, and was buried in Union Cemetery, Hope, Warren County, NJ. Her husband, **Samuel VANSYCKLE**, was born on 30 September 1780. He died on 28 August 1863. and was buried in Union Cemetery. In the 1860 census, Samuel, a farmer, had real estate valued at $400 and personal property worth $200.[39] Samuel and Lavinah had a son:

343 i. **Isaac VANSYCKLE** was born about 1830 in New Jersey. He was a farmer. On 24 September 1853, he married **Luticia RAUB** who was born about 1827, in New Jersey.

68. **Samson ALBERTSON** was born on 5 December 1799 in Frelinghuysen, Sussex County. He died there on 1 November 1858. He was married to **Abigail S. COURSEN** on 20 October 1825 in Frelinghuysen. Abigail S. COURSEN was born on 30 January 1800. She died on 5 September 1845 in Great Meadows, Warren County. Their children were:

344 i. **Garret ALBERTSON** was born on 28 October 1826 in Frelinghuysen, and died on 24 December 1915 in Moundridge, Kansas. He married (1) **Amanda DEMOND,** and (2) **Margaret Jane MCFALL.**

345 ii. **Mary Jane ALBERTSON** was born on 13 March 1828 in Frelinghuysen. She married **Warren I. POTTER** on 17 January 1850.

346 iii. **Emily Elizabeth ALBERTSON** was born on 9 September 1829 in Frelinghuysen. She died on 6 May 1904. She married **Nathan HOAGLAND** on 5 December 1853.

347 iv. **Lydia Ann ALBERTSON** was born on 11 October 1831 in Frelinghuysen, and died on 26 August 1876. She married **Lewis BARNES** on 24 March 1857.

+348 v. **Coursen Henry ALBERTSON.**

349 vi. **Edwin Clark ALBERTSON** was born on 19 August 1836 in Frelinghuysen, and died in Detroit, Wayne County, MI. Edwin served in the Civil War for three years, with Co. B, 15th Regt., NJ Volunteers.

72. **Isaac Read ALBERTSON** was born on 2 November 1809 in Frelinghuysen, Warren County, where he died in 1893. He was married to **Ann UNKNOWN**

---

[39]1860 U.S. Census (population) New Jersey, Warren Co., Hope Twp., p.28, nos.203/201, National Archives Microfilm Publication, M653, roll 711.

about 1837 in Frelinghuysen. Ann UNKNOWN was born in 1816 in NJ. Their children were:[40]

350 i. **Phebe ALBERTSON** was born in 1839 in Frelinghuysen.

351 ii. **Sarah J. ALBERTSON** was born in 1841 in Frelinghuysen, died on 20 April 1889, and was buried in Union Cemetery.

352 iii. **Lemuel E. ALBERTSON** was born in 1844 in Frelinghuysen.

73. **Samuel ALBERTSON** was born on 9 December 1811 in Frelinghuysen, Warren County,where he died in 1897. He married **Mary Aurea J. TREAT** on 1 December 1838 in Warren County.[41] She was born in 1820. Their children were:[42]

353 i. **Edward H. ALBERTSON** was born in 1840 in Frelinghuysen.

354 ii. **Isaiah N. ALBERTSON** was born in 1841 in Frelinghuysen.

355 iii. **Elsey J. ALBERTSON** was born in 1845 in Frelinghuysen.

356 iv. **Nicholas J. ALBERTSON** was born in 1847 in Frelinghuysen.

357 v. **Emma F. ALBERTSON** was born in 1856 in Frelinghuysen.

76. **Margaret HOWELL** was born on 9 May 1794 in Hope, Sussex County. She died on 2 April 1874. She was married to **Consider COOKE** on 29 June 1815 in Sussex County. He was born on 2 November 1793 and died on 9 August 1875. Consider and Margaret were buried in Free Union Cemetery, Mountain Lake, Warren County, NJ. Their children were:[43]

358 i. **Elizabeth COOKE** was born on 6 June 1825 in Warren County, NJ, died on 22 January 1898, and was buried in Free Union Cemetery.

359 ii. **John H. COOKE** was born about 1829 in Warren County, NJ.

360 iii. **Ann COOKE** was born about 1835 in Warren County.

361 iv. **Charles COOKE** was born in 1837 in Warren County.

---

[40]1860 U.S. Census (population) New Jersey, Warren Co., Frelinghuysen, p. 30, nos. 205/214, National Archives Microfilm Publication, M653, roll 711.

[41]Warren County, NJ Marriage Records, LDS Microfilm # 0960890. V. 1, p. 133.

[42]1860 U.S. Census (population) New Jersey, Warren Co., Frelinghuysen, p.30, nos.203/213, National Archives Microfilm Publication, M653, roll 711.

[43]ibid. Hope Twp., p.29, nos. 214/212.

362 v. **Carrie COOKE** was born about 1842 in Warren County.

363 vi. **Lydia Jane COOKE** was born about 1850 in Warren County.

77. **Mary G. HOWELL** was born on 17 July 1796 in Hope, Sussex County, New Jersey. She died on 2 November 1887 in Blairstown, Warren County, NJ. She was buried in Union Cemetery. Mary died of "gradual failure after fracture of the neck of the femur a year prior to death." [44] Mary married **John STRICKLAND,** who was born in 1795 in Sussex County. He died on 22 July 1835 in Warren County, and was buried in Union Cemetery. Mary and John STRICKLAND had one child:

364 i. **Caroline A. STRICKLAND** was born on 4 December 1825, and died on 10 May 1828 in Warren County. She was buried in Union Cemetery.

78. **Charles Wesley HOWELL** was born on 11 May 1801 in Hope, Sussex County, New Jersey, died there on 11 December 1875, and was buried in Union Cemetery. Charles was a stone mason, and a farmer.[45] Charles Wesley HOWELL married **Sarah LETSON**, who was born in 1816. She died on 26 May 1844, and was buried in Union Cemetery. Charles and Sarah had these children:

365 i. **Ellen HOWELL** was born on 31 October 1838 in Warren County. She died on 27 November 1920 in Hope, and was buried in Union Cemetery.

+366 ii. **John Wesley HOWELL.**

79. **Levi HOWELL** was born on 22 May 1802 in Hope, Sussex County. He died on 7 March 1886 in New Jersey, and was buried in Union Cemetery, Hope. He was a farmer. He was married to **Huldah P. WILCOX** on 14 December 1850 in Warren County. [46]Huldah P. WILCOX was born on 29 March 1815. She died on 3 December 1890, and was buried in Union Cemetery. They had these children:

+367 i. **Millard Fillmore HOWELL.**

+368 ii. **Edward A. HOWELL.**(His birth certificate suggests he may have had a male twin.)

+369 iii. **Mary M. HOWELL.**

370 iv. **Anna O. HOWELL** was born on 14 June 1860 in Warren County. She died on 27 November 1923, and was buried in Union Cemetery. She married **Leslie LETSON.**

---

[44]Death certificate for Mary Strickland, signed by John C. Johnson, M.D., dated 2 November 1887.

[45]1850 U.S. Census (population) New Jersey, Warren Co., Hope Twp., p.434, nos.694/726, National Archives Microfilm Publication, M432, roll 465.

[46]Warren County NJ Marriage Records, LDS Microfilm # 0960890, V. 1, p.292.

81. **Abraham S. HOWELL** was born about 1811 in Hope, Sussex County, NJ. He died and was buried in Union Cemetery. He was a laborer. He was married to **Rachael S. WEST** on 15 November 1832 in Warren County.[47] Rachael S. WEST was born in 1816 in Hope, Sussex County, NJ. She died in 1884 in Polkville, Warren County, NJ, and was buried in Union Cemetery. Their children were:[48]

+371 i. **Caleb H. HOWELL.**
+372 ii. **John H. HOWELL.**
+373 iii. **Marshall HOWELL.**
+374 iv. **Martha Ann HOWELL.**
375 v. **Emily HOWELL** was born about 1843. Emily had a son, **Elwell A. HOWELL**, on 17 May 1871.
376 vi. **Sarah Elizabeth HOWELL** was born on 11 November 1854 in Warren County, and died on 24 January 1899 in Portland, Northampton County, PA. She married **George APGAR**. Her obit used this birthdate, but she was said to be 5 on the 1850 census, we aren't certain of the right date.
+377 vii. **Abby Maria HOWELL.**
378 viii. **William HOWELL** was born on 27 April 1851.
379 ix. **Malvene F. HOWELL** was born on 27 June 1853 in Knowlton, Warren County.
+380 x. **Catherine HOWELL.**
+381 xi. **Abraham Brands HOWELL.**

82. **Asa Jacob HOWELL** was born on 8 October 1813 in Hope, Sussex County, NJ. He died on 8 October 1856 in Johnsonburg, Warren County, and was buried in Union Cemetery. Asa was killed while at work in Johnsonburg, NJ. He married **Esther Ann HOPKINS**, who was born on 9 June 1825. She died on 4 May 1881, and was buried in Union Cemetery. She was a seamstress. Their children were:

382 i. **Lahrma Almeda HOWELL** was born on 12 November 1845 in Warren County, where she died on 12 July 1868. She was buried in Union Cemetery.
383 ii. **John C. HOWELL** was born on 29 October 1848 in Hope, Warren County. He died on 28 August 1939 in Mt. Hermon, Warren County, and was buried in Union Cemetery, Hope, Warren County.
384 iii. **Charles T. HOWELL** was born on 29 January 1851 in Hope, Warren County. He died in 1927 in Oxford, and was buried in Union Cemetery.

---

47 Warren County, NJ Marriage Records, LDS Microfilm # 0960890. V.1, p. 71.
48 1850 U.S. Census (population) New Jersey, Warren Co., Hope Twp., p.438, nos. 744/ 779, National Archives Microfilm Publication, M432, roll 465.

385 iv. **Theodore Wesley HOWELL** was born on 18 April 1853 in Hope. He died on 16 December 1908, and was buried in Union Cemetery.

KILLED AS WAS HIS FATHER

Theodore Howell instantly killed through the falling of a heavy drill at the Oxford Furnace.

Theodore Howell, who was killed while at work in the Oxford blast furnace last Wednesday, met a violent death in a manner quite similar to that of his father over 50 years ago. The elder Howell was killed at Johnsonburg on October 9, 1856, while assisting at a pole raising during a political campaign. One of the props gave way, the pole falling and striking him on the head, crushing the skull and causing immediate death.

Theodore, his son, who was killed last week, had been employed at the Oxford Furnace, most of the time as a fireman, since his removal to Oxford in 1882. The accident occurred shortly after 10 0'clock Wednesday morning. Workmen were at the top of the furnace while Howell and three men were at the bottom building a scaffold. A four pound drill got away from the men at the top, rolled across the platform before they could get it and dropped through a crevice in the boards. The heavy iron pierced the skull and dislocated the neck, producing instant death.[49]

386 v. **Jennie Charity HOWELL** was born on 2 June 1857 in Warren County, died in 1929, and was buried in Union Cemetery, Hope, Warren County, NJ.

83. **John H. HOWELL** was born on 2 November 1817 in Hope, Sussex County, NJ. He died on 12 September 1894 in Hope, Warren County, and was buried in Union Cemetery. His farm was located near the Union Cemetery between Hope and Johnsonburg. John had been ailing for some time, when he fell from his porch and died from his injuries.[50] John HOWELL married **Elizabeth S. UNKNOWN**, who was born in 1827. John and Elizabeth had the following children:

387 i. **Lydia A. HOWELL** was born on 21Sep 1846 in Warren County, NJ. She died on 21 July 1848 and was buried in Union Cemetery.

388 ii. **Levi Henry HOWELL** was born on 13 July 1849 in Warren County. He died there on 9 April 1868, and was buried in Union Cemetery.

389 iii. **Sarah L. HOWELL** was born on 15 May 1851 in Warren County, where she died on 26 May 1851.

390 iv. **Emma M. HOWELL** was born on 2 April 1854 in Warren County, NJ.

---

[49]News article, Washington (NJ) Star, 24 December 1908, page 1.

[50]Obituary, Washington (NJ) Star, 20 September 1894.

86. **John Triller HOWELL** was born about 1800. He died on 19 November 1892. He married **Hannah SMITH** on 26 March 1828. Hannah SMITH (daughter of **Joseph SMITH** and **Margaret MOORE**) was born in 1806 in Trafalgar, Halton County, Ontario. She died in 1880. They had one child:

391 i. **Victoria Lambton HOWELL** was born about 1839. She died on 7 January 1842, and was buried in Palermo United Church Cemetery, Trafalgar.

89. **Phebe HOWELL** was born on 7 October 1805 in Hope, Sussex County, NJ. She died on 24 August 1875 in West Jersey, Stark County, IL. She was married to **Thomas PRICE** (son of **Robert PRICE** and **Jemima PARR**) on 11 December 1824 in Sussex County, New Jersey.[51] Their children were:

+392 i. **William Biles PRICE.**

393 ii. **Harriet PRICE** was born in 1834 in Hope, Warren County, NJ. The Warren County Marriage Books record a marriage for a **Harriet PRICE**, to **John BARTOW**, on 27 January 1853, which may be her marriage.[52]

92. **George W. HOWELL** was born in 1812 in Hope, Sussex County, NJ. He died on 29 June 1883 in West Pittston, Luzerne County, PA. George bought from his father, Levi, part of a farm which he and his brothers John and Sampson worked. He was married to **Rachel Harriet STACKHOUSE** (daughter of **James STACKHOUSE** and **Elizabeth POYERS**) on 15 October 1853 in the Methodist Church in Hackettstown, Warren County. Rachel Harriet STACKHOUSE was born in July 1838. She died after 1907 in West Pittston, Luzerne County, PA. Rachel Harriet was apparently known as Harriet, since that is the way she is listed in all censuses. She and George were neighbors in Hope Township, her parents farming a short distance from the Howell farm.

After his marriage to Rachel Harriet, George evidently had financial problems, and sold his share of the farm to John.[53] Later, he is believed to have had other assets which he was forced to turn over to Alpheus Swayze in 1864, to be sold to pay off his creditors.

George and his family were in Northmoreland, Wyoming County at the time of the 1860 census,[54] where he was a farm laborer. By 1870, the family was in Exeter

---

[51] Sussex County Marriage Book A, p. 97.

[52] Warren County, NJ Marriage Records, LDS Microfilm # 0960890. V. 1, p. 344.

[53] Deed , George W. Howell and his wife, Rachel, to John S. Howell and his wife, Ann, Warren County Deed Book 38:343, 24 January 1854.

[54] 1860 U.S. Census (population) Pennsylvania, Wyoming County, Northmoreland Twp., p.224, nos. 852/846, National Archives Microfilm Publication, M653, roll 1197.

Township, Luzerne County, where George claimed to have real estate valued at $400.[55] The post office for this area was in Dallas, which suggests that he was still a farm laborer. By 1880, they were living on Washington Street in West Pittston,[56] which must have been a change for them, since the town was fairly well populated. George listed his occupation as laborer. By 1900, Harriet and Benson were living on Montgomery Street, in one side of a double house, the other side being occupied by her daughter, called Lizzie in the census, her second husband, Melchoir Kintz, and two children from her first marriage. Their children were:

+394	i.	**James Alben HOWELL.**
+395	ii.	**George Marshall HOWELL.**
+396	iii.	**Dorrance W. HOWELL.**
397	iv.	**Benson N. HOWELL** was born in February 1863, and died before 1931 in PA.The 1920 census indicates he was living with his niece, Harriet Wintle PUGH on Spruce Street in West Pittston.
+398	v.	**Helen Elizabeth HOWELL.**

No death certifiacte has ever been found for Rachel Harriet STACKHOUSE.

93. **John Stinson HOWELL** was born on 7 July 1817 in Hope, Sussex County, New Jersey. He died on 1 September 1906 in Avon Twp., Oakland County, Michigan., and was buried in Mt. Avon Cemetery, Rochester, Oakland County. He was married to **Anna A. CORWIN** (daughter of **Nathaniel CORWIN** and **Elizabeth BILES**) on 8 February 1849 in Warren County, New Jersey. Anna A. CORWIN was born on 23 February 1829 in New Jersey. She died on 10 September 1906 in Avon Twp., and was also buried in Mt. Avon Cemetery. John Stinson HOWELL and Anna A. CORWIN had the following children:

399	i.	**Marcus Lafayette HOWELL** was born on 7 October 1849 in Hope.
400	ii.	**Electa A. HOWELL** was born on 28 September 1851 in Hope, and died 15 February 1924. She married **Franklin PARKER** on 31 March 1873 in Macomb County, Michigan. Franklin PARKER died in 1881. Both were buried in Mt. Avon Cemetery.
+401	iii.	**William Biles HOWELL.**
402	iv.	**Mary Elizabeth HOWELL** was born on 28 October 1853 in Hope, Warren County. She died on 20 June 1947, and was buried in Mt. Avon Cemetery. She married **Mervin TURRELL.**

---

[55]1870 U.S. Census (population) Pennsylvania, Luzerne County, Exeter Twp., p. 415, nos.112/114, National Archives Microfilm Publication, M593, roll 1365.
[56]1880 U.S. Census (population) Pennsylvania, Luzerne County, West Pittston Borough, E.D.95, p.43, 379/435, National Archives Microfilm Publication, T-9, roll 1150.

403 v. **Emma Araminta HOWELL** was born in 1856 in Hope, Warren County, New Jersey.

404 vi. **Alice HOWELL** was born on 3 September 1857 in Hope.

405 vii. **Martha E. HOWELL** was born in August 1860, and died on 15 December 1861. Martha is buried next to her grandparents, Levi and Phebe HOWELL in Free Union Cemetery, Mountain Lake, Warren County.

+406 viii. **Franklin A. C. HOWELL.**

99. **Levi HOWELL** was born on 6 March 1809 in Sussex County, New Jersey. He died on 11 April 1882, and was buried in Newton Cemetery, Newton, Sussex County, NJ. Levi's property was midway between Newton and Sparta. The 1860 Sussex County census gives his net worth as $12,000 in real property and $2,000 in personal property.[57] Son Jonah was listed as a farm laborer. Levi married (1) **Mary YOUNG**. Levi HOWELL and Mary YOUNG had one child:

407 i. **Maria HOWELL** was born on 16 December 1833 in Sussex County.

He was married (2) to **Jane SNOOK** (daughter of **William SNOOK** and **Mary CUMMINS**) on 22 December 1838 in Sussex County, New Jersey. Jane SNOOK was born in 1809 in NJ. She died about 1879, and was buried in Newton Cemetery, Sussex County. Levi and Jane had the following children:

+408 i. **Margaret Ann HOWELL.**

+409 ii. **Jonah HOWELL.**

410 iii. **William HOWELL** was born on 18 January 1842. He died young.

411 iv. **Susan E. HOWELL** was born on 1 August 1844 in Sussex County. She married **Abraham MORRIS** on 5 December 1867.

412 v. **Sarah Elizabeth HOWELL** was born on 18 July 1845 in Sussex County. She married **Oliver MORRIS** on 20 April 1870.

+413 vi. **Daniel Webster HOWELL.**

414 vii. **Henderson HOWELL** was born on 23 September 1850 in Newton, Sussex County. He died on 11 February 1870, and was buried in Newton Cemetery, Newton, Sussex County, NJ.

415 viii. **Peter Cummins HOWELL** was born on 12 April 1852 in Newton, Sussex County. He died on 20 March 1861, and was buried in Newton Cemetery.

---

[57]1860 U.S. Census (population) New Jersey, Sussex Co., Newton Twp., p. 613, nos. 308/405, National Archives Microfilm Publication, M653, roll 711.

102. **Daniel P. HOWELL** was born on 23 June 1817 in Sparta, Sussex County, NJ. He died and was buried in Old Newton Burial Ground, Newton, NJ. He was married to **Euphemia COOK** on 21 August 1841 in Newton. Euphemia COOK was born in 1820. She died and was buried in Old Newton Burial Ground, Newton, NJ. Daniel and Euphemia had the following children:

416 i. **Sarah Ellen HOWELL** was born on 26 January 1842 in Sparta. She died and was buried in Old Newton Burial Ground.

417 ii. **Mary E. HOWELL** was born on 29 May 1844, and died on 22 November 1845 in Sparta. She was buried in Old Newton Burial Ground.

+418 iii. **George W. HOWELL.**

419 iv. **Pierson C. HOWELL** was born on 3 November 1848 in Sparta. He died on 5 March 1861, and was buried in Old Newton Burial Ground.

420 v. **Secelia M. HOWELL** was born in 1851 in Sparta.

421 vi. **Esther J. HOWELL** was born on 25 April 1854 and died on 2 December 1856 in Sparta. She was buried in Old Newton Burial Ground.

422 vii. **Levi HOWELL** was born in 1855 in Sparta.

423 viii. **Frances A. HOWELL** was born in 1858 in Sparta.

424 ix. **Rebecca A. HOWELL** was born in May 1859.

425 x. **Ryerson S. HOWELL** was born on 19 April 1862.

103. **Samuel Green HOWELL** was born on 17 January 1822 in Sparta, Sussex County, NJ. He died on 31 July 1866 in Brandon, Oakland County, Michigan. He was married to **Esther (Hester) Bailey EDMONSON** on 4 January 1845 in Newton, Sussex County.[58] Esther (Hester) Bailey EDMONSON was born on 26 January 1827. She died on 19 June 1899 in Independence Twp., Brandon, MI. In 1855, Samuel and Esther traveled to Michigan by way of the Erie Canal, and settled in Independence Twp., Michigan. They had the following children:[59]

+426 i. **Mary Matilda "Tillie" HOWELL.**

427 ii. **Joseph E. HOWELL** was born on 17 April 1847 and died on 17 August 1847 in Sussex County, NJ

+428 iii. **Emma Jane HOWELL.**

429 iv. **Jonah HOWELL** was born on 11 July 1851 in Sussex County, New Jersey. He died on 16 November 1871.

Esther EDMONDSON married (2) **Moses TAYLOR** on 29 October 1868 in Oakland County, Michigan.

---

[58]Sussex County Marriage Book A, page 97.

[59]Information on this family was contributed by Marfy Goodspeed, 136 Locktown-Flemington Rd., Flemington NJ 08822.

106. **Lavinia HOWELL** was born on 30 March 1815 in Sussex County, New Jersey. She died on 3 December 1890 in Frelinghuysen, Warren County, NJ. She was buried in Union Cemetery, Hope, Warren County, NJ. Lavinia married **Hiram SMITH**. Lavinia HOWELL and Hiram SMITH had one child:

430 i. **Mary A. SMITH** was born in Sussex County, New Jersey, and died at 5 months.

107. **William F. B. HOWELL** was born in 1816. He died on 22 January 1890. He was a farmer. He was married to **Clarissa SUTTON** (daughter of **Aaron SUTTON**) on 14 June 1849 in Frelinghuysen, Warren County, New Jersey. [60] Clarissa SUTTON was born in 1818. Their children were:

+431 i. **Watson Vincent HOWELL**.

+432 ii. **Levi C. HOWELL**.

433 iii. **Isaac M. HOWELL** was born on 9 November 1850 in Frelinghuysen, [61] where he died on 16 April 1902. He was buried in Johnsonburg Cemetery, Johnsonburg, NJ.

434 iv. **Martha "Mattie" HOWELL** was born in 1853 in Frelinghuysen.

435 v. **Alvah HOWELL** was born on 9 June 1856 in Frelinghuysen, and died there on 23 November 1856. He was buried in Johnsonburg Cemetery.

436 vi **Lavina Ada HOWELL** was born on 25 September 1857 in Frelinghuysen.

437 vii. **William F. HOWELL** was born in 1858 in Frelinghuysen.

+438 viii. **Clarissa Jennifer HOWELL**.

108. **Mary HOWELL** was born on 25 October 1819 in Sussex County, New Jersey. She died on 30 March 1887, and was buried in Union Cemetery, Hope, Warren County, New Jersey. She married **Edward CHANDLER** on 26 October 1844. [62] Edward CHANDLER was born in 1815 in Connecticut. He died on 13 May 1882, and was buried in Union Cemetery. Mary HOWELL and Edward CHANDLER had these children:

439 i. **Margey CHANDLER** was born in 1846 in Warren County, NJ.

---

[60]Marriage Return for Wm.F.B. Howell & Clarissa Sutton, New Jersey State Archives, Trenton, NJ. Vol. AH, p. 14 NJ State Archives.

[61]Birth Certificate, Vol. AJ, p. 42, Warren Co. NJ. New Jersey State Archives, Trenton, NJ.

[62]Warren County, NJ Marriage Records, LDS Microfilm # 0960890, p. 108.

440 ii. **Elen CHANDLER** was born in 1847 in Warren County.
441 iii. **George CHANDLER** was born in September 1849 in Frelinghuysen, Warren County, NJ. He died on 3 May 1855, and was buried in Union Cemetery.
442 iv. **Sarah CHANDLER** was born about 1851 in Warren County. She died on 6 October 1854, and was buried in Union Cemetery.
443 v. **John CHANDLER** was born about 1853, and died on 30 April 1855 in Frelinghuysen. He was buried in Union Cemetery.
444 vi. **Watson CHANDLER** was born in 1854 in Stillwater, Sussex County, NJ.
445 vii. **Emma CHANDLER** was born in 1856 in Stillwater.
446 viii. **Permila CHANDLER** was born in 1858 in Stillwater.

109. **A. J. HOWELL** was born in Sussex County, New Jersey. A.J. and his family were found in the 1860 census for Blairstown, but not in the 1870 census. He was married to **Calfernia "Cally" DUNHAM** on 22 July 1854 in Farmington, Warren County, PA. Calfernia "Cally" DUNHAM was born in 1835 in NJ. A. J. HOWELL and Calfernia "Cally" DUNHAM had the following children:[63]

447 i. **Lucy HOWELL** was born in 1856.
448 ii. **Jenny HOWELL** was born in 1858.

111. **Anthony Johnson HOWELL** was born on 25 June 1813 in Hope, Sussex County, NJ. He died on 14 March 1844 in NJ, and was buried in Union Cemetery, Hope, Warren County, NJ. Anthony married **Levina ALLEN** on 30 June 1832 in Warren County, NJ.[64] Levina was born in 1813 in NJ. Their children were:

+449 i. **Anna Maria HOWELL.**
+450 ii. **Charles D. HOWELL.**
+451 iii. **Isaac Allen HOWELL.**
+452 iv. **George Green HOWELL.**
+453 v. **Martha J. HOWELL.**
+454 vi. **Euphemia HOWELL.**

According to the information in Levi Howell's biography, Anthony's children were sent to live with Levi in Wyoming County, PA, after Anthony died.[65] Apparently, Levina remained in New Jersey with Euphemia by the time of the 1850 census,

---

[63]Information on this family contributed by Alfred E. Lee, 209 Colony Park Dr., Liverpool NY 13088.
[64]Warren County, NJ Marriage Records, LDS microfilm # 0960890. Vol. 1, p. 67.
[65]H.C. Bradsby, ed., History of Luzerne County, PA., with Biographical Selections, (Chicago:S.B.Nelson & Co.,1893), p.1000.

where she was listed on the farm of John Drake, in Mendham, Morris County, NJ.[66]

112. **Levi HOWELL** was born on 27 February 1817 in Hope, Sussex County, NJ. He died on 13 February 1904 in Trucksville, Luzerne County, PA, and was buried on 15 February 1904 in Cedar Crest Cemetery, Trucksville.[67]

"Levi Howell, farmer, P.O. Trucksville, was born in Hope Township, Warren County, N. J., February 27, 1817, a son of George G. and Lydia Johnson Howell, both of whom were born in the above named place. George G. Howell was a wealthy man, a loyal citizen, a kind accommodating neighbor, an honest and upright man in every respect. His family consisted of 10 children, all of whom are now living, Levi being second in the family. He received his education in the public schools of Hope, NJ, and in 1839, when aged 22 years, he removed to North Moreland Twp., Wyoming Co., Pa., where he purchased 160 acres of land to which he added 94 acres, thus showing his ability in his chosen vocation to manage his affairs and accumulate property. During his residence of 25 years there, he brought under cultivation 200 acres, proving himself to be a thoroughly practical farmer. Selling this property, he moved to Orange, this county, where he purchased a house and lot, but this was farming on too small a scale for a man of his ability, so he sold out and removed to Kingston township, same county, where he purchased a farm of 160 acres, 120 of which are under the plow, his specialties being grain and hay. Mr. Howell has been married four times. For his first wife, he wedded Miss Sarah Luce of New Jersey, by whom he had one daughter, Sarah, now Mrs. Coursen. For his second wife, he married Miss Olivia Smith, by whom he had one daughter, Mollie, wife of William Hatfield. His third wife was Miss Ruth Ann Rogers, and by her had six children, one of whom is now living in Iowa. His fourth wife was Mrs. Vaughan, who bore him six children, four of whom are now living: Levi T. married Miss Kate Schooley, Charles W. married Miss Kate Atherholt, Judson J. married to Miss Carrie Goode, and Emeline married to Walter Badler. Mr. Howell is a man of marked influence in his township, both in social and religious circles. He is a member of the M.E. Church, in politics a Republican, and has held several township offices." [68](The number of children adds to 14, not 10!)
Levi was married (1) to **Sarah Margaret LUCE** (daughter of **Aaron LUCE** and **Elizabeth READ**) on 4 January 1838 in Hardwick Twp., Warren County, NJ. [69] Sarah Margaret LUCE was born on 15 July 1819 in Sussex County. She died on 9 December 1839, and was buried in Union Cemetery, Hope, Warren County, NJ. Levi HOWELL and Sarah Margaret LUCE had one child:

+455 i. **Sarah Elizabeth HOWELL.**

---

[66]1850 U.S. Census (population) New Jersey, Morris Co., Mendham Twp.,p. 123, nos. 195/223, National Archives Microfilm Publication, M432, roll 465.
[67]Luzerne County Death Records 1900-1905,p. 225. LDS microfilm # 0960582
[68]H. C. Bradsby, History of Luzerne County, Pennsylvania, (Chicago: S. B. Nelson & Co., 1893), p. 1000
[69]Warren County, NJ Marriage Records, LDS microfilm # 0960890.

Levi married (2) **Olivia SMITH** (daughter of **Samuel G. SMITH** and **Margaret DEWITT**), in 1841. She was born in February 1818, and died on 1 May 1842. She was buried in Centremoreland Cemetery, Luzerne County, PA. Levi HOWELL and Olivia SMITH had one child:

+456 i. **Mary Ann "Mollie" HOWELL.**

Levi married (3) **Ruth Ann ROGERS**, who was born in January 1825. She died on 14 December 1853, and was buried in Rogers Cemetery, Centremoreland, Luzerne County, PA. Ruth Ann had 6 children, only three of whom have been identified. They were:

+457 i. **David R. HOWELL** was born in 1848 in Franklin Twp., Luzerne County, PA.

458 ii. **Euphame HOWELL** was born in January 1850 in Franklin Twp.

459 iii. **George HOWELL** was born in 1852 in Franklin Twp.

Levi married (4) **Emeline Griffin VAUGHAN**, whowas born on 30 May 1821, and died on 30 November 1898 in Trucksville, Luzerne County, PA.[70] Levi and Emeline had the following children:

+460 i. **Levi T. HOWELL.**

461 ii. **Charles W. HOWELL** was born in August 1856 in Franklin Twp., and died on 6 February 1935. He was buried in Cedar Crest Cemetery, Trucksville. He married **Kate ATHERHOLT.**

+462 iii. **John S. HOWELL.**

+463 iv. **Emeline R. HOWELL.**

464 v. **Kate E. HOWELL** was born on 30 August 1860, died on 21 January 1891, and was buried in Cedar Crest Cemetery. She married **Ziba SCHOOLEY**, who was born in 1859 in Kingston, Luzerne County.

465 vi. **Judson John HOWELL** was borne in 1862 in Franklin Twp. He died in 1938, and was buried in Cedar Crest Cemetery. He married **Carrie GOODE.**

The 1870 census shows Levi and Emeline in Kingston Township, Luzerne County, PA, with their children. Levi's real estate was valued at $9,100, personal property at $17,240.[71]

---

[70]Luzerne County, Pennsylvania Death Records, 1893-1899, p. 247. LDS microfilm #0960581.

[71]1870 U.S. Census (population) Pennsylvania, Luzerne County, Kingston Twp., p. 106, nos. 96/96, National Archives Microfilm Publication, M593, roll 1366.

113. **Samuel G. HOWELL Jr.** was born on 8 January 1819 in Hardwick Twp., Sussex County, NJ. He died in Luzerne, Luzerne County, PA. In the 1850 Warren County, NJ census, he was listed as a farmer, with land valued at $200.[72] By 1870, he was in Lehman Twp. Luzerne County, PA,[73] with his family. His real estate was valued at $2,000, personal property at $2,500 in that census. Samuel married his cousin, **Mercy HOWELL** (daughter of **James HOWELL** and **Hannah TEMPLER**). She was born in 1823 in Canada. Samuel G. HOWELL Jr. and Mercy HOWELL had the following children:

466 i. **Hannah Elizabeth HOWELL** was born on 21 February 1849 in Blairstown, Warren County, NJ.

467 ii. **Unnamed male HOWELL** was born on 11 January 1852 in Blairstown.

468 iii. **Mary C. HOWELL** was born in 1854 in Luzerne, Luzerne County, PA.

+469 iv. **James W. HOWELL.**

470 v. **Lewis J. HOWELL** was born on 11 January 1862 in Lehman Twp., Luzerne County, PA.

115. **Euphemia Osborne HOWELL** was born on 21 January 1822 in Hardwick Twp., Sussex County, NJ. She died on 30 September 1922 in Delaware County, IA, and was buried in Pineview Cemetery, Delaware County, IA. She was married (1) to **Albert THOMPSON** (son of **Luther THOMPSON** and **Ruhamah CHEDISTER**) on 27 November 1841 in Warren County, NJ.[74] Albert THOMPSON was christened on 3 July 1818 in Mendham, Morris County, NJ. He died on 31 October 1848 in Morris County, NJ. Euphemia Osborne HOWELL and Albert THOMPSON had the following children:[75]

+471 i. **Emeline Olivia THOMPSON.**

472 ii. **Anna Mary THOMPSON** was born in 1845 in Morris County, NJ. She married **R. C. WINCH**, and was living in Hopkinton, Iowa when her father died in 1904. She died after 1904, and was buried in Buck Creek Cemetery, Delaware County, Iowa.

After Albert's death, Euphemia married (2) his cousin **Amzi Babbitt THOMPSON** (son of **Daniel THOMPSON** and **Mary AXTELL**) in 1856 in Wilkes Barre, Luzerne County, PA., according to Euphemia's grand-daughter, Verna Bacon Neil. The marriage date is based on the birth date of the first child

---

[72]1850 U.S. Census (population) New Jersey, Warren Co., Blairstown, p.457,nos.1009/1050, National Archives Microfilm Publication, M432, roll 465.
[73]1870 U.S. Census (population)Pennsylvania, Luzerne Co., Lehman Twp., p.206, nos.119/ 117, National Archives Microfilm Publication, M593, roll 1366.
[74]Warren County, NJ Marriage Records, LDS microfilm #0960890. Vol. 1, p. 172.
[75]Family information contributed by Blanche Donovan, 16691 South 18th Way, Phoenix AZ 85048.

born of the marriage, and the fact that Amzi's first wife died in April of 1853. The location of the marriage also cannot be verified, since no records were kept in Pennsylvania until 1885. Amzi Babbitt THOMPSON was born on 7 June 1822, and was christened on 6 July 1822 in Mendham, Morris County, NJ. He died on 3 August 1877 in Grove Creek, IA. Euphemia and Amzi Babbitt THOMPSON had these children:

+473	i.	**Clara C. THOMPSON.**
+474	ii.	**William Howell THOMPSON.**

117. **William HOWELL** was born on 9 March 1826 in Hardwick Twp., Warren County, NJ. He married **Sarah Elizabeth ROGERS** (daughter of **David Banks Wheeler ROGERS** and **Eliza JONES**) on 27 September 1849 in Naperville, Dupage County, IL. Sarah Elizabeth ROGERS was born on 19 November 1828 in Northmoreland, Luzerne County, PA. Their children were:[76]

475	i.	**Lewis R. HOWELL** was born on 26 August 1850 in PawPaw, Lee County, IL.
476	ii.	**Mary E. HOWELL** was born on 4 October 1852 in PawPaw.
+477	iii.	**George Albert HOWELL.**
478	iv.	**Ira Andrew HOWELL** was born on 28 March 1859 in PawPaw.
479	v.	**Hattie Louise HOWELL** was born on 4 April 1861 in PawPaw.
480	vi.	**Cora Ella HOWELL** was born on 11 June 1863 in PawPaw.
481	vii.	**Frank E. HOWELL** was born on 13 January 1867 in PawPaw.
482	viii.	**Fred Curtis HOWELL** was born on 4 January 1871 in PawPaw.

118. **James HOWELL** was born on 9 May 1828 in Hardwick Twp., Warren County, NJ. He died on 23 January 1904 in Dallas Twp., Luzerne County, PA, and was buried on 26 January 1904 in Trucksville Cemetery, Luzerne County, PA. James died of "old age."[77]James married **Catherine STOCKER.** In 1870, the family was in Dallas Township, Luzerne County, PA. His real estate was valued at $8,000, personal property at $2,000.[78] James was a farmer. While both James and Catherine were born in New Jersey, their son, Nelson, was born in Pennsylvania, so it is apparent they had moved to Luzerne county by 1857. Catherine STOCKER

---

[76] Family information was contributed by Denise Prince, 3373 NW 123rd Place, Portland OR 97229.

[77]Luzerne County, PA Death Records, 1900-1905, p. 220. LDS Microfilm #0960582.

[78]1870 U.S. Census (population) Pennsylvania, Luzerne County, Dallas Twp., p.356, nos. 24/25,National Archives Microfilm Publication, M653, roll 1366.

was born in 1833 in Sussex County, New Jersey. (By 1900, Nelson had married and was living on the farm in Dallas Twp. with his parents.) [79] They had a son:

+483 i. **Nelson Whitney HOWELL.**

119. **Ziba O. HOWELL** was born on 23 March 1830 in Hope, Warren County, NJ. He died on 22 July 1878 in Hope, Warren County, NJ. He was buried in Union Cemetery, Hope, Warren County, NJ. Ziba was living with his father in Frelinghuysen in the 1850 census.[80] By 1860, he was farming in Hope, Warren County, NJ, with real estate was valued at $2,000, and personal property at $1,500.[81] and he was listed as a farmer in the 1860 census. All of the family are buried in Hope Union Cemetery. Ziba married **Lydia CORLISS**, who was born in 1832 in NJ. They had these children:

484 i. **Cora Ella HOWELL** was born on 8 August 1855 in Frelinghuysen, Warren County, NJ. She died on 25 September 1872 in NJ.

485 ii. **William Edgar HOWELL** was born on 9 August 1856 in Frelinghuysen. He died on 6 October 1863 in NJ.

120. **George S. HOWELL** was born on 4 January 1832 in Hope, Warren County, NJ. He died on 13 December 1897 in Monroe Twp., Wyoming County, PA. The 1870 census for Wyoming county shows George and Catherine in Monroe Township. He was a farmer, with real estate valued at $5,000 and personal property at $1,000.[82]He was married to **Catherine HIBLER** on 3 November 1855 in Frelinghuysen, Warren County, NJ.[83] George and Catherine had one child:

486 i. **William A. HOWELL** was born on 25 February 1859 in Frelinghuysen.

123. **Ira K. READ** was born on 14 December 1828 in Frelinghuysen, Warren County, NJ. He died on 14 June 1890 in Wilkes Barre, Luzerne County, PA. According to his biography in Bradsby's History of Luzerne County, PA,[84] Ira was a farmer until his health failed, about 1865. The family had moved to Dallas,

---

[79]1900 U.S. Census (population) Pennsylvania, Luzerne County, Dallas Twp., E.D. 39, Sheet 1, line 51, National Archives Microfilm Publication, T623, roll 1431.
[80]1850 U.S. Census (population) New Jersey, Warren Co., Frelinghuysen, p.487, nos.155/167, National Archives Microfilm Publication, M432, roll 465.
[81]1860 U.S. Census (population) New Jersey, Warren County, Hope Twp., p.29, nos. 210/208, National Archives Microfilm Publication, M653, roll 711.
[82]1870 U.S. Census (population) Pennsylvania, Wyoming Co., Monroe Twp., p. 92 nos. 104/123, National Archives Microfilm Publication, M593, roll 1467.
[83]Warren County, NJ Marriage Records, LDS Microfilm # 0960890. Vol. 2, p. 3.
[84]H. C. Bradsby, ed., History of Luzerne County, PA, (Chicago: S.B.Nelson Co., 1893) 1269.

Luzerne County, PA, about 1858. In 1865, they moved to Kingston, where he operated a hardware business for 3 years, and then moved to Wilkes Barre, where he was a salesman for Bertels Company, and later for Payne & Company until his death, in Miners Mills.

After his death, their oldest daughter set up a dressmaking business in the family home, where she, her husband and son lived with her mother. Ira was, according to his biography, a Methodist, and a Republican. The 1870 census showed him to be quite well-to-do, his real estate in Kingston being valued at $12,000.[85] Ira married **Elizabeth HOWELL** (daughter of **Philip Shaver HOWELL** and **Margaret VOUGHT**) on 3 December 1851 in Frelinghuysen, Warren County, NJ.[86] Elizabeth HOWELL was born on 16 August 1831 in Frelinghuysen, Warren County, NJ. She died on 10 May 1912 in Frelinghuysen, Warren County, NJ. Ira K. READ and Elizabeth HOWELL had the following children:

+487 i. **Sarah M. READ.**
+488 ii. **Anna Rebecca READ.**
+489 iii. **Emma A. READ.**

128. **Levi J. HOWELL** was born on 3 January 1826 in Frelinghuysen, Warren County, NJ. He died on 17 December 1899 in Frelinghuysen, and was buried in Union Cemetery. Levi was elected Commissioner of Deeds four times, in March, 1858, April 1867, May 1872, and April 1879. He was Assessor for Frelinghuysen Township 1855 - 1857,and 1867 - 1869. He was chosen a Freeholder of Johnsonburg from 1875 - 1877, and sat on the Town Committee from 1858 to 1860 for Johnsonburg. The 1887 Directory for Hope, NJ, listed Levi as a miller. His death notice reads: "Levi J. Howell's lamp of life went out early on Sunday morning, December 17th, after he had been on a bed of sickness for several weeks. he had been in feeble health for a long time. His age was 73 years, 11 months, 14 days, and is survived by a wife and several children. The funeral services were held at the house Tuesday morning at 11 o'clock; interment in Union Cemetery."[87] Levi was married to **Sarah CASSADY** on 9 March 1859. Sarah CASSADY was born in 1839. She died in 1925 in Frelinghuysen, and was buried in Union Cemetery. Levi and Sarah had these children:

490 i. **Anna M. HOWELL** was born in February 1860 in Frelinghuysen.
491 ii. **Margaret Luella HOWELL** was born on 31 August 1864 in Frelinghuysen. She died on 25 April 1893, and was buried in Union Cemetery.
492 iii. **Amedia Etta HOWELL** was born on 28 October 1865 in Frelinghuysen.

---

[85]1870 U.S. Census (population) Pennsylvania, Luzerne Co., Kingston Borough, p.106, nos.493/496, National Archives Microfilm Publication, M593, roll 1366.
[86]Warren County, NJ Marriage Records, LDS Microfilm # 0960890.
[87]Obituary, Washington (NJ) Star, 21 December 1899.

493 iv. **John C. HOWELL** was born on 11 February 1867 in Frelinghuysen.

494 v. **David Alanson HOWELL** was born in 1874. He married **Ina BARDEN**. He was called Alanson in the 1880 census. He was a graduate of Trenton State Teachers College. He was the supervising principal in the Pompton Lakes School. When he retired, they moved to Newton, Sussex County, NJ, where he died on 23 May 1944. He was buried in Cheshire, Masachusetts.

495 vi. **Sarah HOWELL** was born in 1875, died on 25 September 1961, and was buried in Union Cemetery. She married **Theodore WOODRUFF**, who died before her.

129. **Lucinda Ann HOWELL** was the second wife of **Garret K. HOWELL**. For her family, please see Garret K. HOWELL #151.

130. **Charles Marshall HOWELL** was born on 19 August 1834 in Frelinghuysen, Warren County, NJ. He died, and was buried in Andover Presbyterian Cemetery, Andover, Sussex County, NJ. He married (1) **Phoebe Maria HILL** (daughter of **Samuel HILL** and **Elcey WILCOX**), who was born on 20 June 1837. She died on 19 August 1873, and was buried in Andover Presbyterian Cemetery. Their children were:

496 i. **Elsie F. HOWELL** was born on 9 January 1865 in Andover Twp. She died on 16 September 1893, and was buried in Andover Cemetery.

497 ii. **William W. HOWELL** was born on 8 August 1867. He died on 20 July 1937, and was buried in Andover Presbyterian Cemetery, Andover, NJ.

Charles married (2) **Leonora DAVIDSON**. She was born on 19 November 1843. She died on 5 February 1912, and was buried in Andover Presbyterian Cemetery, Andover, NJ.

133. **Philip Shaver HOWELL** was born on 21 December 1803 in Sussex County, New Jersey. He died on 5 June 1882 in Hope, and was buried in Union Cemetery, Hope. Philip was listed as a farmer in the 1850 census, with land valued at $5,920.[88] He was married to **Margaret VOUGHT** (daughter of **John VOUGHT** and **Sarah MCMURTRIE**) on 26 October 1830 in Frelinghuysen, Warren County, NJ, by Rev. Isaac Winner. [89] Margaret VOUGHT was born on 3 December 1812 in NJ. She died on 28 February 1859 in Frelinghuysen, Warren

---

[88]1850 U.S. Census (population) New Jersey, Warren Co., Hope, p. 485, nos. 119/129, National Archives Microfilm Publication, M432, roll 465.
[89]Warren County, NJ. Marriage Records, LDS Microfilm # 0960890.

County, NJ.[90] The Bible record from which the family information has come also includes information on her parents. Their children were:

498 i. **Elizabeth HOWELL**. married a cousin, **Ira K. READ**. Her family is found with him, #123.

499 ii. **Sarah Sophia HOWELL** was born on 25 March 1833 in Frelinghuysen, and died on 13 March 1909. She married **Abraham SHUSTER** on 21 December 1864 in Frelinghuysen.

500 iii. **Margaret HOWELL** was born on 31 December 1835, and died on 3 November 1921 in Frelinghuysen. She was buried in Union Cemetery. Margaret was unmarried, and lived with her parents.

501 iv. **Isaac Whitfield HOWELL** was born on 4 May 1838 in Frelinghuysen. He died there on 10 October 1838, and was buried in Union Cemetery.

+502 v. **John Wesley HOWELL.**

503 vi. **David HOWELL** was born on 19 October 1842 in Frelinghuysen He died on 5 December 1863 in Wilkes Barre, Luzerne County, PA, when an omnibus upset, between Kingston and Wilkes Barre. He was buried in Union Cemetery.

+504 vii. **Slidell MacKenzie HOWELL.**

505 viii. **Bethena Ann HOWELL** was born on 18 November 1848 and died in 1930 in Frelinghuysen. She was buried in Union Cemetery. She married **Henry LUSE** on 3 January 1873 in Frelinghuysen. Henry LUSE was born in 1848 and died in 1916 in New Jersey. He was buried in Union Cemetery.

506 ix. **Ira VanCleve HOWELL** was born on 24 October 1852 in Frelinghuysen. He died on 25 August 1938, and was buried in Union Cemetery.

134. **Elizabeth HOWELL** was born in 1811 in Sussex County, New Jersey. She married (1) **Henry CORSEN**, and (2) **Robert VANSICKLE**. Robert VANSICKLE was born in 1807 in New Jersey. At the time of the 1860 census, his mother, **Prudence VANSICKLE**, was living with the family. Robert's real estate was valued at $8,500, and personal property at $200.[91] Their children were:

507 i. **Rebecca VANSICKLE** was born in 1840 in Oxford, Warren County, NJ.

508 ii. **Abraham VANSICKLE** was born in 1841 in Oxford.

509 iii. **Prudence VANSICKLE** was born in 1843 in Oxford.

---

[90]Bible records in possession of New Jersey Genealogical Society. #3540.

[91]1860 U.S. Census (population) New Jersey, Warren Co., Oxford, p. 321, nos. 322/318, National Archives Microfilm Publication, M653, roll 711.

510 iv. **Sarah VANSICKLE** was born in 1846 in Oxford.

135. **Susan Ann HOWELL** was born in 1814 in Sussex County, New Jersey. She died on 25 August 1882, and was buried in Union Cemetery. Susan married **John ALBERTSON**, who was born in 1828. John was a carpenter. Susan Ann HOWELL and John ALBERTSON had the following children:

511 i. **James ALBERTSON** was born on 28 August 1848 in Warren County, NJ.
512 ii. **Ariella ALBERTSON** was born on 23 August 1854 in Warren County, NJ.
513 iii. **Isaac ALBERTSON**.
514 iv. **Gideon ALBERTSON**.
+515 v. **Emma E. ALBERTSON.**

136. **David K. HOWELL** was born on 25 September 1816 in Hope, Sussex County, NJ. He died on 18 July 1874, and was buried in Union Cemetery. David was a farmer. He married **Joanna J. OSMUN**, who was born on 19 May 1819 in NJ. She died on 16 December 1895, and was buried in Union Cemetery. David K. HOWELL and Joanna J. OSMUN had the following children:[92]

516 i. **Ziba O. HOWELL** was born on 9 May 1837, and died on 12 October 1865 in New Jersey. He married **Elizabeth B. AYERS** (daughter of **Daniel S. AYERS** and **Pernina VLIET**) on 30 November 1859 in Cadington, Warren County, NJ.[93] Elizabeth B. AYERS was born in 1838 in New Jersey. Ziba was a farm tenant, in the 1860 census, with real property worth $8,000 and personal property valued at $2,000.[94]
517 ii. **Emma S. HOWELL** was born on 14 November 1837, and died on 17 April 1839 in Warren County. She was buried in Union Cemetery.
+518 iii. **Isaac Lemuel HOWELL.**
519 iv. **David HOWELL** was born in Warren County. He died and was buried in Union Cemetery.

138. **Frances HOWELL** was born on 5 June 1806 in Nichols, Tioga County, NY. She died on 20 May 1895. She married **Stephen MOREY**, who was born on 7

---

[92]ibid. Hope Twp., p. 31, nos.216/226.
[93]Return of marriage for Ziba O. Howell and Elizabeth B. Ayers, Volume AH, page 173, Independence, Warren County, NJ, State of New Jersey Archives, Trenton, NJ.
[94]1860 U.S. Census (population), New Jersey, Warren County, Hope Twp., p. 16, nos. 109/108, National Archives Microfilm Publication M653, roll 711.

November 1805, and died on 30 May 1894. Both are buried in Lounsberry Cemetery in Nichols. Frances and Stephen MOREY had one child:

+520 i. **James H. MOREY**.

139. **John L. HOWELL** was born in Nichols, Tioga County, NY on 12 May 1810. He died on 23 August 1895. John married **Almira Ann WEBSTER**, who was born on 7 March 1817, and died on 9 April 1891. John, Almira and their small children were all buried in Asbury Cemetery. Their children were:

521 i. **Elizabeth A. HOWELL** died on 25 June 1892.
522 ii. **Achsah A. HOWELL** was born on 12 August 1838 and died on 17 April 1841.
523 iii. **Frances HOWELL** was born on 14 September 1843 and died on 17 April 1844.
524 iv. **Angeline J. HOWELL** was born on 3 November 1847 and died on 5 December 1859.
+525 v. **John J. HOWELL.**
526 vi. **Unknown female HOWELL** married **Unknown VAN ESS.**
527 vii. **Isadora HOWELL** was born about 1859 and died on 25 February 1885. She married **Charles WHITE.**
528 viii. **Isabelle HOWELL.**

140. **Mary Ann HOWELL** was born about 1813 in Nichols, Tioga County, NY. She died on 1 May 1882. She married **William S. MOREY** who was born about 1812 and died on 8 November 1885. Both are buried in Lounsberry Cemetery. Mary and William MOREY had the following children:

529 i. **Elizabeth MOREY**.
530 ii. **Martha MOREY.**
531 iii. **Robert MOREY.**
532 iv. **Sarah MOREY.**
533 v. **Frances MOREY.**
534 vi. **Emoline MOREY** died 15 August 1862, and was buried in Lounsberry Cemetery, Nichols, NY.

142. **Robert HOWELL** was born on 4 September 1815 in Nichols, Tioga County, NY. He died on 19 October 1891. He was a geologist, mineralogist, and a farmer. Robert was introduced to geology by a book borrowed from a neighbor, while he was young, and the interest grew as he studied the area around his home. He eventually began recording the weather and worked in Washington, D.C. at the weather bureau. He was appointed by the U.S.Geological Survey to prepare reports on the forests in his home area, while he continued to farm his property in Tioga

county.[95] Robert HOWELL married (1) **Rhoda MOREY** (daughter of **Joseph MOREY**). She was born in 1825 in New York. They had a son:

+535 i. **Arthur M. HOWELL.**

Robert HOWELL married: (2) **Julia C. FORMAN** (daughter of **Smith FORMAN** and **Martha MILLER**), who was born in 1840; (3) **Sarah LOUNSBERRY** (daughter of **Pratt LOUNSBERRY** and **Sarah LANNING**), who was born in NY, and died on 20 September 1888, and (4) **Matilda OWENS**. Robert and his wives were buried in Lounsberry Cemetery.

143. **William S. VAN HORN** was born on 19 August 1812 in NJ. He was married to **Macrina JONES** (daughter of **Jonathan JONES**) on 19 June 1851 in NJ. She was born in 1828 in Johnsonburg, Warren County, and died on 31 December 1870. Their children were:

536 i. **Edward Mentor VAN HORN** was born on 8 May 1852 in Frelinghuysen.
537 ii. **Lenora A. VAN HORN** was born on 27 September 1854 in Frelinghuysen.
538 iii. **Laura B. VAN HORN** was born on 9 September 1856 in Frelinghuysen. She died there before 1860.
539 iv. **Rosaline F. VAN HORN** was born on 22 July 1858 in Frelinghuysen.
540 v. **Horace VAN HORN** was born about 1860 and died in infancy.

144. **Isaac H. VAN HORN** was born on 10 March 1814 in New Jersey. He died on 8 December 1858 in Frelinghuysen, and was buried in Johnsonburg Cemetery. He was married to **Rebecca M. STILLWELL** on 18 September 1836 in Johnsonburg, Warren County, NJ.[96] Rebecca M. STILLWELL was born in 1813. She died on 15 May 1882, and was buried in Johnsonburg Cemetery. In 1860, Rebecca was head of household, with real estate valued at $18,110, and personal property valued at $1,500.[97] They had these children:[98]

541 i. **Levinah VAN HORN** was born in 1838 in Frelinghuysen, Warren County, NJ.
542 ii. **George W. VAN HORN** was born in 1839.

---

[95]W. B. Gay, Historical Gazetteer of Tioga County, New York, 1785-1888 (1887; reprint, Bowie, MD: Heritage Books, Inc., 1991)288-289.
[96]Warren County, NJ Marriage Records, LDS Microfilm # 0960890. Vol. 1, p. 114.
[97]1860 U.S. Census (population) New Jersey, Warren Co., Frelinghuysen, p.14, nos.108/114, National Archives Microfilm Publication, M653, roll 711.
[98]James P. Snell, compiler, History of Warren and Sussex Counties, Vol. 2,(1881; reprint: Middletown, NY, Trumbull Publishing Company, 1971) p. 593.

543 iii. **Tobias S. VAN HORN** was born in 1841 in Frelinghuysen.
544 iv. **Alace A. VAN HORN** was born in 1843 in Frelinghuysen.
545 v. **William J. VAN HORN** was born in 1845 in Frelinghuysen.
546 vi. **Henrietta "Nettie" VAN HORN** was born in 1846 in Frelinghuysen.
547 vii. **Theodore F. VAN HORN** was born in 1848 in Frelinghuysen.
548 viii. **Philetus R. VAN HORN** was born in April 1850 in Frelinghuysen.
549 ix. **Sarah Emma VAN HORN** was born in 1852 in Frelinghuysen.
550 x. **Richard Marshall VAN HORN** was born in August 1854 in Frelinghuysen. He died on 27 May 1912.
He married **Ada "Minnie" Minerva READ.**

145. **David Green VAN HORN** was born on 8 October 1816 in NJ. David married **Harriet YOUNG** on 28 November 1838 in Sussex County, NJ. Harriet was born in 1815. Their children were:[99]

551 i. **George VAN HORN** was born in 1842 in Frelinghuysen.
552 ii. **Melville VAN HORN** was born in 1843 in Frelinghuysen.
553 iii. **Mercilia VAN HORN** was born in 1846 in Frelinghuysen.
554 iv. **Silas A. VAN HORN** was born in 1849 in Frelinghuysen.

146. **Abraham Shaver VAN HORN** was born on 27 March 1819 in NJ. Abraham married **Miranda E. UNKNOWN**, who was born in 1825. Abraham and Miranda had the following children:

555 i. **Jacob C. VAN HORN** was born in 1845 in Frelinghuysen.
556 ii. **Mary S. VAN HORN** was born in 1848 in Frelinghuysen.
557 iii. **Alvina VAN HORN** was born in 1849 in Warren County, NJ.
558 iv. **Osten C. VAN HORN** was born in 1852 in Hardwick Twp., Warren County.

---

[99] 1860 U.S. Census (population) New Jersey, Warren County, Frelinghuysen, p. 28, nos. 128/134, National Archives Microfilm Publication, M653, roll 711.

559 v. **Andrew N. VAN HORN** was born in 1853 in Hardwick Twp.
560 vi. **Johnson C. VAN HORN** was born in 1855 in Hardwick Twp.
561 vii. **Garret A. VAN HORN** was born in 1858 in Hardwick Twp.
562 viii. **Rosa M. VAN HORN** was born in May 1860 in Hardwick Twp.

147. **George VAN HORN** was born on 20 April 1822 in Warren County, NJ. George married **Sevilla C. JONES**. Sevilla C. JONES was born in 1825. George was listed as a hotel keeper in the 1850 census. By 1860, George was apparently dead, and Sevilla was listed as a hotel keeper. [100] Their children were:

563 i. **Minerva VAN HORN** was born in 1845 in Warren County, NJ.
564 ii. **Neldon VAN HORN** was born in 1848 in Warren County, NJ.

148. **Aaron Benjamin HOWELL** was born on 4 February 1813 in Independence, Sussex County, NJ. He died on 7 March 1889 in Arlington, and was buried in Tranquility Cemetery, Tranquility, Sussex County, NJ. Aaron HOWELL married **Martha Ann BACON** on 8 February 1840. Martha Ann BACON was born on 17 February 1815 in NJ. She died on 1 October 1887. She was buried in Tranquility Cemetery. Aaron Benjamin HOWELL and Martha Ann BACON had the following children:[101]

+565 i. **Livinia Matilda HOWELL.**
566 ii. **William H. H.(Henry Harrison) HOWELL** was born on 29 November 1840 in Independence. He died on 25 October 1902, and was buried in Tranquility Cemetery.[102]
+567 iii. **George Washington HOWELL.**
+568 iv. **Benjamin B. HOWELL.**
569 v. **Theodore Taylor HOWELL** was born on 1 March 1847 in Independence. He died on 21 July 1866, and was buried in Johnsonburg, Sussex County, NJ.
570 vi. **Sarah S. HOWELL** was born on 11 March 1850 in Independence, and died on 4 December 1864 in NJ.

---

[100]1860 U.S. Census (population) New Jersey, Warren Co., Hope Twp., p. 25, nos. 173/171, National Archives Microfilm Publication, M653, roll 711.
[101]1880 U.S. Census (population) New Jersey, Warren Co., Independence Twp., E.D.200, p.14, nos. 126/134, National Archives Microfilm Publication, T9, roll 799.
[102]Obituary, Washington (NJ) Star, 30 October 1902.

571 vii. **Levi H. HOWELL** was born on 28 April 1853 in Independence, died on 30 July 1853, and was buried in Johnsonburg Cemetery, Johnsonburg, NJ.

572 viii. **Mary Frances HOWELL** was born on 3 August 1854, and died on 18 January 1855 in Independence, Warren County, NJ.

573 ix. **John A. HOWELL** was born on 7 September 1856 in Independence. When his mother died in 1916, he was living in Phillipsburg, NJ

150. **Susan HOWELL** was born in 1818 in Independence, Sussex County, NJ. She died in 1901 in Vienna, Warren County, NJ. She was married to **William Irving ROE, M.D.** on 14 September 1850 in Warren County, NJ. William Irving ROE was born on 22 December 1821 in Milton, Morris County, New Jersey. He died on 11 February 1899 in Danville, Warren County, NJ. They had a son:

574 i. **Jacob Irving ROE** was born on 28 July 1854 in Branchville, NJ. He died on 2 July 1922 in Danville, Warren County, NJ. He married **Susan Irene DALRYMPLE** on 16 September 1875. They lived in Wilkes Barre, Luzerne County, PA. Susan DALRYMPLE died on 31 July 1901.

151. **Garret K. HOWELL** was born on 21 October 1822 in Independence, Sussex County, NJ. He died on 5 January 1863 in Warren County, and was buried in Union Cemetery. He married (1) **Mary Ann JONES** (daughter of **Jonathan JONES** and **Lydia CUMMINS**) who was born in 1822, and died on 16 May 1846.

He was married (2) to **Lucinda Ann HOWELL** (daughter of **Samuel Green HOWELL** and **Eleanor FREESE**) about 1853 in Warren County, NJ. Lucinda Ann HOWELL was born on 9 June 1832 in Frelinghuysen, and died on 23 October 1898, at her brother's home in Howard, NJ.[103] Lucinda was called Annie in her obituary. Garret K. HOWELL and Lucinda Ann HOWELL had these children:

575 i. **George Warren HOWELL** was born on 27 October 1854 in Independence. George moved West, but his mother's obituary gave no other information.

576 ii. **Samuel G. HOWELL** was born on 8 July 1851 in Independence. Samuel lived in Newton, Sussex County, NJ at the time of his mother's death.

153. **Uzal Ogden HOWELL** was born on 3 December 1813 in Newton, Sussex County, NJ. He died on 10 November 1886 in Muskegon, Muskegon County, MI. He married **Martha ELLIS** on 2 April 1846 in S. Dumfries, Ontario. [104] Martha

---

[103]Obituary, Washington (NJ) Star, 2 7 October 1898.

[104]Thomas B. Wilson, Ontario Marriage Notices. (Lambertville, NJ: Hunterdon

ELLIS was born on 20 May 1826, died on 9 November 1896 in Muskegon. Martha and Uzal are buried in Oakland Cemetery in Muskegon. They had these children:[105]

+577	i.	**Nathan A. HOWELL.**
+578	ii.	**David E. HOWELL.**
+579	iii.	**George Wabent HOWELL.**
580	iv.	**John HOWELL** was born in 1859; he is said to have died in Tacoma, Washington.
581	v.	**Martha HOWELL** was born in 1862. She married twice, to **George PLANT** and to **C. O. PHILLABAUM**, order not known.
+582	vi.	**Thomas E. HOWELL.**
583	vii.	**Frances HOWELL** was born about 1868 in Muskegon.

155. **Samson Waugh HOWELL** was born on 19 June 1830 in S. Dumfries, Brant County, Ontario. He died on 25 January 1870 in Brant County, and was buried in St. George United Cemetery, S. Dumfries. He was married to **Jane BRAY** about 1854 in S. Dumfries. Jane BRAY was born in 1833 in S. Dumfries. She died on 21 November 1900, and was buried in Colborne Cemetery, Goderich, Huron County, Ontario. Samson Waugh HOWELL and Jane BRAY had these children:

584	i.	**Thomas HOWELL** was born on 4 May 1854 in S. Dumfries. He died on 27 October 1861, and was buried in St. George United Cemetery.
+585	ii.	**George HOWELL.**
+586	iii.	**Dorothea HOWELL.**
+587	iv.	**Elizabeth Jane HOWELL.**
+588	v.	**Harvey J. HOWELL.**
+589	vi.	**William Nathan HOWELL.**
+590	vii.	**Eliza Jane HOWELL.**

156. **Harvey Clinton HOWELL** was born in 1833 in Brant County, Ontario. He was married to **Eliza MORRIS** in 1858. Harvey Clinton HOWELL and Eliza MORRIS had the following children:

591	i.	**Clara Ell HOWELL** was born about 1859.
592	ii.	**Mary HOWELL** was born about 1864.
593	iii.	**Emma HOWELL** was born about 1879.

157. **Samson G. HOWELL** was born on 2 June 1810 in Sussex County, New Jersey. He died on 16 September 1879 in Sussex County, and was buried in Union Brick Cemetery, Blairstown, Warren County, NJ. Samson was on the town

---

House, 1982), 143.

[105]Information on this family contributed by Carl C. Howell, 6060 S. Shore Dr., Whitehall MI 49461.

committee of Hardwick from 1838 to 1841. He was elected Justice of the Peace on 6 February 1843, a Freeholder of Frelinghuysen Township 1848-1849, and also Collector of the township. He was chosen Freeholder of Johnsonburg 1854-1856. He was a Deacon and an original member of the Christian Church in Hope.

He was married to **Angeline CRISMAN** on 6 November 1834 in Warren County, NJ. [106]Angeline CRISMAN was born on 31 May 1812. She died on 8 April 1886, and was buried in Union Brick Cemetery. Samson G. HOWELL and Angeline CRISMAN had the following children:

594 i. **Jonah HOWELL** was born on 15 December 1833,and died on 12 December 1839 in Warren County..

+595 ii. **Garret C. HOWELL.**

596 iii. **Isaac Christian HOWELL** was born in 1841 in Frelinghuysen. He was living in Seattle, King County, Washington in 1909. He married **Minerva Ellen RAUB** (daughter of **John S. RAUB** and **Elizabeth UNKNOWN**) on 22 February 1872 in Blairstown. [107] Minerva was born in 1852.

597 iv. **John HOWELL** was born about 1842 in Warren County. He died there on 12 March 1845, and was buried in Union Brick Cemetery, Blairstown.

+598 v. **Edgar Crisman HOWELL.**

599 vi. **Susan HOWELL** was born in Warren County, NJ. She died in 1872.

600 vii. **Sarona HOWELL** was born in 1849, and died on 18 July 1851 in Warren County. She was buried in Union Brick Cemetery.

159. **Letitia HOWELL** was born about 1814 in Frelinghuysen, Sussex County, NJ. She married **Peter Shoemaker MILLER** (son of **Jacob C. MILLER** and **Anna C. SHOEMAKER**) on 25 January 1832 in Warren County, NJ. Peter Shoemaker MILLER was born on 2 February 1809 in Hope, and died in 1881 in Hope, Warren County, NJ. He was a farmer. Their children were:

601 i. **William C. MILLER** was born in 1832, in Hope, where he died on 13 February 1899, and was buried in Union Cemetery. He was a butcher, known in Hope as "Butcher Miller" .[108] He and his wife, **Elizabeth JOHNSON**, had no children.

+602 ii. **Angeline MILLER.**

603 iii. **George G. MILLER** was born on 8 May 1843 in Hope.

---

[106]Warren County, NJ Marriage Records, LDS microfilm # 0960890. Vol.1, p. 91.

[107]Return of Marriage for Isaac C. Howell &Minerva E. Raub, Vol. BK, p. 871, Waren Co., NJ, New Jersey State Archives, Trenton, NJ.

[108]Obituary, Washington (NJ) Star, 23 February 1899.

He died on 27 August 1869, and was buried in Little Oxford Cemetery, Hazen, NJ. He married **Abbie UNKNOWN.**

+604 iv. **Euphemia MILLER.**
+605 v. **Garrett MILLER.**
+606 vi. **Gideon H. MILLER.**
607 vii. **Amelia MILLER.**
+608 viii. **Henry MILLER.**
609 ix. **Christine MILLER** was born in September 1849, and died in childhood.
+610 x. **Elizabeth MILLER.**

160. **Gideon Leeds HOWELL** was born on 3 August 1815 in Frelinghuysen, Warren County, NJ. He died on 1 March 1892 in Hope, Warren County, NJ, and was buried on 5 March 1892 in Union Cemetery. [109] He was a bartender and a drover. He later ran the American Hotel, a hotel in Hope, until his death. He was known as Doc, because he had been named for Dr. Gideon Leeds. He served on the town committee in Johnsonburg from 1862 to 1863, and on the town committee of Hope in 1851 and 1855. Gideon married (1) **Sally Maria FREEMAN** on 27 January 1842. Sally Maria FREEMAN was born in 1821, and died on 22 February 1847. She was buried in Union Brick Cemetery, Blairstown. They had a child:

+611 i. **Lydia Ann HOWELL.**

Gideon married (2) **Mary C. UNKNOWN**. She was born on 5 August 1816 in NJ. She died on 28 September 1892, and was buried in Union Cemetery. Mary gave 1819 as her birth date in the 1850 census.[110] After Gideon's death, Mary moved out of the American House, sold Gideon's personal belongings, and moved into a house across the road from the hotel. Gideon and Mary had these children:

+612 i. **Levi H. HOWELL.**
613 ii. **Johanna Elizabeth HOWELL** was born on 28 April 1853 in Hope.
614 iii. **Unknown female HOWELL** was born on 15 January 1859 in Hope.

162. **Elizabeth HOWELL** was born on 11 May 1821 in Sussex County, New Jersey. She died on 13 May 1877, and was buried in Union Brick Cemetery, Blairstown, Warren County, NJ. She was married to **Morris CRISMAN** in 1843 in Sussex County, New Jersey. Morris CRISMAN was born on 16 October 1815. He died on 5 April 1897. He was buried in Union Brick Cemetery, Blairstown, Warren County, NJ. Elizabeth and Morris CRISMAN had the following children:

---

[109] Obituary, Washington (NJ) Star, 10 March 1892.
[110] 1850 U.S. Census (population) New Jersey, Warren Co., Hope Twp., p.426, nos.541/564, National Archives Microfilm Publication, M432, roll 465.

615 i. **James A. King CRISMAN** was born about 1850, and died on 28 January 1855 in Warren County, NJ. He was buried in Union Brick Cemetery.

616 ii. **Susan Alzina CRISMAN** was born about 1854 in Warren County, NJ. She died there on 1 March 1856 and was buried in Union Brick Cemetery.

617 iii. **Cassius CRISMAN** married **Abbie SNYDER.**

618 iv. **J. I. Blair CRISMAN** married **Ella FISHER.**

619 v. **Emma M. CRISMAN** married **Jacob BEDE.**

620 vi. **Josephine CRISMAN** married **Peter YOUNG**.

163. **Susan A. HOWELL** was born on 28 March 1825 in Warren County, NJ. She died on 6 January 1854, and was buried in Union Cemetery. She married **David L. SURLES**, who was born on 2 November 1820. He died on 8 March 1852, and was buried in Union Cemetery. They had these children:

621 i. **Margaret L. SURLES** was born on 29 February 1848 in Hope. She died on 26 March 1850 in Hope, and was buried in Union Cemetery.

622 ii. **Hellen SURLES** died on 21 January, year not readable on her tombstone, at the age of 5 years. She was also buried in Union Cemetery.

164. **Jonah HOWELL** was born on 22 June 1827 in Frelinghuysen, Warren County, NJ. He died on 15 July 1906 in Wyoming, Luzerne County, PA, and was buried in Wyoming Cemetery, Luzerne County, PA.[111] Jonah was a blacksmith, living in Frelinghuysen, Warren County, in the 1850 census, with land valued at $800. He married **Eliza HUFF**, who was born in 1828 in NJ. By 1870, Jonah and Eliza were living in Susquehanna County, PA; in 1880, they were in Pittston, where Jonah was a blacksmith. By 1900, Eliza had apparently died, and Jonah was living on Luzerne Avenue in West Pittston, with Harriet and her husband. Jonah HOWELL and Eliza HUFF had the following children:[112]

623 i. **Austin HOWELL** was born on 12 January 1850 in Frelinghuysen, Warren County, NJ. The 1870 census for West Pittston, Luzerne County, PA, listed Austin as a seaman.

624 ii. **Sarah D. HOWELL** was born on 21 January 1851 in Frelinghuysen.

625 iii. **Mariam B. HOWELL** was born on 9 September 1853

---

[111]Burial record, Wyoming Cemetery, # 522, dated 17 July 1906, for Jonah Howell.

[112]1870 U.S. Census (population) Pennsylvania, Luzerne Co., West Pittston Borough, p.419, nos.27/28, National Archives Microfilm Publication, M593, roll 1365.

in Hope, Warren County. In the 1870 census, she was listed as a milliner, living with her parents in West Pittston, Luzerne County, PA.

626 iv. **Emma G. HOWELL** was born on 3 June 1856 in Hope, Warren County, NJ.

627 v. **Harriet HOWELL.** was born in 1859 in Exeter Twp., Luzerne County, PA. She married, about 1886, **George F. WINTERS** who was a house painter. They had no known children. In 1900, they lived on Luzerne Avenue, West Pittston, with her father.

628 vi. **Archbald HOWELL** was born in 1864 in Exeter Twp. He died on 24 April 1905 in Buffalo, Erie County, New York, and was buried on 27 April 1905 in Wyoming Cemetery, Luzerne County, PA.[113] County records indicate he died of heart trouble.

629 vii. **Ellen HOWELL** was born in 1866 in Exeter Twp., Luzerne County, PA.

630 viii. **Lula HOWELL** was born in 1868 in Exeter Twp.

631 ix. **Frank HOWELL** was born in March 1870 in Exeter Twp.

165. **Jonathan Thompson HOWELL** was born on 12 November 1828 in Frelinghuysen, Warren County, NJ. He died on 13 December 1896 in Centremoreland, and was buried in Centremoreland Cemetery, Luzerne County, PA. He was a drover according to the 1860 census. The 1870 census shows Jonathan and Rachel farming in Franklin Township, Luzerne County, PA., with their children. His real estate was valued at $12,000 in that year.[114]

He married **Rachel Ann NEWMAN** on 13 February 1858 in Hope, Warren County, NJ. [115] She was born on 6 November 1839 in NJ, died on 14 November 1897 in Centremoreland, and was buried in Centremoreland Cemetery. Their children were:

632 i. **Horrace M. HOWELL** was born on 6 October 1858 in Hope.[116]

633 ii. **Cassius HOWELL** was born in 1861 in Hope.

634 iii. **Lawson F. HOWELL** was born on 16 July 1862 in

---

[113]Card index for Wyoming Cemetery, Luzerne County, PA. Burial in lot # 14, on 29 March 1905. No official record for #232, but the death and burial are found in Luzerne County records, Microfilm #LDS 0960582.

[114]1870 U.S. Census (population) Pennsylvania, Luzerne Co., Franklin Twp., p.494, nos. 493/496, National Archives Microfilm Publication, M593, roll 1365..

[115]Return of Marriage for Jonathan T. Howell & Rachel Ann Newman, Vol AH, p. 147, Warren Co., NJ, New Jersey State Archives, Trenton, NJ.

[116]Birth Certificate, Vol. AJ. p. 269, Warren Co., NJ. New Jersey State Archives, Trenton, NJ.

Hope.

635 iv. **John B. HOWELL** was born in 1866 in Hope.

636 v. **Elisabeth HOWELL** was born in 1868 in Hope.

637 vi. **May HOWELL** was born about 1877 in Franklin Twp.[117]

638 vii. **William HOWELL** was born in January 1880 in Franklin Twp.

167. **Alice HOWELL** was born on 3 October 1814 in Sussex County, New Jersey. She died on 14 July 1877 in Delaware Station, NJ. She was buried in Ramsayburg Cemetery, Warren County, NJ.[118] (Some have her named Elsie, born 8 October 1819.) She was married to **William H. HEMINGWAY** about 1830 in Blairstown, Warren County, NJ. He was born on 28 November 1814 in Orange County, NY, died on 12 May 1888 in Delaware, Warren County, NJ., and was buried in Ramsayburg Cemetery, Warren County, NJ. He taught Latin in his home, which was the D L & W railroad station. They had one child:

+639 i. **William A. HEMINGWAY**.

168. **Elizabeth S. HOWELL** was born in 1820 in Sussex County, New Jersey. She died on 8 July 1910 and was buried in Cedar Ridge Cemetery, Blairstown, NJ. She was a milliner. Elizabeth had a son:

+640 i. **William C. HOWELL**.

170. **Ann L. HOWELL** was born in 1824 in Paulina, Warren County, NJ. Ann was appointed Postmaster of Blairstown in 1856. She died in July 1915 in Blairstown, Warren County, NJ, and was buried in Cedar Ridge Cemetery, Blairstown, NJ. She was married to Dr. **John Couse JOHNSON,** M.D. on 15 January 1862 in Blairstown, Warren County, NJ. John Couse JOHNSON was born in 1828 and died in 1907 in NJ. Ann and John C. JOHNSON had a daughter:

641 i. **Sarah Alice JOHNSON** was born in 1865 in Blairstown. She died in 1934, and was buried in Cedar Ridge Cemetery. She was not married.

178. **Laban HOWELL** was born on 6 March 1820 in Hope, Sussex County, NJ. He died on 19 May 1868 in Vincentown, Burlington County, NJ. Laban and his family lived on the farm of William H. Quick, in 1850, where Laban was a laborer. He later had a farm in the Vincentown area, belonged to the Whig Party, and later the Republican Party. He married **Clarissa LAWRENCE** in 1842 in Vincentown, Burlington County, New Jersey. She was born in New Egypt, New Jersey. Their children were:

---

[117] 1880 U.S. Census, Pennsylvania, Luzerne County, Franklin Twp., E.D. 93, p.220, nos 79/84, National Archives Microfilm Publication, T9, roll 1148.
[118] Obituary, Washington (NJ) Star, 19 July 1877.

+642 i. **John Richards HOWELL.**
643 ii. **Aaron HOWELL** was born in 1844 in Southampton Twp., Burlington County, NJ. Aaron was a doctor in Camden, NJ in 1910.
644 iii. **Mary HOWELL** was born in 1847 in Southampton Twp., Burlington County. In 1910, Mary was living in Mt. Holly, Burlington County, NJ.
645 iv. **Adda HOWELL** was born in Vincentown. She married **Sexton FOLWELL.**
646 v. **Ella HOWELL** was born on 18 October 1852 in Southampton Twp.

179. **Thaddeus HOWELL** was born in 1826 in Egg Harbor, Burlington, County, NJ. He married **Emeline UNKNOWN** in Burlington County. Emeline was born in 1830 in NJ. They had these children:

647 i. **Ezekial HOWELL** was born in 1848 in Burlington County, New Jersey.
648 ii. **Sarah Jane** or **Mary L. HOWELL** was born on 2 April 1849 in Springfield, Burlington County, NJ.
649 iii. **Charles W. HOWELL** was born in July 1850 in Washington Twp., Burlington County, NJ.
650 iv. **Thomas A. HOWELL** was born on 1 October 1853 in Washington Twp.
651 v. **Wattson HOWELL** was born on 29 March 1855 in Westhampton, Burlington County, NJ.
652 vi. **Mariah E. HOWELL** was born on 22 September 1858 in Mullica Twp., Atlantic County, NJ.

183. **Alexander Cummins HOWELL** was born on 24 February 1820 in Sussex County, New Jersey. He died on 17 May 1902 in Hackettstown, Warren County, NJ, and was buried in Union Cemetery, Hackettstown, Warren County, NJ. In 1850 he was in Independence, Warren County, working as a turner, with real estate valued at $40.[119] His obituary says he was survived by a son and two daughters, though it doesn't name them.[120] Alexander was a confectioner in Hackettstown, and the first postmaster of the Vienna Post office, when it opened 7 February 1853.

He married (1) **Sarah I. UNKNOWN**, who was born about 1821 in PA. She died on 16 January 1853, and was buried in Methodist Cemetery, Vienna, Warren County, NJ. Their daughter was:

653 i. **Olivia A. HOWELL** was born on 6 December 1850 in

---

[119]1850 U.S. Census (population) New Jersey, Warren Co., Independence, p. 510, nos.92/109, National Archives Microfilm Publication, M432, roll 465.
[120]Obituary, Washington(NJ) Star, 22 May 1902.

Independence, Warren County, NJ.

He was married (2) to **Phebe A. BOSS** in 1855. Phebe A. BOSS was born in October 1827 in NJ. She died in 1913, and was buried in Union Cemetery, Hackettstown. Alexander Cummins HOWELL and Phebe A. BOSS had these children:

654	i.	**Charles P. HOWELL** was born on 9 April 1856 in Independence.
655	ii.	**John B. HOWELL** was born on 5 October 1860 in Independence
+656	iii.	**Bessie HOWELL**.
657	iv.	**Nelly HOWELL** was born about 1869 in Independence.

We have recently learned that there may have been other children who died young. Records of the Union Cemetery in Hackettstown indicate that Mildred, Eddie and Franklin HOWELL are buried in the Alexander Howell plot. The 1880 census names **Eddie BOSS**, a nephew, aged 5, in the home. He may have been the child buried in that plot.

184. **Christeon Goodrech HOWELL** was born on 6 March 1822 in Sussex County, New Jersey. He died on 3 September 1898 in Corning, Steuben County, NY, and was buried in New Hope Cemetery in Corning. His brother, Uzal Hampton Howell, and his son, Frank, are supposed to have written a history of the Sampson Howell family. Unfortunately, no one seems to know what happened to that history.

Christeon and his family left New Jersey in 1845, moving to Pine Street in Corning, where they made their home. He was a tailor for some time, with a shop on Market Street in that town. For a period of time, he operated a factory which made both cloth and paper bags. He also was known to have had a business which sold oils of several varieties, both illuminating and lubricating, and had a kerosene refinery. (Homes had no electricity and were lighted with kerosene lamps in the mid-nineteenth century.) Evidently a well-to-do businessman, he also had investments in real estate in the area.

Christeon erected a monument in the New Hope Cemetery in Corning, NY dedicated to his Howell ancestors. This monument is quite attractive, and can be seen in that cemetery today.

He was married to **Luanna Josephine WALWORTH** on 9 March 1847 in New York, NY. Luanna Josephine WALWORTH was born in 1826. She died in 1902 in Corning, Steuben County, NY. She was buried in New Hope Cemetery, Corning, NY. Christeon Goodrech HOWELL and Luanna Josephine WALWORTH had these children:

+658 i. **Francis "Frank" Jerome HOWELL.**

659 ii. **Albert C. HOWELL** was born on 16 August 1849 in Corning. He died in 1900, of tuberculosis, and was buried in New Hope Cemetery in Corning. Albert studied at Rennselaer Polytechnical Institute in Rochester, NY, and worked in the art field with his brother. He never married.

185. **Uzal Hampton HOWELL** was born on 7 January 1824 in Sussex County, New Jersey. He died on 10 April 1903 in Vienna, Warren County, and was buried on 13 April 1903 in Christian Church Cemetery, Vienna, NJ,[121] but his body was later moved to the Union Cemetery in Hackettstown. Uzal lived in Vienna, NJ at one time, though he may have been the brother who accompanied James HOWELL to Corning, New York. In the 1850 census, he was listed as a tailor, living in Independence, Warren County, with real estate valued at $600. Uzal planted the sugar maples along the road in Vienna, and in his obituary was given credit for naming the town. He died of Grippe followed by heart failure. He belonged to the Christian church in Vienna, NJ. He married **Lucinda M. HANKINSON** (daughter of **Henry Johnson HANKINSON** and **Rebecca EMMONS**) on 10 May 1845 in Independence. Lucinda was born on 9 December 1822 in NJ, and died on 21 June 1885. Their children were:

+660 i. **Ellen HOWELL.**

661 ii. **Russell Irving HOWELL** was born on 11 August 1848 in Independence. Russell was living in Plainfield, Union County, New Jersey in 1916. He was not listed as a survivor of Belden, so is presumed to have died before 1923. Russell married **Anna WARNE,** (daughter of **Daniel WARNE** and **Eliza DAVISON**), on 23 December 1871. Anna was born on 16 April 1851.

+662 iii. **Belden D. HOWELL.**

663 iv. **Francis Henry HOWELL** was born on 13 March 1854 in Independence. He died in December 1916 in Spring City Hospital, La Salle, Illinois, and was buried in Hackettstown Union Cemetery. He was a painter. He moved to Princeton, Illinois about 1903. He contracted tetanus when he was pecked on the hand by a chicken, while at work. Frank married (1) **Lydia LARUE**, who was born on 17 July 1855 in Haughright, Morris County, NJ, and died in 1916. Frank married (2) **Anna THATCHER** on 28 March 1882. Frank's obituary noted that Anna lived in Easton, PA.[122]

---

[121]Obituary, Hackettstown (NJ) Gazette, 17 April 1903.
[122]Obituary, Washington (NJ) Star, 14 December 1916.

664 v. **Harvey Fleming HOWELL** was born on 14 March 1856 in Independence. He died in 1915 in Hackettstown, in a motorcycle accident. He was married to **Emma HALL** on 14 March 1879 in German Valley, Morris County, NJ. Emma HALL was born on 20 August 1861.

665 vi. **Charles Dayton HOWELL** was born on 15 October 1860 in Independence.He died on 23 July 1861 in Warren County, NJ.

666 vii. **William Ellsworth HOWELL** was born on 7 August 1864 in Independence. He died on 26 August 1864, and was buried in Vienna, Warren County, NJ.

+667 viii. **Oren Rockwell HOWELL.**

668 ix. **Willard Parker HOWELL** was born on 12 June 1866 in Independence. He died on 13 June 1867 in Warren County, NJ.

186. **Isaac Byington HOWELL** was born on 1 July 1827 in Hackettstown, Warren County, NJ. He died on 7 April 1896, and was buried in Union Cemetery, Hackettstown. Isaac moved from Vienna to Hackettstown, in 1855, where he built a home at 734 Washington Street. He was a carriage maker, and built furniture. He married **Henrietta ROBERTS** (daughter of **Thomas ROBERTS** and **Margaretta UNKNOWN**) on 20 July 1850.[123] She was born in 1829 in NY, and died on 27 April 1909 in Rockaway, Morris County, NJ[124]. Henrietta had made her home with Margaret and Harry Mutchler, her daughter and son-in-law, for four years before she died. Her funeral took place in Rockaway, and she was buried in the Union Cemetery in Hackettstown. Isaac and Henrietta had the following children:

+669 i. **Robert Ogden HOWELL.**

+670 ii. **Thomas B. HOWELL.**

+671 iii. **Anna Matilda "Mary" HOWELL.**

+672 iv. **Charles E. HOWELL.**

+673 v. **Margaret Roberts HOWELL.**

+674 vi. **Gustavus Ashmead HOWELL.**

675 vii. **Julia Willis HOWELL** was born in 1868 in Warren County. She died in 1930, and was buried in Hackettstown Union Cemetery. Julia married **William B. MCCRACKEN**, and they lived in Madison, NJ. They had no children.

+676 viii. **Emma Louise HOWELL.**

188. **Sampson Ogden HOWELL** was born on 14 March 1834 in Johnsonburg, Warren County, NJ. He died on 10 August 1901 in Vienna, Warren County, NJ, and was buried on 13 August 1901 in Union Cemetery, Hackettstown, Warren

---

[123]Warren County, NJ Marriage records, LDS Microfilm #0960890.

[124]Obituary, Washington(NJ) Star, 6 May 1909.

County, NJ. He was a skilled cabinet maker. Sampson walked from Vienna to Hackettstown to enlist in Company B, 15th Infantry, New Jersey Volunteers, and served 22 months during the Civil War. He was honorably discharged on 21 April 1864, because of physical disability. He was a member of Sedgwick Post No. 18, G.A.R., of Hackettstown. There was a long obituary in the Washington STAR,[125] a New Jersey newspaper, at the time of his death.

Sampson married **Mary Magdalene MCLEAN** (daughter of **Nicholas MCLEAN** and **Elizabeth UNKNOWN**), who was born on 2 March 1828 in German Valley, NJ. She died on 5 January 1901, and was buried in Union Cemetery, Hackettstown, Warren County, NJ. Sampson and Mary had one child:

+677 i. **Austin C. HOWELL.**

195. **Eden S. HOWELL** was born in 1824 in Hope Twp. He died on 18 May 1882 in Warren County, and was buried in Union Cemetery in Hope. He was a farmer and an assessor. He was married to **Sarah K. DAVIS** on 11 May 1845.[126] Sarah K. DAVIS was born in 1823 in Hope, Sussex County, NJ. She died in 1889, and was buried in Union Cemetery. Their children were:

678 i. **Unknown female HOWELL** was born and died on 1 June 1846 in Warren County; she was buried in Union Cemetery.

679 ii. **Anna Matilda HOWELL** was born in 1847 in Warren County. She died in 1923, and was buried in Union Cemetery, Hope, Warren County, NJ.

680 iii. **Mary Elizabeth HOWELL** was born on 16 September 1851, and died on 17 December 1851 in Hope, Warren County, NJ.

681 iv. **Charlotte A. HOWELL** was born on 8 May 1853, and died on 23 April 1877 in Hope. She was buried in Union Cemetery.

682 v. **Asa Corwin HOWELL** was born in 1855, died on 5 December 1855, and was buried in Union Cemetery.

683 vi. **Caleb C. HOWELL** was born on 11 June 1857 in Hope, Warren County, NJ.

684 vii. **Unknown female HOWELL** was born on 15 September 1858 in Hope.

685 viii. **Eleanor R. HOWELL** was born on 24 March 1860 in Hope. She died in 1923, and was buried in Union Cemetery. She married **William H. MERRILL.**

686 ix. **Franklin B. HOWELL** was born on 20 July 1864 in

---

[125]Obituary, Washington (NJ)Star, 15 August 1901.

[126]Warren County, NJ Marriage Records, LDS microfilm # 0960890. V. 1, p. 228.

Hope, Warren County. He died in 1899, and was buried in Union Cemetery. In 1895, Frank was jailed for having forged some checks. More than this is not known.

199. **Margaret C. HOWELL** was born on 23 April 1822 in Sussex County, New Jersey. She died on 7 January 1896, and was buried in Union Cemetery, Hackettstown, Warren County, NJ. She married **John B. INGERSOLL** on 1 August 1840.[127] Marriage records list her as Margaretta HOWELL. John INGERSOLL was born on 19 April 1817, died on 5 November 1894, and was buried in Union Cemetery, Hackettstown, Warren County, NJ. He was a farmer. Their children were:

687 i. **Edward/Edgar INGERSOLL** was born about 1842.
688 ii. **Caleb INGERSOLL** was born about 1845.
689 iii. **Perninah INGERSOLL** was born about 1847.
690 iv. **Margaret INGERSOLL** was born about 1857.

200. **Sarah Mariah HOWELL** was born on 5 February 1824 in Hope, Sussex County, NJ. She died on 20 December 1908 in Hope, Warren County, NJ, and was buried on 23 December 1908 in Moravian Cemetery, Hope, NJ. Sarah's death resulted from a fall early in December, in which it was believed she sustained internal injuries as well as a fractured hip.[128] She married **Caleb SWAYZE** (son of **John SWAYZE** and **Molly DRAKE**) on 18 January 1843. Caleb SWAYZE was born on 22 June 1813, died on 19 May 1894, and was buried in Moravian Cemetery, Hope, NJ. Caleb was a direct descendant of Israel Swayze, an early Welsh immigrant. Sarah and Caleb SWAYZE had these children:[129]

691 i. **Olivia L. SWAYZE** was born in Warren County. She married **T. S. VAN HORN,** and they lived in Newark, NJ.
692 ii. **Savon B. SWAYZE** was born in 1844 in Warren County, died in 1852, and was buried in Moravian Cemetery, Hope, NJ.
693 iii. **Julia C. SWAYZE** was born in 1854 and died in 1881 in Warren County, NJ.
694 iv. **Caleb O. SWAYZE** was born in 1859 in Warren County; he died in 1860, and was buried in Moravian Cemetery.
695 v. **Montgomery SWAYZE** was born in 1861 in Warren County, died in 1863, and was buried in

---

[127]Warren County, NJ Marriage Records, LDS microfilm # 0960890. Vol. 1, p. 171.
[128]Obituary, The Washington (NJ) Star, 24 December 1908.
[129]1860 U.S. Census (population), New Jersey, Warren County, Hackettstown, p. 24, nos. 174/172, National Archives Microfilm Publication, M653, roll 711.

Moravian Cemetery, Hope, NJ.

696 vi. **Erastus SWAYZE** was born in Warren County. He died before 1908.

697 vii. **Sarah H. SWAYZE** married **Rush HARTUNG.** A brief note in the same paper which carried her mother's obituary told of her husband's Christmas gift - a Wagner piano.

204. **Perninah B. HOWELL** was born in March 1831 in Hope, Warren County, NJ. She died on 3 May 1902 in Hope, and was buried on 6 May 1902 in Union Cemetery. Perninah died of heart disease, having been an invalid for many years. Four of her siblings survived her as well as six children, named in her obituary as: Alvah, of Jersey City, Blavilla, Oni, Lillian, Matilda, Mrs. Frank Howell, Mrs. Elwood Ribble, Carrie, and Mrs. Daniel VanCampen. (We cannot identify them further.) Perninah was married to **Ziba O. OSMUN** in Warren County, NJ. Ziba O. OSMUN was born in 1826 in Sussex County, New Jersey. He died in 1882. Ziba was a farmer. Perninah and Ziba O. OSMUN had the following children:

698 i. **Alvah OSMUN** was born in 1853. At the time of his mother's death, he was living in Jersey City, NJ

699 ii. **Abiah OSMUN** was born about 1853 in Hope, Warren County, NJ.

700 iii. **Wilimina OSMUN** was born about 1854. She died on 20 October 1856.

701 iv. **Elwood S. OSMUN** was born on 30 March 1856, and died on 19 October 1856.

702 v. **Brevilla OSMUN** was born on 30 March 1858, and died on 3 April 1911.

703 vi. **Ono J. OSMUN** was born 6 November 1860.

207. **Savilla J. HOWELL** was born in 1838 in Warren County, NJ. She died in 1914. She was buried in Union Cemetery, Hackettstown. Savilla married **Abraham M. VANSICKLE**, who was born in 1841. He died in 1916, and was buried in Union Cemetery, Hackettstown, Warren County, NJ. Their birth and death dates are from their grave stones. Savilla and Abraham M. VANSICKLE had these children:

704 i. **Sarah H. VANSICKLE** was born in 1872. She died in 1948.

705 ii. **Rebecca M. VANSICKLE** was born in 1873. She died and was buried in Union Cemetery, Hackettstown.

706 iii. **Elizabeth M. VANSICKLE** was born in 1875. She died and was buried in Union Cemetery, Hackettstown.

208. **Hester Anne HOWELL** was born on 17 February 1841 in Warren County, NJ. She died on 7 September 1914, and was buried in Union Cemetery, Hope, Warren County, NJ. She was married to **Ozias SHARP** on 12 May 1869. Ozias

SHARP was born on 10 September 1841 in Warren County, NJ. He died on 8 November 1905 in Hope, and was buried in Union Cemetery. Ozias died suddenly of heart failure, having suffered two hemorrhages in the weeks prior.[130] He and Hester had purchased the Howell homestead, and lived there all their married lives. It was near the Union Church cemetery, and he had been active in restoring that cemetery. Hester Anne and Ozias SHARP had the following children:

707 i. **Clinton SHARP** was born on 19 October 1873 in Frelinghuysen, Warren County, NJ. He died on 18 September 1907, and was buried in Union Cemetery, Hope, Warren County, NJ. Clinton was the principal of the Pompton Plains school when his father died.

708 ii.. **Clarence SHARP** was born in 1877 in Frelinghuysen, Warren County, NJ. Clarence was unmarried and living at home when his father died in 1905.

211. **Jonah T. HOWELL** was born in 1817 in S. Dumfries, Brant County, Ontario. He was a farmer. He died on 10 May 1892, and was buried in Baptist Church Cemetery, S. Dumfries. He married **Mary Eliza FARR** (daughter of **Eliza HILTON**). Mary Eliza was born about 1820. She died on 15 March 1901 in Ontario. Jonah T. HOWELL and Mary Eliza FARR had the following children:

+709 i. **Elisa HOWELL.**

+710 ii. **Martha HOWELL.**

711 iii. **Alexander HOWELL** was born in 1852 in S. Dumfries. He died in 1931.

712 iv. **Lydia HOWELL** was born in 1855 in S. Dumfries.

+713 v. **Clark HOWELL.**

+714 vi. **James Arthur HOWELL**

+715 vii. **Frederick Templer HOWELL.**

716 viii. **Alfred HOWELL** was born on 3 September 1869 in S. Dumfries. He died on 26 December 1892, and was buried in the Baptist Church Cemetery in S. Dumfries. He never married.

213. **Mercy HOWELL** was born in 1823 in Canada. She married a cousin, **Samuel G. HOWELL Jr**. For information on her family, see Samuel G. HOWELL, #113.

215. **Sarah HOWELL** was born in 1827 in Ontario, Canada. She married **David COCHRANE**. Sarah HOWELL and David COCHRANE had a son:

717 i. **Samuel W. H. COCHRANE** was born and died in

---

[130]Obituary, Washington (NJ) Star, 16 November 1905.

Ancaster Twp.

216. **Mary Jane HOWELL** was born on 25 September 1831 in Ontario. She died on 1 October 1910, and was buried in Zion Hill Cemetery. She was married (1) to **James WILSON** on 24 January 1852. James WILSON was born in 1824. He died on 20 July 1862 in Ancaster Twp., and was buried in Zion Hill Cemetery. Mary Jane HOWELL and James WILSON had the following children:

718 i. **Elizabeth H. WILSON** was born in 1852 in Ontario.
719 ii. **James H. WILSON** was born in 1854 in Ontario.
720 iii. **Hannah WILSON** was born in 1856 in Ontario.
721 iv. **Isabella G. WILSON** was born in 1857 in Ontario.
722 v. **Lucinda WILSON** was born in 1859 in Ontario.

Mary Jane married (2) **George WILSON** in 1863. He was born in 1837, died on 12 January 1917, and was buried in Zion Hill Cemetery. Mary Jane and George WILSON had these children:

723 i. **William Franklin WILSON** was born in 1864 in Ontario. He died on 29 July 1917, and was buried in Zion Hill Cemetery.
724 ii. **George Woods WILSON** was born in 1867 in Ontario.

218. **Isaac Reid HOWELL** was born in 1812 in Wentworth County, Ontario. He died on 17 November 1877 in Brantford Twp., Brant County, Ontario. He married **Lucinda WELLS**, who was born in 1814 in NY, and died on 8 December 1882 in Brantford Twp. Isaac and Lucinda had the following children:

725 i. **Julia HOWELL** was born in 1838 in Brantford Twp. She died in 1880, and was buried in St. George United Cemetery. She married **Lemuel B. KITCHEN** (son of **Edward KITCHEN** and **Eunice CULVER**) on 19 October 1858.
+726 ii. **John Edward HOWELL.**
727 iii. **Mary A. HOWELL** was born about 1842 in Brantford Twp., Brant County.
+728 iv. **Augustus HOWELL.**
729 v. **Rachel HOWELL** was born in 1847 in Brantford Twp. She died in 1916, and was buried in St. George United Cemetery. She married **Lemuel B. KITCHEN** (son of **Edward KITCHEN** and **Eunice CULVER**), who was born on 25 August 1834 in St. George, and died in 1905. Lemuel had previously been married to her sister, Julia.
730 vi. **Ada HOWELL** was born about 1848 in Brantford Twp.
731 vii. **Wellington HOWELL** was born about 1851 in Brantford Twp., Brant County.
732 viii. **Lucinda Josephine HOWELL** was born about 1852 in

Brantford Twp.

733 ix. **Frederick E. HOWELL** was born about 1854 in Brantford Twp.

222. **Levi D. HOWELL** was born on 6 August 1817 in Wentworth County, Ontario. He died on 8 October 1893 in Ancaster Twp., and was buried in Zion Hill Cemetery, Ancaster Twp. He was a farmer. He was married to **Lucy CUMMINGS** in 1843 in Flamborough, Ontario. Lucy CUMMINGS was born in 1815 in Ohio, and died on 7 January 1897 in Ancaster Twp., and was buried in Zion Hill Cemetery. Levi D. HOWELL and Lucy CUMMINGS had one child:

734 i. **Elizabeth A. HOWELL** was born in 1846.

223. **John HOWELL** was born on 10 October 1818 in Wentworth County, Ontario. He was married to **Elizabeth HOLDSWORTH** on 18 July 1849. Their son was:

+735 i. **Arthur HOWELL.**

225. **William HOWELL** was born in 1821 in Ancaster Twp., Wentworth County, Ontario. He died on 26 May 1898 in Ancaster Twp., and was buried in Zion Hill Cemetery. He was married to **Mary HORNING** on 4 February 1844 in Wentworth County, Ontario. Mary HORNING was born in 1825. She died on 5 December 1907, and was buried in Zion Hill Cemetery. William HOWELL and Mary HORNING had the following children:

736 i. **Isaac Reid HOWELL** was born in 1845 in Ancaster Twp. He died on 18 September 1920 and was buried in Zion Hill Cemetery. He married **Hannah TEMPLER**, who was born in 1845 and died on 27 August 1923. She was also buried in Zion Hill Cemetery.

+737 ii. **John Dennis HOWELL.**

+738 iii. **George Wesley HOWELL.**

+739 iv. **William Triller HOWELL.**

+740 v. **Oliver Alfred HOWELL.**

741 vi. **Mary Orilla HOWELL** was born in 1857 in Ancaster Twp. She married **James ARMSTRONG.**

+742 vii. **Bertha Ann HOWELL.**

743 viii. **Albert A. HOWELL** was born in 1859 in Ancaster Twp. He died on 16 July 1882, and was buried in Zion Hill Cemetery, Ancaster Twp.

+744 ix. **Charles Lewis HOWELL.**

745 x. **Frank Ellsworth HOWELL** was born on 31 December 1866 in Ancaster Twp. He died on 18 September 1868, and was buried in Zion Hill Cemetery.

746 xi. **Henry M. HOWELL** was born in 1871 in Ancaster Twp. He died young.

227. **Mary Eliza FARR** married a cousin, **Jonah T. HOWELL**. Please refer to Jonah T. HOWELL, #211.

229. **Jane HOWELL** was born on 28 September 1817 in S. Dumfries, Brant County, Ontario. She died on 16 November 1864, and was buried in St. George United Cemetery, S. Dumfries. She married **Samuel CASSADA** (CASSADY). Samuel CASSADA was born on 12 April 1816. He died on 7 January 1897, and also was buried in St. George United Cemetery. They had these children:

+747 i. **Isaac CASSADA.**
748 ii. **Sarah CASSADA** was born on 1 December 1839. She married **Hugh Montgomery BONHAM**, who was born about 1839. They had no children.
+749 iii. **Mary Jane CASSADA.**
+750 iv. **Harriet Ann CASSADA.**
+751 v. **Phoebe Eliza CASSADA.**
+752 vi. **Catherine CASSADA.**
+753 vii. **James Albert CASSADA.**
754 viii. **Alice Maria CASSADA.**
755 ix. **William Wallace CASSADA.**
+756 x. **Samuel CASSADA.**

230. **Rachel HOWELL** was born on 24 April 1819 in S. Dumfries, Brant County, Ontario. She died on 18 May 1899 in Ontario, and was buried in St. George United Cemetery, S. Dumfries. She was married to **Alfred KITCHEN** (son of **Edward KITCHEN** and **Eunice CULVER**) on 14 February 1845 in S. Dumfries. He was born on 24 July 1823 in Ontario, died on 28 July 1901, and was buried in St. George United Cemetery. Alfred was a farmer, and a Brant County Warden. Their children were:

+757 i. **Dr. Edward KITCHEN.**
758 ii. **Daniel KITCHEN** was a doctor, born about 1854.
+759 iii. **Eunice KITCHEN.**
760 iv. **Juliaett KITCHEN** died on 29 October 1860, at the age of 9 weeks. The date of death is from her marker.
761 v. **Harriet KITCHEN** was born on 4 December 1850, died on 8 March 1937, and was buried in St. George United Cemetery Harriet was unmarried.
+762 vi. **Isaac C. KITCHEN.**
+763 vii. **Mary Helen KITCHEN.**
764 viii. **Sarah Jane KITCHEN** was born on 4 April 1859 in Ontario. She died on 26 September 1861, and was buried in St. George United Cemetery. Dates of birth and death are from her tombstone.
+765 ix. **James Alfred KITCHEN.**
+766 x. **Carrie Rachel KITCHEN.**

231. **Sarah "Sally" HOWELL** was born on 12 August 1821 in S. Dumfries, Brant County, Ontario. She died on 20 May 1911 in Ontario, and was buried in St. George United Cemetery. She was married to **James Bird KITCHEN** (son of **Edward KITCHEN** and **Eunice CULVER**) on 30 October 1842. James Bird KITCHEN was born on 13 July 1820 in Norfolk County, Ontario. He died on 8 April 1893 in Ontario, and was buried in St. George United Cemetery. Sarah and James had the following children:

+767	i.	**Mary Jane KITCHEN.**
+768	ii.	**Eunice Maria KITCHEN.**
769	iii.	**John M. KITCHEN** was born on 2 June 1858 and died in 1911. He married, in 1880, **Lucy Lucinda MCLEAN**, who was born in 1853, and died in 1944. Both are buried in St. George United Cemetery. One researcher believes he was adopted.

233. **Firman Aikman HOWELL** was born on 22 May 1826 in S. Dumfries, and died there. He was a farmer. Firman and his father, Isaac, who was a joiner, built a home which duplicated the father's home. Some of Isaac's descendants still live in the home. He was married to **Rachel CASSADA** on 28 September 1845 in Brant County, Ontario. Rachel CASSADA was born on 16 July 1829 in S. Dumfries, where she also died. Firman Aikman HOWELL and Rachel CASSADA had the following children:

+770	i.	**Mary Adelaide HOWELL.**
+771	ii.	**James Bird HOWELL.**
+772	iii.	**Sarah Jane HOWELL.**
773	iv.	**Russell HOWELL** was born in Ontario, and died there in childhood.
774	v.	**Isaac HOWELL** was born about 1858 in S. Dumfries.

234. **Lemuel HOWELL** was born on 5 May 1829 in S. Dumfries, Brant County, Ontario. He died in May 1912 , and was buried in St. George United Cemetery. He married (1) **Margaret WAUGH** (daughter of **William WAUGH**) who was born on 23 February 1833. She died on 4 June 1851, of a fever, and was buried in St. George United Cemetery.

Lemuel then married a sister of his first wife, (2) **Helen N. WAUGH** (daughter of **William WAUGH**) who was born on 19 May 1835. She died in September 1928, and was buried in St. George United Cemetery. Lemuel HOWELL and Helen N. WAUGH Had these children:

+775	i.	**Margaret HOWELL.**
+776	ii.	**Osborne HOWELL.**
777	iii.	**Elma HOWELL** was born in Ontario. She married **Joseph MCLEAN.**

778 iv. **Minnie Jane HOWELL** was born on 29 May 1863 in S. Dumfries. She married **Albert BUCK** (son of **Lideral Ensign BUCK** and **Margaret SWARTZ**). Albert BUCK was born on 16 November 1858 and died on 15 May 1940 in South Gate, CA. They had no children.

+779 v. **Morley A. HOWELL.**

236. **Thomas Waugh HOWELL** was born on 20 May 1819 in St. George, Brant County, Ontario. He died on 12 January 1887 in S. Dumfries, Brant County, Ontario. He was a farmer. He was married to **Mary Catherine BOWSLAUGH** on 9 May 1847 in S. Dumfries. Mary Catherine BOWSLAUGH was born on 15 February 1830 in S. Dumfries. Thomas and Mary Catherine had these children:

+780 i. **James Romain HOWELL.**

+781 ii. **William Waugh HOWELL.**

782 iii. **Margaret HOWELL** was born in S. Dumfries in 1853, and died in 1922. She married **Charles BADENOCH**, who was born in 1847 and died in 1923. Both were buried in St. George United Cemetery.

783 iv. **Mary HOWELL** was born in 1854 in S. Dumfries. She married the **Reverend SCOTT**.

784 v. **Thomas Franklin HOWELL** was born in 1858 in S. Dumfries. He married **Elizabeth MILLIARD**, who was born in 1849 and died on 9 February 1926. Both were buried in St. George United Cemetery.

+785 vi. **Herbert Watson HOWELL.**

237. **Hannah HOWELL** was born on 14 April 1821 in Ontario. She died on 21 November 1853, and was buried in St. George United Cemetery. She married **William ELLIS**, who was born about 1818. He died on 9 December 1896, and was buried in St. George United Cemetery. Their children were:

786 i. **Margaret ELLIS** was born about 1842, died on 27 September 1848, and was buried in St. George United Cemetery.

787 ii. **Sarah J. ELLIS** was born in 1844. She married **Albert DIETZ** on 25 December 1868. Albert DIETZ was born in 1847.

788 iii. **Catherine ELLIS** was born about 1849, died on 23 December 1853, and was buried in St. George United Cemetery.

789 iv. **Mary ELLIS** was married to **George BLACK** on 22 September 1858. He was born in County Down, Ireland, in 1826.

790 v. **Jonah ELLIS.**

791 vi. **Alice ELLIS.**

792 vii. **Hannah ELLIS.**

238. **James HOWELL** was born in 1824 in Ontario, died on 25 April 1847, and was buried in St. George United Cemetery. He was married to **Frances L. UNKNOWN**, who was born in 1827, died on 20 January 1890, and was buried in St. George United Cemetery. James and Frances had one child:

793 i. **Thomas HOWELL** was born about 1845. He was a dentist.

239. **Margaret HOWELL** was born in 1832 in Ontario. She married **John VANDUZER** on 22 June 1852. Margaret HOWELL and John VANDUZER had the following children:

794 i. **William VANDUZER.**
795 ii. **George VANDUZER.**
796 iii. **Ira VANDUZER.**
797 iv. **Mary VANDUZER.**
798 v. **Ida VANDUZER.**
799 vi. **Fred VANDUZER.**

240. **Henry HOWELL** was born in 1835 in Ontario. He was a farmer. He died in 1920, and was buried in St. George United Cemetery. He married **Martha COPEMAN**, who was born about 1836 in S. Dumfries. Henry HOWELL and Martha COPEMAN had the following children:

+800 i. **George W. HOWELL.**
+801 ii. **Mary E. HOWELL.**
+802 iii. **Harry B. HOWELL.**
+803 iv. **Sydney HOWELL.**
804 v. **Marthy HOWELL** was born in December 1870 in Ontario.

242. **Hannah HOWELL** was born in 1827 in Ontario. She died before 1885 in Oxford County, Ontario, of typhoid fever, and was buried in Richmond Cemetery, Oxford County. She married **Daniel CASSADA** about 1847. Daniel CASSADA was born on 2 September 1827 in S. Dumfries, and died on 18 April 1906 in Blenheim Twp., Oxford County. Their children were:[131]

+805 i. **Charles William CASSADA.**
+806 ii. **Aurilla CASSADA.**
807 iii. **David CASSADA** was born in 1854, died in 1924 in Ayr, Ontario, and was buried in Ayr Cemetery, N. Dumfries. He married **Mary BURROWS.**

---

[131]Family information contributed by Jane Ellen Rich, 11 Park Plaza Dr., Hamilton, Ontario L5V 5A3

Dumfries. He married **Mary BURROWS**.

808 iv. **Mary CASSADA** was born in 1856.

809 v. **Daniel CASSADA** was born in 1858.

810 vi. **James CASSADA** was born in 1859, and died in 1862 in Blenheim Township, Ontario.

811 vii. **Samuel CASSADA** was born in 1861.

812 viii. **Lemuel CASSADA** was born in 1864 and died on 12 April 1918.

813 ix. **Arthur CASSADA** was born in 1868.

814 x. **James CASSADA** was born in 1870.

243. **Peter M. HOWELL** was born in 1839 in Ontario, Canada. He died on 28 October 1894, and was buried in Zion Hill Cemetery, Ancaster Twp., Wentworth County, Ontario. He married **Dorothy L. WAUGH** (daughter of **William WAUGH**), who was born in 1843, died on 29 November 1907, and was buried in Zion Hill Cemetery. Peter and Dorothy had a son:

815 i. **William M. HOWELL** was born in 1872, died in 1934, and was buried in Zion Hill Cemetery.

247. **William HOWELL** was born in 1843 in S. Dumfries, Brant County, Ontario. He died on 25 April 1920, and was buried in Zion Hill Cemetery. He married **Charlotte BIGGS** (daughter of **Richard BIGGS** and **Elizabeth UNKNOWN**), who was born about 1846. She died on 18 April 1920, and was buried in Zion Hill Cemetery. William HOWELL and Charlotte BIGGS had the following children:

816 i. **Stacy HOWELL**.

817 ii. **Mildred HOWELL** was born in 1879, died in 1910, and was buried in Holy Trinity Anglican Cemetery, Brant County. She married **Unknown LLOYD-JONES.**

248. **Jane A. HOWELL** was born about 1845 in S. Dumfries, Brant County, Ontario. She died on 13 September 1894, and was buried in St. George United Cemetery. She was married to **Hugh RONALD** on 23 May 1866 in Brant County, Ontario. Hugh RONALD (son of **William RONALD** and **Jane BECKETT**) was born in 1837, died on 10 May 1891, and was buried in St. George United Cemetery. Jane A. HOWELL and Hugh RONALD had a daughter:

818 i. **Rosa RONALD** was born about 1873, died on 24 April 1901, and was buried in St. George United Cemetery.

253. **Sadie HOWELL** was born on 28 April 1861 in Ontario. She died on 28 March 1888, and was buried in Burford Cemetery, Brant County, Ontario. She married **Major Robert Cuthbertson MUIR** who was born in 1810, and died on 10 March 1906. Sadie Robert Cuthbertson MUIR had a daughter:

819 i. **Sadie Howell MUIR** was born on 26 March 1888, died on 7 December 1940 in Brantford, and was buried in Burford Cemetery. She married (1) **Wesley J. MERIDITH**, (born in 1890, died in 1928), and (2) **Arthur CALDER.**

262. **Isaac Reid HOWELL** was born on 17 September 1817 in Jerseyville, Ancaster Twp., Wentworth County, Ontario. He died on 21 June 1901, and was buried in Jerseyville Cemetery. He was married (1) to **Nancy MARLATT** on 8 December 1845. Nancy MARLATT was born about 1829. She died on 25 July 1878, and was buried in Jerseyville Cemetery. Isaac and Nancy had one child:

+820 i. **Hettie HOWELL.**

After Nancy's death, Isaac Reid HOWELL married (2) **Esther CROSBY** (daughter of **Horatio CROSBY** and **Sarah UNKNOWN**), who was born in 1841 in Riga, Monroe County, New York. She died on 16 October 1895, and was buried in Ancaster Twp.

264. **George Ferguson HOWELL** was born on 6 April 1820 in Jerseyville, and died on 8 September 1863. He was a wagonmaker. He married (1) on 14 November 1840, **Mary Ann CARSON** who was born in 1820. She died on 7 September 1853 in Jerseyville, and was buried in Jerseyville Cemetery. George Ferguson HOWELL and Mary Ann CARSON had the following children:

821 i. **Martha HOWELL** was born in 1841. She married **Richard MUNSON** on 10 January 1860

822 ii. **Betsy Ann HOWELL** was born in 1845 and died in 1925. She married **George WEAVER** in 1862. George WEAVER was born in 1836 and died on 31 March 1924. Both were buried in Jerseyville Cemetery.

823 iii. **Edgar HOWELL** was born about 1848, died on 28 March 1868, and was buried in Jerseyville Cemetery.

824 iv. **Carson M. HOWELL** was born about 1852, died on 19 October 1894, and was buried in Jerseyville Cemetery.

George married (2) **Catharine SHAVER** (daughter of **Philip SHAVER** and **Margaret SMITH**). Catharine was born on 30 May 1835 in Wentworth County, and died on 2 September 1886 in Ancaster Twp., Wentworth County. George Ferguson HOWELL and Catharine SHAVER had these children:

825 i. **Wellington Rose HOWELL** was born in 1857, died on 31 January 1864, and was buried in Jerseyville Cemetery.

826 ii. **Georgina HOWELL** was born in 1861, and died in

1947. She married the **Rev. George W. HEWITT** on 7 July 1879 in Canada.

827 iii. **George Robert Albert HOWELL** was born about 1862, died on 18 August 1864 and was buried in Jerseyville Cemetery.

265. **Daniel HOWELL** was born on 3 December 1825 in S. Dumfries. He died on 6 November 1889, and was buried in Trinity Anglican Cemetery, North Dumfries, Waterloo County, Ontario. He was married to **Sarah SPENCER** on 14 September 1850 in S. Dumfries. Sarah SPENCER was born about 1821 in S. Dumfries. Daniel HOWELL and Sarah SPENCER had the following children:

828 i. **Mary Alice HOWELL** , birth date unknown, died on 9 December 1854, and was buried in Trinity Anglican Cemetery

+829 ii. **Henry Spencer HOWELL**.

266. **James DEAN** was born about 1804 in Saltfleet, Wentworth County, Ontario. He was buried in Stoney Creek Cemetery, Stoney Creek, Wentworth County. He married **Emily FLETCHER** who was born on 28 February 1810 in Saltfleet. James DEAN and Emily FLETCHER had the following children:

830 i. **Lewis Levi DEAN** was born about 1830 in Saltfleet.

+831 ii. **Samuel DEAN**.

832 iii. **James DEAN Jr**. was born about 1833 in Hamilton, Wentworth County.

833 iv. **John DEAN** was born about 1835 in Strathroy, Wentworth County, Ontario.

+834 v. **Andrew DEAN.**

835 vi. **Dennis DEAN** was born about 1838 in Saltfleet. He married **Barbara KNOWLES,** who was born in 1821 and died in 1882.

836 vii. **Levi DEAN** was born about 1851 in Saltfleet. He married **Lydia UNKNOWN**, who was born about 1851 in Saltfleet.

837 viii. **Albert DEAN** was born about 1855 in Saltfleet.

838 ix. **Garrett DEAN** was born about 1858 in Saltfleet.

271. **Levi DEAN** was born on 1 January 1815 in Saltfleet. He married **Martha BIGGAR** (daughter of **John BIGGAR** and **Margaret FISHER**), who was born about 1816 in Nelson Twp., Halton County, Ontario. Their children were:

+839 i. **Clarisa A. DEAN.**

+840 ii. **Margaret E. DEAN**.

841 iii. **Andrew S. DEAN** was born on 9 August 1843 in Saltfleet.

842 iv. **Ruth M. Dean** was born about 1846 in Saltfleet. She married **R. PATTON**, who was born about 1842 in

Saltfleet.

+843 v. **Martha Florilla DEAN.**
+844 vi. **Anson O. DEAN.**
+845 vii. **Levi Lewis DEAN.**

274. **Ann DEAN** was born on 24 March 1825 in Saltfleet. She married **Christopher BIGGAR**, who was born on 9 October 1819 in Nelson Twp., Halton County, Ontario. They had these children:

+846 i. **Mary Elizabeth BIGGAR.**
+847 ii. **Martha Matilda BIGGAR.**
+848 iii. **Joseph W. BIGGAR.**
+849 iv. **Robert Wellington BIGGAR.**
+850 v. **Emerson Bristol BIGGAR.**
+851 vi. **Selina A. BIGGAR.**
+852 vii. **Walter Elgin BIGGAR.**
+853 viii. **Sanford Dennis BIGGAR.**
+854 ix. **Milton Enos BIGGAR.**

275. **Mary HOWELL** was born on 20 March 1820 in Jerseyville. She was married to **Joseph STEELE** on 6 November 1838. Joseph STEELE was born on 8 February 1817 in St. George, Brant County, Ontario. Mary HOWELL and Joseph STEELE had the following children:

+855 i. **Edwin STEELE.**
+856 ii. **Lydia STEELE.**
+857 iii. **Jennie STEELE.**

276. **Daniel HOWELL** was born on 9 April 1821 in Jerseyville. He died in 1879, and was buried in St. George United Cemetery. He married **Sarah Ann KITCHEN** (daughter of **Edward KITCHEN** and **Eunice CULVER**) on 9 February 1841 in Ontario. She was born on 1 April 1822 in Elgin County, Ontario, died in 1897 in Ontario, and was buried in St. George United Cemetery. Their children were:

858 i. **Eunice Jane HOWELL** was born on 30 November 1845 in Ontario. She died on 11 August 1851, and was buried in St. George United Cemetery.

859 ii. **George M. HOWELL** was born in 1848 in Ontario, and died on 15 August 1851. He was buried in St. George United Cemetery.

860 iii. **Louise Burrows HOWELL** was born on 13 November 1852, and died on 15 June 1942 in Ontario. She was the daughter of **Joseph BURROWS** and **Charlotte UNKNOWN**, adopted after Daniel and Sarah lost their other children to diphtheria. She married **Salem Griswell KITCHEN** (son of **Edward KITCHEN** and **Eunice CULVER**)

on 22 March 1876. Salem was born on 29 June 1843 and died on 1 February 1920. Both were buried in St. George United Cemetery.

861 iv. **Unknown Female HOWELL** was born in 1859.

277. **Philip Stenabaugh HOWELL** was born on 19 November 1822 in Jerseyville. He died on 26 February 1910 in S. Dumfries, and was buried in St. George United Cemetery. He married **Mary Jane GREEN** (daughter of **Richard GREEN** and **Rachel BONHAM**) on 4 February 1846. Mary Jane GREEN was born on 20 June 1826 in Stoney Creek, Wentworth County, died on 23 December 1899 in S. Dumfries, and was buried in St. George United Cemetery. Their children were:

+862 i. **Alice HOWELL.**

863 ii. **Freeman HOWELL** was born on 29 December 1847 in S. Dumfries, where he died on 29 March 1881. He was buried in St. George United Cemetery. He ran a cheese factory on his father's farm. He was single.

864 iii. **Maria Amelia HOWELL** was born on 11 August 1851 in S. Dumfries. She died on 4 July 1938, and was buried in St. George United Cemetery. She was unmarried.

865 iv. **Rachel Melissa HOWELL** was born on 25 April 1854 in S. Dumfries, where she died on 10 June 1912. She was buried in St. George United Cemetery. She was unmarried.

+866 v. **Mary Ellen HOWELL.**

+867 vi. **Herbert Levi HOWELL.**

+868 vii. **Ida Jane HOWELL.**

+869 viii. **Catherine Alberta HOWELL.**

278. **Peter HOWELL** was born on 11 December 1823 in Jerseyville. He died on 26 December 1892, and was buried in Village Cemetery, N. Norwich Twp., Oxford County, Ontario. He married **Margaret SMITH** (daughter of **David SMITH** and **Charity SHAVER**) on 29 December 1852 in Norwich. Margaret SMITH was born on 1 September 1828 in Ancaster Twp., died on 3 May 1917 in N. Norwich Twp., and was buried in the Village Cemetery. Their children were:

870 i. **Catharine HOWELL** was born and died in N. Norwich Twp. She was buried in Milldale Cemetery. She married **George TEDFRY**

871 ii. **Lucy HOWELL** was born and died in Norwich, and was buried in Norwich Gore Cemetery, N. Norwich. She married **William TAPLEY.**

872 iii. **Richmond HOWELL** lived and died in N. Norwich Twp. He was buried in the Village Cemetery, as was his wife, **Maude BUCKRELL.**

+873 iv. **Levi HOWELL.**

279. **Lydia HOWELL** was born on 3 May 1825 in Jerseyville. She was married to **Bruin CORNELL** on 29 June 1845. Lydia and Bruin CORNELL had children:

874 i. **Keturah CORNELL** married **Unknown SHOWLER.**
875 ii. **Samuel CORNELL.**

280. **George M. HOWELL** was born on 21 September 1827 in Jerseyville. He died on 11 March 1908, and was buried in Princeton Cemetery, Blenheim Twp., Oxford County, Ontario. He was a farmer. He was married to **Abigail SHEWERT** (daughter of **Joseph SHEWERT** and **Christianna UNKNOWN**) on 24 May 1860 in Burford Township, Brant County, Ontario. Abigail SHEWERT was born in 1835 in Burford Township. She died on 8 June 1891, and was buried in Princeton Cemetery, Blenheim Twp., Oxford County. Their children were:

876 i. **Elsie HOWELL** was born in 1861 in Burford Twp., and died there in 1936. She was buried in Princeton Cemetery. She married **Arthur BROOKS**.
877 ii. **Edwin HOWELL** was born in 1861 in Burford Township, Brant County.
878 iii. **Florence HOWELL** was born in 1865 in Burford Township, Brant County.
879 iv. **Adelaide HOWELL** was born in 1867 in Burford Township. She died in 1915, and was buried in Princeton Cemetery.
880 v. **George HOWELL** was born in 1870 in Burford Township, Brant County.
+881 vi. **Bertha C. HOWELL.**

281. **Margaret Ann HOWELL** was born on 10 January 1833 in Jerseyville. She died on 4 July 1921, and was buried in St. George United Cemetery. She was married to **Richard GREEN** (son of **Richard GREEN** and **Rachel BONHAM**) on 13 January 1852. Richard GREEN was born on 5 March 1828 in Stoney Creek, Wentworth County, Ontario. He died on 23 June 1901, and was buried in St. George United Cemetery. Margaret Ann and Richard GREEN had these children:

+882 i. **John GREEN.**
883 ii. **Arthur Wellington GREEN** was born on 13 October 1860. He died on 22 April 1881 in Ancaster Twp. He married **Catherine Stewart STEELE**, who was born in 1874, and died on 20 February 1932. Both are buried in St. George United Cemetery.

282. **David HOWELL** was born on 20 May 1809 in Ancaster Twp. where he died on 22 April 1881. He was married to **Jane THATCHER** on 20 January 1831 in Ontario. Jane THATCHER died in Ontario. Their children were:[132]

884 i. **Barbara HOWELL** was born in 1832.

885 ii. **Ann HOWELL** was born on 23 February 1834 in Ancaster Twp. She died January 1916, and was buried in Greenwood Cemetery, Brant Twp. She married **Seth Wesley BRADSHAW** (son of **Walter BRADSHAW** and **Huldah VANSICKLE)** on 4 January 1855 in Ancaster Twp. Seth was born on 25 December 1833 in Belleville, Ontario.[133] He had a wagon and carriage making business, which he sold to his brother when he began to sell sewing machines. He later worked for William Patterson, a member of the Canadian Parliament.

886 iii. **Catherine HOWELL** was born about 1835 in Jerseyville. She married **R. H. HAVITT**.

+887 iv. **Elsie Alice HOWELL**.

+888 v. **Triller HOWELL.**

889 vi. **Olive HOWELL** was born about 1840 in Onondaga Twp., Brant County. She married **Sylvester MISNER** in 1859.

890 vii. **Elizabeth HOWELL** was born about 1842 in Ancaster Twp. She married **William WESTBROOK** in 1860.

891 viii. **Susan HOWELL** was born about 1843 in Ancaster Twp. She married **John W. BUTLER** in 1865.

+892 ix. **Mary HOWELL**.

893 x. **Arthur David HOWELL** was born on 11 July 1849 in Ancaster Twp. He died on 13 July 1855.

286. **Benjamin Ogden HOWELL** was born on 24 May 1816 in Ancaster Twp., and died on 15 March 1900 in Ayr, Waterloo County, Ontario. He was a farmer. He married **Margaret UNKNOWN** who was born in 1818 in Ancaster Twp., and died on 9 January 1855 in W. Dumfries Twp. Their children were:

894 i. **Calista HOWELL** was born about 1840. She married (1) **F. E. DAVIS** on 9 March 1861, and married (2) **Ebenezer CURRIE** (son of **James CURRIE** and **Mary BEATTIE)** on 7 October 1862 in Brant

---

[132]Information on this family was contributed by Nancy Shaver Lytle, 74 Regent Cres., Brandon, MB, Canada R7B 2W9.

[133] George Maclean Rose, A Cyclopaedia of Canadian Biography, (Toronto: Rose Publishing Co., 1886) p. 604

County. Ebenezer CURRIE was born in Scotland.

895 ii. **Thomas M. HOWELL** was born about 1843.

896 iii. **Ann Elizabeth HOWELL** was born on 25 June 1850, and baptized on 18 April 1853 in Ayr.

287. **Isaac Lanning HOWELL** was born on 9 July 1818 in Ancaster Twp. He died on 5 January 1887 in Brantford Twp., Brant County, Ontario, where he had a 150 acre farm[134]. The family moved to Brantford Township in 1854 and settled near the town of Paris, Brant County. Isaac married **Harriet Eliza WAUGH** on 19 January 1847 in Brantford Twp. Their children were:

897 i. **Marcia A. HOWELL** was born in 1848.

898 ii. **Alice Elisa HOWELL** was born in 1851.

899 iii. **Franklin HOWELL**.

+900 iv. **Cordelia M. HOWELL**.

901 v. **Emmerata HOWELL** was born in 1856 in Brantford Twp.

902 vi. **James Albert HOWELL** was born in 1860 in Brantford Twp.

903 vii. **Isaac Franklin HOWELL** was born in 1862 in Brantford Twp.

904 viii. **Herbert Benjamin HOWELL** was born in 1864 in Brantford Twp.

290. **Levi C. HOWELL** was born on 20 May 1825 in Ancaster Twp., Wentworth County, Ontario. He died about 1860. He was married to **Mary Margarett AIKMAN** (daughter of **Alexander AIKMAN** and **Mary SPRINGER**) in 1853. Mary Margarett AIKMAN was born on 16 November 1832. She died on 25 October 1915 in Niagara Falls, Ontario. Their children were:

+905 i. **Ada Matilda HOWELL**.

906 ii. **Levi HOWELL**, Ada's twin, was born about 1854, and died soon afterward.

907 iii. **Madella Anne HOWELL** was born in 1856 in North Dumfries, Waterloo County, Ontario. She died on 16 December 1938, of cerebral thrombosis, [135] and was buried on 19 December 1938.

908 iv. **Mary Alevia HOWELL** was born in 1858 in North Dumfries. She died on 25 September 1938 in

---

[134]Warren & Beers, History of the County of Brant, Ontario, (1883, publisher unknown) 574.

[135]Cemetery Record, Resthaven Cemetery, Scarboro, Ontario, Block E, Section 307, Lot 2.

294. **George Miller HOWELL** was born on 25 July 1815 in Jerseyville. He died on 26 January 1899, and was buried in Jerseyville Cemetery. He was married (1) to **Rebecca Belle MCCAY** on 6 March 1839 in Canada. Rebecca Belle MCCAY was born on 31 December 1817 in Nelson Twp., Halton County, Ontario. She died on 14 September 1851 in Jerseyville, probably in childbirth, and was buried in Jerseyville Cemetery. George and Rebecca had the following children:

909 i. **Edwy Ryerson HOWELL** was born about 1840. He died and was buried in Ancaster Twp. He married **Maria SWARTY** (daughter of **Peter SWARTY**) in 1862 in Ontario.

910 ii. **Phoebe W. HOWELL** married **Daniel PICKETT** in 1865.

911 iii. **Infant HOWELL** died on 26 September 1851, and was buried in Jerseyville Cemetery.

George Miller HOWELL married (2) **Mary I. DAVIDSON**, who was born about 1833. She died on 7 April 1894, and was buried in Jerseyville Cemetery. They had one child:

+912 i. **Elwood Usher HOWELL.**

295. **Sarah HOWELL** was born in 1817. She died on 7 December 1860 in London, England, and was buried in Ancaster Twp. She married **Burdge MCCAY** (son of **Moses MCCAY**), who was born in 1811 in Nelson Twp., Halton County, Ontario. He died on 25 August 1853 in Jerseyville, and was buried in Jerseyville Cemetery. There were two children of this marriage, the name of the second unknown. (Sometimes the last name is MCCAY and sometimes MCCOY.) Their one known child was:[136]

+913 i. **Catherine Burdge MCCAY.**

296. **Jane HOWELL** was born in 1820. She died on 7 January 1859, of consumption, and was buried in Jerseyville Cemetery. She married **Murray MCCAY** (son of **Moses MCCAY**) on 22 May 1839.[137] They had 7 children, only one of whom is known. Murray MCCAY died on 3 November 1900, and was buried in Greenwood Cemetery, Brant Twp., Brant County, Ontario. The only child known was:

914 i. **Peter MCCAY** died in childhood.

---

[136]Informationon this family contributed by Debbie Reynen, Box 10, Site 1, R.R.#2, Lacombe, Alberta T0C 1S0.

[137]Thomas B. Wilson, Ontario Marriage Notices, (Lambertville, NJ: Hunterdon House, 1982) 52.

298. **Catharine HOWELL** was born in 1824. She died on 16 October 1851 in Jerseyville, and was buried in Jerseyville Cemetery. Her obituary said she was survived by her husband and two daughters. She was married to **Michael FICHT** on 5 October 1847. The only child known was:

915 i. **Mary E. FICHT** was born about 1849, died on 13 December 1881, and was buried in Jerseyville Cemetery.

301. **Harriet HOWELL** was born on 27 August 1833; she died on 8 March 1878, and was buried in Jerseyville Cemetery. She was married to Rev. **James HARRIS** on 19 June 1855.[138] James HARRIS was born in 1827 in Stockport, England. He died in 1914 in Guelph, Wellington County, Ontario, and was buried in Jerseyville Cemetery. They had these children:

916 i. **Willie Arthur HARRIS** was born on 24 August 1851, died three days later, and was buried in Jerseyville Cemetery.

917 ii. **Minnie HARRIS** was born about 1863. She died on 6 April 1865, and was buried in Jerseyville Cemetery

303. **Sophia HOWELL** was born on 2 June 1823 in Jerseyville. She died there on 26 August 1850, and was buried in Jerseyville Cemetery. She married **Morris ANDERS** on October 13, 1841; he died in 1902. Their only child was:

918 i. **Zypha ANDERS** was born on 5 September 1844 in Jerseyville, and died in December 1887 in Brantford Twp., Brant County, Ontario.

304. **Wesley HOWELL** was born on 28 January 1825 in Jerseyville. He died on 28 July 1903 in Brantford Twp., Brant County. He married **Emma VANDERLIP** (daughter of **Edward VANDERLIP** and **Elizabeth UNKNOWN**) on 8 February 1848 in Brant County. Emma VANDERLIP was born in 1826 in Brantford Twp. She died on 13 May 1895 in Brantford Twp. Both were buried in Greenwood Cemetery. Wesley and Emma had these children:

919 i. **Corwin O. HOWELL** was born in 1848 in Brantford Twp. He made his home in Chicago, Cook County, Ilinois, where he died in December 1907.

920 ii. **Martha HOWELL** was born about 1849 in Brantford Twp. She married **Unknown SHUTTLEWORTH**. They lived in London, Ontario.

921 iii. **Emily C. HOWELL** was born in 1867 in Brantford Twp. She died in 1942, and was buried in

---

[138]Thomas B. Wilson, Ontario Marriage Notices, (Lambertville, NJ: Hunterdon House, 1982) 287.

Greenwood Cemetery. She married **Levi SEACORD**.

922 iv. **Lottie Elizabeth HOWELL** was born in 1867 in Brantford Twp. She died in November 1942, and was buried in Greenwood Cemetery.

923 v. **Frederick J. HOWELL** was a Colonel in the Canadian Army. He lived in Hamilton, Wentworth County.

924 vi. **Osmond C. HOWELL** lived in Coshocton, Coshocton County, Ohio.

305. **Nelson HOWELL** was born on 27 January 1827 in Jerseyville. He died on 18 January 1912 in Brantford Twp., Brant County, Ontario, and was buried in Jerseyville Cemetery. He married (1) **Mary Jane CAMPBELL** on 11 October 1848 in Brantford Twp. Mary Jane CAMPBELL was born about 1829. She died on 27 March 1862 in Jerseyville, and was buried in Jerseyville Cemetery. Their children were:

925 i. **Unknown female HOWELL.**

926 ii. **Unknown male HOWELL** was born on 17 March 1862.

927 iii. **Unknown female HOWELL.**

Nelson was married (2) to **Annie KEAGY** on 28 May 1863 in West Flamboro, Wentworth County, Ontario. Annie KEAGY was born about 1834, died on 1 September 1868, and was buried in Jerseyville Cemetery. They had one child:

928 i. **Sarah Louise HOWELL** was born about 1868, died on 29 April 1872, and was buried in Jerseyville Cemetery.

Nelson was married (3) to **Mary SHAW** on 22 December 1869 in Ontario. Mary SHAW was born in 1853. She died in 1886, and was buried in Mt. Vernon United Cemetery, Brant County, Ontario. He married (4) **Hattie WOODYAT** in August 1888 in Ontario. She died on 19 July 1912 in Brantford Twp.

306. **Morris HOWELL** was born on 14 December 1828 in Jerseyville. He died on 4 May 1912 in Vineland, NJ., and was buried in Jerseyville Cemetery. Morris and his family moved to Vineland, New Jersey about 1876. He was married (1) to **Jane LYMBURNER** on 17 June 1853 in Brantford Twp., Brant County, Ontario. She was born in 1834, died on 11 August 1855 of consumption, in Jerseyville, and was buried in Jerseyville Cemetery. They had one child:

+929 i. **Moses Hazen HOWELL.**

Morris married (2) **Letitia PALMERS** on 28 March 1861 in Ancaster Twp., Wentworth County, Ontario.

307. **Ruth HOWELL** was born on 8 February 1831 in Jerseyville. She died on 22 December 1910 in Cainsville, Brantford, Ontario, and was buried in Greenwood Cemetery, Brant Twp. She married **Justus VANDERLIP** (son of **Edward VANDERLIP** and **Elizabeth UNKNOWN**) on 13 February 1852 in Jerseyville. Justus VANDERLIP was born on 7 June 1828 in Brantford Twp. Ruth HOWELL and Justus VANDERLIP had these children:

930 i. **Taylor VANDERLIP.**
931 ii. **Orpha VANDERLIP** married **Unknown SUMLER.**
932 iii. **Mary H. VANDERLIP** married **Unknown TAYLOR.**
933 iv. **Libbie VANDERLIP.**
934 v. **John VANDERLIP.**
935 vi. **Clark VANDERLIP** died at 15 in Cainsville. He drowned in the Grand River at Cainsville.

309. **Obed HOWELL** was born on 19 June 1835 in Jerseyville. He died on 16 December 1887 in Brantford Twp., of typhoid fever, and was buried in Jerseyville Cemetery. He was a timberman. He married **Esther Louisa TOWN** on 31 December 1867 in Nunda, New York. Esther Louisa TOWN was born about 1847 in NY; she died on 22 September 1887 in Brantford Twp., of typhoid fever, and was buried in Jerseyville Cemetery. Their children were:

936 i. **Harry E. HOWELL** was born about 1868.
937 ii. **Louise HOWELL** was born in 1872; she died in 1951, and was buried in Jerseyville Cemetery.
938 iii. **Pearl HOWELL.**
939 iv. **Roy C. HOWELL** was born about 1885.

311. **Clark HOWELL** was born on 25 November 1838 in Jerseyville He operated a heating & plumbing business. He was married to **Frances TAYLOR** (daughter of **Edward TAYLOR** and **Jane UNKNOWN**) on 4 July 1863. Frances TAYLOR was born on 10 August 1843 in Craigs, Antrim, Ireland. Clark and Frances had the following children:

940 i. **Grant HOWELL** was born on 9 June 1865; he died on 9 June 1865, and was buried in Forest Lawn Cemetery, Erie County, New York.
941 ii. **William Clark HOWELL** was born on 16 January 1869, and died on 17 January 1869, in Rochester, NY. He was buried in Mount Hope Cemetery, Rochester, Monroe County, New York.
+942 iii. **Obed Ernest HOWELL.**

312. **Lydia HOWELL** was born on 16 November 1840 in Jerseyville. She died on 17 April 1912 in Buffalo, Erie County, New York, and was buried in Jerseyville Cemetery. She married **Lewis Wilson BAXTER** on 23 December 1856 in Ontario. Lewis Wilson BAXTER was born in 1832 in Bertie, Welland County, Ontario; he died in 1909, and was buried in Jerseyville Cemetery. Their children were:

943 i. **Alfred E. BAXTER** was born in Jerseyville.
944 ii. **Howell BAXTER** was born in November 1862 in Jerseyville. He died on 30 January 1863, and was buried in Jerseyville Cemetery.

318. **Nancy HOWELL** was born on 10 June 1831. She died on 26 December 1914 in Mt. Brydges, Caradoc Twp., Middlesex Co., Ontario. She married **Daniel BURNHAM**, who was born in 1823, and died on 19 June 1897. Nancy and Daniel BURNHAM had the following children:

945 i. **Mahalah Jane BURNHAM** was born in 1849. She died in 1923.
946 ii. **Matilda BURNHAM** was born in 1853. She died on 19 November 1943.
947 iii. **Isaac Howell BURNHAM** was born on 5 March 1855. He died in 1875.
948 iv. **Violetta BURNHAM** was born in 1857 and died in 1936.
+949 v. **Clarissa Bell BURNHAM**.

319. **Elizabeth HOWELL** was born on 29 December 1833, and died on 6 April 1913 in London, Ontario. She was married to **Robert GULLEN**, who was born on 9 September 1823, and died on 10 June 1873. The GULLEN children were:

+950 i. **Minnie GULLEN**.
951 ii. **Arthur GULLEN** was born on 5 March 1869. He died on 23 August 1938.
+952 iii. **Ella GULLEN.**
953 iv. **Albert GULLEN** was born on 15 August 1872. He died on 24 March 1962.

320. **Lois Ann HOWELL** was born in 1846. She died on 4 August 1888 in Mt. Brydges, Caradoc Twp., Middlesex Co. She married **Jeremiah BRYAN**. Lois and Jeremiah BRYAN had the following children:

954 i. **Martha E. BRYAN** was born on 26 May 1863, and died on 28 February 1901 in Mt. Brydges.
955 ii. **George Dennis BRYAN** was born 24 July 1865, and died 27 November 1944.
956 iii. **Edmund Arthur BRYAN** was born on 29 June 1867, and died on 12 May 1934.
957 iv. **Henry Franklin BRYAN** was born on 9 January 1870. He died in 1902.
958 v. **James Lewis BRYAN** was born on 9 April 1872. He died on 9 August 1952.
959 vi. **Jeremiah William BRYAN** was born on 14 July 1875.
960 vii. **Annie V. BRYAN** was born on 22 May 1876, and died on 8 August 1892 in Mt. Brydges.

961 viii. **Herman Ross Howell BRYAN** was born on 31 October 1879.

962 ix. **Ethel Frances BRYAN** was born on 29 August 1883, and died on 10 December 1924.

337. **Alexander James HOWELL** was born on 27 November 1837 in Onondaga Twp., Brant County, Ontario. He died on 23 May 1922, and was buried in Greenwood Cemetery, Brant Twp., Brant County. He married (1) **Elizabeth LINCOLN** on 27 March 1861 in Brant County. Elizabeth LINCOLN was born about 1843. She died on 2 October 1873, and was buried in Greenwood Cemetery. Alexander and Elizabeth had one child:

+963 i. **Marion Elizabeth HOWELL.**

Alexander married (2) **Alice SHUTTLEWORTH**.

338. **Isaac HOWELL** was born on 22 March 1839 in Onondaga Twp., Brant County, Ontario. He died on 13 July 1898 in Onondaga Twp., and was buried in Brant Cemetery, Brantford Twp., Brant County. He was married to **Mary Alice HOLMES** in 1875 in Brant County. Mary Alice HOLMES was born about 1846. She died on 14 July 1933, and was buried in Brant Cemetery. Their children were:

+964 i. **Melvin HOWELL.**

+965 ii. **Harold HOWELL.**

966 iii. **Edgar A. HOWELL** was born on 27 August 1881 in Onondaga Twp. He died there on 25 July 1885, and was buried in Brant Cemetery.

340. **William Hamilton HOWELL** was born in 1843 in Onondaga Twp., Brant County, and died in 1920. He was a farmer. He married **Helen SUTTON** in 1876 in Brant County, Ontario. Their children were:

967 i. **Isabella HOWELL.**

+968 ii. **Laura Grace HOWELL.**

969 iii. **Edwin HOWELL.**

William and his brother Isaac lived with their families on their parents' farm, along with their widowed mother. [139]

---

[139]Warren & Beers, History of the County of Brant, Ontario, (1883, publisher not known) 643.

EUPHEMIA OSBORNE HOWELL THOMPSON
on her 100th birthday.

SIXTH GENERATION

348. **Coursen Henry ALBERTSON** was born on 26 March 1833 in Frelinghuysen, Warren County, NJ. In the 1860 census for Vienna, Warren County, NJ., Coursen's real estate was valued at $2,500, and his personal property at $1,800. Coursen married **Clarissa WHITE** (daughter of **John WHITE**), who was born in 1834 in NJ. They had the following children:

970 i. **Fanny ALBERTSON** was born in 1856 in Vienna.
971 ii. **John ALBERTSON** was born in 1859 in Vienna.
972 iii. **Kerr ALBERTSON** was born about 1861. In the 1880 census, he was said to be a law student.[140]
973 iv. **Anna B. ALBERTSON** was born about 1863.
974 v. **William ALBERTSON** was born about1865.
975 vi. **Milton ALBERTSON** was born about 1869.
976 vii. **Jennie ALBERTSON** was born about 1872.

359. **John H. COOKE** was born about 1829 in Warren County, NJ. He married **Sarah UNKNOWN**, who was born about 1838. John was a farmer. He and Sarah had the following children:[141]

977 i. **George COOKE** was born in 1860.
978 ii. **Matilda M. COOKE** was born in 1861.
979 iii. **Charles W. COOKE** was born in 1863.
980 iv. **Samuel H. COOKE** was born in 1866.
981 v. **Anna Elizabeth COOKE** was born in 1868.
982 vi. **Edwin COOKE** was born in 1871.

366. **John Wesley HOWELL** was born on 1 March 1841. He died on 4 December 1864 and was buried in the Union Cemetery in Hope. John Wesley Howell married, but his wife's name is **UNKNOWN**. Their child was:

983 i. **Charles W. HOWELL** was born in September 1861, and died in 1930. He married **Jennie M. UNKNOWN**, who was born in June 1871 and died in 1952. Both were buried in Union Cemetery.

367. **Millard Fillmore HOWELL** was born on 11 April 1852 in Hope, Warren County, NJ. He died on 10 February 1924 in West Livingston, NJ, and was buried in Union Cemetery, Hope, Warren County, NJ. He was a farmer. Millard, called Fillmore, was living in Summit in 1899, when his brother died. His own obituary

---

[140] 1880 U.S. Census(population, New Jersey, Warren County, Vienna, p. 123, nos. 24/24, National Archives Microfilm Publication, T9, roll

[141] 1870 U.S. Census (population) New Jersey, Warren Co., Hope Twp., p. 146, nos.164/171, National Archives Microfilm Publication, M593, roll 892

called him Miller F. Howell.[142] He was married to **Sarah Catherine SNYDER** on 20 December 1882 in Broadway, Sussex County, New Jersey. Sarah Catherine SNYDER was born on 30 March 1858. She died on 30 March 1934 in Livingston, Essex County, NJ.[143] Their children were:

984 i. **Evert HOWELL.**
985 ii. **Blair HOWELL.**
986 iii. **George HOWELL.**
987 iv. **Mabel HOWELL** married **Unknown SERGENT**, and lived in Livingston, NJ. in 1934.

368. **Edward A. HOWELL** was born on 2 April 1854 in Hope, Warren County, NJ[144]. He died on 10 February 1899, and was buried in Moravian Cemetery, Hope, NJ. [145] Edward was a deacon in the Christian Church in Hope, NJ. (He had a twin brother, not named.) Edward died of pneumonia and pleurisy. His obituary described him as "a gentleman in every sense of the word. He was ever kind to those socially or otherwise beneath him; he had a word of greeting for all the children, and was liberal in all benevolent work. Though he had a mind of his own, he was rarely heard to express publicly his sentiments or to engage in any debate where his own affairs were not especially concerned." Edward A. HOWELL married **Hannah J. UNKNOWN**, who was born on 20 February 1860, died on 29 August 1950, and was buried in Moravian Cemetery, Hope, NJ. Edward and Hannah had one child:

988 i. **Turner HOWELL** was born in March 1888.

After Edward's death, Hannah married **John FLUMMERFELT**.

369. **Mary M. HOWELL** was born on 21 April 1856 in Hope, Warren County, NJ. She died in 1930 in Hope, and was buried in Union Cemetery. She married **Jacob E. WEST**, who was born in 1855. He died in 1931, and was buried in Union Cemetery. Mary and Jacob had these children:

989 i. **Grace H. WEST** was born in October 1881 in Warren County, NJ.
990 ii. **Florence E. WEST** was born in February 1883 in Warren County, NJ.
+991 iii. **Robert M. WEST.**

371. **Caleb H. HOWELL** was born on 23 August 1833 in Hope, Warren County, NJ. He died on 29 July 1911 in Chicago, Cook County, IL, and was buried in

---

[142]Obituary, Washington(NJ) Star, 14 February 1924.
[143]Obituary, Washington (NJ) Star, 6 April 1934
[144]Birth Certificate showing twin boys, Vol. AJ, p. 148, Warren Co., NJ. New Jersey State Archives, Trenton, NJ.
[145]Obituary , Washington (NJ) Star, 23 February 1899.

Oxford Twp. Cemetery, Oakland County, MI. He was married to **Harriet E. ALLEN** on 31 December 1861. Caleb and his family moved to Michigan, settling in the town of Oxford, Oakland County, MI. In 1902, Caleb went to Chicago to live with his daughter, Nettie and her husband, where he died. He was buried from the home of his sister-in-law, **Mrs. O. H. MILLSPAUGH**.[146] Harriet E. ALLEN was born on 19 September 1840, died on 4 May 1886 in Oxford, and was buried in Oxford Twp. Cemetery. Caleb and Harriet had the following children:

992 ii. **Charles W. HOWELL** was born on 28 October 1862. He died on 8 April 1884 in Oxford Twp.

993 iii. **Nettie HOWELL** was born in 1863 , and died in 1940 in Oxford. She married **John W. WULFF**, who was born in 1869, and died in 1940.

372. **John H. HOWELL** was born on 23 August 1835 in Hope, Warren County, NJ. He died on 5 June 1921 in Bloomsbury, Hunterdon County, New Jersey. He was buried in Lower Harmony Cemetery, Harmony, Warren County, NJ. He was a farmer. John was a private in Captain C.F. Fernalde's Co. M, 2nd Regiment, New Jersey Cavalry, enlisted 25 August 1864, and discharged 29 June 1865 at Vicksburg, Mississippi.

He was married to **Hannah Etta GREEN** (daughter of **Jeremiah K. GREEN** and **Azannah ADAMS**) on 28 September 1867 in Independence, Warren County, NJ. Hannah Etta GREEN was born on 2 March 1843 in Warren County, NJ. She died on 7 February 1920 in Harmony.[147] She was buried in Lower Harmony Cemetery. John and Hannah Etta had these children:

994 i. **Janson Deckert HOWELL** was born on 12 July 1868 in Warren County. He died on 14 December 1930, and was buried in Fairmount Cemetery, Phillipsburg, Warren County. He was a clerk in Philliipsburg, in 1920 when his mother died. He married **Phoebe STOUT** (daughter of **Jacob STOUT** and **Mary HINELINE**) on 10 September 1902. Phoebe was was born in 1876, died on 17 November 1947 in Easton, Northampton County, PA. and was buried in Fairmount Cemetery.

995 ii. **Emily Azannah HOWELL** was born on 28 September 1869 in Warren County. She died on 29 August 1906, of consumption, in Harmony, and was buried in Lower Harmony Cemetery.[148]

996 iii. **Jeremiah Green HOWELL** was born on 14 March 1871; he died of diphtheria on 25 March 1874 in

---

[146]Obituary, unknown Oakland County (MI) newspaper, 1911.
[147]Obituary, Washington (NJ) Star, 12 February 1920.
[148]Obituary, Washington (NJ) Star, 6 September 1906.

Warren County, and was buried in Green's Chapel Cemetery, Hope, Warren County, NJ.

997 iv. **George H. HOWELL** was born on 7 December 1872, and died on 16 January 1878 in Warren County, NJ, of diphtheria. He was buried in Green's Chapel Cemetery.

998 v. **Frank G. HOWELL** was born on 18 August 1874, died on 2 February 1878 of diphtheria, and was buried in Green's Chapel Cemetery.[149]

+999 vi. **Charles Milton HOWELL.**

+1000 vii. **John Manning HOWELL.**

+1001 viii. **Ephriam Clarke HOWELL.**

+1002 ix. **Obadiah Titman HOWELL.**

+1003 x. **Robert Carter HOWELL.**

373. **Marshall HOWELL** was born on 30 November 1838 in Hope, Warren County, NJ. He died on 30 May 1915 in Pen Argyl, and was buried in Fairview Cemetery, Pen Argyl, Northampton County, PA. Marshall enlisted 3 October 1861, in Company H, 8th Regiment, New Jersey Volunteers, was promoted to corporal, fought in 47 battles and was frequently cited for bravery in the field. He was discharged 12 July 1865, after the war ended. He was married to **Anna M. CASSADY** on 27 November 1866 in Newton, Sussex County, NJ. Anna M. CASSADY was born on 15 December 1842, died on 2 June 1902, and was buried in Fairview Cemetery, Pen Argyl, Northampton County, PA. Their children were:

+1004 i. **William V. HOWELL.**

+1005 ii. **Leslie A. HOWELL.**

374. **Martha Ann HOWELL** was born in October 1843 in Warren County, NJ. She died in 1901. She was buried in Brooklyn, Kings County, New York. She married (1) **Jesse EILENBERGER**, of Upper Mt. Bethel, PA, on 6 September 1862[150]. Jesse EILENBERGER was born on 29 September 1839. He died on 12 January 1873 in Ramsayburg, Warren County, New Jersey. Their children were:[151]

+1006 i. **John E. EILENBERGER.**

+1007 ii. **Osmond Perle Eilenberger HOWELL.**

+1008 iii. **James Prall Eilenberger HOWELL.**

+1009 iv. **Elizabeth EILENBERGER.**

Martha married (2) **Peter SCHERER.**

---

[149]Death notice, Washington(NJ)Star, 21 Feb 1878.

[150]Warren County, NJ Marriage Records, LDS Microfilm # 0960890. V. 2, p. 242.

[151]Information on this family contributed by: Louise Ponce, 584 Elm St., Maywood NJ 07607, and by Robert Howell, 725 Scott St., Stroudsburg PA 18360.

377. **Abby Maria HOWELL** was born about 1848. She died on 25 November 1884, and was buried in the Johnsonburg cemetery. She married **Judson KITTLE** on 19 January 1874 in Hope, Warren County, NJ.[152] Judson KITTLE was born on 8 July 1849 in NJ. He died on 8 September 1903 in Allamuchy, Warren County, and was buried in Johnsonburg Cemetery. They had these children:

1010 i. **Delvene KITTLE** was born about 1873 in Warren County.
1011 ii. **John KITTLE** was born about 1876 in Warren County.
1012 iii. **Alice KITTLE** was born on 8 August 1877,[153] died on 19 October 1896, and was buried in Johnsonburg Cemetery. The birthdate on her tombstone is 1877, but her birth certificate says she was born in April 1878. Alice committed suicide by taking poison.
1013 iv. **Catherine KITTLE** was born about 1878 in Warren County.
1014 v **Frank KITTLE**.

380. **Catherine HOWELL** was born on 5 May 1860 in Knowlton, Warren County, NJ. She died on 8 February 1944 in Smithfield Twp., Monroe County, PA, and was buried in Stroudsburg Cemetery, Monroe County, PA. She was married (1) to **John THATCHER** on 17 March 1877 in Belvidere, Warren County, NJ. Catherine HOWELL and John THATCHER had one child:

1015 i. **Isaac J. THATCHER** was born in 1878. He was living in Easton in 1944, and may have used the surname DILDINE.

Some time later, Catherine HOWELL married (2) **Lorenzo DILDINE**. Catherine's obituary gives her name as Mary, so perhaps her name was Mary Catherine. Their children were:[154]

1016 i. **George DILDINE** lived in Easton, Northampton County, PA, in 1944.
1017 ii. **Emma DILDINE** was married to **Edward STONE**. She died in East Stroudsburg, Monroe County, PA on 25 February 1963. [155]
1018 iii. **Nettie DILDINE** married **Sterling STAPLES**, and was living in Cheyenne, Wyoming in 1963.

381. **Abraham Brands HOWELL** was born on 6 February 1857 in Zions Chapel, Delaware, Warren County, NJ. He died on 7 July 1938, and was buried in Hazen

---

[152]Marriage license return, Hope Twp.,Warren County, NJ, Vol. BM, page 839.
[153]Birth Certificate, New Jersey Archives, Vol. CP, p. 440, gives date as 1878.
[154]Obituary for Mary Dildine, Easton (PA) Express, 10 Feb 1944.
[155]Obituary, Easton (PA) Express, 25 February 1963.

Cemetery, Hazen, Warren County, NJ. He was a farmer. Although the 1860 census lists Abraham as a 3 year old child, his descendants believe he was born in 1861, and his tombstone uses the date 24 March 1861. The International Genealogical Index records his birthdate as February 1857, and based on the census and IGI, we have used 1857 as his birth date.

Abraham was married to **Rosa VANDERGRIFT** (daughter of **William VANDERGRIFT** and **Rebecca Ann PITTENGER**) on 4 November 1882 in Blairstown, Warren County, NJ. Rosa VANDERGRIFT was born on 8 October 1864 in Oxford, Warren County, NJ. She died on 14 June 1938, and was buried in Hazen Cemetery. They had the following children:

+1019 i. **Vandy W. HOWELL.**
+1020 ii. **Evan John HOWELL.**
+1021 iii. **Rachel Rebecca Ann HOWELL.**
1022 iv. **Elmer HOWELL** was born on 7 July 1890. He died on 1 October 1891, and was buried in Portland Cemetery, Portland, Northampton County, PA.
+1023 v. **Eugene B. HOWELL.**
1024 vi. **Charles L. HOWELL** was born on 16 May 1894. He died on 3 February 1939, and was buried in Hazen Cemetery, Hazen , Warren County, NJ.
+1025 vii. **Ellis Oliver HOWELL.**
+1026 viii. **Alvin C. HOWELL.**
+1027 ix. **Ruth HOWELL.**

392. **William Biles PRICE** was born on 14 April 1832 in Hope, Warren County, NJ. He died on 17 January 1895 in Spirit Lake, Dickinson County, Iowa. William was a veteran of the Civil War; he served with Company F, 112th Illinois Infantry Volunteers, having enlisted while living in Toulon, Stark County, Illinois, in 1862. He took his family to Illinois in 1856, moved to Calhoun County, Iowa in 1868, and to Webster County, Iowa in 1869, then to Humboldt County, and in 1884, they moved to Dickinson County, Iowa. He was married to **Euphemia Elizabeth POYER** (daughter of **Abiathar POYER** and **Louisa STACKHOUSE**) on 22 December 1855 in Hope, Warren County, NJ.[156] Euphemia Elizabeth POYER was born on 31 July 1835 in Warren County, NJ. She died on 22 May 1905 in Spirit Lake, Dickinson County, Iowa. Their children were:

+1028 i. **Norman Augustus PRICE.**
+1029 ii. **Thomas Henderson PRICE.**
+1030 iii. **Charles Warren PRICE.**
+1031 iv. **Phoebe Louisa PRICE.**

394. **James Alben HOWELL** was born on 15 August 1854 in Hope, Warren County, NJ. He was a Constable in West Pittston, Luzerne County, PA, between

---

[156]Warren County, NJ Marriage Records, LDS Microfilm # 0960890. Vol. 2, p. 2.

1900 and 1904. He died after 1931 in Wyoming, Luzerne County, PA. The 1900 census listed James as a railroad conductor, though later he became a constable in West Pittston. Most of the information on this branch of the family has come from letters from (Marion) Ethel Howell Phethean, James' granddaughter. (Ethel did not maintain contact with her cousins after she married, and didn't know the names of the husbands in most cases. I have verified some of the names and ages with the census records, but still have some loose ends to trace.) James Alben was married to **Bridget MCHUGH** about 1874 in West Pittston, Luzerne County, PA. Bridget MCHUGH was born in July 1854. She died in West Wyoming, Luzerne county, PA, at the home of her daughter, Eva (HOWELL) PRICE.[157] Their children were:

+1032 i. **Eva Frances HOWELL.**
+1033 ii. **Mary A. HOWELL.**
+1034 iii. **Benson W. HOWELL.**
+1035 iv. **George HOWELL.**
+1036 v. **Charles Joseph HOWELL.**
1037 vi. **Guy E. HOWELL** was born on 4 September 1889 in Luzerne County, and died in May 1980 in Wyoming, Luzerne County. He was a printer. He married **Ariel UNKNOWN**, and they lived on 5th Street in Wyoming.[158] They had no children.
1038 vii. **Gertrude HOWELL** was born in 1892 in West Pittston, died on 8 November 1896, of diphtheria, and was buried in West PittstonCemetery. [159]

395. **George Marshall HOWELL** was born in June 1857 in NJ. He died before 1931 in Pittston, Luzerne County, PA. He was married to **Alice UNKNOWN** about 1883. Alice UNKNOWN was born in June 1865. Their children were:

1039 i. **Harry HOWELL** was born in July 1884 in Pittston.
+1040 ii. **Joseph HOWELL.**
+1041 iii. **Wilbur HOWELL.**
1042 iv. **Anna HOWELL** was born in September 1890 in Pittston.
+1043 v. **George HOWELL.**
1044 vi. **Mary HOWELL** was born in June 1894 in Pittston.
1045 vii. **Raymond HOWELL** was born in May 1897 in Pittston.
1046 viii. **Edna HOWELL** was born in 1909 in Pittston.

396. **Dorrance W. HOWELL** was born on 19 December 1859 in Franklin Twp., Luzerne County, PA. He died of tuberculosis, on 3 October 1931 in West Pittston, and was buried on 6 October 1931 in West Pittston Cemetery. He had been a railroad conductor, had driven a laundry wagon, and had worked in the mines as a

---

[157]Letter from Marion Ethel Howell Phethean to Jeannette Jones Phethean.
[158]ibid.
[159]Luzerne County, PA Death Index 1900-1905, LDS Microfilm #0960582.

young man. At the time of his death, he was the secretary of a railroad brotherhood. He was married to **Sarah Jane (Jenny) ROBERTS** (daughter of **Robert ROBERTS** and **Ann DAVIDSON**) on 13 February 1886 in West Pittston.[160] Sarah Jane (Jenny) ROBERTS was born on 20 September 1862 in West Pittston.. She died on 31 May 1940 in West Pittston, and was buried on 3 June 1940 in West Pittston Cemetery. Sarah Jane was known as Jenny by her contemporaries. She was active in the Methodist Church, where she belonged to a large Sunday School class, which held monthly social meetings at members' homes, and she enjoyed the quilting circle which met at the church. This group assembled quilt tops which had been "pieced" by local ladies, and quilted them. Many of these quilts may still be in existence. Dorrance and Jenny had these children:[161]

+1047 i. **Ann Charlotte HOWELL.**
1048 ii. **Harriet Rachel HOWELL** was born on 27 December 1887 in West Pittston, died on 24 November 1907, of a ruptured appendix, and was buried in West Pittston Cemetery. She had just completed her apprenticeship as a dressmaker when she died.
+1049 iii. **Robert HOWELL.**
+1050 iv. **Jean Louise HOWELL.**
+1051 v. **Helen Elizabeth HOWELL.**

398. **Helen Elizabeth HOWELL** was born in January 1869 in West Pittston. She died after 1931 in Mehoopany, Wyoming County, PA. Helen, known as Lib, was married (1) to **Charles WINTLE** on 26 September 1885 in West Pittston.[162] Charles WINTLE was born in England. Their children were:

+1052 i. **Harriet WINTLE.**
1053 ii. **Harry WINTLE** was born in December 1888 in West Pittston.

"Lib" was married (2) to **Melchoir KINTZ** in 1892 in West Pittston. No date can be identified, but she stated to the census taker that they had been married 8 years. The couple was living at 720 Montgomery Ave. West Pittston, at the time of the 1900 census.[163] "Lib" was married (3) to **Merritt KISHPAUGH** in PA. She was identified as Mrs. Merritt Kishpaugh of Mehoopany, Wyoming County, PA, in

---

[160]Marriage certificate issued by West Pittston Methodist Church, 13 February 1886, copy in possession of Jeannette Phethean. (No state marriage certificates were issued at the time.)
[161]Personal knowledge of Jeannette Phethean , and Bible record.
[162]Marriage record in West Pittston Methodist Church archives, 1875-1923. LDS film # 1671296.
[163]1900 U.S. Census, Pennsylvania, Luzerne County, West Pittston Borough, E.D. 147, Sheet 14, line 11, National Archives Microfilm Publication, T623, roll 1435.

Dorrance Howell's obituary in October 1931. Merritt KISHPAUGH was born in 1859. He died in Mehoopany, Wyoming County, PA.

401. **William Biles HOWELL** was born on 28 September 1851 in Hope, Warren County, NJ. [164] William had a farm known as Linden Lawn Place. He died on 31 March 1935, and was buried in Mt. Avon Cemetery, Rochester, Oakland County, MI. He married **Alice NEWBERRY** (daughter of **Milo P. NEWBERRY** and **Mary HOYT**) about 1881. Alice was born on 18 June 1859 in Rochester, died on 24 March 1924, and was buried in Mt. Avon Cemetery. Their children were:

1054	i.	**Mabel HOWELL** was born in November 1881.
1055	ii.	**C. Arthur HOWELL** was born in April 1883.
1056	iii.	**Anna A. HOWELL** was born in October 1887.
+1057	iv.	**John Stinson HOWELL.**
+1058	v.	**Milo Max HOWELL.**
1059	vi.	**Leah R. HOWELL** was born about 1901 in Avon Twp., Oakland County, MI.

406. **Franklin A. C. HOWELL** was born in April 1870 in Avon Twp., Oakland County, MI. He died on 30 March 1904, and was buried in Mt. Avon Cemetery. He was married to **Effie A. UNKNOWN** about 1896. Effie A. UNKNOWN was born in October 1879. Their children were:

1060	i.	**Merle J. HOWELL** was born in June 1897 in Michigan.
1061	ii.	**Mertie L. HOWELL** was born in November 1898 in Michigan.

408. **Margaret Ann HOWELL** was born on 11 November 1839 in Sussex County, New Jersey. She died in 1908, and was buried in Newton Cemetery, Newton, Sussex County. She married **George CURRENT**, who was born in 1840, died in 1902, and was buried in Newton Cemetery. Their children were:

1062	i.	**Charles CURRENT** was born about 1863.
1063	ii.	**Georgeanna CURRENT** was born about 1870.
1064	iii.	**Elizabeth CURRENT** was born in 1871 and died in 1904. She was buried in Newton Cemetery.
1065	iv.	**Irene CURRENT** was born in 1874; she died in 1878, and was buried in Newton Cemetery.
+1066	v.	**Almira Current YOUNG.**
1067	vi.	**Mary CURRENT** died at 8 months, and was buried in Newton Cemetery.
1068	vii.	**Milly CURRENT** died at 8 months, and was buried in Newton Cemetery.

---

[164] Birth Certificate, Vol. AJ, p. 86, Hope Twp., Warren Co., NJ. New Jersey State Archives, Trenton, NJ.

409. **Jonah HOWELL** was born on 21 May 1841 in Andover, Sussex County, NJ, died on 1 March 1900 in Pinckneyville, Sussex County, and was buried in Newton Cemetery. Jonah was born on the old Howell farm near Pinckneyville, in Andover Township. He was a farmer, following his father in working the family acreage. He died there, a highly respected member of his community. He married (1) **Salina STRADER** on 2 December 1863 in Sussex County, New Jersey. Salina STRADER was born about 1844. She died on 27 January 1866, and was buried in Newton Cemetery. Their child was:

1069 i. **Florence A. HOWELL** was born on 14 December 1864 in Andover, where she died on 9 January 1879, and was buried in Newton Cemetery.

Jonah was married (2) to **Ila Jane HAMMOND** (daughter of **Andrew HAMMOND**) on 27 November 1879 in Sussex County, New Jersey. Ila Jane HAMMOND was born in April 1861 in New Jersey. She died in 1948, and was buried in Newton Cemetery. Their children were:

+1070 i. **Levi A. HOWELL**.
1071 ii. **Obediah P. HOWELL** was born in 1882; he died in 1888, and was buried in Newton Cemetery.
+1072 iii. **William S. HOWELL**.
1073 iv. **Evelyn HOWELL** was born on 6 February 1892 and died in 1972. She was buried in Newton Cemetery. She married **John S. SIMMONS**, and they lived in Lafayette Twp., NJ.
1074 v. **John C. HOWELL** was born on 2 November 1895; he died in 1900, and was buried in Newton Cemetery.

413. **Daniel Webster HOWELL** was born on 2 August 1846 in Sussex County, New Jersey. He died in 1932, and was buried in Newton Cemetery. He married **Phebe J. UNKNOWN** who was born in 1851, died in 1924, and was buried in Newton Cemetery. Daniel and Phebe had the following children:

1075 i. **Ellen HOWELL** was born about 1872.
1076 ii. **Augusta HOWELL** was born about 1877.
1077 iii. **Fred HOWELL** was born in 1885, died in 1948, and was buried in Newton Cemetery.

418. **George W. HOWELL** was born about 1846 in Sparta, Sussex County, NJ. He died and was buried in Old Newton Burial Ground, Newton, NJ. He was married to **Marietta OLMSTEAD** on 31 December 1867 in Hope, Warren County, NJ. George W. HOWELL and Marietta OLMSTEAD had one child:

1078 i. **Almira HOWELL** was born about 1869.

426. **Mary Matilda "Tillie" HOWELL** was born on 13 November 1845 in Newton, Sussex County, NJ. She died on 26 January 1926 in Clarkston, Oakland

County, MI. She was married to **Harrison WALTER** on 15 December 1864 in Brandon, Oakland County, Michigan. [165] Mary Matilda "Tillie" HOWELL and Harrison WALTER had the following children:

1079 i. **Edith WALTER** was born in 1865, and died in 1876 in Clarkston.
+1080 ii. **Agnes Emma WALTER**.
1081 iii. **Gertrude WALTER** was born in 1876, and died about 1894, in Clarkston..
1082 iv. **Eva Esther "Tessie " WALTER** was born in 1877.
1083 v. **Samuel J. WALTER** was born in 1879. He married **Nina M. BRYAN** in 1907.

428. **Emma Jane HOWELL** was born on 20 September 1848 in Howellsville, Sussex County, NJ. She married **Henry Harmon HOWE**. Emma Jane and Henry Harmon HOWE had the following children:

+1084 i. **Edith HOWE**.
1085 ii. **Rose Z. HOWE**.

431. **Watson Vincent HOWELL** was born on 19 December 1849 in Frelinghuysen, Warren County, NJ. He died on 24 October 1934. The 1880 Hanover Township, Luzerne County, PA census named his wife Ruth.[166] We believe that **Ruth E. HOWELL**, who is buried in Carverton Cemetery, Luzerne County, PA, may have been his first wife. She died 26 October 1881, at the age of 21 years, 8 months and 3 days, which would give her a birth date of 23 February 1860. If this is true, his marriage to Mehitable Ann GRIFFIN would have been his second marriage. **Mehitable Ann GRIFFIN** was born in June 1857. She died in 1922, and was buried in Centremoreland Cemetery. [167] Their children were:[168]

1086 i. **Clara Asha HOWELL** was born in July 1885. She died on 26 April 1943.
1087 ii. **Edith HOWELL** was born on 31 December 1886, and died on 6 October 1978.
+1088 iii. **Harrison Morton HOWELL.**
1089 iv. **Emma HOWELL** was born on 7 October 1890. She died on 6 February 1969.
1090 v. **Freda HOWELL** was born on 9 September 1892. She

---

[165]Marriage notice pasted in Howell family Bible.
[166]1880 U.S. Census (population) Pennsylvania, Luzerne County, Hanover Twp., E.D.109, p. 29, nos. 245/245, National Archives Microfilm Publication, T9, roll 1149.
[167]1900 U.S. Census, Pennsylvania, Luzerne County, Hanover Twp., E.D. 56, Sheet 22, line 46, National Archives Microfilm Publication, T623, roll 1432.
[168]Information on this family contributed by Barbara Crane, RR4, Box 326C, Dallas PA 18612.

died on 9 June 1980.
+1091 vi. **Ethel HOWELL.**
+1092 vii. **Finley HOWELL.**

432. **Levi C. HOWELL** was born on 9 November 1850 in Frelinghuysen, Warren County, NJ. [169] He died on 3 July 1905, and was buried in Johnsonburg Cemetery, Johnsonburg, NJ. Quote from a local paper: "Levi C. Howell of Johnsonburg committed suicide on Monday by blowing out his brains with a shot gun. A string was tied to the trigger and the other to his toe, and the gun was discharged while he lay full length upon the bed. Strange to say, Howell's brother committed suicide in identically the same manner and in the same bed and room about two years ago. It is supposed that Howell's mind was affected by financial trouble. He is survived by a son."[170]

Levi was married to **Emma J. DRAKE**. Emma was born in 1856, and died in 1885. She was buried in Johnsonburg Cemetery, Johnsonburg, NJ. Levi C. HOWELL and Emma J. DRAKE had one child:

1093 i. **Selah J. HOWELL** was born in February 1885 in Johnsonburg.

438. **Clarissa Jennifer HOWELL** was born on 10 March 1861 in Hope, Warren County, NJ. Clarissa married **Unknown VAIL**, and they had these children:

1094 i. **Ethel VAIL.**
1095 ii. **Olga VAIL.**

449. **Anna Maria HOWELL** was born on 22 October 1832 in Hope, Warren County, NJ. She died on 9 October 1901, and was buried in Johnsonburg Cemetery, Johnsonburg, NJ. The 1860 census shows Anna's brother, Charles HOWELL, was living with the family; he was 24 at the time.[171] Anna Maria was married to **Frederick SAVERCOOL** about 1853. Frederick was born about 1825 in Hardwick Twp., Warren County, NJ. He was a farmer, and they lived in Hardwick. They had the following children:

1096 i. **Emma SAVERCOOL** was born in 1854 in Hardwick Twp.
1097 ii. **Theodore SAVERCOOL** was born in 1856 in Hardwick Twp.
1098 iii. **George G. SAVERCOOL** was born about 1858 in Hardwick Twp.

---

[169]Birth Certificate, Vol. AJ, p. 42, Warren Co., NJ. New Jersey State Archives, Trenton, NJ.
[170]News item, Washington (NJ) Star, 6 July 1905.
[171]1860 U.S. Census (population) New Jersey, Warren Co., Blairstown, p. 73, nos. 543/543, National Archives Microfilm Publication, M653, roll 711.

1099 iv. **Anna SAVERCOOL** was born about 1861 in Warren County, NJ.

1100 v. **Isaac SAVERCOOL** was born about 1863 in Warren County, NJ.

1101 vi. **Edwin SAVERCOOL** was born about 1866 in Warren County, NJ.

1102 vii. **William SAVERCOOL** was born about 1868 in Warren County, NJ.

1103 viii. **Alva SAVERCOOL** was born in 1872 in Warren County, NJ.

1104 ix. **Frederick SAVERCOOL** was born in 1874 in Warren County, NJ.

450. **Charles D. HOWELL** was born on 27 February 1836 in Hope, Warren County, NJ. He died on 4 February 1895 in Phillipsburg, and was buried in Old Cemetery, Phillipsburg. He married **Temperance V. LEA**, who was born on 20 June 1835 in NJ. She died on 15 January 1911, and was buried in Old Cemetery, Phillipsburg, NJ. Her death notice reads: "Mrs. Temperance V. Howell, a Bennett street woman, died Sunday night from a complication of diseases. She was 79 years old and leaves two daughters, Carrie and Jennie." Their children were:[172]

1105 i. **Carrie Marie HOWELL** was born in 1873 in Warren County, and died on 16 September 1939. She was buried in Fairmount Cemetery, Phillipsburg. Her year of birth was taken from her tombstone.

1106 ii. **Jennie May HOWELL** was born in 1876 in Warren County, died on 1 March 1947, and was buried in Fairmount Cemetery,.

451. **Isaac Allen HOWELL** was born on 29 March 1839 in Hope, Warren County, NJ. He died after 1920 in West Pittston, Luzerne County, PA. (We have not been able to learn where he is buried, but he is not buried in Wyoming Cemetery, where his wife was buried.) According to "History of Luzerne County",[173] Isaac's father died when Isaac was only a child, and he came to Pennsylvania to live with his uncle Levi Howell in Luzerne county. He was educated by his uncle, and stayed with him until 1861, when he enlisted in Company F, 53rd Pennsylvania Volunteer Infantry, with the rank of sergeant. He was quickly promoted to lieutenant and then to captain, and took part in many battles. He married Lydia Houser while still in service. After the war, he returned to farming, in North Moreland and Franklin Township, and later moved to Kansas for four years. He came back to Luzerne County, where he farmed and raised dairy cattle for years.[174]

---

[172] Obituary, Washington (NJ) Star, 15 January 1911.

[173] H.C. Bradsby, ed., History of Luzerne County, PA., with Biographical Selections, (Chicago: S. B. Nelson & Co.,1893) p. 998.

[174] ibid. p. 999.

Isaac was married to **Lydia A. HOUSER** (daughter of **Henry HOUSER** and **Maggie MITZGER**) on 14 January 1864. Lydia A. HOUSER was born on 21 December 1839 in Stroudsburg, Pennsylvania. She died on 4 April 1932 in West Pittston, Luzerne County, PA, and was buried on 7 April 1932 in Wyoming Cemetery, Luzerne County. [175] Although we cannot say certainly where the couple was prior to 1900, at that time they were living on Eighth Street in Wyoming, Luzerne County, PA. [176]Their children were:

+1107 i. **Mary Ellen HOWELL.**
+1108 ii. **Eva HOWELL.**

452. **George Green HOWELL** was born on 30 June 1840 in Hope, Warren County, NJ. He died on 7 April 1934 in Roxburg, Warren County, NJ, and was buried in Belvidere Cemetery, Belvidere, Warren County, NJ. He was married to **Mary Jane GINGLES** on 9 January 1862 in Hope. Mary Jane GINGLES was born on 15 August 1841; she died on 18 January 1931, and was buried in Belvidere Cemetery. George Green HOWELL and Mary Jane GINGLES had the following children:[177]

+1109 i. **Lavenia Arzella HOWELL.**
+1110 ii. **Stella HOWELL.**
1111 iii. **Unknown HOWELL** was born on 11 September 1874 in Oxford, Warren County, NJ. He died in infancy.

453. **Martha J. HOWELL** was born about 1842 in Hope, Warren County, NJ. She died in 1927, and was buried in Moravian Cemetery in Hope. She was married to **Cornell T. HARTMAN** on 15 January 1873 in Warren County. Cornell T. HARTMAN was born in 1842 in NJ. He died in 1913, and was buried in Moravian Cemetery. Martha and Cornell T. HARTMAN had these children:

1112 i. **George W. HARTMAN** was born in December 1873 in Knowlton, Warren County, NJ., and died in 1958. He married **Annie H. UNKNOWN**, who was born in 1879 and died in 1966. Both were buried in Moravian Cemetery.
1113 ii. **Laura HARTMAN** was born about 1879 in Knowlton, Warren County, NJ.
1114 iii. **Charles HARTMAN** was born in December 1881. He

---

[175]Cemetery record #1984, dated 5 April 1932, for burial of Mrs. Lydia Howell, Wyoming Cemetery, Luzerne County, PA.
[176]1900 U.S. Census,(population), Pennsylvania, Luzerne County, Wyoming, E.D.189, Sheet 16, line 69, National Archives Microfilm Publication, T623, roll 1434.
[177]Information on this family contributed by John Butler, 6201 Lasngate Rd., Midlothian VA 23112.

married **Katherine COOK.**

454. **Euphemia HOWELL** was born on 19 November 1844 in Hope, Warren County, and died there on 1 January 1911. She was buried in Union Cemetery. She married **Solomon F. WILSON**, who was born on 23 April 1842 and died on 31 July 1910 in Warren County. He was buried in Presbyterian Cemetery, Oxford, Warren County. In 1880, Solomon and Euphemia were farming in Hanover Twp., Luzerne County, PA,[178] very near Watson Vincent HOWELL and his wife, Ruth. By 1900, we think Solomon and Euphemia had returned to Warren County, NJ. Solomon and Euphemia had these known children:

1115 i. **Melvin J. WILSON** was born about 1867 in Philadelphia.
1116 ii. **Ella WILSON** was born about 1869 in PA.
1117 iii. **Myron WILSON** was born about 1871 in PA.

455. **Sarah Elizabeth HOWELL** was born in 1839. After her mother's death, Sarah was apparently raised by grandparents, since she did not appear in the census with Levi in Pennsylvania. She married **Andrew Jackson COURSEN** on 25 November 1857[179] in Warren County, and they later lived in Kingston, Luzerne County, PA. The 1880 census located them on Parrish Street, in the 14th ward of Wilkes Barre, where Andrew was a retail grocer.[180] Their children were:

1118 i. **Isaac COURSEN** was born in 1860 in Dallas Twp., Luzerne County, PA.
1119 ii. **Emma A. COURSEN** was born in 1862 in Dallas Twp., Luzerne County, PA.

456. **Mary Ann "Mollie" HOWELL** was born on 19 July 1841 in Northmoreland, Luzerne County, PA. She was married to **William HATFIELD** on 22 November 1864 in Northmoreland. William HATFIELD was born on 17 December 1833 in Northmoreland. He died about 1902 in Springfield, Ohio. William was a butcher, and in 1870, the family lived in West Pittston, Luzerne County.[181] In the following years, the family moved frequently, according to information from a descendant. Their children were:[182]

---

[178] 1880 U.S. Census (population), Pennsylvania, Luzerne Co., Hanover Twp., E.D. 109, sheet 29, nos.244/244. national Archives Microfilm Publication, T9, roll 1149.

[179] Warren County, NJ Marriage Records, LDS Microfilm # 0960890. V. 2, p. 24.

[180] 1880 U.S. Census, Pennsylvania, Luzerne County, Wilkes Barre, E.D. 125, p. 41,nos. 369/383, National Archives Microfilm Publication, T9, roll 1150.

[181] 1870 U.S. Census (population) Pennsylvania, Luzerne Co., West Pittston Borough, p.429, nos. 166/178, National Archives Microfilm Publication, M593, roll 1365.

[182] 1880 U.S. Census, Pennsylvania, Luzerne County, West Pittston Borough, E.D. 95, p. 238, nos. 84/92, National Archives Microfilm Publication, T9, roll 1148.

+1120 i. **Frank Leroy HATFIELD**.
1121 ii. **Olivia HATFIELD** was born on 24 January 1869. She died in 1896. She married **Vernon B. SWEET**.

457. **David R. HOWELL** was born in 1848 in Luzerne County, PA. He was a farmer, living with his family in Franklin Twp., Luzerne County in 1880. He married **Ruth Ann LORD** (daughter of **John** and **Elizabeth LORD**) about 1871. Ruth Ann died on 24 March 1898, of blood poisoning. Since her husband wasn't named in the records, but her parents were, we think David had already died. Ruth Ann was buried in the Mt. Zion Cemetery, Luzerne County. David and Ruth Ann had three known children:[183]

1122 i. **John W. HOWELL** was born about 1872 in Franklin Twp.
1123 ii. **Nellie B. HOWELL** was born in January 1875 in Franklin Twp. She and Levi were on the farm at the time of the 1900 census.
1124 iii. **Levi HOWELL** was born in June 1880 in Franklin Twp.

460. **Levi T. HOWELL** was born in 1854 in Franklin Twp., Luzerne County, PA. He died in 1930, and was buried in Cedar Crest Cemetery, Trucksville, Luzerne County, PA. He married **Catherine "Kate" SCHOOLEY** (daughter of **Joseph SCHOOLEY** and **Lydia FRANTZ**). Kate was born in 1855. She died in 1925. Levi T. HOWELL and Catherine "Kate" SCHOOLEY had the following children:

1125 i. **Ziba HOWELL** was born in 1884. He died in 1929.
1126 ii. **Clifford HOWELL**. Clifford lived in Florida.
1127 iii. **Marjorie HOWELL** married **Unknown MARINO**. They lived in New York.

462. **John S. HOWELL** was born on 14 September 1857 in Carverton, Luzerne County, PA. He died on 16 October 1889 in Evans Falls, Wyoming County, PA. and was buried in Cedar Crest Cemetery, Trucksville. John was married to **Martha E. MOYER** on 5 December 1883 in Centremoreland, Wyoming County, PA. Martha E. MOYER was born on 10 May 1866 in Evans Falls, Wyoming County, PA, and died on 16 February 1921 in Damascus, PA, where she was buried. Their children were:[184]

1128 i. **Emeline Annetta HOWELL** was born on 15 January 1885 in Evans Falls, Wyoming County, PA. She

---

[183]1900 U.S. Census, Pennsylvania, Luzerne County, Franklin Twp., E.D. 53, Sheet 4, line 89, National Archives Microfilm Publication, T623, roll 1431.
[184]Information on this family contributed by Mildred Law, 599 Galloping Ghost Lane, Anderson SC 29624.

died on 5 February 1968 in Wilkes Barre,Luzerne County, PA., and was buried in Fern Knoll Cemetery, Dallas, Luzerne County. She married **Harold BYLE Sr.** on 14 August 1906.

1129 ii. **Walter Bodle HOWELL** was born on 27 October 1887.

John S. Howell's will in the Wyoming County Court House states that John died in Monroe Twp. on 16 October 1889. The bond was signed by Levi Howell, J. W. Roberts, and G. C. Lyman. The estate apparently was valued at $3000, and the widow renounced her claim to the farm in favor of her father-in-law, Levi Howell. She remarried within 6 months, perhaps in order to support her children.

463. **Emeline R. HOWELL** was born in January 1859 in Luzerne County, PA. She married **Walter BODLE** about 1877. He was born on 1 July 1844 in Pennsylvania, and died on 18 January 1905. He was a farmer; they lived in Franklin Twp., Luzerne County. They had two living children in 1900, one having died prior to that time. The children were:[185]

1130 i. **Kate H. BODLE** was born in January 1879 in Franklin Twp.

1131 ii. **John BODLE** was born in June 1883 in Franklin Twp.

469. **James W. HOWELL** was born in June 1855 in Luzerne, Luzerne County, PA. He married **Martha UNKNOWN** about 1878 in Luzerne. Martha was born in February 1856 in Pennsylvania. He was a mine laborer. The 1900 census said there had been 5 children, 2 of whom survived:[186]

1132 i. **Samuel HOWELL** was born in February 1879.

1133 ii. **Arthur HOWELL** was born in September 1880.

471. **Emeline Olivia THOMPSON** was born on 4 July 1843 in Morris County, NJ. She died on 16 June 1864 in Iowa. She was married to **Edward SIPERLY** on 26 July 1860 in Delhi, IA. Edward SIPERLY was born about 1833. Emeline Olivia THOMPSON and Edward SIPERLY had the following children:

1134 i. **Frank Oliver SIPERLY** was born on 11 December 1862, and died on 27 October 1863. He was buried in Grove Creek Cemetery, Delaware County, Iowa.

+1135 ii. **Alida Euphemia SIPERLY**.

---

[185] 1900 U.S. Census (population) Pennsylvania, Luzerne County, Franklin Twp., E.D. 53, Sheet 4, line 72, nos. 90/91National Archives Microfilm Publication, T623, roll 1431.

[186] 1900 U.S. Census, Pennsylvania, Luzerne County, Luzerne Borough, E.D. 85, Sheet 17, line 2, National Archives Microfilm Publication, T623, roll 1432.

473. **Clara C. THOMPSON** was born on 23 August 1856 in Mendham, Morris County, NJ. She died on 29 August 1944 in Delaware County, Iowa, and was buried in Pineview Cemetery, Delaware County. She was married to **Henry Clay FEAR** in February 1885 in Iowa. Henry Clay FEAR died in 1900 in IA. Clara C. THOMPSON and Henry Clay FEAR had the following children:

1136	i.	**Rolf FEAR** died in infancy.
+1137	ii.	**Albert "Bert" FEAR**.
1138	iii.	**Roy FEAR** was born on 8 June 1893 in Iowa.
1139	iv.	**Lee FEAR** was born on 5 April 1897 in Iowa.
+1140	v.	**Female FEAR**.

474. **William Howell THOMPSON** was born on 20 January 1862 in Hope, Warren County, NJ. He died on 11 December 1904 in Hopkinton, Delaware County, Iowa. William committed suicide, apparently depressed about his life.[187] He was married to **Charity Ann GARVIN** (daughter of **David GARVIN** and **Sarah SHEPPARD**) on 29 March 1882. Charity Ann GARVIN was born on 12 September 1862. She died on 24 September 1958 in IA. Their children were:

1141	i.	**Maude Euphemia THOMPSON** was born on 28 September 1883 in Iowa. She died on 22 May 1974 in Indiana. She married (1) **William MOORE** on 8 September 1915. She married (2) **Edward THOMAS,** M.D. She had no children.
+1142	ii.	**Anna Pearl THOMPSON**.
+1143	iii.	**William Bert THOMPSON**.
+1144	iv.	**Glenn David THOMPSON**.
+1145	v.	**Blanche Berniece THOMPSON**.
+1146	vi.	**Dewitt Howell THOMPSON**.
+1147	vii.	**DeWain Garvin THOMPSON**.

477. **George Albert HOWELL** was born on 26 March 1857 in PawPaw, Lee County, IL. He died on 23 March 1913 in Hood River, Hood River County, OR. He married **Mary Magdalene KLUCKNER** (daughter of **Ernest KLUCKNER** and **Adeline FALLER**) on 30 December 1884. Their children were:

+1148	i.	**Arthur F. HOWELL**.
+1149	ii.	**Frank HOWELL**.
1150	iii.	**Alta Mae HOWELL** was born on 23 October 1889 in Frankfort, Marshall County, Kansas, and died on 22 July 1954 in New Mexico. She married (1) **Thomas BISHOP**, and (2) **Claude G. MOORE** on 5 September 1915 in Hood River, OR.

---

[187]News item and obituary from an unknown Delaware County, Iowa newspaper, 9 December 1904.

+1151 iv. **Harry Albert HOWELL.**
+1152 v. **Blanche Elizabeth HOWELL.**
+1153 vi. **Grace Ann HOWELL.**
+1154 vii. **Ruth Eleanor HOWELL.**
+1155 viii. **Roy Earl HOWELL.**
+1156 ix. **Carolyn Madeline HOWELL.**
+1157 x. **Walter Claire HOWELL.**
+1158 xi. **Ira Edward HOWELL.**

483. **Nelson Whitney HOWELL** was born on 27 May 1857 in Dallas, Luzerne County, Pennsylvania. Nelson was a farmer. He married **Nancy LORD** (daughter of **Stephen LORD** and **Elizabeth DEWITT**) on 14 December 1881 in Carverton, Luzerne County. Nancy LORD was born on 9 May 1859 in Mt. Zion, Luzerne County.[188] In 1937, Nelson and Nancy celebrated their 56th wedding anniversary, as noted in the Times Leader. Nelson and Nancy had one child:

+1159 i. **Harry E. HOWELL.**

487. **Sarah M. READ** was born in April 1853 in New Jersey. She married **Henry BACHMAN** in Luzerne County, PA. By 1900, Henry BACHMAN was apparently dead, and Sarah and her son lived with her mother; she had a large dressmaking business in the home in Miners Mills, Luzerne County. Sarah M. READ and Henry BACHMAN had a son:[189]

1160 i. **Arthur R. BACHMAN** was born in December 1881.He was listed as a clerk in the 1900 census.

488. **Anna Rebecca READ** was born about 1855 in New Jersey. She married **James L. RIBBLE** in Wilkes Barre, Luzerne County, PA. James L. RIBBLE was a harness-maker in Wilkes Barre. Anna and James L. RIBBLE had a son:

1161 i. **Willard A. RIBBLE.**

489. **Emma A. READ** was born about 1860 in Luzerne County, PA. She married **William ALLEN** in Wilkes Barre. William Allen was head plasterer for Charles Shiver, a contractor in Wilkes Barre. Emma and William ALLEN had a son:

1162 i. **Ira W. ALLEN.**

502. **John Wesley HOWELL** was born on 29 February 1840 in Frelinghuysen, Warren County, NJ. He died on 18 April 1917 in Wilkes Barre, Luzerne County, PA, and was buried on 21 April 1917 in Presbyterian Cemetery, Andover, Sussex

---

[188]News item, Times Leader, Wilkes Barre, PA. 14 December 1937.
[189]1900 U.S. Census (population), Pennsylvania, Luzerne County, Miners Mills, E.D. 88, Sheet 4, line 97, National Archives Microfilm Publication, T623, roll 1433.

County, NJ. He was a farmer. John died in a sanitarium in Wilkes Barre, apparently a sufferer from tuberculosis, though his obituary did not say that.[190] His funeral was held at the home of Bethena Ann Howell LUSE, his sister, in Ebenezer, NJ. John was married to **Mary Melissa KISHPAUGH** (daughter of **James KISHPAUGH** and **Elizabeth SUTTON**) on 28 December 1864 in Vienna, Warren County, NJ.[191] Mary Melissa KISHPAUGH was born on 19 June 1841, died on 18 June 1888, and was buried in Presbyterian Cemetery. They had these children:

1163 i. **Carrie Aurelia HOWELL** was born on 11 October 1866, died on 26 August 1868, and was buried in Presbyterian Cemetery.

1164 ii. **Elber Clement HOWELL** was born on 28 May 1872, died on 20 May 1883, and was buried in Presbyterian Cemetery.

504. **Slidell MacKenzie HOWELL** was born on 30 March 1845 in Frelinghuysen, Warren County, NJ. He died on 26 February 1900 in Beemerville, Sussex County, NJ.[192] He was buried in Beemerville Cemetery, Beemerville, Sussex County, NJ. Slidell loved horses; he was pushed against a stall by one of them, and injured. His injuries led to Bright's disease, from which he died. He was married to **Harriet Estella WYKER** on 8 February 1865 in Wantage, Sussex County, NJ. Harriet Estella WYKER was born on 6 October 1843. She died on 4 March 1932 in Succasunna, Morris County, NJ, and was buried in Beemerville Cemetery. Slidell and Harriet had these children:[193]

+1165 i. **David Clarence HOWELL**.

+1166 ii. **Orange Judd HOWELL**.

+1167 iii. **Elizabeth Victoria HOWELL**.

1168 iv. **Margaret Estelle HOWELL** was born on 24 June 1876 in Beemerville. She died in 1959, and was buried in Beemerville Cemetery.

515. **Emma E. ALBERTSON** married **Daniel I HILDEBRANT** on 8 March 1856.[194] Emma died of heart disease. Emma and Daniel had these children:

1169 i. **Winfield S. HILDEBRANT**.

1170 ii. **Unknown Female HILDEBRANT** married **Caleb GIBBS**, and they lived in Pen Argyl, Northampton

---

[190]Obituary, Washington (NJ) Star, 26 April 1917.

[191]Return of marriage for John W. Howell & Mary Kispaugh, Vol. AH, p.258, New Jersey State Archives, Trenton, NJ

[192]Obituary, Washington (NJ) Star, 8 March 1900.

[193]Information on this family contributed by Evan Howell, Little Philadelphia Rd., Washington NJ 07882.

[194]Warren County, NJ Marriage Records, LDS Microfilm # 0960890. Vol. 2, p. 7.

County, PA.

1171 iii. **Unknown Female HILDEBRANT** married **George DECKER**.

518. **Isaac Lemuel HOWELL** was born in August 1840 in Warren County, NJ. He died in 1926, and was buried in Union Cemetery, Hope, Warren County, NJ. Isaac was a farmer, and a Civil War veteran.

Isaac was married to **Lucy A. AYERS** (daughter of **Daniel S. AYERS** and **Pernina VLIET**) on 30 November 1864 in Petersburg, Warren County, NJ. [195] Lucy A. AYERS was born on 1 June 1843. She died in 1925, and was buried in Union Cemetery. Isaac and Lucy had the following children:

1172 i. **Sarah Ella HOWELL** was born on 19 September 1873 in Independence, died on 4 March 1898, and was buried in Union Cemetery.

1173 ii. **Robert Cecil HOWELL** was born on 31 August 1878 in Independence, died on 10 March 1885, and was buried in Union Cemetery.

520. **James H. MOREY** was born on 4 August 1835, and died on 30 July 1907. He married Prudence **LOUNSBERRY**, who was born on 16 September 1834 and died on 22 January 1919. Both are buried in Lounsberry Cemetery, in Nichols. They had three children:

1174 i. **George Morey** was born on 16 November 1858 and died on 10 February 1859. He was buried in Lounsberry Cemetery.

1175 ii. **Frederick J. MOREY** was born on 25 July 1860 and died on 28 February 1861. He was buried in Lounsberry Cemetery.

1176 iii. **Fred H. MOREY** was born on 10 November 1863, died on 17 October 1881 and was buried in Lounsberry Cemetery.

525. **John J. HOWELL** was born in 1853, and died in November 1908. He married **UNKNOWN**. Their children were:

1177 i. **Nellie HOWELL** was born in 1873 and died on 7 March 1909. She married **Guy CARPENTER**, who was born in Waverly, Tioga County, NY.

1178 ii. **Unknown female HOWELL** married **Luther COBURN**. They lived in Connecticut.

---

[195] Return of marriage for Isaac L. Howell and Lucy Ayers, Vol. AH, p. 258, Warren Co., NJ, New Jersey State Archives, Trenton, NJ.

535. **Arthur M. HOWELL** was born on 6 August 1842 in Nichols, Tioga County, NY, and died on 25 February 1909. He was a farmer. He married **Helen PALMER**, who was born in 1842. Both are buried in Lounsberry Cemetery.Their children were:

+1179 i. **William Praul HOWELL.**
+1180 ii. **Mary Amelia HOWELL.**
1181 iii. **Ida HOWELL** was born in 1869. She married **Unknown THOMPSON.**
1182 iv. **Grace HOWELL** was born in 1871. She married **Charles Jay QUICK**, who was born on 27 December 1867.
1183 v. **Charles HOWELL** died young, and was buried in Lounsberry Cemetery.
1184 vi. **Jessie HOWELL** died young, and was buried in Lounsberry Cemetery.

565. **Livinia Matilda HOWELL** was born in 1833 in Independence, Warren County, New Jersey. She died on 15 March 1916 in Easton, Northampton County, Pennsylvania, and was buried in Tranquility Cemetery, Tranquility, New Jersey. Livinia was always called Matilda. She married **William HAMILTON**. William HAMILTON was born in 1828, and died in 1891. They had these children:

1185 i. **William HAMILTON** was living in Hackettstown, Warren County, NJ when his mother died in 1916.
1186 ii. **Howell HAMILTON** was born in 1855. He died in 1930. He is buried in Tranquility Cemetery. In 1916, he was living in Greensburg, NJ.
1187 iii. **James HAMILTON**. In 1916, he was living in Johnsonburg, Warren County, NJ.

567. **George Washington HOWELL** was born on 14 October 1842 in Independence, Warren County, New Jersey. He died on 6 November 1926 in Newark, NJ, and was buried in Tranquility Cemetery, Sussex County, NJ. When his sister Matilda died, he lived in Vienna, NJ. His brief obituary in the Star, Washington, NJ, states that he had been a resident of Great Meadows, but was living in Newark with his daughter, prior to death. He was married to **Sarah E. BEDFORD** on 29 November 1865. Sarah E. BEDFORD was born on 16 March 1846 in NJ. She died on 22 December 1877, and was buried in Tranquility Cemetery. George Washington HOWELL and Sarah E. BEDFORD had one child:

1188 i. **Sarah Francis HOWELL** was born on 19 July 1866 in Independence, Warren County, NJ, and died on 15 December 1934 in Maplewood, Essex County, NJ. She married **McClellan GARRIS**, who died on 26 March 1931. Both are buried in Pequest Cemetery,

Great Meadows, NJ.[196]

568. **Benjamin B. HOWELL** was born on 20 November 1844 in Independence, Warren County, NJ. He died on 13 May 1906. He was buried in Pequest Union Cemetery, Great Meadows, Warren County, NJ. He was a farmer. He was married to **Catherine Gertrude DEETS** on 19 January 1871 in Warren County, NJ. Catherine Gertrude DEETS was born on 19 August 1854, died on 30 November 1921 in Vienna, Warren County, NJ, and was buried in Pequest Union Cemetery. They had the following children:[197]

1189 i. **Marcella HOWELL** was born in 1872 in Warren County, NJ.

+1190 ii. **Aaron B. HOWELL.**

1191 iii. **Sarah "Sadie" HOWELL** was born on 30 July 1876 in Warren County. She died on 23 February 1940 in Orange, NJ. She was a secretary. She was married (1) to **UNKNOWN**, and (2) to **Tobias V. HENDERSHOT**, who was born on 13 October 1870, and died on 12 January 1940. Both were buried in Pequest Cemetery.

577. **Nathan A. HOWELL** was born in July 1850 in Hamilton, Wentworth, Ontario, Canada. He died on 23 June 1932 in Muskegon, Muskegon County, MI, and was buried in Oakwood Cemetery, Muskegon, MI. He married **Mary Ann RADLEY** in 1879 in Muskegon. She was born about 1858, died on 1 September 1932 in Muskegon, and was buried in Oakwood Cemetery. They had these children:

+1192 i. **Maude B. HOWELL.**

+1193 ii. **Carl Coulton Radley HOWELL.**

578. **David E. HOWELL** was born on 7 September 1851 in Hamilton, Wentworth, Ontario, Canada. He died on 21 October 1900 in Delmar, Clinton County, Iowa, and was buried in Evergreen Cemetery, Delmar, Iowa. He married **Louisa ESTEY** on 18 May 1879 in Delmar. Louisa ESTEY was born on 1 March 1861 in Iowa. She was buried in Evergreen Cemetery. Their children were:[198]

+1194 i. **Ralph C. HOWELL.**

1195 ii. **Willy HOWELL** was born about 1882 in Clinton County, IA.

---

[196] Obituary, Washington (NJ) Star, 27 December 1934.

[197] 1880 U.S. Census (population) New Jersey, Warren Co., Independence Twp., E.D.200, p. 14, nos. 123/131, National Archives Microfilm Publication T9, roll 799.

[198] Information on this family contributed by Jackie Rudolph, 6517 Roe Ave., Prairie Village KS 66208.

1196 iii. **Jessie H. HOWELL** was born in May 1885. His wife was **Frances E. UNKNOWN.**

1197 iv. **George W. HOWELL** was born on 5 April 1887. He died on 16 January 1891 in Delmar, Clinton County, IA, and was buried in Evergreen Cemetery.

+1198 v. **Fern Ruth HOWELL.**

579. **George Wabent HOWELL** was born on 14 November 1856 in Hamilton, Wentworth, Ontario, Canada. He died on 31 December 1928 in Muskegon, Muskegon County, MI. He was buried in Oakwood Cemetery. He was married to **Sarah BELL** on 22 June 1882 in Van Buren, MI. Sarah BELL was born in 1861 in Ravenna, OH. She died on 30 May 1914, and was buried in Oakwood Cemetery. George Wabent HOWELL and Sarah BELL had the following children:

1199 i. **Chester M. HOWELL** was born on 10 September 1883 in Muskegon, and died on 8 May 1965 in Saginaw, Saginaw County, Michigan. He was married to **Clara BRICKER** on 29 June 1910 in Saginaw.

1200 ii. **Belle A. HOWELL** was born in August 1885 in MI. She died in Tacoma, Pierce County, WA.

1201 iii. **Dwight HOWELL** was born on 10 December 1888 in MI. He died in March 1963 in Illinois.

1202 iv. **Walter HOWELL** was born in February 1893 in Michigan. He married **Alberta BALL.**

582. **Thomas E. HOWELL** was born in August 1864 in Muskegon, Muskegon County, MI. He died in Tacoma, WA. He was married to **Letitia UNKNOWN**, who was born in May 1868 in Canada. Thomas E. HOWELL and Letitia UNKNOWN had the following children:

1203 i. **Maude HOWELL** was born in September 1887 in Canada.

1204 ii. **Jaslas HOWELL** was born in August 1889 in Canada.

1205 iii. **Thomas F. HOWELL** was born on 25 July 1893 in MI. He died in July 1977 in Pinellas County, FL.

1206 iv. **Maggie HOWELL** was born in January 1897 in MI.

1207 v. **Letitia HOWELL** was born in September 1899 in MI.

585. **George HOWELL** was born in December 1855 in S. Dumfries, Brant County, Ontario. He died in Des Moines, Polk County, IA. George was a veterinarian. He married **Josephine POINTER**, who was born in April 1860 in Canada. George HOWELL and Josephine POINTER had the following children:

1208 i. **Margaret HOWELL** was born in March 1883 in Des Moines.

1209 ii. **Ella B. HOWELL** was born in July 1887 in Iowa.

586. **Dorothea HOWELL** was born in October 1857 in S. Dumfries, Brant County, Ontario. She died in June 1922, and was buried in Colborne Cemetery, Goderich, Huron County, Ontario. She married **James WATSON**, who was born in October 1851. He died in June 1923, and was buried in Colborne Cemetery. James, a farmer, was killed when a team of horses ran over him. Dorothea HOWELL and James WATSON had the following children:

1210 i. **William WATSON** was born in 1886 and died in 1963. He was buried in Colborne Cemetery, Goderich. He married **Lillian MCPHEE**, who was born in 1898 and died in 1972.

1211 ii. **Marian WATSON** was born in 1890 and died in 1949. She married **Arthur FULFORD**, who was born in 1878 and died in 1961.

+1212 iii. **Allen WATSON.**

587. **Elizabeth Jane HOWELL** was born in 1859 in S. Dumfries, Brant County, Ontario. She died in 1925 in Holland, Michigan, and was buried in Colborne Cemetery, Goderich, Huron County, Ontario. She married **Frederick YONKERS**, a doctor. He was born in 1857, and died in 1923. Their children were:

1213 i. **William YONKERS** died in a train accident.

1214 ii. **Charles YONKERS** was born on 3 February 1883. He married William's widow, **Maybelle UNKNOWN,** who was born on 1 January 1890 and died in March 1965. Charles died in October 1969 in Grand Rapids, MI.[205]

1215 iii. **Katheryn YONKERS**.

588. **Harvey J. HOWELL** was born on 14 February 1863 in S. Dumfries, Brant County, Ontario. He died on 2 June 1896 in Colborne, Huron County, Ontario, and was buried in Colborne Cemetery, Goderich, Huron County, Ontario. His wife was **Cassie POTTER**. They had the following children:

1216 i. **Esther HOWELL**.

1217 ii. **Myrtle HOWELL** lived in Winnipeg.

589. **William Nathan HOWELL** was born about 1865 in Brant County, Ontario. He died and was buried in Colborne Cemetery, Goderich, Huron County, Ontario. William Nathan HOWELL owned a store at Colborne, then moved to Saskatoon, where he ran the ferry on the Utana River. One of his sons was killed either by or on this ferry. He was married to **Winogene Evangeline BISSET** on 11 June 1886 in Goderich, Huron County, Ontario. William and Winogene had the following children:

---

[205]Social Security Death Index, Ancestry, Inc.

1218 i. **Unknown male HOWELL.**
1219 ii. **Unknown male HOWELL.**

590. **Eliza Jane HOWELL** was born on 4 December 1867 in Goderich, Huron County, Ontario. She died on 20 September 1944 in Ontonagon, Michigan, and was buried in Riverside Cemetery, Ontonagon. She married **Joseph TROYER** on 12 January 1886 in Colborne, Huron County, Ontario. Joseph TROYER was born on 3 July 1860 in Vaughn, York County, Ontario, died on 4 December 1936 in Ontonagon, and was buried there. Eliza and Joseph TROYER had these children:

+1220 i. **Raymond Claude TROYER.**
+1221 ii. **Jesse Howell TROYER.**
+1222 iii. **Lucy Jane TROYER.**

595. **Garret C. HOWELL** was born on 5 January 1838 in Frelinghuysen, Warren County, NJ. He died on 18 March 1923, and was buried in Johnsonburg Cemetery, Johnsonburg, Warren County, NJ. [199] Garret was a farmer, with a home near Hope. He was married (1) to **Anna E. KING** on 6 February 1866. [200] Anna E. KING was born in 1843. She died on 15 August 1870, and was buried in Green's Chapel Cemetery, Hope, Warren County, NJ.

Garret married (2) **Leonora VANSYCKLE**, who was born in 1851. She died in 1888, and was buried in Union Brick Cemetery, Blairstown, Warren County, NJ. Garret and Leonora had the following children:

+1223 i. **Anna Bertha HOWELL.**
+1224 ii. **Frank C. HOWELL.**
1225 iii. **George V. HOWELL** was born on 27 May 1876 in Warren County, and died in 1941. He married **Luella H. UNKNOWN**, who died in 1957. Both were buried in Johnsonburg Cemetery.
1226 iv. **Jeremiah King HOWELL** was born on 4 February 1878 in Warren County, NJ. He died there in 1899.
1227 v. **Leonora Belle HOWELL** was born on 22 October 1879, and died in infancy.
+1228 vi. **Dewitt C. HOWELL.**
1229 vii. **Emma HOWELL** was born on 30 January 1883,and died in infancy.
1230 viii. **John V. HOWELL** was born on 27 July 1884 in Warren County, and died there on 25 November 1945.[201] He married **Sadie R. MILLER** (daughter of **Delmar MILLER**), in January 1909.

---

[199]Obituary, Washington (NJ) Star, 15 March 1923.
[200]Warren County, NJ Marriage Records, LDS Microfilm # 0960890. V. 2, p. 144.
[201]Funeral Notice, Easton Express, 30 November 1945.

She was born on 22 February 1887 in Great Meadows, and died on 15 November 1981. Both are buried in Free Union Cemetery, Mountain Lake, Warren County, NJ.

1231 ix. **Edgar C. HOWELL** was born on 2 August 1886 in Warren County. He died on 30 August 1964 in Irvington, NJ. Edgar was employed by Bond Bakery in Newark until he retired in the 1950's. He had lived in the Irvington area for 60 years. He married **Anna Rose UNKNOWN**, who was born in 1880. She was not named in Edgar's obituary, so she may have predeceased him. Both were buried in the Moravian Cemetery in Hope.[202]

1232 x. **M. Alice HOWELL** was born on 27 November 1887 in Warren County, and died in 1888.

Garret married (3) **Charlotte WILLETT** about 1891. Charlotte WILLETT was born in January 1842 in NJ, died in 1921, and was buried in Johnsonburg Cemetery, Johnsonburg, NJ.

598. **Edgar Crisman HOWELL** was born in September 1846 in Warren County, NJ. He died on 27 December 1909 in Morris Plains, NJ, and was buried on 30 December 1909 in Union Brick Cemetery, Blairstown, Warren County, NJ[203]. He was a farmer. The 1880 census indicated they were living in Hope and his mother and a sister-in-law, Althea, were living with them. Edgar suffered a stroke three years before he died, and had been in poor health. He was confined to the State hospital in Morris Plains after his mind began to fail, and he died there. He was married to **Emma L. AYERS** on 15 January 1870 in Marksboro, Warren County, NJ.[204] Emma L. AYERS was born in April 1844. She died in 1919. She was buried in Union Brick Cemetery, Blairstown, Warren County, NJ. Emma was an invalid when her husband died. Edgar and Emma had one child:

+1233 i. **Alvah S. HOWELL**.

602. **Angeline MILLER** was born on 6 November 1834 in Hope, Warren County, New Jersey.When her borother William died in 1899, Angeline and her family were living in Hackettstown. She married **George W. GIBBS** on 12 May 1854. Angeline MILLER and George W. GIBBS had the following children:

+1234 i. **Edwin P. GIBBS**.

+1235 ii. **Isaac A. GIBBS**.

1236 iii. **William H. GIBBS** was born on 19 April 1859. He

---

[202]Obituary, Washington (NJ) Star, 10 September 1964.

[203]Obituary, Washington (NJ) Star, 30 December 1909.

[204]Warren County, NJ Marriage records, LDS Microfilm #0960890. Vol. 2, p.199.

+1235 ii. **Isaac A. GIBBS.**
1236 iii. **William H. GIBBS** was born on 19 April 1859. He married **Addie STAPLES.**
+1237 iv. **Emma A . GIBBS.**
1238 v. **Julia H. GIBBS** was born on 15 January 1863.
+1239 vi. **John D. GIBBS.**
+1240 vii. **Luella V. GIBBS.**
+1241 viii. **Sampson Howell GIBBS.**
+1242 ix. **Frank L. GIBBS.**
1243 x. **George H. GIBBS** was born on 25 March 1875.
+1244 xi. **Lavina G. GIBBS.**
1245 xii. **Marie Etta GIBBS** was born on 12 November 1878.

604. **Euphemia MILLER** was born in 1839 in Hope, Warren County, NJ. She died in 1877 in Hope. She was married to **William A. CRUSEN**. Euphemia and William had one child:

+1246 i. **Frederick F. CRUSEN.**

605. **Garrett MILLER** was born in 1842 in Hope, Warren County, NJ. We think he died before his brother William. Garrett was married to **Susan VAN KIRK**. Their children were:

1247 i. **William MILLER.**
1248 ii. **Emma MILLER.**
1249 iii. **Daisy MILLER.**

606. **Gideon H. MILLER** was born in 1844 in Hope, Warren County, NJ. In 1916, Gideon and his family lived in Stroudsburg, Monroe County, PA. Gideon was married to **Charlotte SWARTWOOD**. Their children were:

+1250 i. **Stewart MILLER.**
+1251 ii. **Wirt D. MILLER.**
1252 iii. **Olive L. MILLER** died before 1916.
+1253 iv. **Frank H. MILLER.**

607. **Amelia MILLER** was born in 1845 in Hope, Warren County, NJ. She died on 16 March 1904 in Anita, Cass County, Iowa. She was married (1) to **William RETALLIC** (son of **John RETALLIC**) on 25 December 1869 in Hope. William RETALLIC died in Hope. Amelia and William RETALLIC had one child:

1254 i. **Albert G. RETALLIC** was born on 5 January 1874 in Hope. He was a farmer and stockman in Atlantic, Cass County, IA. He married **Mary M. BEEKMON** (daughter of **Casper BEEKMON** and **Elizabeth SCHAIN**) on 25 June 1911 in Anita, IA.

Amelia married (2) **Andrew TRIMMER**, who died on 20 March 1900 in Anita. Their children were:

1255 i. **Andrew C. TRIMMER** was born on 7 September 1879 in Anita, IA. He was a farmer and stockman in Wiota, Cass County, IA. He married **Minerva MCCUE** (daughter of **William Henry MCCUE** and **Emaline CARLTON**) on 28 April 1910 in Greenfield, Adair County, IA.

1256 ii. **Stewart A. TRIMMER** was born on 6 April 1881 in Anita. He married **Nellie FAULKNER** (daughter of **Daniel FAULKNER** and **Elvira LEWIS**) on 21 March 1906 in Anita.

+1257 iii. **Mayme E. TRIMMER**.

1258 iv. **Max G. C. TRIMMER** was born in 1885. He died on 6 June 1896.

608. **Henry MILLER** was born on 22 February 1846 in Warren County, NJ. He died on 31 August 1898 in Dallas Twp., Luzerne County, PA. He was married to **Sarah SMITH** (daughter of **Theodore SMITH** and **Mary Ann WATSON**) on 25 October 1875 in Franklin Twp., Luzerne County. Sarah SMITH was born on 3 March 1851. Henry MILLER and Sarah SMITH had the following children:

+1259 i. **Annie MILLER**.

+1260 ii. **Letitia MILLER**.

+1261 iii. **Jennie MILLER**.

1262 iv. **Josephine MILLER** was born on 29 January 1890 in Dallas Twp.

1263 v. **Gideon MILLER** was born on 6 March 1892 in Dallas Twp.

610. **Elizabeth MILLER** was born in Hope, Warren County, NJ. When her brother died in 1899, Elizabeth and her family were living in Newark, Essex County, NJ. Elizabeth married **Joseph TERWILLIGER**. Elizabeth MILLER and Joseph TERWILLIGER had one child:

1264 i. **Roland TERWILLIGER**.

611. **Lydia Ann HOWELL** was born on 9 July 1844 in NJ; she died on 6 January 1895, and was buried in Moravian Cemetery, Hope, NJ. She was married to **William BOWERS**. William BOWERS was born on 20 May 1844, and died on 21 September 1925. Lydia and William BOWERS had these children:

1265 i. **Mabel BOWERS** was born in 1887. She was the second wife of **Alvah S. HOWELL**. She died in 1956, and was buried in the Moravian Cemetery, Hope, Warren County, NJ.

1266 ii. **Gideon H. BOWERS** was born in 1877 and died in

He married **Belle S. SWAYZE,** who was born in 1872 and died in 1954.

612. **Levi H. HOWELL** was born on 5 April 1852 in Hope, Warren County, NJ. He died on 26 March 1878, and was buried in Union Brick Cemetery, Blairstown, Warren County, NJ. He married **Mary A. WEST** (daughter of **Mathias WEST** and **Caroline UNKNOWN**) on 14 January 1873[205]. She was born on 19 February 1853, died on 28 August 1880, of consumption, and was buried in Union Brick Cemetery. Levi and Mary had the following children:

1267 i. **Clinton HOWELL** was born about 1873 in Warren County, NJ.
1268 ii. **Carrie F. HOWELL** was born on 1 October 1876 in Warren County, NJ. She died on 3 December 1895, and was buried in Union Brick Cemetery.
1269 iii. **Luella HOWELL** was born about 1878 in Warren County, NJ.

639. **William A. HEMINGWAY** was born 14 June 1851 in Trenton, Mercer County, NJ. He married **Mary J. LINN** (daughter of **Judge Samuel LINN**), who was born about 1854. William worked for the DL&W Railroad at Delaware, Warren County, NJ, and later moved to Middletown, Orange County, NY, where he worked as a hospital nurse for 25 years. He died in November 1929 in Middletown. William A. HEMINGWAY and Mary J. LINN had these children:

1270 i. **Edith B. HEMINGWAY** was born about 1876 in NJ.
+1271 ii. **Samuel Linn HEMINGWAY**.

640. **William C. HOWELL** was born in 1843 and died in 1922 in NJ. He was the postmaster in Blairstown during the presidency of William Howard Taft, whose inauguration he attended. William married **Henrietta PARSONS** (daughter of **Elisha PARSONS**) who was born in 1840 in CT. She died in 1932 in NJ. William C. HOWELL and Henrietta D. PARSONS had one child:

1272 i. **Elizabeth Marie HOWELL** was born in Blairstown, Warren County, NJ. She married **Frank WILKINS** in Edge Hill, NJ.

642. **John Richards HOWELL** was born on 1 January 1844 in Vincentown, Burlington County, NJ. He operated a general store in Vincentown, and later bought his father's farm. He exchanged it for a store and business in Medford, which he ran for five years(1871). He was elected Surrogate of Burlington County in 1876, serving for 10 years. During that period he also was secretary of the Mt. Holly Insurance Company. After leaving office, he ran an insurance business. He

---

[205]Warren County, NJ Marriage Records, LDS Microfilm # 0960890. V. 2, p.258.

was a member of F&AM, Lodge 44, Vincentown, and the BPOE. John was married (1) to **Ann Eliza PRICKETT** (daughter of **Clayton PRICKETT** and **Maria EAYRE**) on 1 January 1867. Ann Eliza PRICKETT died in 1879 in Vincentown. John Richards HOWELL and Ann Eliza PRICKETT had one child:

1273 i. **Laura Clarissa HOWELL** was born on 23 July 1868 in Vincentown, Burlington County, NJ.

John was married (2) to **Susan Deacon LANGSTAFF** on 28 April 1886 in Mt. Holly, NJ. Susan Deacon LANGSTAFF was born in Mt. Holly, Burlington County, NJ.

656. **Bessie HOWELL** was born on 2 November 1864 in Independence, Warren County, NJ. In 1900, Bessie was in her parents' home, listed in the census as Bessie Howell, with a daughter, Grace. She was divorced, had 2 living children, but only Grace was named. Bessie and **UNKNOWN** had one known child:

1274 i. **Grace UNKNOWN** was born in July 1892.

658. **Francis "Frank" Jerome HOWELL** was born on 26 December 1847 in Corning, Steuben County, NY, where he died on 25 August 1927. He was buried in New Hope Cemetery, Corning. Frank was troubled by the fact that he had so many daughters, and his only son committed suicide. The family lived at 248 Pine Street in Corning. Frank was married to **Emily LITSCHKE** on 28 May 1896 in Corning. Francis and Emily had these children:

1275 i. **Frances Evaline HOWELL** was born in 1898; she died in December 1969, and was buried in New Hope Cemetery, Corning, NY.

1276 ii. **Luanna Pauline HOWELL** was born in 1899. She died in Corning, and was buried in New Hope Cemetery.

1277 iii. **Emily Louise HOWELL** was born in 1901, died in 1966, and was buried in New Hope Cemetery. She was married to **Floyd L. TEWKSBURY** who was born in 1901 and died in 1966.

1278 iv. **Christeon Goodrech HOWELL** was born on 5 April 1903. He died on 12 April 1927, and was buried in New Hope Cemetery.

1279 v. **Alice Verona HOWELL** was born on 3 December 1906, died on 13 August 1978, and was buried in New Hope Cemetery.

1280 vi. **Nelly Walworth HOWELL** was born on 31 May 1908. She lived in Lynbrook, Nassau County, NY

+1281 vii. **Matilda Cummins HOWELL** was born on 7 February 1911.

660. **Ellen Rebecca HOWELL** was born on 17 March 1846 in Independence, Warren County, NJ. She died on 4 March 1901, and was buried in Union Cemetery, Hackettstown, Warren County, NJ. Ellen married **William Emery CUMMINS** who was born on 4 July 1845. They had these children:

1282 i. **Charles Rockwell CUMMINS** was born on 19 September 1868, and died on 9 October 1868 in Vienna, Warren County, NJ.

1283 ii. **Jennie Howell CUMMINS** was born on 13 September 1869.

1284 iii. **Carrie Emery CUMMINS** was born on 20 June 1875 in Washington, Warren County, NJ.

1285 iv. **Mary Welch CUMMINS** was born on 20 October 1879 in Washington, NJ.

662. **Belden D. HOWELL** was born on 26 August 1851 in Independence, Warren County, NJ. He died in April 1923 in Clinton, Hunterdon County, NJ, and was buried on 9 April 1923 in Riverside Cemetery, Clinton.[206] He was a dentist, was called Bell. He was married to **Cynthia C. GILLEN** on 26 May 1877 in Lebanon, Hunterdon County, NJ. Cynthia C. GILLEN was born in 1862; she died in 1918, and was buried in Riverside Cemetery. Belden D. HOWELL and Cynthia C. GILLEN had the following children:

1286 i. **Harvey Clearfield HOWELL** was born on 29 June 1879. Harvey lived in Bogota, Bergen County, NJ when his father died, in 1923.

+1287 ii. **Sylvester Vansyckle HOWELL**.

667. **Oren Rockwell HOWELL** was born on 16 February 1869 in Independence, Warren County, NJ. He died in 1927, and was buried in Tranquility Cemetery, Tranquility, NJ. Oren was living in New York City in 1903, when his father died. By 1923, when Belden died, he was in Hoboken, Hudson County, NJ. He was a painter. He was married to **Nina A. RUNION** on 13 September 1888. Nina A. RUNION was born in November 1873 in Warren County, NJ. Oren and Nina had one child:

1288 i. **Lewis HOWELL** was born in June 1889.

669. **Robert Ogden HOWELL** was born on 23 November 1851 in Hackettstown, Warren County, NJ. He died on 21 January 1921 in Binghamton, NY. Robert moved to Binghamton, Broome County, NY after Anna's death, where he worked for the police department. Robert married (1) **Anna WEIR**, who was born in 1856. Robert Ogden HOWELL and Anna WEIR had one child:

+1289 i. **Charles Evans HOWELL**.

---

[206]Obituary, Hunterdon County Democrat (NJ), 12 April 1923.

Robert Ogden HOWELL married (2) **Lydia COLE**. They had two children:

+1290 i. **Robert Ernest HOWELL.**
1291 ii. **Lucy Cole HOWELL** was born in 1891.

670. **Thomas B. HOWELL** was born in 1853 in Hackettstown, Warren County, NJ. He died in 1926. In 1904, when brother Gustavus died, he was living in Hope. He operated a restaurant and bakery, as well as a catering business on Main Street in Hackettstown for many years. After he sold this business he opened a steam laundry on Main Street in that town, until he retired. Thomas married (1) **Lydia SAVACOOL**. Lydia L. SAVACOOL was born in 1850, died in 1889, and was buried in Union Cemetery, Hackettstown, Warren County, NJ. Thomas and Lydia had these children:

+1292 i. **Elizabeth Weise HOWELL.**
1293 ii. **Willard B. HOWELL** was born in 1879, died in 1880 in Warren County, and was buried in Union Cemetery, Hackettstown, Warren County, NJ.

Thomas was married (2) to **Luella C. CLAUSEN** on 4 May 1890. Luella C. CLAUSEN was born in 1854. She died in 1933.

671. **Anna Matilda "Mary" HOWELL** was born on 30 January 1858 in Hackettstown, Warren County, NJ. She died in 1930. She and her family were living in Phillipsburg in 1904, when Gustavus died. In her mother's obituary, she was called Mary Hess (1909). She married **John HESS**, who died in 1912. Anna Matilda "Mary" HOWELL and John HESS had one child:

1294 i. **John Royden HESS** was born in 1882. He married **Ethyl SMITH**.

672. **Charles HOWELL** was born on 10 July 1860 in Hackettstown, Warren County, NJ. He died on 30 March 1936. Charles worked in the carriage manufacturing industry, and later was a sign painter in Hackettstown. In 1904, he was living in Brooklyn, according to his father's obituary. By 1909, when his mother died, he was living in Hope, NJ. At the time of his death, he was living in Hackettstown. Charles married **Anna SMALL**, who was born in 1864. She died in 1949. Their children were:

1295 i. **Walter Thomas HOWELL** was born in 1885 and died in 1961. He was the postmaster in Hackettstown. On 8 September 1908, he married **Jane C. LAKE**, (daughter of **Jacob LAKE** and **Margaret LARSON**) who was born on 2 November 1882 in Drakestown, NJ. She died in Hackettstown in 1974. Both are buried in Union Cemetery, Hackettstown.
1296 ii. **Elva Small HOWELL** was born on 29 May 1889 in Brooklyn, Kings County, New York. She died in

March 1972 in Hackettstown, and was buried in Union Cemetery, Hackettstown. Elva was a nurse.

1297 iii. **Ebell HOWELL** died in infancy.

673. **Margaret Roberts HOWELL** was born on 11 January 1863 in Hackettstown, Warren County, NJ. She died in 1942. Margaret was living in Rockaway in 1904, when her brother Gustavus died. She married **Harry W. MUTCHLER** on 19 March 1883. Margaret and Harry W. MUTCHLER had the following children:

1298 i. **Mabel MUTCHLER** was born in 1884, and died in 1889.

1299 ii. **Raymond MUTCHLER**.

674. **Gustavus Ashmead HOWELL** was born on 26 October 1865 in Hackettstown, Warren County, NJ. He died on 21 April 1904 in Hackettstown, of rheumatism of the heart and pneumonia. He was buried in Union Cemetery, Hackettstown. He was head baker at Thomas Howell's bakery, which was operated by his brother, Thomas B. HOWELL, in Hope. He was a member of St. James Episcopal Church in Hope. Just before Gustavus' death, his wife, **Harriet Jane RICE**, was taken to Morristown Memorial Hospital, where she had surgery. She was recovering, but was unable to attend her husband's funeral. According to Gustavus' obituary, there were three children, all under the age of ten, when he died.[207] Harriet Jane RICE was born about 1876. They had these children:

+1300 i. **Mildred Julia HOWELL**.

1301 ii. **Henrietta Roberts Howell** was born about 1897 in Warren County. She died in 1945. She married **Leslie HANKINSON**.

1302 iii. **Lewis Rice HOWELL** was born about 1898 in Warren County, NJ. He was an Episcopal priest.

676. **Emma Louise HOWELL** was born on 14 February 1871 in Warren County, NJ. She died on 14 October 1959, and was buried in Union Cemetery, Hackettstown, Warren County, NJ. Emma married **John Bonnett ROE**, who was born on 5 July 1871, and died on 19 June 1950. In 1904, Emma and her family lived in Canton, NY. They lived in Passaic, Passaic County, NJ when Emma's mother died. Their children were:

1303 i. **Thomas Howell ROE**.

1304 ii. **James Bryon ROE**.

1305 iii. **Esther Mildred ROE**.

677. **Austin C. HOWELL** was born on 26 April 1859 in Independence, Warren County, NJ. He died on 11 March 1929, having suffered a heart attack while

[207]Obituary, Washington (NJ) Star, 28 April 1904.

trying to put out a fire at the post office he operated. He was buried in Union Cemetery, Hackettstown, Warren County, NJ. He was a house painter and interior decorator. Austin was the postmaster at Vienna, NJ at the time of his father's death in 1901, having been appointed to the post on 10 May 1897, by President William McKinley. Austin was married to **Arisena BERRY** in 1905. Arisena BERRY was born in 1865, and died in 1959. She was buried in Union Cemetery, Hackettstown. She was a teacher in the Newark, NJ schools. They had one child:

+1306 i. **Samson Austin HOWELL**.

709. **Elisa HOWELL** was born about 1848 in S. Dumfries, [208]Brant County, Ontario. She was married to **John W. GREENE** M.D. (son of **Almanzo GREENE** and **Viletta JOHNSON**) on 18 July 1871. John W. GREENE M.D. was born in 1836 in West Laurens, Otsego County, NY. He was a physician and surgeon in Otsego County. John W. Green became a member of Company G, 78th New York Cavalry, served eleven months and was mustered out with his regiment. He served for some time as warden in a hospital in Washington, D.C., afterward studied medicine, and graduated from the Bellevue Hospital Medical College in 1881. Elisa HOWELL and John W. GREENE M.D. had these children:

1307 i. **Frederick H. GREENE** was born in 1872 in West Laurens, Otsego County. Frederick was a school teacher for at least five years as a young man.
1308 ii. **Mary Eliza GREENE**.
1309 iii. **Evalena GREENE**.
1310 iv. **Olive Viletta GREENE** was born in 1877 in West Laurens.

710. **Martha HOWELL** was born about 1850 in S. Dumfries, Brant County, Ontario. She married **James FARROW**. Martha and James FARROW had these children:

1311 i. **Charles FARROW**.
1312 ii. **Jennie FARROW**.
1313 iii. **Thomas FARROW**.

713. **Clark HOWELL** was born about 1856 in S. Dumfries, Brant County, Ontario. He died and was buried in Baptist Church Cemetery, S. Dumfries. He married **Martha BOUGHNER**, who was born in 1869; she died in 1931, and was buried in Baptist Church Cemetery, S. Dumfries. Clark HOWELL and Martha BOUGHNER had these children:

1314 i. **Alex HOWELL**.
1315 ii. **Edith HOWELL**.

---

[208]Biographical Review: Biographical Sketches of the Leading Citizens of Otsego County, NY, (1893; reprint, Bowie, MD: Heritage Books, Inc., 1994), 264-265.

714. **James Arthur HOWELL** was born in 1861 in S. Dumfries, Brant County, Ontario. He died in 1941 in S. Dumfries, and was buried in Baptist Church Cemetery, S. Dumfries. He married **Sarah Maria ROSEBRUGH**, who was born in 1857. She died in 1927, and was buried in Baptist Church Cemetery, S. Dumfries. James Arthur HOWELL and Sarah Maria ROSEBRUGH had children:

+1316 i. **Mary "Mae" Rosebrugh HOWELL.**
+1317 ii. **Alice HOWELL.**
+1318 iii. **Cuthbert HOWELL.**
1319 iv. **Bertha HOWELL.**
1320 v. **Florence HOWELL.**

715. **Frederick Templer HOWELL** was born in 1866 in S. Dumfries, Brant County, Ontario. He died in 1936, and was buried in St. George United Cemetery, S. Dumfries. Frederick married **Elizabeth ROSEBRUGH**, who was born in 1867. She died in 1955, and was buried in St. George United Cemetery. Frederick Templer HOWELL and Elizabeth ROSEBRUGH had the following children:

1321 i. **Ada HOWELL** was born in 1887. She died in 1987, and was buried in St. George United Cemetery.
1322 ii. **Gladys HOWELL.**

726. **John Edward HOWELL** was born in 1840 in Brantford, Brant County, Ontario. He married **Anne Jane SHARP** on 24 October 1866. She was born in 1837. Their children were:

1323 i. **Mary HOWELL** was born about 1868.
1324 ii. **Florence HOWELL** was born in 1871.

728. **Augustus HOWELL** was born in 1844 in Brantford, Brant County, Ontario. He was a farmer. He was married to **Sarah Abigail CHITENDEN** (daughter of **George CHITENDEN**) about 1868 in Brantford. Sarah was born in Paris, Brant County, Ontario. Their children were:

1325 i. **Eva Gertrude HOWELL** was born about 1869 in Brantford.
1326 ii. **Florence Edna HOWELL** was born about 1871 in Brantford.

735. **Arthur HOWELL** was born on 3 March 1857 in Woodstock, Oxford County, Ontario. He died on 23 February 1938 in Pullman, Whitman County, Kansas, and was buried in Maplewood Cemetery, Emporia, Lyon County, KS. He married **Emma Francis SPENCE** (daughter of **William Bates SPENCE** and **Mary Helen NETTLETON**). She was born on 18 August 1860 in Griggsville, Pike County, Illinois, died on 21 May 1924 in Wichita, Sedgwick County, KS, and was buried in Maplewood Cemetery, Emporia. She was a teacher. Arthur HOWELL and Emma Francis SPENCE had these children:

1327 i. **May Odessa HOWELL** was born on 24 May 1882, died on 13 October 1944 in Pullman. She married **Elmer COLPITTS** on 15 June 1910.

1328 ii. **Ada Pearl HOWELL** was born on 2 April 1884, died on 20 May 1933, and buried in Quincy, Greenwood County, KS. She married **Herman STECKEL** on 4 August 1909.

1329 iii. **Grace Elizabeth HOWELL** was born on 31 May 1885, died on 9 November 1975 in Santa Maria, Santa Barbara County, CA. She married **John Calvin FUNK** on 5 August 1914.

1330 iv. **Ivan HOWELL** was born on 4 April 1888. He died on 5 May 1906 in Emporia, Lyon County, Kansas.

1331 v. **Edith Helen HOWELL** was born on 25 March 1892 in Sabetha, Nemaha County, KS. She died on 30 July 1977 in Santa Maria, Santa Barbara County, CA, and was buried in Sterling, Rice County, KS. She married **Lewis Floyd BALDWIN** 15 June 1916.

737. **John Dennis HOWELL** was born in 1848 in Ancaster Twp., Wentworth County, Ontario. He was a farmer. He died in 1925 in Ontario, and was buried in Zion Hill Cemetery. John married **Mary GARLAND** in 1869 in Wentworth County. Mary GARLAND was born in 1842. She died in 1916 in Ontario, and was buried in Zion Hill Cemetery. John and Mary had the following children:

+1332 i. **Aleatha HOWELL**.

1333 ii. **Herbert J. W. HOWELL** was born in 1875, died on 26 April 1880, and was buried in Zion Hill Cemetery.

1334 iii. **Laughlin HOWELL** was born in 1878 in Ancaster Twp., and died in 1950 in Ontario, and was buried in Zion Hill cemetery. His wife, **Alice UNKNOWN**, was born in 1877, died in 1948 and was buried in Zion Hill Cemetery.

738. **George Wesley HOWELL** was born in 1850, and died on 7 January 1893 in Ancaster Twp. He married **Rebecca Ann WILKINS**, who was born in 1852. She died on 19 June 1939 in Ontario, and was buried in Zion Hill Cemetery. George and Rebecca had the following children:

1335 i. **Ann Gertrude HOWELL** was born on 25 February 1874 in Ancaster Twp. She died on 8 July 1958, and was buried in Zion Hill Cemetery.

1336 ii. **Etta Mabel HOWELL** was born on 1 July 1875 in Ancaster Twp. She died on 18 February 1922, and was buried in Zion Hill Cemetery.

1337 iii. **Clara E. HOWELL** was born in 1877 in Ancaster Twp.

1338 iv. **Harris W. HOWELL** was born in 1885, died on 15

May 1886, and was buried in Zion Hill Cemetery.

1339 v. **Frank C. HOWELL** was born in 1887, died on 15 March 1888, and was buried in Zion Hill Cemetery.

1340 vi. **Beulah HOWELL** was born in 1887, died on 24 August 1888, and was buried in Zion Hill Cemetery.

1341 vii. **Mary M. HOWELL** was born in April 1890, died on 14 September 1890, and was buried in Zion Hill Cemetery.

+1342 viii. **Gordon E. HOWELL**.

739. **William Triller HOWELL** was born in 1852 in Ancaster Twp. He died on 12 November 1924 in Ontario, and was buried in Zion Hill Cemetery. William Howell was killed when he was kicked in the face by a horse while driving some horses through a lane. He married **Eliza Jane KITCHEN**, who was born in 1854. She died in 1929 in Ontario, and was buried in Zion Hill Cemetery. William Triller HOWELL and Eliza Jane KITCHEN had these children:

1343 i. **Blanche Ella HOWELL** was born in 1880. She died in 1964, and was buried in Zion Hill Cemetery.

1344 ii. **Mildred M. HOWELL** was born in 1883. She died in 1932 and was buried in Zion Hill Cemetery.

1345 iii. **Winetta HOWELL**.

1346 iv. **Jessie Louise HOWELL**.

1347 v. **Cecil E. HOWELL** was born in 1885 and died in 1953. His wife, **Beatrice KENDRICK**, was born in 1890 and died after 1900. Both are buried in Zion Hill Cemetery.

740. **Oliver Alfred HOWELL** was born in 1855 in Ancaster Twp. He died in 1912 in Ontario, and was buried in Zion Hill Cemetery. He was married to **Susan KELLY** (daughter of **David KELLY** and **Asenath DARROW**) on 5 December 1877 in Ontario. Susan KELLY was born in 1857, died in 1915 in Ontario, and was buried in Zion Hill Cemetery. Oliver and Susan had the following children:

+1348 i. **Fred L. HOWELL**.

1349 ii. **William D. HOWELL** was born in 1882 in Ontario. He died in 1950 in Ontario, and was buried in Zion Hill Cemetery.

1350 iii. **Albert W. HOWELL** was born on 6 February 1886, died on 26 June 1943, in Ontario, and was buried in Zion Hill Cemetery. His wife, **Mary Thelma HAMILTON**, was born on 15 September 1894, died on 23 July 1924, and was buried in Zion Hill Cemetery.

1351 iv. **Elizabeth HOWELL** was born in 1888 in Ontario, died in 1976 in Ontario, and was buried in Zion Hill Cemetery.

742. **Bertha Ann HOWELL** was born in 1859 in Ancaster Twp. She died in 1913 in Ontario, and was buried in Zion Hill Cemetery. She married **James BURNSIDE**, who was born in 1859. He died in 1927, and was buried in Zion Hill Cemetery. Bertha Ann HOWELL and James BURNSIDE had one child:

1352 i. **Alma L. BURNSIDE** was born in 1888, died in 1889, and was buried in Zion Hill Cemetery.

744. **Charles Lewis HOWELL** was born in 1865, and died in 1934 in Ontario. He married **Marion CLARK**, who was born in 1867, and died in 1926. Charles and Marion had the following children:

1353 i. **Lindsay HOWELL**.
1354 ii. **Olive HOWELL**.
1355 iii. **Floyd HOWELL**.

747. **Isaac CASSADA** was born in 1836. He married **Mary HILL**, who was born about 1836. Isaac CASSADA and Mary HILL had the following children:

1356 i. **Frank CASSADA**.
1357 ii. **Melissa CASSADA**.
1358 iii. **Ella CASSADA**.
1359 iv. **William CASSADA**.
1360 v. **Fred CASSADA**.
1361 vi. **James Samuel CASSADA**.
1362 vii. **Maude CASSADA**.
1363 viii. **Harry CASSADA**.

749. **Mary Jane CASSADA** was born on 2 November 1843. She married **George** VAN EVERY (son of **Andrew VAN EVERY** and **Mary UNKNOWN**) on 29 January 1866 in Brant County, Ontario. George VAN EVERY was born in 1842. Mary and George VAN EVERY had the following children:

1364 i. **Russell VAN EVERY**.
1365 ii. **Allen VAN EVERY**.

750. **Harriet Ann CASSADA** was born on 2 November 1843. She married **Jeriah BONHAM**, who was born about 1843. Their children were:

1366 i. **Samuel BONHAM**.
1367 ii. **James BONHAM**.
1368 iii. **Sidney BONHAM**.
1369 iv. **Edith BONHAM**.
1370 v. **Bessie BONHAM**.

751. **Phoebe Eliza CASSADA** was born on 21 May 1846. She died on 13 January 1929, and was buried in St. George United Cemetery, S. Dumfries, Brant

County, Ontario. She was married to **William GERMAN** on 1 January 1868. William GERMAN was born on 4 August 1842 in S. Dumfries. He died on 29 October 1915 in S. Dumfries. Phoebe and William GERMAN had these children:

+1371 i. **Herbert GERMAN**.

1372 ii. **Myrtle May GERMAN** was born on 17 September 1883 in S. Dumfries, and died on 13 April 1975 in Brantford. She married **Alvah MCINTYRE** on 19 February 1908. Alvah was born on 4 September 1880 in Onondaga Twp., Brant County, died on 16 July 1950 in Brantford Twp., and was buried in St. George Cemetery.

752. **Catherine CASSADA** was born about 1847. Catherine married **Edgar VAN EVERY**. Catherine and Edgar VAN EVERY had the following children:

1373 i. **Nellie VAN EVERY**.
1374 ii. **Bert VAN EVERY**.
1375 iii. **George VAN EVERY**.
1376 iv. **John VAN EVERY**.
1377 v. **Lillie VAN EVERY**.
1378 vi. **James VAN EVERY**.

753. **James Albert CASSADA** was born on 7 June 1850. He married **Ethel HERRINGTON**, who was born about 1850. James Albert CASSADA and Ethel HERRINGTON had the following children:

1379 i. **Nina CASSADA**.
1380 ii. **Clarence CASSADA**.

756. **Samuel CASSADA** was married (1) to **UNKNOWN**, and (2) to **Jane MURRAY**. Samuel CASSADA and Jane MURRAY had the following children:

1381 i. **Gertrude CASSADA.**
1382 ii. **Robert CASSADA.**

757. **Edward KITCHEN** was born on 4 January 1855, died on 1 January 1944 and was buried in St. George United Cemetery. He married (1) **Elizabeth ANDERSON**, who was born on 14 May 1858 and died on 8 August 1892. She also was buried in St. George United Cemetery. Edward KITCHEN and Elizabeth ANDERSON had the following children:

1383 i. **Gladys KITCHEN**.
1384 ii. **Hazel KITCHEN**.
1385 iii. **Percy KITCHEN**.

Edward KITCHEN married (2) **Elizabeth MCTAGGERT**, and they had these children:

1386 i. **Edward KITCHEN**.
1387 ii. **Revel KITCHEN**.

759. **Eunice KITCHEN** was born in 1853, and died on 23 February 1915. She married **Milburn BONHAM**, who was born in 1854 and died on 17 April 1916. Both are buried in St. George United Cemetery. Eunice KITCHEN and Milburn BONHAM had the following children:

1388 i. **Alfred BONHAM**.
1389 ii. **Myrtle BONHAM**.
1390 iii. **Gordon BONHAM**.
1391 iv. **Helen BONHAM**.

762. **Isaac C. KITCHEN** was born in 1851 in Ontario. He died on 17 July 1939. He married **Elizabeth Gillespie PATTEN** (daughter of Aaron PATTEN and **Sophia KITCHEN**), who was born on 4 April 1850 in S. Dumfries Twp., Brant County, Ontario. She died on 15 February 1920 in St. George, Ontario.[209] Isaac C. KITCHEN and Elizabeth Gillespie PATTEN had the following children:

1392 i. **Edith KITCHEN** was born on 13 November 1877, and died on 25 November 1962. She married **Charles MOODIE**, who was born on 20 June 1885, and died on 23 November 1968. Both were buried in St. George United Cemetery.
+1393 ii. **Frank KITCHEN**.

763. **Mary Helen KITCHEN** was born on 21 March 1858 in Brant County, Ontario. She died on 6 July 1957 in Bethel Nursing Home, Brantford, Ontario. She was married to Finlay Allison PATTEN (son of **Hugh PATTEN** and **Martha Ann MALCOLM**) on 8 April 1885 in St. George, Brant County. Finlay Allison PATTEN was born in 1852 in St. George, died on 10 September 1930 and was buried in St. George United Cemetery.[210] Mary Helen and Finlay Allison PATTEN had these children:

+1394 i. **Fred J. PATTEN**.
1395 ii. **Harry PATTEN** died in Burlington, Ontario.
+1396 iii. **Culver Finlay PATTEN**.
1397 iv. **Alfred Hugh PATTEN** died on 23 February 1960 in Englehart Hospital, Ontario, and was buried in Englehart Cemetery.[211] He was a conductor on the Northern Ontario Railway, and a veteran of WWI.
1398 v. **Norman PATTEN** was born in 1902 in Harrisburg,

---

[209]Obituary, Brantford Expositor, Brant County, Ontario, 16 February 1920, p. 2.
[210]Obituary , Brantford Expositor, Brant county, Ontario, 11 September 1930, p.6.
[211]Obituary, Brantford Expositor, 24 September 1960, page 2.

Ontario. He died on 16 December 1962 in St. Joseph's Hospital, Brantford, and was buried in St. George United Cemetery. He had been employed by Robbins & Myers Company.

+1399 vi. **Eva H. PATTEN**.

1400 vii. **Helen Mary PATTEN** was married to **Russell B. HAWTHORNE** on 3 September 1924 in St. George Baptist Church, S. Dumfries. She died in Inglewood, Los Angeles County, CA.

765. **James Alfred KITCHEN** was born in 1861 in Ontario. He died in 1934. Alfred was a farmer. He married **Mary HANDY**, who was born in 1868 and died in 1909. Both are buried in St. George United Cemetery. James Alfred KITCHEN and Mary HANDY had the following children:

1401 i. **Erle KITCHEN**.
1402 ii. **Clarence KITCHEN**.
1403 iii. **Perry KITCHEN**.
1404 iv. **Edward KITCHEN**.
1405 v. **Alfred KITCHEN**.
1406 vi. **Donald KITCHEN**.
1407 vii. **Rachel KITCHEN**.
1408 viii. **Ethel KITCHEN**.
1409 ix. **Grace KITCHEN**.

766. **Carrie Rachel KITCHEN** was born in 1863 in S. Dumfries, Brant County, Ontario. She died on 13 October 1904 in St. George, Brant County. She was married to **Sidney J. PATTEN** (son of **Hugh PATTEN** and **Martha Ann MALCOLM**) in 1889. Sidney J. PATTEN was born in 1860 in Canada West. He died on 6 August 1921 in St. George. Carrie and Sidney had one child:

+1410 i. **Anna Rachel PATTEN**.

767. **Mary Jane KITCHEN** was born on 19 May 1843. She died in 1920. She was married to **Charles Franklin BELL** on 9 February 1869. Charles Franklin BELL was born in 1839, and died in 1886. Mary Jane KITCHEN and Charles Franklin BELL had the following children:

+1411 i. **Edward BELL**.
1412 ii. **Frank K. BELL** was born in 1866 and died in 1929.
1413 iii. **Louise BELL** was born in 1868 and died in 1926. She married **Norman BUTLER**.
1414 iv. **Benjamin BELL** was born in 1870 and died in 1941. He married **Alice CRANEY**.
1415 v. **Cyrus BELL** was born in May 1881.
1416 vi. **Aggie BELL** was born in 1872, and died on 26 November 1876.
+1417 vii **Charles BELL**.

1418 viii. **Alice BELL** married **Cyrus GRIFFITH**.
+1419 ix **James BELL**.
+1420 x. **Mary Josephine BELL**.

768. **Eunice Maria KITCHEN** was born on 25 August 1845. She was married to **David HUNTER** on 25 August 1875. Eunice Maria KITCHEN and David HUNTER had the following children:

+1421 i. **James HUNTER** .
1422 ii. **Hallum HUNTER** married **Kathryn BOLEYN**.
1423 iii. **Eva HUNTER** married **Charles HERSEE**.
1424 iv. **Spencer HUNTER** married **Pearl WARDELL**.

770. **Mary Adelaide HOWELL** was born about 1846 in S. Dumfries, Brant County, Ontario. She was married to **John KINNEY** on 8 February 1865 in Brant County. Their children were:

1425 i. **James T. KINNEY** was born on 19 November 1872 and died on 4 May 1962. He married (1) **Larissa NELDA**, who was born on 6 April 1867, and died on 26 December 1923. He married (2) **Ethyl G. HOWELL**, who was born on 29 July 1882 and died on 11 March 1948. He married (3) **Olive SUMMERHAYES**. All are buried in St. George United Cemetery.
1426 ii. **Addie KINNEY** was married twice, to **James MCEWEN**, and to **William KINSEY**.
+1427 iii. **William KINNEY**.
+1428 iv. **Russell KINNEY**.
+1429 v. **Edna KINNEY**.
+1430 vi. **Elma KINNEY**.

771. **James Bird HOWELL** was born on 13 December 1849 in S. Dumfries, Brant County, Ontario. He died on 2 November 1932 in Ontario, and was buried in St. George United Cemetery. James Bird was Warden of Brant County in 1904. James was married to **Rachel E. LAWRASON** on 14 September 1873 in Ontario. Rachel E. LAWRASON was born on 13 November 1852 in S. Dumfries. She died on 17 May 1915, and was buried in St. George United Cemetery. James and Rachel had the following children:

1431 i. **Alice Florence HOWELL** was born on 13 June 1876 in S. Dumfries, and died on 19 January 1960 in Brantford General Hospital. She was buried in St. George United Cemetery. She married **Arthur Elam GREEN**, her second cousin. Arthur was born on 4 April 1869 and died on 4 March 1957. They had no children.
+1432 ii. **Firman Aikman HOWELL**.

+1433	iii.	**William Nelson HOWELL.**
+1434	iv.	**John Roy HOWELL.**

772. **Sarah Jane HOWELL** was born in 1854 in S. Dumfries, Brant County, Ontario. She died in 1923, and was buried in St. George United Cemetery. She married **John Peter WOOD**, who was born in 1851. He died in 1923, and was buried in St. George United Cemetery. Sarah and John had these children:

+1435	i.	**Louis WOOD.**
1436	ii.	**Rachel WOOD.**

775. **Margaret HOWELL** was born on 12 May 1852 in Dumfries, Brant County, Ontario, and died on 28 May 1937 in Hamilton, Ontario. She married **James Henry BUCK** (son of **Lideral Ensign BUCK** and **Margaret SWARTZ)** on 21 September 1875 at St. George, Ontario. James Henry BUCK was born on 20 January 1839 and died on 31 December 1922 in Port Dover, Ontario. They had these children:

+1437	i.	**Lideral William Morley BUCK.**
+1438	ii.	**James Orton BUCK.**

776. **Osborne HOWELL** was born in 1866 in S. Dumfries, Brant County, Ontario. He died on 14 June 1943, and was buried in St. George United Cemetery. He married (1) **Annie MCLEAN** who was born on 21 October 1864. She died on 2 May 1887, and was buried in St. George United Cemetery. Osborne HOWELL and Annie MCLEAN had these children:

+1439	i.	**Orton Stanley HOWELL.**
1440	ii.	**Beaulah HOWELL.**

Osborne married (2) **Jane KEACHIE**. Jane was born in 1870, died in 1965, and was buried in St. George United Cemetery.

779. **Morley A. HOWELL** was born on 8 March 1873 in Ontario. He died on 16 May 1972, and was buried in St. George United Cemetery. He married **Annie Louise BOWLBY**. Their children were:

1441	i.	**Roger HOWELL.**
1442	ii.	**Morgan HOWELL.**
1443	iii.	**Helen HOWELL.**
1444	iv.	**Lucille HOWELL.**
1445	v.	**Rosalie HOWELL.**

780. **James Romain HOWELL** was born about 1849 in S. Dumfries. He married **Elizabeth FONGER**. James and Elizabeth had one child:

1446	i.	**May HOWELL.**

781. **William Waugh HOWELL** was born about 1851 in S. Dumfries. He married **Margaret MCGREGOR**. William Waugh HOWELL and Margaret MCGREGOR had the following children:

1447	i.	**John HOWELL**.
1448	ii.	**Thomas HOWELL**.
1449	iii.	**Beatrice HOWELL**.
1450	iv.	**Phebe HOWELL**.

785. **Herbert Watson HOWELL** was born on 15 August 1860 in S. Dumfries. He died on 14 August 1933, and was buried in St. George United Cemetery. Herbert and his family lived in St. George until 1910 and then went west to Headingly, Manitoba. They settled in Beamsville and were fruit farmers. Herbert married **Ida Jane HOWELL** (daughter of **Philip Stenabaugh HOWELL** and **Mary Jane GREEN**) She was born on 7 September 1862 in S. Dumfries, died on 5 September 1945, and was buried in St. George United Cemetery. Herbert Watson HOWELL and Ida Jane HOWELL had these children:

1451	i.	**Winnifred Kate HOWELL** was born in 1883 in St. George, Brant County, Ontario. She died in February 1966 in St. George, and was buried in St. George United Cemetery. She never married.
1452	ii.	**Charles Edmund HOWELL** was born in 1886 in St. George; he died in December 1947, and was buried in St. George United Cemetery. He was not married.
+1453	iii.	**Thomas Leslie HOWELL**.
+1454	iv.	**Alice Mary HOWELL**.
+1455	v.	**Herbert William HOWELL**.
+1456	vi.	**Jean Alberta HOWELL**.

800. **George W. HOWELL** was born in 1855 in S. Dumfries. He died in 1924, and was buried in St. George United Cemetery. He married **Larissa WOOD**, who was born in 1854. She died in 1912, and was buried in St. George United Cemetery. George and Larissa had the following children:

1457	i.	**Jennie HOWELL** was born in 1870 in Ontario. She died in 1876 in Ontario, and was buried in St. George United Cemetery.
1458	ii.	**Reginald HOWELL** was born in 1884 in Ontario. He died in 1954 and was buried in St. George United Cemetery. He married **Maude UNKNOWN**, who was born in 1886 and died in 1918. She also was buried in St. George United Cemetery.
1459	iii.	**Myrtle HOWELL**.
1460	iv.	**Ethel HOWELL**.

801. **Mary E. HOWELL** was born in 1857 in S. Dumfries. She died in 1937 in Ontario, and was buried in St. George United Cemetery. She married **James ROSEBRUGH**, who was born in 1853. He died in 1931. Mary E. HOWELL and James ROSEBRUGH had the following children:

1461	i.	**Lillian ROSEBRUGH**.
1462	ii.	**Pearl ROSEBRUGH**.
1463	iii.	**Oscar ROSEBRUGH**.
1464	iv.	**Henry ROSEBRUGH**.
1465	v.	**Ernie ROSEBRUGH**.

802. **Harry B. HOWELL** was born in 1863 in Ontario. He married **Lucy KITCHEN**. Harry B. HOWELL and Lucy KITCHEN had the following children:

1466	i.	**Benjamin HOWELL**.
1467	ii.	**Louie HOWELL**.

803. **Sydney HOWELL** was born in 1866 in Ontario. He married **Lottie WOOD**. They had a daughter:

1468	i.	**Cora HOWELL**.

805. **Charles William CASSADA** was born in 1849 in Oakland Township, Ontario. He died on 5 October 1918 in Ayr, and was buried in Ayr Cemetery, N. Dumfries, Waterloo County, Ontario. He married **Annie HUNTER**. Charles William CASSADA and Annie HUNTER had the following children:

1469	i.	**Sara CASSADA**.
1470	ii.	**Florence CASSADA** married **Cameron RUPERT**.
1471	iii.	**Hunter CASSADA**.
1472	iv.	**Ernest CASSADA**.
1473	v.	**Olive CASSADA** married **Robert MCARTHUR**.
1474	vi.	**William Roy CASSADA** was born in 1885. He died in 1950.
1475	vii.	**Annie Edna CASSADA** was born on 23 September 1903, and died on 26 October 1906 in Ayr, Ontario.

806. **Aurilla CASSADA** was born on 5 May 1852 in Oakland Township, Brant County, Ontario. She died on 18 January 1929 in Smiths Falls, Lanark County, Ontario. Aurilla reportedly contracted the flu during a visit to her daughter in Smiths Falls in 1929, which caused her death. She married **John PETRIE** (son of **John PETRIE** and **Phoebe GLASS**) on 31 December 1873 in Blenheim Township, Ontario. John PETRIE was born on 2 July 1841 in Stoney Creek, Wentworth County, Ontario. He died on 8 October 1920 in S. Dumfries, Brant County, Ontario. He was buried in Ayr Cemetery, N. Dumfries, Waterloo County, Ontario. John operated Hillcrest, a successful 100 acre farm. Their children were:

1476	i.	**Jane (Jenny) PETRIE** was born on 12 September 1874

in South Dumfries, and died on 21 November 1930 in Ayr, Ontario.

1477 ii. **John Alexander PETRIE** was born on 28 April 1876 in S. Dumfries. He died on 18 October 1951 in Montreal, Quebec. John was a minister, and lived in Ayr. He married **Janet BROWN**.

1478 iii. **A. Daniel C. PETRIE** was born on 5 October 1878 in S. Dumfries. He died there in 1913 and was buried in Ayr Cemetery. He married **Mary FALLS**.

1479 iv. **Mary Helen "Nellie" PETRIE** was born on 11 June 1882 in S. Dumfries. She married **Ivan FOLSETTER**, a storekeeper in S. Dumfries. He died in 1913 of tuberculosis, and was buried in Ayr Cemetery.

+1480 v. **Margaret PETRIE**.

820. **Hettie HOWELL** was born about 1858. She died on 17 February 1878, and was buried in Jerseyville Cemetery. She married the **Rev. William GALBRAITH**. They had one child:

1481 i. **Clara L. H. GALBRAITH** was born about 1876, died on 2 July 1887, and was buried in Jerseyville Cemetery.

829. **Henry Spencer HOWELL** was born on 5 July 1857. He was married to **Frances Annie DODD** on 18 October 1883 in Australia. He was a world traveler, and wrote articles and brochures for magazines, and a travel book which was published in 1892.[212] Henry and Frances Annie were buried in Trinity Anglican Cemetery, North Dumfries, Waterloo County, Ontario. They had one child:

1482 i. **Laurence Clifford HOWELL** was born on 26 March 1885.

831 **Samuel DEAN** was born on 4 June 1831 in Hamilton, Wentworth County, Ontario. He married **Emma Jane NORVILL** was born on 12 July 1843 in Passaic, NJ. They had these children:

+1483 i. **George Samuel DEAN**

+1484 ii. **David Lorenzo DEAN**.

+1485 iii. **James Riley DEAN**.

1486 iv. **Emma Jane DEAN** was born on 14 February 1863 in North Ogden, Utah.

1487 v. **Rachel Ann DEAN** was born on 27 January 1865 in

---

[212]Henry J. Morgan, ed.; The Canadian Men and Women of the Time; (Toronto:W. Briggs; 1898) p. 479.

North Ogden.

1488 vi. **John Andrew DEAN** was born on 10 January 1867 in North Ogden.

1489 vii. **Mary Theresa DEAN** was born on 20 August 1868 in North Ogden. Her husband, **W. D. OLDEN**, was born in 1864 in North Ogden.

1490 viii. **Rose Elvina DEAN** was born on 11 December 1870 in North Ogden.

+1491 ix. **Martha Matilda DEAN**.

1492 x. **Charles Albert DEAN** was born on 13 October 1875 in North Ogden.

834. **Andrew DEAN** was born about 1836 in Hamilton, Wentworth, Ontario. He married **Caroline CORNEY** who was born about 1841 in Burlington Beach, Wentworth County. Their children were:

1493 i. **Harriet E. DEAN** was born about 1859 in Saltfleet, Wentworth County.

1494 ii. **Barbara E. DEAN** was born about 1860 in Saltfleet.

839. **Clarisa A. DEAN** was born on 19 June 1838 in Saltfleet. She married **John STEWART** who was born about 1836 in Saltfleet. Clarisa A. DEAN and John STEWART had the following children:

1495 i. **Levi STEWART** was born about 1860 in Saltfleet.

1496 ii. **Mariett STEWART** was born about 1862 in Saltfleet.

1497 iii. **Martha M. STEWART** was born about 1864 in Saltfleet.

1498 iv. **Ella J. STEWART** was born about 1866 in Saltfleet.

1499 v. **Clarisa A. STEWART** was born about 1869 in Saltfleet.

1500 vi. **Thomas STEWART** was born about 1871 in Saltfleet.

1501 vii. **May STEWART** was born about 1873 in Saltfleet.

1502 viii. **Georgina STEWART** was born about 1875 in Saltfleet.

1503 ix. **Stanley STEWART** was born about 1877 in Saltfleet.

1504 x. **John STEWART** was born about 1879 in Saltfleet.

840. **Margaret E. DEAN** was born on 4 April 1841 in Saltfleet. She married **Alexander GLOVER** who was born about 1842 in Saltfleet. Their children were:

1505 i. **Martha GLOVER** was born in 1868 in Grimsby, Lincoln County, Ontario.

1506 ii. **Maude GLOVER** was born in 1870 in Grimsby.

1507 iii. **Sarah GLOVER** was born in 1872 in Grimsby.

1508 iv. **Alexander GLOVER** was born in 1874 in Grimsby.

1509 v. **Herbert Dean GLOVER** was born in 1876 in Grimsby.

843. **Martha Florilla DEAN** was born on 28 March 1851 in Saltfleet. She married **Emerson GAGE** who was born in 1847 in Saltfleet. Martha and Emerson GAGE had the following children:

1510 i. **Lily GAGE** was born in 1872 in Saltfleet, Wentworth County, Ontario.
1511 ii. **Ella GAGE** was born in 1875 in Saltfleet.

844. **Anson O. DEAN** was born on 22 November 1854 in Saltfleet. His wife, **Priscilla SHOULDICE**, was born on 16 June 1854 in Nelson Twp., Halton County, Ontario. Their children were:

1512 i. **Gertrude DEAN** was born in 1878 in Nelson Twp., Halton County, Ontario.
1513 ii. **George W. DEAN** was born in 1880 in Wentworth County, Ontario.

845. **Levi Lewis DEAN** was born about 1861 in Saltfleet. His wife, **Sarah BURT**, was born in 1865 in Saltfleet. Levi and Sarah had the following children:

1514 i. **Earle DEAN** was born in 1887 in Saltfleet.
1515 ii. **Ray DEAN** was born in 1889 in Saltfleet.
1516 iii. **Percy DEAN** was born in 1891 in Saltfleet.

846. **Mary Elizabeth BIGGAR** was born about 1843 in Saltfleet. Her husband, **Ezra CHRYSLER**, was born about 1838 in Ontario. Mary Elizabeth BIGGAR and Ezra CHRYSLER had children:

1517 i. **Andrew CHRYSLER** was born in 1868 in Saltfleet.
1418 ii. **Douglas E. CHRYSLER** was born in 1870 in Saltfleet.
1519 iii. **Frederick CHRYSLER** was born in 1871 in S. Dumfries.
1520 iv. **Harry CHRYSLER** was born about 1874 in S. Dumfries.
1521 v. **Louis CHRYSLER** was born about 1876 in S. Dumfries.
1522 vi. **Louise CHRYSLER** was born about 1876 in S. Dumfries.
1523 vii. **Russell CHRYSLER** was born about 1878 in S. Dumfries.
1524 viii. **Albert CHRYSLER** was born about 1880 in S. Dumfries.

847. **Martha Matilda BIGGAR** was born on 7 March 1845 in Saltfleet. Her husband, **Elijah B. SMITH**, was born on 23 January 1845 in Saltfleet. Martha and Elijah B. SMITH had the following children:

1525 i. **Frank SMITH** was born about 1871 in Saltfleet.

1526 ii. **Claude SMITH** was born about 1873 in Saltfleet.

848. **Joseph W. BIGGAR** was born about 1847 in Saltfleet. He married **Marrilla M. SMITH** who was born on 21 January 1848 in Saltfleet. Joseph W. BIGGAR and Marrilla M. SMITH had one child:

1527 i. **Nora BIGGAR**.

849. **Robert Wellington BIGGAR** was born about 1849 in Saltfleet. His wife, **Ida UNKNOWN**, was born in 1851 in Saltfleet. Robert Wellington BIGGAR and Ida UNKNOWN had the following children:

1528 i. **William BIGGAR** was born about 1875 in Saltfleet.
1529 ii. **Emerson BIGGAR** was born about 1877 in Saltfleet.

850. **Emerson Bristol BIGGAR** was born about 1853 in Saltfleet. His wife, **Augusta UNKNOWN** was born in 1857 in Saltfleet. Emerson and Augusta had the following children:

1530 i. **Helen BIGGAR** was born about 1879 in Saltfleet.
1531 ii. **Ruth BIGGAR** was born about 1881 in Saltfleet.

851. **Selina A. BIGGAR** was born about 1855 in Saltfleet. Her husband, **Lewis L. HAGAR**, was born about 1853 in North Grimsby, Lincoln County, Ontario. Selina and Lewis L. HAGAR had these children:

1532 i. **Ethel Louise HAGAR** was born on 17 February 1878 in Ontario.
1533 ii. **Charles Biggar HAGAR** was born on 8 August 1880 in Ontario.
1534 iii. **Roy Hamilton HAGAR** was born on 5 June 1883 in Ontario.

852. **Walter Elgin BIGGAR** was born on 21 September 1857 in Saltfleet. He married **Cynthia VANWAGNER** who was born in 1857 in Saltfleet. Walter and Cynthia had the following children:

1535 i. **Walter Elgin BIGGAR** was born on 9 October 1879 in Saltfleet.
1536 ii. **George BIGGAR** was born in 1881 in Saltfleet.
1537 iii. **Laura BIGGAR** was born in 1883 in Saltfleet.
1538 iv. **Harry Burton BIGGAR** was born in 1885 in Saltfleet.
1539 v. **Nellie BIGGAR** was born in 1887 in Saltfleet.
1540 vi. **Elizabeth BIGGAR** was born in 1889 in Saltfleet.
1541 vii. **Jennie BIGGAR** was born in 1902 in Saltfleet.

853. **Sanford Dennis BIGGAR** was born about 1862 in Saltfleet. He married **Charlotte ARMSTRONG**, who was born in 1866 in Saltfleet. Sanford and Charlotte had the following children:

1542 i. **Howard BIGGAR** was born in 1888 in Saltfleet.
1543 ii. **Ralph BIGGAR** was born in 1890 in Saltfleet.
1544 iii. **Warren BIGGAR** was born in 1892 in Saltfleet.
1545 iv. **Sanford BIGGAR** was born in 1894 in Saltfleet.
1546 v. **Lena BIGGAR** was born in 1896 in Saltfleet.
1547 vi. **Annie BIGGAR** was born in 1898 in Saltfleet.

854. **Milton Enos BIGGAR** was born about 1865 in Saltfleet. He married **Ada BEDDELL** who was born in 1869 in Saltfleet. Milton Enos BIGGAR and Ada BEDDELL had the following children:

1548 i. **Archibald BIGGAR** was born in 1891 in Saltfleet.
1549 ii. **Edith BIGGAR** was born in 1893 in Saltfleet.
1550 iii. **Pearl BIGGAR** was born in 1895 in Saltfleet.
1551 iv. **Clifford BIGGAR** was born in 1897 in Saltfleet.

855. **Edwin STEELE** was born on 28 July 1840 in Paris, Brant County, Ontario. He married **Sarah WHITE** who died in 1921. Edwin STEELE and Sarah WHITE had the following children:

+1552 i. **Mary STEELE**.
+1553 ii. **Albert Edwin STEELE**.

856. **Lydia STEELE** married **Unknown DEPUE**. Lydia and Unknown DEPUE had these children:

1554 i. **Herbert DEPUE**.
1555 ii. **George DEPUE**.
1556 iii. **Edwin DEPUE**.

857. **Jennie STEELE** married **Unknown MILLYARD**. Their children were:

1557 i. **Edwin MILLYARD**.
1558 ii. **William MILLYARD**.

862. **Alice HOWELL** was born on 29 November 1846 in S. Dumfries, Brant County, Ontario. She died on 25 March 1882 in Kintore, Oxford County, Ontario, and was buried in St. George United Cemetery. She married **Rev. Peter W. JONES**. Alice HOWELL and Rev. Peter W. JONES had one child:

1559 i. **Frank JONES** died at the age of nine months.

866. **Mary Ellen HOWELL** was born on 7 June 1856 in S. Dumfries. She died there on 1 May 1939, and was buried in St. George United Cemetery. Mary Ellen

married **John WALLEY**. John WALLEY was born in 1855 in England. He died on 17 July 1942, and was buried in St. George United Cemetery. Mary Ellen HOWELL and John WALLEY had the following children:

+1560 i. **Ernest Albert WALLEY**.
+1561 ii. **Ella May WALLEY**.
+1562 iii. **Alice Evelyn WALLEY**.

867. **Herbert Levi HOWELL** was born on 10 July 1859 in S. Dumfries, died there on 26 December 1941, and was buried in St. George United Cemetery. His wife, **Sarah Jane ROBB**, was born in Troy, Ontario, and died on 5 November 1953 in S. Dumfries. She was buried in St. George United Cemetery. Herbert Levi HOWELL and Sarah Jane ROBB had the following children:

+1563 i. **Ernest Wellesley HOWELL**.
+1564 ii. **Herbert Robb HOWELL**.
+1565 iii. **Ivah HOWELL**.
+1566 iv. **Philip Samuel HOWELL**.

868. **Ida Jane HOWELL** married **Herbert Watson HOWELL**, a cousin. Please refer to # 781, Herbert Watson HOWELL, for details.

869. **Catherine Alberta HOWELL** was born on 11 March 1869 in S. Dumfries, where she died on 4 March 1951. She was married to **Herbert GERMAN** (son of **William GERMAN** and **Phoebe Eliza CASSADA**) on 10 June 1903. Herbert GERMAN was born on 5 December 1869 in S. Dumfries; he died on 11 November 1968 in Brantford, Brant County, Ontario. Their children were:

+1567 i. **Evelyn Mabel GERMAN.**
+1568 ii. **Cecil Bruce GERMAN**.
+1569 iii. **Ethel Mildred GERMAN**.
+1570 iv. **Flossie May GERMAN**.

873. **Levi HOWELL** married **Mary HEIGHT**. Both were buried in Norwich Village Cemetery, Norwich Twp., Oxford County, Ontario. Levi HOWELL and Mary HEIGHT had the following children:

1571 i. **Ethel HOWELL** married **Roy MCKENZIE**.
1572 ii. **Ada HOWELL** married **W. MORLAY**.

881. **Bertha C. HOWELL** was born in 1877. She died in 1952. She was buried in Princeton Cemetery, Blenheim Twp., Oxford County, Ontario. Her husband, **Frederick BROOKS** was born in 1867. He died in 1941, and was buried in Princeton Cemetery. Bertha and Frederick BROOKS had one child:

1573 i. **Alma BROOKS** was born about 1905, died on 6 August 1907, and was buried in Princeton Cemetery.

882. **John GREEN** was born on 21 March 1860. He was married to **Charity Benjamina GULLEN** on 17 September 1880 in S. Dumfries, Brant County, Ontario. Charity Benjamina GULLEN was born on 22 March 1858 in Quebec City, Quebec, Canada. John and Charity had children:

+1574 i. **Herbert Richard GREEN**.
1575 ii. **Reginald GREEN** died about 1947 in California.

887. **Elsie Alice HOWELL** was born on 31 January 1837 in Onondaga Twp., Brant County, Ontario. She died on 19 December 1924 in Brantford Twp., Brant County. She was married to **William Robert SHAVER** (son of **Philip SHAVER** and **Margaret SMITH**) on 18 October 1854. William Robert SHAVER was born on 1 February 1834 in Ancaster Twp., Wentworth County. He died on 31 October 1895 in Cayuga County, Ontario. Elsie and William Robert SHAVER had these children:

1576 i. **Cyrus Hilliard SHAVER** was born on 26 July 1856 in Cayuga County, and died on 30 March 1912. He was married to **Sarah Martha STEWART** in August 1880.
1577 ii. **Rosella SHAVER** was born on 18 April 1858 in Cayuga County, and married **James Alexander LONE** on 1 July 1876.
1578 iii. **Robert Howard SHAVER** was born on 23 November 1861 in Cayuga County, and died in October 1922. He married **Margaret BOYER**.
1579 iv. **William Arthur SHAVER** was born on 5 August 1861 in Cayuga County, and died on 9 January 1933 in Killarney, Manitoba. He married **Margaret JOHNSON** on 8 April 1885.
1580 v. **Richard Truman SHAVER** was born on 7 December 1862 in Cayuga County, and died about 1942. He married (1) **Margaret E. WATERS** on 8 February 1892. He married (2) **Ann MILLER**.
+1581 vi. **John Wesley SHAVER**.
1582 vii. **Pheobe Violette SHAVER** was born on 31 October 1866 in Cayuga County, Ontario, where she died on 18 November 1866.
1583 viii. **Elsie Catherine SHAVER** was born on 30 September 1868 in Cayuga County, and died there on 29 October 1868.
1584 ix. **Ortan Calvin SHAVER** was born on 28 September 1869 in Cayuga County.
1585 x. **Clarissa Edith SHAVER** was born on 25 August 1873 in Cayuga County. She married **James ENBANK**.
1586 xi. **Fred Trillar SHAVER** was born on 17 December 1874 in Cayuga County. He married **Annie WARD**.
1587 xii. **Catherine Mabel SHAVER** was born on 27 January

1877 in Cayuga County. She married **Ezra DREHMER**.

1588 xiii. **George Henry SHAVER** was born on 9 June 1880 in Cayuga County. He married **Mary HIRON**.

888. **Triller HOWELL** was born on 1 January 1839 in Jerseyville. He died on 16 July 1922, and was buried in Mount Hope Cemetery, Brant County, Ontario. They lived at 314 Dalhousie Street in Brantford Township, Brant County, Ontario. Triller married **Angeline DERBYSHIRE**, who was born in 1843. She died on 7 July 1920, and was buried in Mount Hope Cemetery. Their children were:

1589 i. **Effie Gertrude HOWELL** was born on 14 June 1865 in Ancaster Twp. She died on 13 May 1953, and was buried in Mount Hope Cemetery. She married **Davis Francis ROY** on 19 September 1879.

1590 ii. **Emma Jane HOWELL** was born in 1866 in Brantford Twp.

1591 iii. **Lucy HOWELL** was born in 1868 in Brantford Twp. She died and was buried in Mount Hope Cemetery.

1592 iv. **Laura HOWELL** was born in 1871 in Brantford Twp.

1594 v. **Harry HOWELL** was born on 17 April 1878 in Brantford Twp. He committed suicide on 9 January 1913, and was buried in Mount Hope Cemetery. He married **Helen MARR** (daughter of **William MARR** and **Janet THOMSON**) in November 1911 in Brantford Twp. Helen was born on 11 October 1877 in Streetville, Ontario, and died on 31 December 1911 of peritonitis. She was buried in Mount Hope Cemetery.

892. **Mary HOWELL** was born about 1847 in Ancaster Twp. She died there in 1918. She was married to **William H. SHAVER** on 18 August 1864. William H. SHAVER was born in 1842 in Ancaster Twp., and died there in 1921. Mary HOWELL and William H. SHAVER had the following children:

1594 i. **Alfonzo Desmond SHAVER** was born on 26 August 1866, in Ancaster Township, where he died on 26 July 1869.

1595 ii. **Bertha "Bertie" SHAVER** was born on 5 August 1868 in Ancaster Twp.,where she died on 13 November 1938.

1596 iii. **Harry SHAVER**.

1597 iv. **Frederick SHAVER**.

1598 v. **Minnie SHAVER** was born on 22 April 1877 in Ancaster Twp., and died on August 1877.

1599 vi. **Edith May SHAVER**.

1600 vii. **Agnes G. SHAVER**.

900. **Cordelia M. HOWELL** was born on 28 August 1854 in Brantford Twp., and died there on 17 March 1932. She was buried in Paris Cemetery, Paris, Brant County, Ontario. She was married to **Marshall GREEN**, who was born on 7 February 1863 in S. Dumfries, Brant County, Ontario. He died on 15 September 1931 in Paris, Brant County, Ontario, and was buried in Paris Cemetery. They had a child:

+1601 i. **Harriet Howell GREEN**.

905. **Ada Matilda HOWELL** was born about 1854. She married **John BROWN**. Their children were:

+1602 i. **Rita BROWN**.
1603 ii. **Adele BROWN**.
1604 iii. **George BROWN**.

912. **Elwood Usher HOWELL** was born on 24 May 1859. He died on 26 March 1945, and was buried in Jerseyville Cemetery. He married **Anna Elizabeth TEMPLER** (daughter of **John TEMPLER** and **Priscilla VANSICKLE**). Anna was born on 9 November 1860. She died on 10 August 1922, and was buried in Jerseyville Cemetery. Elwood and Anna had the following children:

1605 i. **Wilfred T. HOWELL** was born in 1885 and died in 1950. He married **Mary HAMMILL**.
1606 ii. **George Nelson HOWELL** was born in April 1887; he died on 23 September 1887 in Ancaster Twp., and was buried in Jerseyville Cemetery.
+1607 iii. **J. Stanley HOWELL**.

913. **Catherine Burdge MCCAY** was born in 1845 in Ontario. She married **John M. CRAMER**. Catherine Burdge MCCAY and John M. CRAMER had one child:

+1608 i. Harry **Milton CRAMER**.

929. **Moses Hazen HOWELL** was born about 1855 in Jerseyville. He was married to **Susan Melinda LINEN** in North Carolina. Moses Hazen HOWELL and Susan Melinda LINEN had one child:

+1609 i. **Jose Corwin HOWELL**.

942. **Obed Ernest HOWELL** was born on 4 May 1870 in Buffalo, Erie County, New York. He was born at 224 6th Street, Buffalo, New York. He was married to **Antoinette Evelyn DULL** (daughter of **Cornelius DULL** and **Elizabeth Ann RICE**). Antoinette Evelyn DULL was born on 13 June 1870 in Swoopes, Augusta County, VA. Obed and Antoinette had these children:

1610 i. **Minnie Louise HOWELL** was born on 27 April 1895

in Charleston, WV.

1611 ii. **Francis Rice HOWELL** was born on 3 September 1903 in Charleston, WV.

949. **Clarissa Bell BURNHAM** was born in 1860, and died in 1932. Her husband, **Bannon LIPSIT**, was born in 1859, and died in January 1945. Clarissa and Bannon LIPSIT had the following children:

1612 i. **George LIPSIT** was born in 1883. He died on 20 June 1943.

1613 ii. **Ethel LIPSIT** was born in 1884. She died on 15 January 1944.

1614 iii. **Ernest A. LIPSIT** was born in 1887, and died on 5 September 1949 in Mt. Brydges, Caradoc Twp., Middlesex County.

950. **Minnie GULLEN** was born on 13 October 1867, and died in June 1899. She married **William LAUGHTON** He was born on 6 August 1855, and died in October 1927. Their children were:

1615 i. **Luella LAUGHTON**.

1616 ii. **Archie LAUGHTON** died in 1911.

+1617 iii. **Samuel LAUGHTON**.

1618 iv. **Robert LAUGHTON** was born in August 1890.

952. **Ella GULLEN** was born on 14 November 1870, and died on 12 December 1954 in London, Ontario. She married **John NORTON**. He was born on 14 September 1870, and died on 10 January 1945 in London, Ontario. Ella GULLEN and John NORTON had the following children:

1619 i. **Verna May NORTON** was born on 27 June 1891, and died on 28 March 1968.

1620 ii. **Bessie NORTON** was born on 18 December 1894, and died on 24 September 1951 in London, Ontario.

1621 iii. **Clarence Leslie NORTON** was born on 28 April 1898.

1622 iv. **Ethal Wilma NORTON** was born on 18 August 1901.

+1623 v. **William Albert NORTON**.

963. **Marion Elizabeth HOWELL** was born in 1862 on Manitoulin Island. She died in 1944. She married **Simon McQuarrie FRASER**. He was born in 1854, and died in 1936. They had a child:

+1624 i. **Donald Scott FRASER**.

964. **Melvin HOWELL** was born in 1876; he died in 1950, and was buried in Maitland Cemetery, Goderich Twp., Ontario. His wife, **Mary Ellen CROZIER**, was born in 1872. She died in 1964, and was buried in Maitland Cemetery. Melvin and Mary Ellen had the following children:

1625 i. **Everett H. HOWELL** was born in 1906, and died in 1909.
1626 ii. **E. Melva HOWELL** was born in 1915, and died in 1920.
1627 iii. **Robert W. HOWELL** was born in 1916, and died in 1920.

965. **Harold HOWELL** was born in 1880. He died in 1944. He married, but his wife's name is **UNKNOWN**. Harold HOWELL and UNKNOWN had one child:

1628 i. **Helen HOWELL.**

968. **Laura Grace HOWELL** was born on 13 August 1880 in Onondaga Twp., Brant County, Ontario, and died on 4 April 1965 in Detroit, Wayne County, Michigan. She married (1) **Horace Willoughby MITCHELL**, who was born on 28 November 1876 in London, Ontario, and died on 31 March 1918 in Dearborn, Wayne County. Laura and Horace MITCHELL had the following children:[213]

1629 i. **Hubert (Hugh) MITCHELL** was born in 1903, and died in 1988 in Silver Springs, Maryland.
+1630 ii. **Donald Horace MITCHELL.**
1631 iii. **Bryan MITCHELL** was born in 1908. He moved west from Detroit in the 1920's, and lost contact with his family after that date.

Horace deserted this family, and Helen was married (2) to **Hal ORCUTT** in 1922 in Detroit. Hal ORCUTT died in 1958 in Detroit.

---

[213]Information on this family was contributed by Douglas A. Mitchell, 8846 Whitlock, Dearborn MI 48129.

ISAAC ALLEN HOWELL
1839 - about 1920

SEVENTH GENERATION

991. **Robert M. WEST** was born on 17 February 1889 in Blairstown, Warren County, NJ. He died in January 1971 in Phillipsburg, Warren County, NJ, and was buried in Moravian Cemetery, Hope, NJ. He was a farmer. His wife's name is **UNKNOWN**. Robert and his wife had these children:

1632 i. **Almer WEST**.
1633 ii. **Unknown female WEST** married **Ralph ALBERTSON**.

999. **Charles Milton HOWELL** was born on 22 March 1875 in Warren County, New Jersey. He died on 22 June 1959, and was buried in S. Easton Cemetery, Easton, Northampton County, Pennsylvania. Ephraim's obituary says that Charles, known as Milton, was living in Forks Twp., PA. In 1920, when his mother died, he lived in Easton, PA. He was married to **Sarah Minerva RICE** on 15 April 1896. Sarah Minerva RICE was born on 22 April 1875. She died on 19 December 1949, and was buried in S. Easton Cemetery. Charles Milton HOWELL and Sarah Minerva RICE had the following children:

+1634 i. **Robert Earl HOWELL**.
+1635 ii. **Hazel HOWELL**.
1636 iii. **Claire HOWELL** married **Fred WELLER**.
1637 iv. **Meryl HOWELL** was born in 1908, and died in 1983. She was buried in Fairmount Cemetery, Phillipsburg, Warren County, NJ. She married **Robert BABINGTON**, who was born in 1913 and died in 1986.

1000. **John Manning HOWELL** was born on 29 April 1878 in Warren County, New Jersey. He married **Cora DUCKWORTH** on 4 July 1900. He died on 1 March 1947, and was buried in Belvidere Cemetery, Belvidere, Warren County. John was living in Roxburg NJ when Ephraim died in 1936. Cora DUCKWORTH was born in 1882. She died on 19 December 1963 in Oxford, Warren County, and was buried in Belvidere Cemetery. Their children were:

1638 i. **Flossie HOWELL** was born on 5 February 1901. She died on 8 February 1958. She married **William HESS** (son of **John HESS** and **Anna BEERS**) on 22 September 1917. In 1933, they lived in Raubsville, Pennsylvania.
+1639 ii. **Clark C. HOWELL**.
1640 iii. **Grace HOWELL** was married on 2 August 1912 to **Marcus BEERS**.

1001. **Ephriam Clarke HOWELL** was born on 7 December 1879 in Polkville, Warren County, NJ. He died on 17 January 1936 in Phillipsburg, Warren County, NJ, and was buried in Lower Harmony Cemetery, Harmony, NJ.[214] Ephraim lived in Harmony in 1920, when his mother died. He was employed at Ingersoll Rand Company. He was married (1) to **Belle SWAYZE** in 1901. They had these children:

1641 i. **Mildred H. HOWELL** was born on 9 May 1902, and died on 22 October 1904 in Harmony, Warren County, and was buried in Lower Harmony Cemetery. Her obituary reads: "Mildred, daughter of Mr. and Mrs. Ephraim C. Howell, died at the home of her parents last week from morphine poisoning. The child's aunt laid several morphine pills within reach, and she thought they were candy and ate them. She died 15 minutes later. Her age was two years, five months and thirteen days. The funeral took place Monday afternoon interment in the Methodist cemetery at Harmony. The bereaved parents thank friends and neighbors for sympathy and assistance."[215]

Ephriam was married (2) to **Carrie Belle KINNAMAN** (daughter of **James KINNAMAN** and **Eva KRIES**) on 14 October 1919 in Washington, Warren County, NJ. Carrie Belle KINNAMAN was born on 21 September 1904 in Foul Rift, NJ. She died on 10 August 1969 in Trenton, Mercer County, NJ, and was buried in Lower Harmony Cemetery. In her early twenties, Carrie suffered a mental breakdown, and she was confined to a mental hospital in Trenton, NJ, where she remained for the rest of her life. She didn't recognize her children when they visited. Ephriam and Carrie Belle had these children:

+1642 i. **Willard Janson HOWELL.**
+1643 ii. **Wilmer Ephriam HOWELL.**
+1644 iii. **Helen Mae HOWELL.**
+1645 iv. **Stanley Robert HOWELL.**

1002. **Obadiah Titman HOWELL** was born on 1 October 1882 in Polkville, Warren County, NJ. He died on 25 October 1961 in Phillipsburg, Warren County, NJ, and was buried in Lower Harmony Cemetery. He was a farmer. When his mother died in 1920, Obadiah was living in Harmony, NJ. In 1936, when Ephraim died, Obadiah was living in Stewartsville, NJ. Obadiah was married to **Edith ENGLER** on 17 June 1908. Edith ENGLER was born on 7 December 1886. She

---

[214]Obituary, <u>Washington (NJ) Star,</u> 23 January 1936.
[215]Obituary, <u>Washington (NJ) Star</u>, 27 October 1904.

died on 9 August 1958, and was buried in Lower Harmony Cemetery. Obadiah Titman HOWELL and Edith ENGLER had the following children:

1646 i. **Martin Engler HOWELL** was born on 7 April 1909 and died on 6 March 1980. He was buried in Lower Harmony Cemetery. He married **Quinta C. STANTON**, who was born on 24 June 1919.

+1647 ii. **John Obadiah HOWELL.**

1003. **Robert Carter HOWELL** was born on 11 October 1885 in Warren County, NJ. He died on 23 October 1980, and was buried in Pompton Lakes Cemetery, Pompton Lakes, Passaic County, NJ. In 1920, he lived in Linden, NJ, and in 1936, when Ephraim died, Robert was living in Pompton Lakes, NJ. He was married to **Ethel SCHIFFERT** on 2 February 1912. Ethel SCHIFFERT was born on 6 September 1887. She died on 2 January 1939. Their children were:

+1648 i. **Clayton HOWELL.**
+1649 ii. **Ette HOWELL.**
+1650 iii. **Marion HOWELL.**
+1651 iv. **Robert HOWELL.**

1004. **William V. HOWELL** was born on 7 June 1869; he died in 1949, and was buried in Fairview Cemetery, Pen Argyl, Northampton County, PA. He married **Hattie BRUGH** who was born in 1871. She died in 1923, and was buried in Fairview Cemetery. William and Hattie had these children:

+1652 i. **Clarence M. HOWELL.**
+1653 ii. **William L. HOWELL.**

1005. **Leslie A. HOWELL** was born on 26 September 1873; he died in 1927, and was buried in Fairview Cemetery, Pen Argyl, Northampton County, PA. He was a railroad conductor. He was married to **Mary J. SANDERS** on 19 March 1898. Mary J. SANDERS was born in 1881, died in 1941, and was buried in Fairview Cemetery. Leslie and Mary had the following children:

1654 i. **Anna HOWELL** married **Ralph ACKERMAN**.
1655 ii. **Marion HOWELL** married **William HUGHES**.

1006. **John E. EILENBERGER** was born on 6 July 1863 in Portland, Northampton County, PA. He died on 19 June 1931 in Weehawken, Hudson County, NJ, and was buried in Machpelah Cemetery, N. Bergen, Bergen County, NJ. His marriage return states he was a "segar" maker.[216] He was married to **Louisa MEYERS** (daughter of **Jacob MEYERS** and **Elisab. ROEDER**) on 22 March 1884 in New York, NY. Louisa was born on 16 November 1865 in New

[216] Marriage license return for John Eilenberger and Louisa Meyers, #3021, Bureau of Vital Statistics, City of New York, NY.

York City, NY. She died on 6 July 1919 in Bronx, New York, and was buried in Lutheran Cemetery, Middle Village, NY. Their children were:

+1656 i. **Louis Eilenberger HOWELL.**
+1657 ii. **Emma EILENBERGER.**
+1658 iii. **John E. EILENBERGER.**
+1659 iv. **Louisa "Minnie" EILENBERGER.**
1660 v. **Lizzie EILENBERGER** was born on 9 September 1895. She died on 10 October 1912, and was buried in Lutheran Cemetery, Middle Village, NY.
+1661 vi. **Edward Osmund EILENBERGER.**
1662 vii. **William EILENBERGER.**
1663 viii. **Grace EILENBERGER.**

1007. **Osmond Perle Eilenberger HOWELL** was born on 17 October 1867 in Warren County, NJ. He died on 27 December 1926, of wood alcohol poisoning. He had adopted the last name HOWELL. Osmond married (1) **Emma GREENFELDER**, who was born in June 1866 in Germany. She died on 14 June 1900 in Manhattan, New York City, NY. Two of their children, born prematurely, died and were buried with their grandmother. Osmond and Emma had one surviving child:

1664 i. **Florence Bertha EILENBERGER** was born in January 1888, and died on 30 November 1937 in New York City, NY.

Osmond married (2) **Anna SHEARER**. She was born on 7 January 1881 in Scotland. She died on 5 June 1952, and was buried in Cypress Hills Cemetery, Brooklyn, New York. Their children were:

1665 i. **Elma Virginia HOWELL** was born on 12 February 1902, and died on 5 August 1902.
+1666 ii. **Janet Olive HOWELL.**
+1667 iii. **Milton Howard HOWELL.**
+1668 iv. **Euphemia Perle HOWELL.**
+1669 v. **Ruth Clarice HOWELL.**
+1670 vi. **Mildred HOWELL.**
1671 vii. **Osmond Jesse HOWELL** was born on 26 November 1913. He married **Peggy AYRES.**
+1672 viii. **Marguerita Amelia HOWELL.**
1673 ix. **Albert William HOWELL** was born on 13 November 1917. He died on 4 January 1937, of Hodgkins disease.

1008. **James Prall Eilenberger HOWELL** was born on 28 July 1869 in Hope, Warren County, NJ. He died on 10 February 1949 in Brooklyn, Kings County, New York. James also adopted the last name HOWELL, in 1918, because his import business was not doing well under a German name. He was married to

Dora POPP. Dora POPP was born on 30 June 1872 in Melrose, NY, and died on 9 February 1961 in Oceanside, NY. James Prall Eilenberger HOWELL and Dora POPP had the following children:

1674 i. **Elizabeth "Lizzie" HOWELL** was born on 31 March 1892. She died on 13 December 1968 in Long Island. She married **William SWAGER**, who was born on 29 December 1897. They were caterers, and entertainers, and reportedly once catered a party for Lucky Luciano.

1675 ii. **Kathryn HOWELL** was born on 15 March 1894 in New York City. She died in Bethpage, NY on 2 January 1977. She married **Harry WALTON** on 10 July 1921. He was born on 26 May 1883 and died on 14 November 1954 in Bethpage.

+1676 iii. **Martha Jesse HOWELL**.

+1677 iv. **Robert Marshall HOWELL**.

1678 v. **Louisa Princess HOWELL** was born on 13 September 1905, and died on 22 March 1967. She married **Frank RULAND**, who was born on 22 December 1907 and died in 1986.

1679 vi. **Flora HOWELL** was born on 7 January 1908 in Bayonne, NY. She married **Edward PRESCOTT**.

1680 vii. **Howard Halley HOWELL** was born on 18 May 1910. He died on 6 August 1966. He married **Lillian UNKNOWN**, who was born on 17 February 1908.

1009. **Elizabeth EILENBERGER** married **Julius SPECHT**. Their children were:

1681 i. **Julius SPECHT**.

1682 ii. **Oliver SPECHT**.

1683 iii. **Mabel SPECHT**.

1019. **Vandy W. HOWELL** was born on 13 December 1883. He died on 24 October 1933. He was buried in Butzville Cemetery, Butzville, Warren County, New Jersey. He was a watchman at Manunka Chunk, NJ, for the Pennsylvania Railroad. He was married to **Clara L. SMITH** on 26 May 1910. Clara L. SMITH was born in 1894. She died in 1935. She was buried in Butzville Cemetery, Butzville, Warren County, New Jersey. Vandy W. HOWELL and Clara L. SMITH had the following children:

+1684 i. **Mary L. HOWELL**.

1685 ii. **William Lewis HOWELL** was born on 20 April 1917.

1686 iii. **Gladys HOWELL** was born on 11 September 1918; she died in 1927, and was buried in Butzville Cemetery.

+1687 iv. **Lavina HOWELL**.

1688 v. **Elva HOWELL** married **Frank YONOCSKO** (son of **Frank YONOCSKO** and **Helen HELSNSKI**), who was born on 2 August 1923 in Oxford, Warren County, died on 3 May 1996 in Phillipsburg, Warren County, NJ, and was buried in St. Patrick's Cemetery, Belvidere.

1689 vi. **Walter HOWELL**.

1690 vii. **Richard S. HOWELL** was born in 1920; he died in 1942, and was buried in Butzville Cemetery. Richard was a paratrooper in WWII.

1691 viii. **Earl HOWELL**.

1692 ix. **Betty Jane HOWELL**.

+1693 x. **George HOWELL**.

1694 xi. **Unknown HOWELL** married **Robert SMITH**.

1020. **Evan John HOWELL** was born on 1 November 1885, in Delaware, Warren County, NJ. He died on 25 December 1958 in Phillipsburg, and was buried in Fairmount Cemetery, Phillipsburg, Warren County, NJ. The 1920 census lists him as John J. Howell. He married **Jennie RISSMILLER** who was born in 1888. She died on 16 March 1960, and was buried in Fairmount Cemetery. Evan worked at the Warren Foundry & Pipe Company in Phillipsburg for many years. Evan John HOWELL and Jennie RISSMILLER had the following children:

1695 i. **Gertrude HOWELL** was born in 1911; she married **Donald SMITH**, and lived in Fairlawn, NJ at the time of her father's death.. She died before her brother, Walter.[217]

1696 ii. **John E. HOWELL** was born on 2 February 1913 in Belvidere, Warren County, NJ, and died on 7 February 1979 in Lopatcong Twp, NJ. He married **Dorothy B. CULVER** (daughter of **Henry CULVER** and **Martha POYER**), who was born on 27 June 1914 and died on 13 September 1978. Both were buried in Fairmount Cemetery.

+1697 iii. **Walter R. HOWELL**.

1021. **Rachel Rebecca Ann HOWELL** was born on 24 January 1888 in Butzville, Warren County, New Jersey. She died on 13 February 1964 in Phillipsburg, Warren County, NJ, and was buried in Phillipsburg Cemetery, Phillipsburg, NJ. She married **Leo EHLY**. Rachel and Leo EHLY had the following children:

+1698 i. **Helen EHLY**.

+1699 ii. **Mary Catherine EHLY**.

---

[217]Obituary for Walter R. Howell, Times-Express, Phillipsburg, NJ, 24 April 1999.

+1700 iii. **Leo EHLY**.
+1701 iv. **Charles L. EHLY**.

1023. **Eugene B. HOWELL** was born on 27 July 1892. He died in 1957, and was buried in Belvidere Cemetery, Belvidere, Warren County, NJ. He married **Tekla W. HOWELL**. Tekla W. HOWELL was born on 25 September 1891 in Finland. She died in March 1987, and was buried in Belvidere Cemetery. Eugene B. HOWELL and Tekla W. HOWELL had the following children:

1702 i. **Gertrude HOWELL** was born in 1917.
1703 ii. **Elizabeth HOWELL** was born in 1919.
1704 iii. **Irene HOWELL**.

1025. **Ellis Oliver HOWELL** was born on 22 January 1898 in Delaware, Warren County, New Jersey; he died on 25 December 1953 in Belvidere, after a heart attack, and was buried in Hazen Cemetery, Hazen, Warren County. He married **Velma L. UNKNOWN**, who was born on 8 June 1907. She was buried in Hazen Cemetery. Ellis and Velma had the following children:

+1705 i. **Elmer Richard HOWELL**.
1706 ii. **Nancy Jane HOWELL**.

1026. **Alvin C. HOWELL** was born on 6 May 1900. He died on 5 January 1966 in Phillipsburg, Warren County, NJ, and was buried in Hazen Cemetery, Hazen, Warren County, NJ. He was a millman. He married **Carrie J. REESE**. She was born on 13 March 1903 in Belvidere, Warren County. She died in June 1991, and was buried in Hazen Cemetery. Their children were:

1707 i. **Grace HOWELL** married **Elmer HOTCHKIN**.
+1708 ii. **Robert C. HOWELL**.

1027. **Ruth HOWELL** was born on 21 December 1903 in Belvidere, Warren County, New Jersey. She died on 27 March 1984 in Phillipsburg, Warren County, and was buried in Bloomsbury Cemetery, Bloomsbury, Hunterdon County, New Jersey. Ruth died of a heart attack. She was married to **Austin R. TRIMMER** (son of **Edward TRIMMER** and **Jenny BENWARD**) on 14 April 1923 in Butzville, Warren County. Austin R. TRIMMER was born on 23 January 1898 in West Portal, Hunterdon County, NJ. He died on 31 October 1993 in Easton, Northampton County, PA, and was buried in Bloomsbury Cemetery. He was a security guard. Ruth and Austin had the following children:

+1709 i. **Rose TRIMMER**.
+1710 ii. **Austin R. TRIMMER Jr**.
1711 iii. **Robert H. TRIMMER** was born on 8 August 1928 in Phillipsburg, Warren County, NJ. He died in 1982 in Phillipsburg, and was buried in Bloomsbury Cemetery.
1712 iv. **Richard E. TRIMMER** was born in 1929 in NJ.

1713 v. **Jack R. TRIMMER** was born in 1931 in NJ.
1714 vi. **Wanda TRIMMER** was born in 1932 in NJ. She married **Carl SCHWAR**.
1715 vii. **Edward William TRIMMER** was born in 1934 in NJ.
1716 viii. **Ruth TRIMMER** was born in 1936 in NJ. She married **Arthur BUDD**.
1717 ix. **Donald Wayne TRIMMER** was born in 1938 in NJ.
1718 x. **Nancy TRIMMER** was born in 1941 in NJ. She married **Dennis MILLS**.
1719 xi. **Marianne TRIMMER** was born in 1943 in NJ. She married **William BISCHOFF**.
1720 xii. **Linda TRIMMER** was born in 1946 in NJ. She married **James SMITH**.

1028. **Norman Augustus PRICE** was born on 2 February 1857 in West Jersey, Stark County, Illinois. He died on 18 January 1932 in Sioux Falls, Minnehaha County, South Dakota. Norman was a stone mason, and superintendent of construction on a number of court house buildings in Iowa. He was married to **Nancy Jane "Jennie" SPOHN** on 25 March 1877 in Lotts Creek, Kossuth County, Iowa. Norman Augustus PRICE and Nancy Jane "Jennie" SPOHN had the following children:

1721 i. **Kenneth Llewellyn PRICE** was born on 6 April 1878 in Rutland, Humboldt County, IA.
+1722 ii. **Vida Igerna PRICE**.
1723 iii. **Gwen Howell PRICE** was born on 24 May 1885 in Grant City, Sac County, IA. She died on 2 June 1919 in Jefferson, Greene County, IA.
1724 iv. **Max Whitney PRICE** was born on 5 June 1888 in Grant City. He died there on 22 March 1890.
1725 v. **Norman Donald PRICE** was born on 13 August 1891 in Carroll, Carroll County, IA. He died in December 1969 in Oregon.
+1726 vi. **Malcolm Poyer PRICE**.

1029. **Thomas Henderson PRICE** was born on 25 December 1864 in Joliet, Will County, Illinois. He died on 26 December 1942. Thomas was a builder, who built many homes and business buildings in Eureka, where the family moved in 1906, from Spirit Lake. He was married to **Hannah Jane THOMAS** on 22 February 1889 in Spirit Lake, Dickinson County, Iowa. Hannah Jane THOMAS died on 9 March 1935 in Eureka, Lincoln County, Montana. Hannah was a nurse/midwife in Eureka for many years, and was reported to have attended the births of more than 300 babies, there. She also nursed the sick and injured in her home, since there was no hospital in the town. Thomas and Hannah Jane had the following children:

+1727 i. **Edna Mae PRICE**.
+1728 ii. **Ethel Daisy PRICE**.
1729 iii. **Sarah Edith PRICE** was born on 26 December 1896 in

IA. She married **Unknown ANDERSON**.

+1730 iv. **Thomas Edward PRICE**.

1030. **Charles Warren PRICE** was born on 26 September 1868 in Yatesville, Calhoun County, Iowa. He died on 10 April 1942 probably in Iowa. He was married to **Sarah THOMAS** (daughter of **Webb THOMAS** and **Mary MORGAN**) on 27 November 1890. Sarah THOMAS was born on 3 October 1870 in Spirit Lake, Dickinson County, Iowa. She died on 26 August 1946 in Spirit Lake, and was buried in Lakeview Cemetery, Spirit Lake. Charles and Sarah had these children:

+1731 i. **Myrtle Veda PRICE**.
+1732 ii. **Mary Euphemia PRICE**.
+1733 iii. **Virginia Viola PRICE**.

1031. **Phoebe Louisa PRICE** was born on 17 April 1871 in Otho, Webster County, Iowa. She died on 22 September 1951 in Spokane, Spokane County, Washington. She was married to **Edward THOMAS** (son of **Webb THOMAS** and **Mary MORGAN**) on 3 December 1889 in Spirit Lake, Dickinson County, Iowa. Edward THOMAS was born on 2 May 1866 in New Media, Pennsylvania. He died in May 1930 in Bonners Ferry, Boundary County, Idaho. Phoebe and Edward had these children:

1734 i. **Lloyd THOMAS** was born in Spirit Lake, Dickinson County, Iowa. He died in infancy.
+1735 ii. **Mary Elizabeth THOMAS**.
+1736 iii. **Mabel Etta THOMAS**.
1737 iv. **William Webb THOMAS** was born on 24 September 1896 in Spirit Lake, and died on 26 February 1955 in Laredo, Webb County, Texas. He married **Katherine BREWER** on 25 July 1928. William served in the 19th Military Police, at Camp Dodge, Iowa, and was discharged on 17 February 1919 at Camp Lewis, Washington.
+1738 v. **Lettie Mae THOMAS**.
+1739 vi. **Richard Morgan THOMAS**.
+1740 vii. **Arthur Edward THOMAS**.
+1741 viii. **Robert Charles THOMAS**.
+1742 ix. **Louise Mildred THOMAS**.

1032. **Eva Frances HOWELL** was born in April 1875 in West Pittston, Luzerne County, Pennsylvania. She was married to **Azariah PRICE** on 31 March 1898 in West Pittston.[218] Azariah PRICE was born in Pennsylvania in August 1870; he was a laborer on the railroad. Their children were:

---

[218]Marriage Record in the West Pittston Methodist Church records, 1872 - 1923. LDS microfilm # 1671296.

+1743 i. **Ethel May PRICE**.

1744 ii. **Ruth Evelyn PRICE** was born on 1 April 1903, and died after 1985. Ruth worked for Fowler's department store in Binghamton, New York[219].

1745 iii. **Gordon Howell PRICE** was born on 4 December 1906 in West Pittston. He died in Binghamton, NY before 1985. He married twice; his second wife was named **Sylvia UNKNOWN**. He worked for IBM in Binghamton.

1033. **Mary A. HOWELL** was born in September 1876. Mary, known as Mame, lived with her son on Warren Street in West Pittston. She was married to **Alexander "Sandy" SOMERVILLE** on 29 January 1901 in West Pittston, Luzerne County, PA.[220] Alexander "Sandy" SOMERVILLE was born in 1874. Mary A. HOWELL and Alexander "Sandy" SOMERVILLE had one child:

1746 i. **Harold Robert SOMERVILLE** was born on 14 August 1905 in West Pittston. He died before 1985.

1034. **Benson W. HOWELL** was born in April 1880 in West Pittston, Luzerne County, Pa. He was married to **Nellie M. UNKNOWN** in 1901 in PA. Nellie M. UNKNOWN was born in 1883 in PA. Benson W. HOWELL and Nellie M. UNKNOWN had the following children:[221]

1747 i. **Beatrice HOWELL** was born in 1904 in Tamaqua, PA.

1748 ii. **Elise HOWELL** was born about 1907 in Tamaqua.

1749 iii. **Doris M. HOWELL** was born in 1909 in Tamaqua.

1750 iv. **Florence K. HOWELL** was born in 1913 in Tamaqua.

1751 v. **Elva HOWELL** was born in 1915 in Tamaqua.

1035. **George E. HOWELL** was born in August 1882 in Luzerne County. Quite possibly he was living in Susquehanna County by 1904, since newspaper clippings tell of Constable Howell visiting his son in that county. Other articles mention Mrs. A. J. HOWELL and her sister, Mrs., A SUMMERVILLE visiting relatives in Montrose, Susquehanna County. A 1908 article relates: "George Howell, son of Constable Howell, leaves today for Wonder, Nevada, at which place he will make his home for the future." [222]The 1920 census of Susquehanna County, PA shows George HOWELL with his wife, Ethel, and three children living there, which indicates that they returned to Pennsylvania, probably about 1917. (We believe that they later moved to West Pittston, Luzerne County, but this has not been proved.)

---

[219]Letter from Marion Ethel Howell Phethean to Jeannette Jones Phethean

[220]Marriage record in the West Pittston Methodist Church Records, 1872 - 1923 LDS Film # 1671296

[221]1920 U.S. Census (population) Soundex H400, Pennsylvania

[222]Pittston, (PA) Gazette, West Side Brevities, 26 December 1908, page 8.

Ethel UNKNOWN was born about 1891 in Kansas.[223] Children of George E. HOWELL and Ethel UNKNOWN were:

1752 i. **George E. HOWELL** was born about 1911 in Texas.
1753 ii. **Harold R. HOWELL** was born about 1912 in Texas.
1754 iii. **Mildred J. HOWELL** was born about 1917, probably in Susquehanna County, PA.

1036. **Charles Joseph HOWELL** was born on 28 September 1886 in PA. He was a Railroad employee between 1930 and 1950 in Pittston, Luzerne County, PA. He died on 26 February 1958 in Wyoming, Luzerne County, PA. He was buried on 1 March 1958 in Memorial Shrine Cemetery, Carverton, PA. The family lived on Luzerne Avenue in West Pittston when (Marion) Ethel was born, but they moved to Wyoming when she was small. Charles married **Ethel May GARNETT** on 15 June 1910 in Wilkes Barre, Luzerne County, PA. Ethel May GARNETT was born on 25 December 1888 in Wyoming, Luzerne County, PA, and died there on 29 September 1945.Their children were:[224]

1755 i. **Rhea Thelma HOWELL** was born on 9 February 1915 in West Pittston, and died there in February 1976. She worked for many years at J. C. Penney in Pittston. She married (1) **Alexander SPAIDE** about 1940 in Wyoming. Alex was employed by an electric company, and was killed during an electrical storm, while working on a pole.[225]Rhea married (2) **Everett LABARRE** about 1970 in West Pittston. He was a widower with one daughter. Rhea had no children by either husband.
1756 ii. **Blanche Verda HOWELL**, known as "Bea" was born on 14 October 1918 in West Pittston. She died on 15 August 1967 in Harrisburg, Dauphin County, PA. She married **Harold WEIR**. They had no children.
+1757 iii. **Marion Ethel HOWELL**.

1040. **Joseph HOWELL** was born in September 1886 in Pittston, Luzerne County, Pennsylvania. He was married to **Agnes UNKNOWN** about 1912 in Pittston. Agnes UNKNOWN was born in 1893 in PA. Joseph HOWELL and Agnes UNKNOWN had the following children:

1758 i. **Ruth HOWELL** was born in 1913 in Pittston.
1759 ii. **Kathryn HOWELL** was born in 1915 in Pittston.

---

[223]1920 U.S. Census (population) Pennsylvania, Susquehanna Co., E.D. 65, sheet 1, line 90, nos.44 /47, National Archives Microfilm Publication
[224]Letter from Marion Ethel Howell Phethean to Jeannette Jones Phethean.
[225]Personal knowledge of Jeannette Phethean.

1041. **Wilbur HOWELL** was born in November 1888 in Pittston, Luzerne County, Pennsylvania. He was married to **Anna KIERAN** about 1914 in Pittston. Their children were:

1760	i.	**George HOWELL** was born in 1914 in Pittston.
1761	ii.	**Wilbur HOWELL** was born in July 1917 in Pittston.
1762	iii.	**Mary HOWELL** was born in December 1918 in Pittston.

1043. **George HOWELL** was born in July 1892 in Pittston, Luzerne County, Pennsylvania. He was married to **Ruth UNKNOWN** about 1917 in Pittston. Ruth UNKNOWN was born in 1897 in PA. George and Ruth had one known child:

1763	i.	**Charles HOWELL** was born in 1918 in Pittston.

1047. **Ann Charlotte HOWELL** was born on 1 December 1886 in West Pittston, Luzerne County, Pennsylvania. She died on 26 May 1973 in West Pittston, and was buried on 29 May 1973 in West Pittston Cemetery. Her death resulted from a fall in which she broke a hip. She had worked, after her husband's death, as a secretary for Sutherland and MacMillan, a wholesale grocery in Pittston. She sang in the choir of the West Pittston Methodist Church. She was married to **Charles Augustus JONES** on 16 October 1916 in West Pittston. Charles Augustus JONES died about 1932 in West Pittston, and was buried in West Pittston Cemetery. Ann and Charles Augustus JONES had the following children:

+1764	i.	**Sarah Virginia JONES**.
+1765	ii.	**Helen Elizabeth JONES**.

1049. **Robert HOWELL** was born on 17 August 1891 in West Pittston, Luzerne County, Pennsylvania. He died on 22 November 1936 in West Pittston, and was buried in West Pittston Cemetery. Bob was a salesman for a paper company, and sang in the choir at the Trinity Episcopal Church in West Pittston. He and his family lived with her parents on Montgomery Avenue. He was married to **Sarah WATKINS** in Pittston, Luzerne County, where Sarah was born on 14 January 1895. She died on 17 October 1972 in West Pittston, and was buried in West Pittston Cemetery. They had a daughter:

+1766	i.	**Gladys Jane HOWELL**.

1050. **Jean Louise HOWELL** was born on 9 February 1894 in West Pittston. She died there on 10 December 1979, and was buried on 13 December 1979 in Mt. Zion Cemetery, Harding, Luzerne County. She was married to **Seth WRIGLEY** on 15 January 1915 in West Pittston. They were later divorced. She worked at Drury's grocery store as a bookkeeper, until the store closed about 1945. She then was a bookkeeper for Sidney Friedman's grocery and later for Brennan and Roberts Grocery in Pittston. She was an attendance officer for West Pittston schools for many years. They had one child:

+1767 i. **Jane Louise WRIGLEY**.

1051. **Helen Elizabeth HOWELL** was born on 10 October 1896 in West Pittston, where she died on 19 September 1951. She was buried on 22 September 1951 in West Pittston Cemetery. Helen worked for George T. Bell, a grocer in Pittston when she was young. About 1940, she went back to work at Brennan and Roberts Grocery, as a clerk. About 1949, she developed cancer of the bladder, from which she died following several operations. She was married to **William Evans JONES** (son of **James JONES** and **Jeannette EVANS**) on 21 November 1921 in Wilkes Barre, Luzerne County.[226] He was born on 19 October 1895 in Wilkes Barre, Luzerne County. He died on 23 November 1970 in West Pittston, and was buried on 26 November 1970 in West Pittston Cemetery. He was an inheritance tax appraiser for the state of Pennsylvania, working out of the Luzerne County courthouse, until he retired in 1955. Helen and William Evans JONES had the following children:

+1768 i. **Jeannette Ann JONES**.
+1769 ii. **Harriet Elizabeth JONES**.

1052. **Harriet WINTLE** was born in September 1886 in West Pittston, Luzerne County, Pennsylvania. She died in West Pittston. Hattie was never called Harriet, so far as is known. Hattie married **Solomon PUGH**, who was born in July 1883 in PA. He died in West Pittston, Luzerne County. Sol worked in the coal mines in and around Pittston. Harriet WINTLE and Solomon PUGH had the following children:

1770 i. **Laine PUGH** was born in West Pittston. She married **Harry BLACK**, a widower with several grown children. They had no children.
+1771 ii. **Dolores PUGH**.
1772 iii. **Melchoir PUGH** was born on 14 June 1911 in West Pittston, and died there in November 1968. Mel was a policeman. He married **Eleanor SHOOK**, who was born on 1 August 1914 and died in July 1987 in West Pittston. They had no children.
+1773 iv. **Shirley PUGH**.

1057. **John Stinson HOWELL** was born in April 1891 in Michigan. He died on 16 June 1950. He married **Arvella BANOKE** who was born in 1889 in Arizona. She died on 3 March 1959 in Rochester, Oakland County, MI, and was buried in Mt. Avon Cemetery, Rochester. They had one child:

1774 i. **William Donald HOWELL** was born on 12 May 1910

---

[226]Marriage certificate for William E. Jones and Helen E. Howell, issued by the Puritan Congregational Church , Sherman Street, Wilkes Barre. Certificate in possession of Harriet Jones Davies.

in CA. He died on 4 January 1918 in Rochester, and was buried in Mt. Avon Cemetery.

1058. **Milo Max HOWELL** was born on 18 July 1896 in Avon Twp., Oakland County, Michigan. He died on 26 June 1959. Milo was a Corporal in the Michigan 39th Field artillery during World War I. He married **Harriet Florence OWENS** who was born on 11 August 1895 in Coller, Ohio. She died on 24 December 1979, and was buried in Mt. Avon Cemetery. They had one child:

1775 i. **Harold HOWELL** was born on 15 June 1922 in Avon Twp. He died on 15 June 1922 in Avon Twp., and was buried in Mt. Avon Cemetery.

1066. **Almira Current YOUNG** was born in 1876. She died on 29 April 1904 of consumption in Marksboro, Warren County, NJ, and was buried in Newton Cemetery, Newton, Sussex County, NJ. She married **Clyde WINFIELD**. Almira Current YOUNG and Clyde WINFIELD had one child:

1776 i. **Unknown male WINFIELD**.

1070. **Levi A. HOWELL** was born on 30 November 1881. He died on 12 December 1961, and was buried in Newton Cemetery, Newton, Sussex County, NJ. Levi was a mailman in Newton, NJ. He married **Hannah Venelia BENNETT**, who was born on 14 July 1882. She died on 19 June 1963, and was buried in Newton Cemetery. Levi A. HOWELL and Hannah Venelia BENNETT had these children:

1777 i. **Frank HOWELL**.
1778 ii. **William HOWELL**.
1779 iii. **Ila HOWELL**.
1780 iv. **Florence HOWELL**.
1781 v. **Carman J. HOWELL** was born on 31 July 1903. He died on 22 August 1916, and was buried in Newton Cemetery.

1072. **William S. HOWELL** was born on 22 April 1886. He died in 1949, and was buried in Newton Cemetery. He was married to **Almeda B. VAN HORN** on 28 December 1911. Almeda B. VAN HORN was born on 4 February 1887. She died in April 1970, and was buried in Newton Cemetery. William S. HOWELL and Almeda B. VAN HORN had the following children:

1782 i. **Evelyn May HOWELL** was born in 1917. She died and was buried in Newton Cemetery.
1783 ii. **Thelma HOWELL**.

1080. **Agnes Emma WALTER** was born on 22 May 1870 in Clarkston, Oakland County, Michigan. She died on 12 September 1905 in Detroit, and was buried in Clarkston. She married **John Whitaker GOODSPEED** on 12 January 1892. He was born on 30 May 1859 in Ypsilanti, MI, and died on 15 January 1937 in East Grand Rapids, MI. Their children were:

+1784 i. **Harrison LeGrande GOODSPEED**
1785 ii. **John Whitaker GOODSPEED** was born on 23 May 1901, and died soon after.
1786 iii. **Walter Stuart GOODSPEED** was born on 17 November 1902. He died about 1968 in Grand Rapids.

1084. **Edith HOWE** was born in 1887. She died after 1974 in Delray Beach, Florida. She married (1) **Charles Webster**, and (2) **Rollan GREEN**. Edith HOWE and Rollan GREEN had one child:

1787 i. Marion GREEN.

1088. **Harrison Morton HOWELL** was born on 23 September 1888 in Pennsylvania. He died on 11 February 1963 in Kingston, Luzerne County, PA. He married **Florence Maria SIEGEL**, who was born on 13 July 1889, and died on 31 March 1970. Their children were:

1788 i. **Florence HOWELL** was born and died in 1914.
+1789 ii. **Ethel Fern HOWELL**.
1790 iii. **Jean Louise HOWELL** was born on 30 July 1920 in Luzerne County. She married (1) **Charles MCCULLOUGH**, and (2) **Bryce MAJOR**.
+1791 iv. **Harry Morton HOWELL**.
+1792 v. **Shirley Ruth HOWELL**.

1091. **Ethel HOWELL** was born on 9 September 1893. She died on 29 June 1959. She was married to **Harry Pritchard LEWIS** on 3 September 1927. Harry Pritchard LEWIS was born on 26 January 1882. He died on 7 October 1936. Ethel HOWELL and Harry Pritchard LEWIS had the following children:

+1793 i. **Harry Watson LEWIS**.
1794 ii. **Elizabeth Mary LEWIS** was born on 11 October 1929.
+1795 iii. **Ethel Ruth LEWIS**.
+1796 iv. **Edith Ann LEWIS**.

1092. **Finley HOWELL** was born in August 1895. Finley was married to **Ethel MIDDLETON**. Finley HOWELL and Ethel MIDDLETON had one child:

1797 i. **Dennis HOWELL**.

1107. **Mary Ellen HOWELL** was born on 4 October 1864 in Luzerne County, PA.. She died on 8 February 1908 in Clam Falls, Polk County, WI., and was buried on 10 February 1908 in Lorain Twp. Cemetery, Polk County, WI. She was married to **Flavius Earl ROOT** (son of **Velorus ROOT** and **Syble Maria**

WESTCOTT) on 17 February 1886 in Orange, Luzerne County, PA. Flavius Earl ROOT was born on 4 October 1859 in Brooklyn Twp., Green Lake County, WI. He died on 21 February 1929 in Centuria, Polk County, WI., and was buried on 24 February 1929 in Lorain Twp. Cemetery. [227] Their children were:[228]

1798 i. **Isaac Earl ROOT** was born on 24 December 1886 in Brooklyn Twp., Green Lake County, WI. He died on 12 October 1965 in Tomah, WI.

+1799 ii. **Edna Pearl ROOT**.

+1800 iii. **Leda Marie ROOT**.

1801 iv. **Grover Clyde ROOT** was born on 29 June 1892 in Brooklyn Twp., Green Lake County, WI. He died on 22 July 1918 in France.

+1802 v. **Ethel May ROOT**.

+1803 vi. **Frances "Frank" George ROOT**.

+1804 vii. **Lin Howell ROOT**.

+1805 viii. **Mary Lucille ROOT**.

1108. **Eva HOWELL** was born in 1868 in PA. She married (1) **Thomas N. CHESWORTH**. Eva HOWELL and Thomas N. CHESWORTH had one child:

+1806 i. **Thelma CHESWORTH**.

After Thomas CHESWORTH died, Eva married (2) **Corey W. DRAKE**, but the marriage lasted only a short time, and they divorced.

1109. **Lavenia Arzella HOWELL** was born on 9 January 1863 in Warren County, NJ. She died on 18 December 1917 in Belvidere, Warren County, NJ, and was buried in Belvidere Cemetery, Belvidere, Warren County, NJ. Lavenia married **George VAN HORN**. They had one child:

+1807 i. **Melvin H. VAN HORN**.

1110. **Stella HOWELL** was born in 1872 in NJ. She died on 16 December 1948 in Belvidere, Warren County, NJ., and was buried in Belvidere Cemetery. She was married to **William Taylor BUTLER** on 10 January 1894 in Belvidere. William Taylor BUTLER was born on 2 September 1860 in Belvidere. He died on 22 May 1944, and was buried in Belvidere Cemetery. Their children were:

1808 i. **Walter B. BUTLER** was born on 22 January 1897 in Belvidere. He died on 27 August 1901.

+1809 ii. **Hilton Laire BUTLER**.

---

[227]Obituary, Green Lake Co. (WI) Reporter, 21 March 1929.

[228]Information was contributed by Kathy L. Armstrong, 2326 Hwy SS, Rice Lake WI 54868.

1120. **Frank Leroy HATFIELD** was born on 12 May 1867 in Centremoreland Cemetery, Luzerne County, PA. He died on 25 October 1935 in New York, New York. He was married to **Mary Elizabeth HARMSTON** on 26 September 1889 in Trumansburg, New York. Mary Elizabeth HARMSTON was born on 30 July 1870 in Trumansburg, New York. She died in 1956 in Wilkinsburg, PA. Frank Leroy HATFIELD and Mary Elizabeth HARMSTON had the following children:[229]

+1810	i.	**Elma Hermione HATFIELD.**
+1811	ii.	**Ethel Winifred HATFIELD.**
+1812	iii.	**Vernon Leroy HATFIELD.**
+1813	iv.	**Helyn Elizabeth HATFIELD.**

1135. **Alida Euphemia SIPERLY** was born on 11 October 1861. She married **J. Murray BACON**. Alida Euphemia SIPERLY and J. Murray BACON had the following children:

1814	i.	**Ray BACON.**
1815	ii.	**Verna M. BACON** was born on 17 June 1886, and died on 9 February 1985 in Manchester, Delaware County, Iowa. She attended Lenox College, and was a DAR member for 50 years. She married **Marshal NEIL** on 3 September 1913. He died in 1974.
+1816	iii.	**Louis BACON.**

1137. **Albert "Bert" FEAR** was born on 20 June 1891 in Delaware County, Iowa. He died on 11 January 1966 in Hopkinton, Delaware County, and was buried in Hopkinton Cemetery. He was a farmer. He was married (1) to **Gertrude LITTLE**. She died before 1943 in Hopkinton. Their children were:

1817	i.	**Faybin FEAR.**
+1818	ii.	**Clayton FEAR.**

Bert and Gertrude also had 5 daughters, names unknown.

Bert was married (2) to **Lola BROWN** on 12 February 1943. Lola BROWN died on 19 January 1954. Lola worked for a company named Collins Radio in Cedar Rapids, Linn County,, Linn County,, Linn County,, Linn County,, Linn County,, Iowa, and drove to work each day from Hopkinton with a car pool. On January 19, 1954, in a fog, they had an accident, and Lola was killed. Albert "Bert" FEAR and Lola BROWN had the following children:

1819	i.	**James FEAR.**
1820	ii.	**Lynn FEAR.**
1821	iii.	**Dennis FEAR.**

---

[229]Family ArchiveCD#5, World Family Tree, 1996, #3842, submitted by William M. Whitlock, Portland, OR. Copyright Broderbund Software Inc.

1140. **Unknown Female FEAR** was born in IA. She married **Thomas A. BLANCHARD**. They had one child:

1822 i. **Pearl BLANCHARD**.

1142. **Anna Pearl THOMPSON** was born on 6 November 1886 in IA. She died on 14 October 1974 in IA., and was buried in Buck Creek Cemetery, Delaware County, Iowa. She was married to **Harold Arthur "Hap" STEAD** (son of **Frank STEAD** and **Lula BALCH**) on 18 December 1907 in IA. Harold was born in 1887, and died in 1946 in IA. He was a farmer with a farm near Hopkinton, Iowa. After his death, Anna Pearl moved to Monticello, Iowa where she taught school. Anna and "Hap" had the following children:

1823 i. **Donald STEAD** was born and died in 1916 in Hopkinton.

1824 ii. **Infant Son STEAD** was born and died in 1917 in Hopkinton.

+1825 iii. **Victor STEAD**.

+1826 iv. **W. Vance STEAD**.

+1827 v. **Gordon Frank STEAD**.

1828 vi. **Beverly STEAD** was born on 22 March 1933. She died on 15 October 1993 in Indiana. She married **Donald Theodore CASPER**, a Methodist minister, and they had children, whose names are not known. After Beverly's death, Donald remarried and is retired from the ministry.

1143. **William Bert THOMPSON** was born on 27 February 1889 in Hopkinton, Delaware County, Iowa. He died on 19 September 1968 in Manchester, IA., in an automobile accident. He was married to **Lena Mary FLANNAGAN** (daughter of **John FLANNAGAN** and **Mary BEITZ**) on 20 June 1906 in Manchester, IA. Lena Mary FLANNAGAN was born on 8 February 1886 in Union Twp., Delaware County, and died on 1 March 1967 in Iowa., of heart disease. Their children were:

1829 i. **William Howard THOMPSON** was born on 14 January 1907, and died on 23 January 1907 in IA.

+1830 ii. **Bernard Clark THOMPSON**.

1831 iii. **Harold Walter THOMPSON** was born on 1 July 1911 in Union Twp., Delaware County, IA. He married **Goldie MCMANNIS** on 2 November 1935; they divorced in October 1942. "Brownie" joined the Army on 21 June 1943, and went overseas with the 5th Army, 36th Texas Infantry in November 1943. He was wounded three times, serving in France, Italy, Netherlands and Germany, and was killed near Wissembourg. He and Goldie had no children.

+1832 iv. **Maude Alberta THOMPSON**.

+1833 v. **Mildred Mae THOMPSON**.

+1834 vi. **Vernon Bert THOMPSON**.
1835 vii. **Raymond Paul THOMPSON** was born on 29 August 1922 in Hopkinton. He died on 2 June 1983 in Iowa City, IA, of heart disease. He married **Wilma Lorena OSTERKAMP** on 1 October 1941. She was born in 1921.
+1836 viii. **William John THOMPSON**.

1144. **Glenn David THOMPSON** was born on 25 December 1891 in IA. He died on 23 October 1963 in IA. He was married to **Edna SAUNDERS** (daughter of **John SAUNDERS** and **Martha FINLAY**) on 9 August 1911 in IA. Edna SAUNDERS was born on 26 September 1890. She died on 29 September 1962 in IA. Glenn David THOMPSON and Edna SAUNDERS had the following children:

+1837 i. **Gertrude THOMPSON**.
+1838 ii. **Wayne "Buzzy" THOMPSON**.
+1839 iii. **Bernard THOMPSON**.
+1840 iv. **Glenn David THOMPSON**.

1145. **Blanche Berniece THOMPSON** was born on 23 June 1898 in Hopkinton, Delaware County, Iowa. She died on 16 July 1995 in Venice, Sarasota County, Florida. She was married to **Wilbur R. CARTANO** (son of **Richard CARTANO**) on 28 June 1922 in Monticello, Jones County, IA. Wilbur R. CARTANO was born on 13 August 1897 in IA. He died on 23 July 1972 in Venice. Wilbur and Blanche lived around Monticello, Iowa most of their lives. They were farmers. After he retired he and Blanche moved to Venice, Florida. Blanche died of colon cancer at 97. She had been a teacher. The children were:

1841 i. **Carol Anne CARTANO** was born on 4 July 1923 in Monticello. She died on 25 February 1992 in Venice, FL. She married (1) **Chaunce FRENCH** about 1940, and (2) **Warren RUSSO** about 1950. She had no children.
+1842 ii. **Richard Bruce CARTANO**.
+1843 iii. **David CARTANO**.
1844 iv. **Larry CARTANO** was born on 7 November 1938. He was married (1) to **Patricia HUBERT** about 1970, and (2) to **Melissa Lindsay MARTIN** in 1982. Larry had no children.

1146. **Dewitt Howell THOMPSON** was born on 23 February 1904 in Iowa. He died on 14 September 1971 in Florida. He was married to **Lucille HOGAN** (daughter of **Michael HOGAN** and **Agnes KEHOE**) in 1922 in IA. Dewitt Howell THOMPSON and Lucille HOGAN had the following children:

+1845 i. **Betty THOMPSON**.
+1846 ii. **Jean K. THOMPSON**.
+1847 iii. **Margaret "Peggy" THOMPSON**.

1147. **DeWain Garvin THOMPSON** was born on 23 February 1904 in Iowa, where he died on 20 January 1962. He married **Kathryn Elzina DESHAW** (daughter of **Unknown DESHAW** and **Agnes HAYLE**) on 27 August 1939. She was born in 1916. DeWain and Kathryn had the following children:

+1848	i.	**Stephen William THOMPSON.**
+1849	ii.	**Roger THOMPSON.**

1148. **Arthur F. HOWELL** was born on 16 September 1885 in Frankfort, Marshall County, Kansas. He died on 25 September 1963 in Hood River, Hood River County, Oregon. He married **Margaret CARNES** (daughter of **James CARNES** and **Barbara Ann UNKNOWN**) on 17 April 1909 in Hood River. Their children were:

+1850	i.	**Barbara Ann HOWELL.**
+1851	ii.	**Helen Virginia HOWELL.**
1852	iii.	**Male HOWELL.**

1149. **Frank HOWELL** was born on 10 July 1887 in Frankfort, Marshall County, Kansas. He died on 14 December 1954. He was married to **Phoebe COUGHENNOWER** in January 1916 in Hood River, Hood River County, Oregon. They had the following children:

1853	i.	**Victor HOWELL** was born and died in Hood River.
1854	ii.	**George Albert HOWELL** was born in Hood River. He married **Lucille UNKNOWN.**

1151. **Harry Albert HOWELL** was born on 15 October 1890 in Frankfort, Marshall County, KS. He died on 5 March 1962 in Hood River, Hood River County, OR. He was married to **Lacey Mabel TUCKER** (daughter of **Walter TUCKER** and **Callie HAND**) on 7 December 1918 in Hood River, Hood River County, OR. Harry and Lacey had these children:

+1855	i.	**Eila Maxine HOWELL.**
+1856	ii.	**Eileen Francis HOWELL.**
+1857	iii.	**Harriet Elizabeth HOWELL.**
+1858	iv.	**Blanche La Rayne HOWELL.**
+1859	v.	**Harry Lee HOWELL.**

1152. **Blanche Elizabeth HOWELL** was born on 21 February 1894 in Frankfort, Marshall County, KS. She died on 8 August 1975 in Portland, Multnomah County, Oregon. She was married to **Clyde Lester EATON** (son of **Job EATON** and **Sally CAMPBELL**) on 17 June 1914 in Coquille, Coos County, OR. Blanche Elizabeth HOWELL and Clyde Lester EATON had the following children:

+1860	i.	**Ira Miles EATON.**
+1861	ii.	**Glenn Alan EATON.**

1862 iii. **Leonard Wayne EATON** was born on 6 June 1918 in Portland. He died in 1943 in the Baltic Sea, in WWII. He married **Patricia WARD**.

1863 iv. **Irvin Ray EATON** was born on 25 July 1920 in Portland. He married **Geraldine POWELL**.

+1864 v. **Robert Lester EATON**.

1865 vi. **Charles Edwin EATON** was born on 5 August 1925 in Portland, and died on 26 December 1954 in Mosier, OR. He married **Mildred LAMBERT.**

1866 vii **David Lee EATON** was born on 31 January 1931 in Portland. He married **Kathy BOSTWICK**

1153. **Grace Ann HOWELL** was born on 11 September 1895 in Imbler, OR. She died on 17 November 1916. She was married to **Peter Marye KOONTZ** (son of **John KOONTZ** and **Serah RUFFNER**) in 1914 in Vancouver, Clark County, Washington. Grace Ann HOWELL and Peter Marye KOONTZ had one child:

+1867 i. **Wanona Maxine KOONTZ**.

1154. **Ruth Eleanor HOWELL** was born on 20 May 1897 in Hood River, Hood River County, OR. She died on 6 April 1978 in Redondo Beach, Los Angeles County, California. She married **Frank KOONTZ** (son of **John KOONTZ** and **Serah RUFFNER**) on 26 December 1917 in Vancouver, Clark County, WA. Ruth Eleanor HOWELL and Frank KOONTZ had the following children:

+1868 i. **Thelma Anita KOONTZ**.

+1869 ii. **Frank Emmett KOONTZ**.

1155. **Roy Earl HOWELL** was born on 4 February 1899 in Hood River, Hood River County, OR. He died on 16 February 1960 in Palmdale, Los Angeles County, CA. He married **Wynona Louise KEYS** on 20 September 1924. Roy Earl HOWELL and Wynona Louise KEYS had the following children:

1870 i. **Don Royal HOWELL** was born on 25 March 1925.

1871 ii. **Dell Roy HOWELL** was born on 25 March 1925.

+1872 iii. **Dorothy Darlyne HOWELL**.

+1873 iv. **Eva Mardell HOWELL**.

1156. **Carolyn Madeline HOWELL** was born on 8 August 1902 in Hood River, Hood River County, OR. She died on 25 February 1995 in Portland, Multnomah County, Oregon, and was buried in Lincoln Memorial Park Cemetery, Portland. She was married to **Elmer Arthur LARSON** (son of **Joseph LARSON** and **Amanda KAURIN**) on 2 January 1923 in Portland. Elmer Arthur LARSON was born on 21 November 1899, and died in March 1968 in OR. Their children were:

+1874 i. **Elaine La Verne LARSON**.

1875 ii. **Wayne Howell LARSON** was born on 30 January 1926 in Portland. He died in Jacksonville, Duval County,

+1876 iii. **Donna Claire LARSON.**

1157. **Walter Claire HOWELL** was born on 21 February 1905 in Hood River, Hood River County, Oregon., and died on 29 June 1947 in Vancouver, Clark County, Washington. He married **Leta Emma HUDSON** (daughter of **Leonard HUDSON** and **Emma HILLER**) on 12 August 1929 in Vancouver. Their children were:

+1877 i. **Wayne HOWELL.**
+1878 ii. **Lois Lucille HOWELL.**
+1879 iii. **Victor Alan HOWELL.**
1880 iv. **Gordon Edwin HOWELL.**
1881 v. **Diane Jane HOWELL** was born on 23 August 1942.
1882 vi. **Alta Mae HOWELL** was born on 28 July 1947.

1158. **Ira Edward HOWELL** was born on 8 October 1909 in Hood River, Hood River County, Oregon. He died on 6 March 1986 in Oceanside, San Diego County, California. He was married to **Ethel Robbins BURCH** on 19 December 1930 in Riverside, Riverside County, California. Ira Edward HOWELL and Ethel Robbins BURCH had a daughter:

1883 i. **Janette HOWELL** was born on 6 October 1937 in Escondido, San Diego County, CA.

1159. **Harry E. HOWELL** was born on 25 July 1886 in Dallas Township, Luzerne County, Pennsylvania. He was married to **Bernice DYMOND** (daughter of **James DYMOND** and **UNKNOWN**) on 30 October 1915 in Dallas Township, Luzerne County, PA. Bernice DYMOND was born on 27 October 1887 in Dallas Township.[230] This newspaper article concerns their 50th wedding anniversary. Harry was in the coal hauling business in Dallas, an important trade in that community. Their children were:

1884 i. **Alberta HOWELL** was born in Dallas Twp. Alberta was a teacher in the Philadelphia, PA schools.
1885 ii. **Lois HOWELL** was born in Dallas Twp. She married **I. Frederick MYERS**. The names of their two children are not known.

1165. **David Clarence HOWELL** was born on 28 November 1865 in "Old" Boonton, Morris County, New Jersey, died on 28 January 1950 in Beemerville, Sussex County, NJ, and was buried in Beemerville Cemetery. He married **Isabella Mary SMITH** on 13 October 1887 in Warren County, NJ. Isabella Mary SMITH was born in 1866, and died in 1936. She was buried in Beemerville Cemetery. Their children were:

---

[230]News item Times Leader-Evening News, Wilkes Barre, PA., 27 October 1965.

+1886 i. **John Smith HOWELL.**
+1887 ii. **Leon Judd HOWELL.**
1888 iii. **Veola E. HOWELL** was born on 29 September 1891 in Beemerville. She died on 13 February 1913, and was buried in Beemerville Cemetery. She married **Oliver W. STRUBLE** on 25 December 1912.
1889 iv. **Olive V. HOWELL** was born in 1894 and died in 1973. She was buried in Beemerville Cemetery. She married **William H. STEPHENS** on 27 November 1913. He was born in 1892 and died in 1940. He was buried in Beemerville Cemetery.
1890 v. **C. Slidell HOWELL.**
1891 vi. **Virginia H. HOWELL** was born in 1910, and died in 1988. She married **Unknown WARNER**.

1166. **Orange Judd HOWELL** was born on 30 September 1868 in Old Boonton, Morris County, NJ. He died on 22 April 1947. He was married to **Bertha ATCHLEY**, who was born in Dobbs Ferry, NY. Orange Judd HOWELL and Bertha ATCHLEY had the following children:

+1892 i. **Horace Beemer HOWELL.**
1893 ii. **William HOWELL** was born in Dobbs Ferry, NY. He died young
1894 iii. **Thelma HOWELL** was born on 4 March 1905 in Dobbs Ferry. She died on 11 September 1983. She married **Walter CLAUS**.
+1895 iv. **Atchley HOWELL.**
+1896 v. **Ruth HOWELL.**

1167. **Elizabeth Victoria HOWELL** was born on 2 October 1873 in Old Boonton, Morris County, NJ. She died on 23 October 1934. She was buried in Union Cemetery, Hackettstown, Warren County, NJ. She was married (1) to **Edward Frederick Schwaedler CLEGG** on 5 October 1898. Edward Frederick Schwaedler CLEGG died before 1912 in Warren County, NJ. Their children were:

1897 ii. **Barbara CLEGG** was born in 1900 in Allamuchy, Warren County, NJ. She died in 1996.
1898 iii. **Victoria CLEGG** was born in 1906. She died in 1984. There is a question as to Victoria's date of birth. The 1920 census says she was 17 at that time. The dates here are from her grave stone.

She was married (2) to **John Sharp MACLEAN** on 26 November 1912. John Sharp MACLEAN was born in 1874. He died in 1967. In 1920, the family was living in Allamuchy Twp., Barbara and Victoria were at home, and Hattie, her mother, was living with them

1179. **William Praul HOWELL** was born on 19 October 1862 in Tioga County, New York. He died on 26 April 1929 in Willard, NY. William moved from Nichols to Camillus, NY, where he worked for Camillus Cutlery. He married **Anna Sabrina MARTIN**, who was born on 21 January 1865, and died on 2 March 1934. Both were buried in Maplewood Cemetery, Camillus. They had these children:

+1899 i. **Ralph Lester HOWELL.**
1900 ii. **Clarence HOWELL** was born in 1896. Clarence was killed on the railroad tracks in 1917. He was buried in Maplewood Cemetery.

1180. **Mary Amelia HOWELL** was born on 18 August 1869, and died on 10 June 1950. She married **Andrew David QUICK**, who was born on 9 June 1863 and died on 18 August 1939. Their children were:

1901 i. **Helen QUICK** was born on 15 June 1892.
1902 ii. **Mabel Howell QUICK** was born on 17 June 1893
1903 iii. **Robert H. QUICK** was born on 1 November 1895; he married **Cora Betty Phillips**.
1904 iv. **Charles Arthur QUICK** was born on 25 October 1896. He married **Neva Agnes BENDER**, who was born on 23 November 1899.

1190. **Aaron B. HOWELL** was born on 21 March 1873 in Warren County, NJ. He died in 1950, in Arlington, NJ, and was buried in Fairview Cemetery, Blairstown, Warren County. Aaron had been a superintendent at the Borden Co. plant in Newark, NJ. He married **Vesta LOLLER** (daughter of **Jefferson LOLLER** and **Emma UNKNOWN**), who was born on 7 November 1875 in Mt. Hermon, Warren County. She died on 23 October 1976, and was buried in Fairview Cemetery. Their children were:

1905 i. **Alice Beatrice HOWELL** was born on 6 August 1907. She married **Wayne S. HOLBROOK** and they lived in Pittsfield, Massachusetts.
1906 ii. **Sarah Emily HOWELL** was born on 18 May 1911 and died on 16 November 1973. She was buried in Fairview Cemetery, Blairstown, NJ. She married **Max PLADEX**, and they lived in Arlington, NJ.

1192. **Maude B. HOWELL** was born in April 1884 in Muskegon, Muskegon County, Michigan. She married **Joseph CANTON**. Maude B. HOWELL and Joseph CANTON had the following children:

1907 i. **Marie Howell CANTON** married **H. RODRIGUEZ.**
1908 ii. **Vivian CANTON** died in 1984.
1909 iii. **William CANTON.**

1193. **Carl Coulton Radley HOWELL** was born in December 1890 in Muskegon, Muskegon County, MI. He died on 9 September 1958 in Muskegon, and was buried in Evergreen Cemetery, Muskegon, MI. He married **Myrtle POMEROY**, who was born on 23 June 1895 in Trumond. She died in October 1982 in Muskegon. Carl Coulton Radley HOWELL and Myrtle POMEROY had the following children:

+1910 i. **Virginia HOWELL**.
+1911 ii. **Dorothy HOWELL**.
+1912 iii. **Carl Clayton HOWELL**.

1194. **Ralph C. HOWELL** was born on 6 April 1880 in Muskegon, Muskegon County, MI. He died on 12 March 1955 in St. Louis, St. Louis County, MO. He married **Emma Dorothy PILGRIM**, who was born in 1880. She died in 1958. Ralph C. HOWELL and Emma Dorothy PILGRIM had one child:

1913 i. **Harlan Ralph HOWELL** was born on 1 May 1905. He died in May 1977 in San Diego, California.

1198. **Fern Ruth HOWELL** was born on 2 January 1896 in Clinton County, IA. She died on 29 April 1929 in Green Bay, Brown County, Wisconsin. She was buried in Laona Cemetery, Laona, WI. She was married to **Robert Erwin THOMPSON** on 11 January 1912 in St. Paul, Minnesota. Robert Erwin THOMPSON was born in 1886, and died in 1959. Fern and Robert Erwin THOMPSON had these children:

+1914 i. **Samuel David THOMPSON**.
+1915 ii. **Robert John THOMPSON**.
+1916 iii. **Ervin THOMPSON**.
+1917 iv. **Julia Louise THOMPSON**.
+1918 v. **Clarence Joseph THOMPSON**.
+1919 vi. **Marie Grace THOMPSON**.
+1920 vii. **Florence Agnes THOMPSON**.
1921 viii. **Margaret Mary THOMPSON** was born and died in 1924.

1212. **Allen WATSON** was born in 1895, and died in 1991. He married **Olive A. UNKNOWN**, who was born in 1908. She died in 1983, and was buried in Colborne Cemetery, Goderich, Huron County, Ontario. They had one child:

1922 i. **Ivan J. WATSON** was born in 1938. He died in 1967, and was buried in Colborne Cemetery.

1220. **Raymond Claude TROYER** was born on 12 December 1887 in Canada. He died on 23 June 1970 in Eagle River, WI. He was married to **Hilda HEITI** on 25 December 1910. Hilda HEITI was born on 14 July 1889 in Finland. She died on 16 October 1962 in Eagle River, WI. Their children were:

+1923 i. **Dorothy Margaret TROYER.**
1924 ii. **Raymond Claud TROYER** was born in 1914 in Eagle River, WI. He died on 25 January 1940.
+1925 iii. **Ruth Elizabeth TROYER.**

1221. **Jesse Howell TROYER** was born on 1 February 1890, and died on 27 September 1973 in Pontiac, Oakland County, Michigan. He married **Ethel May PIERCE** on 18 June 1916 in Winegar, Wisconsin. Ethel May PIERCE was born on 14 November 1895 in Nottawa Twp., Isabella County, WI. She died on 27 November 1979 in Pontiac, MI., and was buried in Lakeview, MI. They had these children:

+1926 i. **Donald Pierce TROYER.**
+1927 ii. **Phyllis Ann TROYER.**
+1928 iii. **Alice Jane TROYER.**

1222. **Lucy Jane TROYER** was born on 15 May 1891 in Rhinelander, Oneida County, Wisconsin. She died in April 1952, and was buried in St. Mary's Cemetery in Rhinelander. She married, on 10 April 1912, **Frank Henry LAUNDRIE**, who was born on 22 September 1887 in Peshtigo, Marinette County, Wisconsin. He died on 22 November 1971, and was buried in St. Mary's Cemetery, also. Their children were:

+1929 i. **Jess Francis LAUNDRIE.**
+1930 ii. **Norene Lucille LAUNDRIE.**
+1931 iii. **Mary Odeal LAUNDRIE.**

1223. **Anna Bertha HOWELL** was born on 25 December 1873 in Warren County, NJ. She died on 18 October 1972. She was married to **Jacob CRUSEN** in 1891. Jacob CRUSEN was born in 1841 in NJ. He died in 1921; both were buried in Moravian Cemetery, Hope, NJ. Anna was Jacob's second wife. He served in Company G, unknown regiment in the Civil War. They had one child:

1932 i. **Arthur CRUSEN** was born in 1894 in NJ. He died in 1916, in World War I. He had been with the 7th Infantry, Company K. He was buried in Moravian Cemetery.

1224. **Frank C. HOWELL** was born on 1 February 1875 in Warren County, NJ. He died on 4 July 1953 in Newton, Sussex County, NJ. and was buried in Moravian Cemetery, Hope, NJ. He was a butcher. He married **Lillie O. OSMUN** about 1898. Lillie O. OSMUN was born on 2 December 1870 in NJ. She died on 26 August 1955 in Newton, and was buried in Moravian Cemetery. Their children were:

+1933 i. **Jonah HOWELL.**
1934 ii. **Lucy A. HOWELL** was born 31 March 1901. She died in 1991. She was married to **John HOOVER.**

+1935 iii. **Brevilla HOWELL**

1228. **Dewitt C. HOWELL** was born on 9 February 1882 in Warren County, NJ. He died on 14 November 1968, and was buried in Pequest Union Cemetery, Great Meadows, NJ. He lived in Milton, Delaware. He was married (1) to **Mary C. SMITH** on 4 February 1905. [239] Mary C. SMITH was born in 1882. She died on 2 March 1906, and was buried in Pequest Union Cemetery. Dewitt and Mary had a son:

1936 i. **Herbert B. HOWELL** was born about February 1906 in Warren County, NJ

Dewitt C. HOWELL married (2) **Lucinda (Lulu) COURTRIGHT**, who was born on 22 August 1891 and died in June 1979. They had these children:

1937 ii. **Charles C. HOWELL** was born about 1913 in Warren County, NJ.

1938 iii. **Harry R. HOWELL** was born on 15 June 1913 in Warren County. He died in May 1980.

1233. **Alvah S. HOWELL** was born in February 1877 in Warren County, NJ. He died in 1946, and was buried in Moravian Cemetery, Hope, Warren County. He was a store owner and postmaster in Hope. He was married (1) to **Diza M. LANCE** (daughter of **Isaiah LANCE** and **Kasiah TITMAN**) on 29 August 1900. Diza M. LANCE was born in 1879 in Walnut Valley, NJ. She died on 27 August 1930, and was buried in Moravian Cemetery. Alvah and Diza had one child:

+1939 i. **Gladys L. HOWELL**.

Alvah married (2) **Mabel BOWERS** (daughter of **William BOWERS** and **Lydia Ann HOWELL**). Mabel was born in 1887; she died in 1956, and was buried in Moravian Cemetery.

1234. **Edwin P. GIBBS** was born on 5 October 1855. He was called Edwin P. in one paragraph in the Michael Shoemaker Book,[240] and Edward P. in another, so perhaps that was his proper name. Edwin married **Alice CAVANAUGH**. Edwin P. GIBBS and Alice CAVANAUGH had the following children:

+1940 i. **Grace Anna GIBBS**.
+1941 ii. **Josephine GIBBS**.
1942 iii. **Edith GIBBS**.
1943 iv. **Yale GIBBS**.
1944 v. **Walter Wayne GIBBS**.

---

239 Notice of marriage, Washington (NJ) Star 13 Feb 1905.
240 Williams T. Blair, The Michael Shoemaker Book, 1924, Scranton, PA, International Textbook Press. p. 318.

1945 vi. **Viola Marion GIBBS.**

1235. **Isaac A. GIBBS** was born on 12 May 1857. He married **Phebe QUICK**. Their children were:

+1946 i. **Harry GIBBS.**
+1947 ii. **Freda GIBBS.**
+1948 iii. **Fannie GIBBS.**
1949 iv. **Lena GIBBS** married **Fred DEREMER**.
1950 v. **Stella GIBBS.**
1951 vi. **Angeline GIBBS** married **Unknown MYERS**.
1952 vii. **Clarence GIBBS.**
1953 viii. **Claude GIBBS.**

1237. **Emma A . GIBBS** was born on 25 April 1861. Since she was not named as a survivor in her brother William's obituary, she can be presumed to have died before 1899. Emma married **John WHITESELL**. Their children were:

1954 i. **George WHITESELL** married **Olive CUMMINGS**.
1955 ii. **William WHITESELL** married **Mary GREEN**.

1239. **John D. GIBBS** was born on 15 March 1865. John married (1) **Anna MARLOTT**. John D. GIBBS and Anna MARLOTT had one child:

1956 i. **Andrew GIBBS.**

John D. GIBBS married (2) **Alice PAULISON**.

1240. **Luella V. GIBBS** was born on 25 November 1868. She was married to **William H. BALL**, (son of **John Snover BALL** and **Mary TUNNISON**) on 15 February 1888. Their children were:

1957 i. **Leon C. BALL** was born on 4 June 1890 in Wharton, Morris, NJ. Leon was employed by the Wharton Steel Company. He became a draftsman, and, in 1916, was Chief draftsman in the Ordnance Department of the U. S. Army, with an office in the Dover, New Jerey Arsenal.
1958 ii. **Floyd S. BALL** was born on 19 December 1891.
1959 iii. **Jessie M. BALL** was born on 13 September 1893, and married **Eugene OPDYKE** (son of **Archibald OPDYKE**) on 30 December 1911 in Wharton, NJ.
1960 iv. **Earl G. BALL** was born on 2 February 1897.
1961 v. **Vida L. BALL** was born on 3 March 1899.

1241. **Sampson Howell GIBBS** was born on 10 August 1870. Sampson married **Lizzie SKILLMAN**. Sampson and Lizzie had one child:

1962 i. **Myrtle V. GIBBS.**

1242. **Frank L. GIBBS** was born on 10 November 1872. Frank married **Ada SCHOCH**. Frank L. GIBBS and Ada SCHOCH had the following children:

1963 i. **Gladys GIBBS.**
1964 ii. **Paul GIBBS.**

1244. **Lavina G. GIBBS** was born on 12 November 1877. She married **William A. COLE**. Lavina G. GIBBS and William A. COLE had the following children:

1965 i. **Frederick M. COLE.**
1966 ii. **William Olice COLE.**

1246. **Frederick F. CRUSEN** was born in Hope, Warren County, NJ. Fred was in the farm products business in Brooklyn, NY in 1916. He married **Lillian BOWLES**. They had one child:

1967 i. **Ruth Euphemia CRUSEN.**

1250. **Stewart MILLER** married **Mamie SWETTON**. Their children were:

1968 i. **Donald MILLER.**
1969 ii. **Edith MILLER.**

1251. **Wirt D. MILLER** was a merchant in Stroudsburg, PA in 1916. He married **Emma WILLIAMS**. Wirt D. MILLER and Emma WILLIAMS had the following children:

1970 i. **Frederick MILLER.**
1971 ii. **Robert MILLER.**

1253. **Frank H. MILLER**. Frank and his family lived in Fort Collins, Colorado in 1916. He married **Della CRAWFORD**. Frank H. MILLER and Della CRAWFORD had one child:

1972 i. **Frank Howell MILLER.**

1257. **Mayme E. TRIMMER** was born on 20 January 1883 in Anita, Cass County, Iowa. She was married to **Dr. C. J. WAINWRIGHT** (son of **John WAINWRIGHT** and **Laura HOOVER**) on 20 January 1909 in Anita. Dr. Wainwright graduated from Nebraska State University as a physician in 1905, and began practice in Anita that year. In 1911, they moved to Giltner, Nebraska, where he died on 13 January 1914. Mayme stayed in Giltner after his death. They had one child:

1973 i. **Maxwell T. WAINWRIGHT** was born on 27 November 1910 in Giltner, NE.

1259. **Annie MILLER** was born on 29 April 1877 in Dallas Twp., Luzerne County, Pennsylvania. She died on 23 April 1914 in Port Blanchard, Luzerne County. She married **George L. BRITTON** (son of **John BRITTON** and **Anna SNELL**) on 26 October 1895 in Dallas Twp. They had these children:

1974 i. **Lilian BRITTON** was born on 2 January 1899.
1975 ii. **Robert BRITTON** was born on 17 December 1901.
1976 iii. **Sarah BRITTON** was born on 11 September 1903.
1977 iv. **Gertrude BRITTON** was born on 3 November 1905.
1978 v. **Lawrence BRITTON** was born on 29 October 1908.
1979 vi. **Arthur BRITTON** was born on 7 April 1910.

1260. **Letitia MILLER** was born on 14 February 1879 in Dallas Twp., Luzerne County, PA. She was married to **Samuel Arthur FREAR** (son of **Elisha Harding FREAR** and **Elnora GOBLE**) on 26 April 1905. Samuel Arthur FREAR was born on 17 December 1877. They had one child:

1980 i. **Donald Elisha FREAR** was born on 16 September 1906 in Eatonville, Wyoming County, Pennsylvania.

1261. **Jennie MILLER** was born on 18 January 1885 in Dallas Twp., Luzerne County, Pennsylvania. She married **Lorenzo D. FITCH**. Jennie MILLER and Lorenzo D. FITCH had these children:

1981 i. **Laura FITCH** was born on 26 July 1904 in Pittston, Luzerne County, PA.
1982 ii. **Alice FITCH** was born on 7 May 1906 in Pittston.
1983 iii. **Florence FITCH** was born on 18 May 1908 in Pittston.
1984 iv. **Ralph FITCH** was born on 10 February 1910 in Pittston.

1271. **Samuel Linn HEMINGWAY** was born about 1877 in New Jersey. He married **UNKNOWN**. They had one child:

+1985 i. **Margery HEMINGWAY** .

1279. **Alice Verona HOWELL** was born on 3 December 1906. She married **Benjamin D. CONDIT**, who was born on 26 June 1901 and died on 17 October 1973. Alice died on 13 August 1978. Both are buried in New Hope Cemetery. They had two daughters:

1986 i. **Virginia Elizabeth CONDIT** was born on 28 December 1942.
+1987 ii. **Mary Alice CONDIT**.

1281. **Matilda Cummins HOWELL** was born on 7 February 1911. She married **Leonard SMEDES**. Their daughter was:

+1988 i. **Alice SMEDES.**

1287. **Sylvester Vansyckle HOWELL** was born on 21 April 1895 in Clinton, Hunterdon County, NJ. He died on 20 February 1966 in Flemington, Hunterdon County, and was buried in Riverside Cemetery, Clinton, Hunterdon County.[231] Sylvester was called Lester in his father's obituary. He was living in West Orange, NJ at that time. He purchased a farm in the Cokesbury area in 1948. He was a graduate of Clinton High School and Lafayette College. He was a vice president of Caroon and Reynolds Insurance Company of New York, though he had not been active in the business for some time before his death. He had also been a director of the Insurance Federation of New York. He was a veteran of the Signal corps in WWI. He was married to **Thusnelda UNKNOWN**. Their children were:

1989 i. **John D. HOWELL** was living in Arlington, Virginia, a retired Captain of the US Navy, at the time of his father's death, in 1966.

1990 ii. **Cynthia C. HOWELL** married **Unknown CRAGIN**. They lived in rural Lebanon, New Jersey in 1966.

1289. **Charles Evans HOWELL** was born on 19 November 1876. He died on 3 February 1949. He married **Ida WHEELER**. Charles Evans HOWELL and Ida WHEELER had the following children:

1991 i. **Gladys HOWELL.**

1992 ii. **Unknown male HOWELL** was killed by an out-of-control car which ran into the yard where he was playing.

1993 iii. **Herbert HOWELL.**

1290. **Robert Ernest HOWELL** was born on 1 August 1887 in Binghamton, NY. He died on 28 October 1918. He was a machinist. He married **Frances Emma OAKEY**, who was born on 14 April 1887 in Hednesford, Shropshire, England. She died on 10 May 1940. Their children were:

1994 i. **Richard Henry HOWELL**. was born on 23 September 1909. He died on 10 March 1971. He married **Lucille Caroline PERSBACKER**, who was born on 1 April 1907.

1995 ii. **Marion Louise HOWELL** was born on 27 November 1914. She was a dental hygienist.

1292. **Elizabeth Weise HOWELL** was born in 1876 in Warren County, NJ. She died in 1969, and was buried in Union Cemetery, Hackettstown, Warren County. She married **Carter Martin LABAR**, who was born in 1877. He died in 1947 in Warren County, NJ. Elizabeth and Carter LABAR had one child:

---

[231]Obituary, The Democrat, (Flemington, NJ) 24 February 1966, p. 7.

1996 i. **Thomas B. Howell LABAR** was born in 1902.

1300. **Mildred Julia HOWELL** was born about 1895 in Warren County, NJ. She died in 1973, and was buried in Union Cemetery, Hackettstown, Warren County. She married **Russel VLIET**. Mildred and Russel VLIET had one child:

1997 i. **Lewis VLIET**.

1306. **Samson Austin HOWELL** was born on 6 June 1906 in Vienna, Warren County, NJ. He died on 13 November 1994 in Bethlehem, Northampton, County, PA, and was buried in Union Cemetery, Hackettstown, Warren County. [232] Samson was a CPA, employed by J. S. Teunon and Co. in Trenton, Mercer County, NJ before retiring in 1970. He was married to **Mabel S. DOOLEY** (daughter of **George S. DOOLEY** and **Ann SMILEY**) on 15 June 1935 in Philadelphia, Philadelphia County, PA. Mabel S. DOOLEY was born on 3 August 1908 in Philadelphia. She died on 30 March 1997 in Bethlehem, and was buried on 12 April 1997 in Union Cemetery, Hackettstown.[233] Mabel lived in Bethlehem after 1993, having moved from Vincentown, NJ. where she had lived from 1975 to 1993. Prior to that time, she had lived in Trenton, NJ from 1936 to 1975. She had been a private secretary for Curtis Publishing Co. in Philadelphia, retiring in 1935. Samson and Mabel had one child:

1998 i. **Edna HOWELL** married **Unknown UPDIKE**, and was living in Bethlehem, PA in 1997. She is said to have 3 children.

1316. **Mary "Mae" Rosebrugh HOWELL** was born on 4 January 1889 in S. Dumfries, Brant County, Ontario. She was buried in St. George United Cemetery, S. Dumfries. She was married to **Herbert Robb HOWELL** (son of **Herbert Levi HOWELL** and **Sarah Jane ROBB**) on 21 September 1910 in S. Dumfries. Herbert Robb HOWELL was born on 21 May 1889 in S. Dumfries. He died on 9 September 1974. and was buried in St. George United Cemetery. Their children are:

+1999 i. **Dorothy Leone HOWELL**.
+2000 ii. **Lloyd Herbert HOWELL**

1317. **Alice HOWELL** was born on 5 May 1893. She died on 7 July 1963, and was buried in St. George United Cemetery. She married **Fernie TAYLOR**, who was born on 28 January 1891. He died on 19 October 1962, and was buried in St. George United Cemetery. Their children were:

2001 i. **Ross TAYLOR**.
2002 ii. **Joyce TAYLOR**.

---

[232]Obituary, Easton (PA) Express, 14 November 1994.
[233]Obituary, Easton (PA) Express, 2 April 1997.

2003 iii. **Leone TAYLOR**.
2004 iv. **Howard TAYLOR**.

1318. **Cuthbert HOWELL** was born in 1900. He died on 1 May 1950, and was buried in St. George United Cemetery. He married **Gladys PRINE**, who was born on 29 August 1896. She died on 21 August 1984, and was buried in St. George United Cemetery. Cuthbert and Gladys had one child:

2005 i. **Elizabeth HOWELL** was married to **Glen SMITH**.

1332. **Aleatha HOWELL** was born in 1870 in Ancaster Twp., Wentworth County, Ontario. She died in 1916 in Ontario, and was buried in Zion Hill Cemetery, Ancaster Twp. She married **William POTTER**. Aleatha HOWELL and William POTTER had the following children:

2006 i. **Mary K. POTTER** died in 1911, and was buried in Zion Hill Cemetery.
2007 ii. **William POTTER** was born in 1883, died in 1966 and was buried in Zion Hill Cemetery. He married **Florence Emily UNKNOWN**, who was born in 1899,died in 1973, and was buried in Zion Hill Cemetery.

1342. **Gordon E. HOWELL** was born in 1891. He died in 1970, and was buried in Zion Hill Cemetery. He married **Helen M. TREDWAY**, who was born in 1895. She died in 1972, and was also buried in Zion Hill Cemetery. Gordon E. HOWELL and Helen M. TREDWAY had one child:

2008 i. **Peggy Ann HOWELL** was born in 1915 and died in 1963. She married **Ronald ARDON**, who was born in 1911 and died in 1974. Both were buried in Zion Hill Cemetery.

1348. **Fred L. HOWELL** was born in 1880 in Ancaster Twp., Wentworth County, Ontario. He died in 1940, and was buried in Ancaster Twp. He married **Leona Ethel BILLIALD**, who was born in 1883. She died on 11 March 1968, and was buried in Ancaster Twp. Fred L. HOWELL and Leona Ethel BILLIALD had one child:

2009 i. **Alfred Leslie HOWELL**.

1371. **Herbert GERMAN** was born on 5 December 1869 in S. Dumfries, Brant County, and died on 11 November 1968 in Brantford, Brant County. He married **Catherine Alberta HOWELL** (daughter of **Philip Stenabaugh HOWELL** and **Mary Jane GREEN**) on 10 June 1903. Please refer to Catherine Alberta HOWELL # 869.

1393. **Frank KITCHEN** was a farmer. He was married to **Edith BOWLBY** on 2 September 1908 in Toronto, Ontario. Frank KITCHEN and Edith BOWLBY had the following children:

2010 i. **Harold KITCHEN**.
2011 ii. **Russell KITCHEN**.

1394. **Fred J. PATTEN** was born in 1887 in Harrisburg, Ontario. He died on 31 March 1965 in St. Joseph's Hospital, Brantford, Ontario. His wife was **Eva SMITH**. Fred and Eva had these children:

2012 i. **Doris PATTEN** married **Richard EARL**. They lived in Palmetto, Florida.
2013 ii. **Jeanne PATTEN** married **Roy ABRAM**; they lived in Northfield, Ohio.
2014 iii. **Frank PATTEN**.
2015 iv. **Joyce Almira PATTEN** was born in May 1935. She died on 10 August 1936.

1396. **Culver Finlay PATTEN** was born on 8 November 1889 in St. George, Brant County, and died on 5 April 1960 in Brantford General Hospital. He married **Janet T. MCNEIL**, and they had one child:.

2016 i. **Eva PATTEN** married **Frank ARCHER**.

1399. **Eva H. PATTEN** was married (1) to **W. W. ROBERTSON**. Eva married (2) **Samuel J. CHERRY** on 12 February 1919 in Harrisburg, Ontario. They had these children:

2017 i. **Isabel CHERRY**.
2018 ii. **Harold CHERRY**.

1410. **Anna Rachel PATTEN** was born in Brant County. She was married to **Earl Kelsey HOPKINS** on 29 October 1919 in St. George, Brant County, Ontario. Their children were:

+2019 i. **Marion HOPKINS**.
2020 ii. **Mary HOPKINS** was born and died on 13 October 1920 in S. Dumfries.

1411. **Edward BELL** married **Jessie PHARRISH**. They had one child:

2021 i. **Bertram BELL** was born about 1883 and died on 24 January 1886.

1417. **Charles BELL** married **Annie MCKAY**. Charles BELL and Annie MCKAY had one child:

2022 i. **Claude BELL**

1419. **James BELL** married **Helen HEALY**. James and Helen had these children:

2023 i. **Mildred BELL**.
2024 ii. **Alice BELL**.
2025 iii. **Douglas BELL**.

1420. **Mary Josephine BELL** was born in 1881, and died in 1951. She married **Benjamin Bell PATTEN**, who was born in 1880, and died in 1958. Their children were:

+2026 i. **Laurie Alice PATTEN**.
2027 ii. **Helen PATTEN**.

1421. **James HUNTER** married **Gussie CALVERT**. James and Gussie had these children:

2028 i. **Augusta HUNTER**.
2029 ii. **Calvert HUNTER**.

1427. **William KINNEY** married **Mabel RICHARDS**, and they had one child:

2030 i. **Elizabeth KINNEY**.

1428. **Russell KINNEY** married **Emma WORTHINGTON**, and they had two children:

2031 i. **Kathleen KINNEY**.
2032 ii. **Jack KINNEY** was married to **Grace MITCHELL**.

1429. **Edna KINNEY** married **Graydon SWARTZ**. Their children were:

2033 i. **Glen SWARTZ**.
2034 ii. **Marguerite SWARTZ**.
2035 iii. **Clifford SWARTZ**.

1430. **Elma KINNEY** married **James HUNT**, and they had these children:

2036 i. **Fernie HUNT**.
2037 ii. **May HUNT**.
2038 iii. **Sinclair HUNT**.

1432. **Firman Aikman HOWELL** was born on 14 February 1878 in S. Dumfries. He died there on 29 March 1944, and was buried in St. George United Cemetery. He married his second cousin, **Ella May WALLEY** (daughter of **John WALLEY** and **Mary Ellen HOWELL**) on 2 November 1910 in Birtle, Manitoba. Ella May was born on 12 May 1885 in Birtle. She died on 5 May 1967 in Brantford Twp., Brant County, Ontario, and was buried in St. George United Cemetery. Their children were:

2038 i. **Alice Evelyn HOWELL** was born on 30 July 1911. She taught in Brant County schools for 21 years, and in Puslich for 2 years. She married **Edwin Simon SHANTZ** on 9 July 1941. He was born on 1 April 1878 in Wilmont, Waterloo County, Ontario, and died in Hespeler, Ontario. He was buried in Wanner Cemetery in Hespeler.

2040 ii. **Margaret Fern HOWELL** was born on 31 October 1914. Margaret never married. She was a chicken farmer and worked at Spruceleigh Farms.

1433. **William Nelson HOWELL** was born on 17 December 1881 in S. Dumfries, Brant County, Ontario. He died on 1 September 1962 in Ontario, and was buried in St. George United Cemetery. In 1941, he was elected Warden of Brant County, and served as Reeve of the county from 1940 through 1942. He was married (1) to **Emma Pauline WILSON** (daughter of **John WILSON** and **Annie COUSE**) on 7 October 1908 in Marsville, Dufferin County, Ontario. Emma Pauline WILSON was born on 27 January 1884 in Marsville. She died in S. Dumfries, Brant County, Ontario. Their children were:

+2041 i. **James Wilson HOWELL**.

2042 ii. **Marjorie Anna Pauline HOWELL** was born on 2 April 1915 in S. Dumfries. Marjorie was a teacher. She married **William MCCREA** on 16 October 1943 in St. George. He died on 10 March 1965 in Brantford Twp. They had no children.

After marrying (2) **Anne RICHARDS**, William retired from farming, and moved into St. George. His son, James, took over the farm.

1434. **John Roy HOWELL** was born on 31 March 1885 in S. Dumfries. He died on 19 November 1973 in Brantford Twp., and was buried in St. George United Cemetery. He married **Gladys Norma KITCHEN** (daughter of **Edward Collver KITCHEN** and **Lizzie ANDERSON**) on 28 August 1912. She was born on 30 March 1890, and died on 23 April 1974 in Brantford Twp. They had a son:

+2043 i. **John Arthur HOWELL**.

1435. **Louis WOOD** married **Inez NEALE**. Louis WOOD and Inez NEALE had one child:

2044 i. **Margaret WOOD**.

1437. **Lideral William Morley BUCK** was born on 6 November 1876, and died on 10 March 1948in Birmingham, AL. He married **Catherine COMER** (daughter of **Braxton Bragg COMER** and **Eva Jane HARRIS**), on 7 January 1908 in Birmingham, AL. Catherine COMER was born in Alabama on 20 December 1882 and died on 13 February 1968 in Delray Beach, FL. William operated the Orchard Beach Hotel, first opened by his father. They had three children:

+2045	i.	**William Morley BUCK**.
+2046	ii.	**John Harris BUCK**.
+2047	iii.	**Edward Comer BUCK**.

1438. **James Orton BUCK** was born on 10 September 1880 in Brantford. The family moved to Port Dover in 1886. At 19, James went to Boston, where he worked for R. G. Dun & Co., which later became Dun & Bradstreet. He stayed with the firm until retirement, having served as manager of the Bridgeport CT and Portland ME offices. He died in Lake Wales, Fl on 6 March 1965. James married **Myra Estelle WOOSTER** (daughter of **Albert Mills WOOSTER** and **Fannie Brounley BOWEN**) on 5 June 1912 in Bridgeport CT. Fannie was born in Washington, D.C. on 23 June 1879, and died on 15 August 1969 in DeBary, FL. Their children were:

+2048	i.	**James Orton BUCK**.
2049	ii.	**Beverley BUCK** was born on 10 January 1916 in Bridgeport, Fairfield County, CT.
+2050	iii.	**Julian Randolph BUCK**.
2051	iv.	**Beatrice BUCK** was born on 21 August 1918 in Portland, ME.

1439. **Orton Stanley HOWELL** was born on 17 July 1884 in St. George, Brant County, Ontario. He died on 27 June 1967 in Galt, Waterloo County, Ontario, and was buried in St. George United Cemetery. He was a farmer. He married (1) **Alice Mary HOWELL** (daughter of **Herbert Watson HOWELL** and **Ida Jane HOWELL**) who was born in 1890 in St. George, died in December 1928 in Dundas, Ontario, and was buried in St. George United Cemetery. Their only child was:

+2052	i.	**Orton Bertrum McLean HOWELL**.

Orton married (2) **Annie Elizabeth MCLEAN**, who was born in 1891. She died in 1966, and was buried in St. George United Cemetery. Orton and Annie Elizabeth had one child:

2053	i.	**Shirley Diane McLean HOWELL**.

1453. **Thomas Leslie HOWELL** was born on 28 December 1889 in St. George, Brant County, Ontario. He died on 16 June 1950 in Chatham, Ontario, and was buried in Chatham. Thomas L. Howell served in WWI and then joined the Ontario Provincial Police. He was stationed at Dresden until 1949, and then in Chatham,

Ontario. He was married to **Ina Mae STAFFORD** (daughter of **Charles STAFFORD** and **Blanche WELDON**) on 2 March 1932 in Shedden, Ontario. Ina Mae STAFFORD was born on 14 February 1907 in Shedden, Ontario. Thomas Leslie HOWELL and Ina Mae STAFFORD had the following children:

+2054	i.	**Leslie Weldon HOWELL.**
+2055	ii.	**Maxwell Glen HOWELL.**
+2056	iii.	**Maxine Lucille HOWELL.**

1454. **Alice Mary HOWELL** was born in 1890 in St. George, Brant County, Ontario. She died in December 1928 in Dundas, Ontario, and was buried in St. George United Cemetery. Please see **Orton Stanley HOWELL** , # 1439, above.

1455. **Herbert William HOWELL** was born on 16 September 1894 in St. George, Brant County, Ontario. He died on 15 November 1970 in Aurora, Ontario. He was married to **Florence Ann PICKESS** (daughter of **William PICKESS** and **Jane SADLER**) on 1 August 1919 in the Registry Office, England. Florence Ann PICKESS was born on 25 September 1896 in London, England. She died on 1 April 1971 in Aurora, Ontario, Canada. Their children were:

+2057	i.	**Muriel Grace HOWELL.**
+2058	ii.	**Jean Alva HOWELL.**
+2059	iii.	**Wayne Bertrum HOWELL.**
2060	iv.	**Leslie Watson HOWELL** was born on 1 June 1924 in Beamsville, Ontario.
2061	v.	**Donald HOWELL** was born on 14 August 1926 in Beamsville, Ontario.
2062	vi.	**Gerald L. HOWELL** was born on 8 October 1935 in Guelph, Wellington County, Ontario.

1456. **Jean Alberta HOWELL** was born on 20 February 1898 in St. George, Brant County, Ontario. She was married to **James Wendel SIMPSON** M.D. on 4 October 1922 in Winnipeg, Manitoba. James Wendel SIMPSON M.D. was born on 18 November 1896 in Ashton, Carleton County, Ontario. Jean Alberta HOWELL and James Wendel SIMPSON M.D. had the following children:

+2063	i.	**James Holmes SIMPSON.**
+2064	ii.	**Patricia Ann SIMPSON.**
+2065	iii.	**Jean Elizabeth SIMPSON.**
+2066	iv.	**Janet Elaine SIMPSON.**

1480. **Margaret PETRIE** was born on 4 August 1890 in South Dumfries. She died on 4 February 1964 in Smiths Falls, Lanark County, Ontario, and was buried in Maple Vale Cemetery, Smiths Falls. She was married to **Jackson Graham DAVIDSON** on 10 July 1911 in Paris, Brant County, Ontario. Jackson Graham DAVIDSON was born on 26 March 1889 in Cainsville, Brant County, Ontario. He died on 5 December 1970 in Smiths Falls, and was buried in Maple Vale

Cemetery. Graham was a veterinarian, a graduate of University of Toronto. He was a government meat inspector, touring farms to test cattle for tuberculosis. He also traveled overseas frequently, on government business. They had these children:

+2067 i. **Helen Elizabeth DAVIDSON**.
+2068 ii. **Margaret Graham DAVIDSON**.
+2069 iii. **Dorothy Irene DAVIDSON**.
+2070 iv. **Jackson Graham DAVIDSON**.

1483. **George Samuel DEAN** was born on 26 August 1857 in North Ogden, Weber County, Utah. He married **Alice Sarah DANIELS**, who was born on 18 May 1867 in Tillshead, Wiltshire, England. George Samuel DEAN and Alice Sarah DANIELS had the following children:

2071 i. **George Samuel DEAN Jr**. was born on 14 September 1885 in North Ogden. He married (1) **Pearl WEATHERMAN**, who was born in 1889 in North Ogden, and (2) **Faye WILSON**, also born in 1889 in North Ogden.

2072 ii. **Inez Emma DEAN** was born on 23 March 1888, in North Ogden. She married **Joseph SPACKMAN**, who was born on 8 October 1887 in Pleasant View, Weber County, UT.

2073 iii. **Irene Elizabeth DEAN** was born on 23 March 1888 in North Ogden. She married **William Mathias ALVORD**, who was born on 27 November 1888 in North Ogden.

2074 iv. **John William DEAN** was born on 1 November 1889 in North Ogden. He married **Myrtle COUEY**, who was born on 21 April 1886 in Boyd, Chippewa County, WA.

2075 v. **Lester Clyde DEAN** was born on 30 September 1891 in North Ogden. He married (1) **Roella CASHIN**, who was born in 1895 in North Ogden. Lester married (2) **Merle Elizabeth WISEMAN**, who was born in 1895 in North Ogden.

2076 vi. **Alice Mary DEAN** was born on 10 August 1893 in North Ogden.

2077 vii. **Levi Norvill DEAN** was born on 20 August 1897 in North Ogden. He married **Lucile Adina WALDRAM,** who was born on 27 January 1896 in North Ogden.

2078 viii. **Beatrice Violet DEAN** was born on 20 August 1897 in North Ogden. She married **Clarence Arthur DAVIS**, who was born in 1893 in North Ogden.

2079 ix. **Melba DEAN**.

1484. **David Lorenzo DEAN** was born on 25 May 1859 in North Ogden, Weber County, Utah. He married **Alice Ann JENKINS** was born on 21 August 1865 in Salt Lake City, Salt Lake County, Utah. David and Alice had one child:

2080 i. **Thomas J. DEAN** was born in 1885 in Logan, Cache County, Utah.

1485. **James Riley DEAN** was born on 1 April 1861 in Pleasantview, Utah. His wife was **Lucinda Elizabeth EVELAND**, who was born on 4 September 1874 in Clay, Clay Center County, Kansas. James and Lucinda had one child:

2081 i. **Nellie Elizabeth DEAN** was born on 26 April 1897 in North Ogden. She married **Edward Franklin GLINES**, who was born on 9 October 1890 in Vernal, Uintah County, UT.

1491. **Martha Matilda DEAN** was born on 29 June 1872 in North Ogden. She married **George Edgar WORTON**, who was born in 1868 in North Ogden. They had one child:

2082 i. **Mabel L. WORTON** was born on 29 November 1900 in North Ogden.

1552. **Mary STEELE** was born in 1865. She died in 1957. She married **George PARKHILL** who was born in 1859. He died in 1938. They had one child:

+2083 i. **Fred PARKHILL**.

1553. **Albert Edwin STEELE** was born on 24 May 1870 in Paris, Brant County, Ontario. He died in 1944. He was married to **Minnie MIDGLEY** in 1891. Minnie MIDGLEY was born in 1872. Albert Edwin STEELE and Minnie MIDGLEY had one child:

+2084 i. **Grace STEELE**.

1560. **Ernest Albert WALLEY** was born on 11 October 1883 in Birtle, Manitoba. He died in 1966. He was married to **Maude Effie CHRISTIE** (daughter of **Jonas CHRISTIE** and **Margaret THOMAS**) on 27 December 1911 in Glenboro, Manitoba. Maude Effie CHRISTIE was born on 16 July 1890 in Glenboro, Manitoba. Ernest Albert WALLEY and Maude Effie CHRISTIE had the following children:

+2085 i. **John Earlington "Jack" WALLEY**.
+2086 ii. **Irene Marguarite WALLEY**.
+2087 iii. **Kathleen Maude WALLEY**.
2088 iv. **Jean Merle WALLEY** was born on 26 June 1918 in Glenboro, Manitoba. She died on 4 October 1929 in Birtle, Manitoba, of diphtheria.

+2089 v. **Ernest Christie WALLEY**.

1561. **Ella May WALLEY** was born on 12 May 1885 in Birtle, Manitoba, and died on 5 May 1967 in Brantford Twp., Brant County, Ontario. She was buried in St. George United Cemetery. She was married to **Firman Aikman HOWELL** (son of **James Bird HOWELL** and **Rachel E. LAWRASON**) on 2 November 1910 in Birtle, Manitoba. Please refer to **Firman Aikman HOWELL**, # 1432.

1562. **Alice Evelyn WALLEY** was born in 1889 in Birtle, Manitoba. She died in 1974 in Winnipeg, Manitoba. She was married to **Albert Summerfield HAMES** on 10 July 1913 in Glenboro, Manitoba. Albert Summerfield HAMES was born in 1882 in Meadow Lea, Manitoba. He died in 1963 in Winnipeg, Manitoba. Alice Evelyn WALLEY and Albert Summerfield HAMES had the following children:

+2090 i. **Marie Evelyn HAMES**.
+2091 ii. **Ellen Berta HAMES**.
+2092 iii. **Elizabeth Jean HAMES**.

1563. **Ernest Wellesley HOWELL** was born in 1888 in S. Dumfries. He died in 1972, and was buried in St. George United Cemetery. He married **Pearl Mary ROSEBRUGH**, who was born in 1889. She died in 1978, and was buried in St. George United Cemetery. Ernest Wellesley HOWELL and Pearl Mary ROSEBRUGH had one child:

2093 i. **Ruth HOWELL** was born in 1913.

1564. **Herbert Robb HOWELL** was born on 21 May 1889 in S. Dumfries. He died on 9 September 1974, and was buried in St. George United Cemetery. He was married to **Mary "Mae" Rosebrugh HOWELL** (daughter of **James Arthur HOWELL** and **Sarah Maria ROSEBRUGH**) on 21 September 1910 in S. Dumfries. Please refer to **Mary "Mae" Rosebrugh HOWELL** #1316.

1565. **Ivah HOWELL** was born on 26 December 1892 in Prospect Hill, Ontario. She died in 1957She was married to **James Dafoe MULHOLLAND** on 23 February 1921 in Galt, Waterloo County, Ontario. James Dafoe MULHOLLAND was born on 30 April 1890 in Branchton, Ontario. He died on 1 May 1957 in Calderbank, Saskatchewan, and was buried in Central Butte Cemetery, Calderbank, Saskatchewan. Ivah and James Dafoe MULHOLLAND had the following children:

2094 i. **Alma May MULHOLLAND** was born on 14 December 1924 in Calderbank. She died on 29 May 1925.
+2095 ii. **Cecil James MULHOLLAND**.

1566. **Philip Samuel HOWELL** was born on 12 November 1895 in S. Dumfries, Brant County, Ontario. He died on 26 April 1985 in Brantford, Brant County, Ontario. He was married (1) to **Helen Irene KER** (daughter of **William Holmes KER** and **Lucy Jane BULLOCK**) on 16 June 1920 in St. George, Brant County,

Ontario. Helen Irene KER was born on 20 June 1899 in St. George, Ontario. She died on 9 April 1994 in Paris, Brant County, Ontario, and was buried on 12 April 1994 in Paris Cemetery, Paris, Brant County, Ontario. Philip Samuel HOWELL and Helen Irene KER had the following children:

+2096 i. **Marion Helen HOWELL.**
+2097 ii. **Jack Philip HOWELL.**
+2098 iii. **William Herbert HOWELL.**
+2099 iv. **Gordon Ker HOWELL.**
+2100 v. **Jean Louise HOWELL.**

Philip left his wife, Helen Irene KER and married (2) **Harriet Margaret GRINYER** (daughter of **Edward GRINYER** and **Mary ALPINE**) was born on 29 August 1904 in Caledonia, Ontario. She died on 2 June 1976, and was buried in Mt. Zion Cemetery, Wentworth County, Ontario. Their children were:

+2101 i. **Kenneth Philip HOWELL.**
+2102 ii. **Margaret Joyce HOWELL.**
+2103 iii. **Donald Howard HOWELL.**
+2104 iv. **Edwin Allen HOWELL.**
+2105 v. **James Edgar HOWELL.**
2106 vi. **Unknown male HOWELL** was born in 1947 in Brantford Twp, died a few days after birth, and was buried in St. George United Cemetery.
+2107 vii. **Mary Elizabeth HOWELL.**

1567. **Evelyn Mabel GERMAN** was born on 18 April 1904 in S. Dumfries, Brant County, Ontario. She was married to **Charles Clifton Alexander LYONS** (son of **Alexander LYONS** and **Jenny Lamb GOODBRAND**) on 4 October 1930 in S. Dumfries. Charles Clifton Alexander LYONS was born on 11 August 1901 in Ancaster Twp., Wentworth County, Ontario. He died on 22 February 1983 in Brantford Twp., Brant County, Ontario. Evelyn and Charles had these children:

+2108 i. **Glen Clifton LYONS.**
2109 ii. **Howard Gordon LYONS** was born on 14 April 1933 in S. Dumfries. He died on 23 April 1956 in Toronto, Ontario, and was buried in St. George United Cemetery.

1568. **Cecil Bruce GERMAN** was born on 3 January 1906 in S. Dumfries. He died on 31 December 1991 in Brantford Twp., Brant County, Ontario. He was married to **Edythe Mary FITZGERALD** on 5 September 1936 in Thorndale, Ontario. Edythe Mary FITZGERALD was born on 22 June 1902 in Thorndale, Ontario, and died on 30 May 1986 in Brantford Twp. Their children were:

+2110 i. **Herbert Edward GERMAN.**
+2111 ii. **William Bruce GERMAN.**
+2112 iii. **Raemond Fitzgerald GERMAN.**

1569. **Ethel Mildred GERMAN** was born on 26 December 1907 in Brantford Twp., Brant County, Ontario. She died on 30 April 1978 in Brantford Twp. She was married to **Gavin Thomas MCCLURE** on 21 November 1942 in S. Dumfries. Gavin Thomas MCCLURE was born on 28 December 1901 in Brantford Twp. He died there on 3 June 1979, and was buried in Mt. Hope Cemetery, Brantford Twp. Ethel Mildred and Gavin Thomas MCCLURE had the following children:

+2113 i. **Katharine Jane MCCLURE**.
2114 ii. **John Gavin MCCLURE** was born on 28 February 1945 in Brantford Twp. He married **Corrinne Pearl KINGHAM** on 17 November 1984 in Brantford Twp. She was born on 9 May 1948 in Kitchener, Waterloo County, Ontario.
+2115 iii. **Donald Morton MCCLURE**.

1570. **Flossie May GERMAN** was born on 28 November 1908 in S. Dumfries. She was married to **Harold Bentley BUCHANAN** on 21 October 1933 in S. Dumfries. Harold Bentley BUCHANAN was born on 27 April 1908 in Zone Township, Kent County, Ontario. He died on 10 June 1981 in Brantford Twp., Brant County, Ontario. Flossie May and Harold Bentley BUCHANAN had the following children:

+2116 i. **John Herbert BUCHANAN**.
+2117 ii. **Evelyn Mae BUCHANAN**.
+2118 iii. **Richard Bentley BUCHANAN**.

1574. **Herbert Richard GREEN** was born on 25 April 1882 in Brantford Twp., Brant County, Ontario. He married **Eva VANLOON**. Herbert Richard GREEN and Eva VANLOON had the following children:

2119 i. **Dorothy GREEN** married **Unknown HUTCHISON**.
2120 ii. **Marion GREEN** married **Unknown HILL**.
2121 iii. **Kenneth McClure GREEN**.
2122 iv. **Margaret Eleanor GREEN**.

1581. **John Wesley SHAVER** was born on 26 February 1863 in Cayuga County, Ontario, and died on 9 November 1942 in Winnipeg, Manitoba. He married (1) **Hannah Maria WATERS** on 19 November 1889 in Manitou, Manitoba. Hannah was born on 7 February 1872 in Waterloo, Waterloo County, Ontario, and died on 5 February 1907 in Morden, Manitoba. Their children were:

2123 i. **Earnest T. SHAVER** was born on 20 November 1890 in Kaleida, Manitoba.
2124 ii. **Robert Wesley SHAVER** was born on 20 November 1890 in Kaleida. He died on 22 January 1963 in Ft. Lauderdale, Broward County, FL. He married **Ruby E. KNOX**.
2125 iii. **Norman Riley SHAVER** was born on 10 March 1894

in Kaleida. He died on 26 March 1970 in Vancouver, British Columbia. He married (1) **Elizabeth "Bessie" SMITH**, (2) **Elsie FINDLAY**, and (3) **Unknown HARESNAPE**.

2126 iv. **Luta Belle SHAVER** was born on 21 June 1896 in Kaleida, and died on 15 June 1984 in Arden, Manitoba. She married **Henry Johnston LEWIS** on 16 December 1914.

+2127 v. **Cyrus George SHAVER**.

2128 vi. **Elizabeth May "Bessie" SHAVER** was born on 31 May 1910 in Kaleida, and died on 28 June 1990 in Winkler, Manitoba. She married **Clifford MCLEAN**.

2129 vii. **Olive SHAVER** was born on 1 July 1903 in Kaleida. She married **Harold SOMMERFIELD**.

He was married (2) to **Jane (Jennie) MCKEEN** about 1907.

1601. **Harriet Howell GREEN** was born on 28 April 1888 in Canning, Ontario. She died on 1 September 1955 in St. Thomas, Brant County, Ontario. She was buried in Paris Cemetery, Paris, Brant County, Ontario. She married **Nelson W. MULLOY**, who was born on 24 May 1878 in Elmira, Ontario. He died in January 1955 in St. Thomas, and was buried in Paris Cemetery. They had one child:

+2130 i. **Margaret Kathleen MULLOY**.

1602. **Rita BROWN** was born in 1889. She died on 17 October 1970 in Falls Church, VA. She married **Fred GALBRAITH**. Rita BROWN and Fred GALBRAITH had one child:

2131 i. **Fred E. "Teddy" GALBRAITH**.

1607. **J. Stanley HOWELL** was born on 8 January 1889. He died on 11 April 1961, and was buried in Jerseyville Cemetery. He married **Alma Ruth BAKER**, who was born on 15 November 1909. She died on 16 August 1968, and was buried in Jerseyville Cemetery. Thay had one child:

2132 i. **Nelson HOWELL**.

1608. **Harry Milton CRAMER** was born in 1889. He married **Iva May HUDKINS**. Harry Milton CRAMER and Iva May HUDKINS had one child:

+2133 i. **Alta Doreen CRAMER**.

1609. **Jose Corwin HOWELL** was born on 27 April 1875 in Burlington, North Carolina. He died in Burlington, North Carolina. He was married to **Harriet Pearl MARKHAM** (daughter of Rev. **George Phillips MARKHAM** and **Vesta**

MCINTYRE) on 9 May 1912. Harriet Pearl MARKHAM was born on 10 May 1887 in Hoosick Falls, NY. Their children were:

2134 i. **Joseph Corwin HOWELL** was born on 3 March 1913 in Orlando, Orange County, FL.
2135 ii. **George Markham HOWELL** was born on 21 July 1914 in Orlando, where he died in January 1984.
2136 iii. **Theodore Morris HOWELL** was born on 24 October 1920 in Orlando.

1617. **Samuel LAUGHTON** was born on 29 November 1888, and died on 1 April 1944. He married **Edith POGUE**, who was born on 15 June 1892. Their children were:

2137 i. **Luella LAUGHTON** was born in 1911.
2138 ii. **Verna LAUGHTON** was born on 16 April 1913.
2139 iii. **Clifford LAUGHTON** was born on 15 April 1915.
2140 iv. **Robert LAUGHTON** was born on 14 February 1918.
2141 v. **Loy LAUGHTON** was born on 6 March 1920.
2142 vi. **Florence LAUGHTON** was born on 6 April 1922.
2143 vii. **Hughie LAUGHTON** was born on 5 September 1924.

1623. **William Albert NORTON** was born on 23 March 1905. He died in 1980 in London, Ontario. He married **Opal Isabell CORNELL**, who was born on 22 February 1909. She died in 1981 in London, Ontario. William Albert NORTON and Opal Isabell CORNELL had one child:

2144 i. **Lorne Albert NORTON** was born on 5 April 1929.

1624. **Donald Scott FRASER** was born in 1897. He died in 1961. His wife, **Ella May BRIGGS** was born in 1903. She died in 1932. Donald Scott FRASER and Ella May BRIGGS had one child:

2145 i. **Donald Blair FRASER** was born in 1929.

1630. **Donald Horace MITCHELL** was born on 4 September 1905 in Detroit, Wayne County, Michigan, and died on 31 March 1988. He was married (1) to **Ruth Esther GUENTHER** on 24 October 1931. They lived in Morrow, Ohio. Ruth Esther GUENTHER was born on 27 July 1911. She died on 16 April 1978. Donald Horace MITCHELL and Ruth Esther GUENTHER had these children:

+2146 i. **Donald Horace MITCHELL**.
+2147 ii. **Charles Theodore MITCHELL**.

He was married (2) to **Lucille MENKE** in 1981.

THE FAMILY OF FRANK LAUNDRIE
Norene, Frank, Jess, Lucy Jane and Mary

EIGHTH GENERATION

1634. **Robert Earl HOWELL** was born on 30 October 1896. He died on 1 February 1966, and was buried in Arndt's Cemetery, Easton, Northampton County, PA. He married **Miriam M. WALTERS** (daughter of **Oscar WALTERS** and **Mary WOODRING**). Miriam was born on 6 October 1902 in Easton. She died on 10 September 1971 in Easton, and was buried in Arndt's Cemetery. Robert Earl HOWELL and Miriam M. WALTERS had the following children:

+2148 i. **Ruth Elizabeth HOWELL.**
2149 ii. **Unnamed HOWELL** was born and died in 1920 in New Jersey and was buried in Arndt's Cemetery.

1635. **Hazel HOWELL** was born on 5 July 1902. She died on 25 January 1978 in Phillipsburg, Warren County, New Jersey. She married **Osmun LAUBACH**, and they had these children:

+2150 i. **Lawrence H. LAUBACH.**
+2151 ii. **Kenneth M. LAUBACH.**
+2152 iii. **Meryl "Bobbie" LAUBACH.**
+2153 iv. **Harriet LAUBACH.**
+2154 v. **Mark R. "Mickey" LAUBACH.**
+2155 vi. **William M. LAUBACH.**
2156 vii. **Thomas Clair LAUBACH** was born in 1938, and died in 1989 in an auto accident.

1639. **Clark C. HOWELL** was born on 21 April 1904. He died on 3 February 1933 in Roxburg, Warren County, NJ, and was buried in Belvidere Cemetery, Belvidere, Warren County. Clark committed suicide while suffering from melancholy. He had been employed as milling machine operator in the Phillipsburg plant of Ingersoll Rand, but had been laid off in 1931. He married **Edna RUSH**, who was born in Stewartsville, NJ. Clark C. HOWELL and Edna RUSH had the following children:

+2157 i. **Robert L. HOWELL.**
+2158 ii. **Walter HOWELL.**

1642. **Willard Janson HOWELL** was born on 24 July 1920 in Harmony, Warren County, NJ. He died on 10 November 1992 in Phillipsburg, Warren County. He was an auto mechanic. He married and was divorced from **Arlene A. FENSTERMACHER**, (daughter of **James FENSTERMACHER** and **Elsie CAHILL**) was born on 30 October 1918 in Easton, Northampton County, PA. She died on 5 July 1980, and was buried in Easton Heights Cemetery, Easton. Willard Janson HOWELL and Arlene A. FENSTERMACHER had the following children:

+2159 i. **Mary Lou HOWELL.**
+2160 ii. **Andrea Lee HOWELL.**

1643. **Wilmer Ephriam HOWELL** was born on 10 July 1921 in Harmony, Warren County, NJ. He died on 14 October 1983 in Lopatcong, Warren County, and was buried in St. Philip & James Cemetery, Phillipsburg, Warren County. He was a sheet metal worker. Wilmer served with the US Air Corps during WWII. When he sent for a copy of his birth certificate, he found he was registered as Wilmer E. Howell. Since he had never liked the name Ephriam, he called himself Wilmer Earl Howell. He was baptized in the Methodist faith, but, after his marriage to Doris, he joined the Catholic Church. Wilmer was married to **Doris Mae TUCKER** on 12 February 1955 in Phillipsburg. Doris Mae TUCKER (daughter of **Addison Clifford TUCKER** and **Anna WALSH**) was born on 12 April 1933 in Phillipsburg. Their children are:

+2161 i. **Melody Ann HOWELL**.

2162 ii. **Joan Lee HOWELL** was born on 3 June 1957 in Phillipsburg. She is a product safety engineer. She was married to **Patrick LILLY** on 20 June 1987 in Lopatcong, Warren County, NJ. Patrick LILLY was born on 20 February 1956 in Easton, Northampton County, PA.

+2163 iii. **Phyllis Jean HOWELL**.

2164 iv. **Patrice Janel HOWELL** was born on 18 July 1965 in Phillipsburg. She is a sales clerk. She married **Raymond ROSSI**, who was born on 27 January 1966 in Phillipsburg. He is a drywall finisher.

2165 v. **Janel Marie HOWELL** was born on 28 November 1967 in Phillipsburg. She is a secretary.

+2166 vi. **Michele Ann HOWELL**.

2167 vii. **Melissa-Jo HOWELL** was born on 8 October 1972 in Phillipsburg. She is a day care worker.

1644. **Helen Mae HOWELL** was born on 11 September 1923 in Harmony, Warren County, NJ. Because of her mother's illness, Helen lived with Mr. and Mrs. William Demass. Helen married (1) **Harold RUSSELL Sr**., and they divorced about 1957. They had these children:

+2168 i. **Harold Walter RUSSELL Jr**.

+2169 ii. **Gary RUSSELL**.

+2170 iii. **William Fraley RUSSELL**.

Helen married (2) **Donald BALABAN**, who was born on 22 May 1918 in Albany, Albany County, NY. He died in February 1984 in Tampa, Hillsborough County, FL. The BALABAN children are:

+2171 i. **Donald BALABAN Jr**.

+2172 ii. **Helen "Honeygirl" BALABAN**.

2173 iii. **John BALABAN** was born on 22 November 1961 in Tampa. He married **Linda UNKNOWN**, who was born on 28 April 1949 in West Virginia.

1645. **Stanley Robert HOWELL** was born on 21 June 1927 in Easton, Northampton County, PA. He died on 16 December 1993 in Phillipsburg, Warren County, and was buried in Lower Harmony Cemetery, Harmony, NJ. He was a forklift operator. He married (1) **Luanne SCHERER** on 29 June 1957. The daughter of **Henry SCHERER** and **Laura FRUTCHEY**, Luanne was born on 5 July 1940, and died on 31 October 1979 in Phillipsburg. She was buried in Bloomsbury Cemetery, Bloomsbury, Hunterdon County, New Jersey. Their children are:

2174 i. **Janson Robert HOWELL** was born on 1 March 1964. He married **Apryl LIGHTCAP** in Roxburg, Warren County, NJ.

2175 ii. **Jared David HOWELL** was born on 27 August 1976 in Phillipsburg. He died on 21 May 1992 in Carpentersville, Warren County, NJ, and was buried in Lower Harmony Cemetery.

Stanley married (2) **Virginia Lynn BOWERS**, who was born on 23 March 1962.

1647. **John Obadiah HOWELL** was born on 27 October 1911. He died on 12 January 1960, and was buried in Stewartsville Cemetery, Stewartsville, NJ. He was married to **Eleanor SMITH** on 26 July 1935. Eleanor SMITH was born on 10 September 1916. Their children were:

+2176 i. **Robert John HOWELL**.

+2177 ii. **Doris Marie HOWELL**.

1648. **Clayton HOWELL** was born on 12 August 1912. He died in April 1985 in Pompton Lakes, Passaic County, NJ. He was married to **Doris MANDEVILLE** on 12 February 1942. Doris MANDEVILLE was born on 2 July 1913, and died in January 1985. Clayton and Doris had the following children:

2178 i. **James HOWELL** was born on 19 June 1942.

2179 ii. **Jean HOWELL** was born on 30 November 1943.

2180 iii. **Carolyn HOWELL** was born on 28 October 1945.

2181 iv. **Susan HOWELL** was born on 1 November 1958.

1649. **Ette HOWELL** was born on 30 March 1915 in New Jersey. She died on 3 November 1995. She married **Floyd HAMILL**. Ette and Floyd HAMILL had these children:

2182 i. **Diane HAMILL** was born on 28 September 1941.

2183 ii. **Lynn HAMILL** was born on 27 November 1945.

1650. **Marion HOWELL** was born on 16 February 1918. She was married to **Francis HALLEY**, who was born on 7 May 1912 and died in February 1985 in Pompton Plains, Morris County, NJ. They had one child:

2184 i. **William HALLEY**.

1651. **Robert HOWELL** was born on 25 March 1922. He was married to **Florence POST** on 29 January 1955. Robert HOWELL and Florence POST had the following children:

2185 i. **John HOWELL** was born on 12 September 1957.
2186 ii. **Stephen Lee HOWELL** was born on 23 August 1960.

1652. **Clarence M. HOWELL** was born in 1889 in Pen Argyl, Northampton, Pennsylvania. He died in May 1941, and was buried in Fairview Cemetery, Pen Argyl. He married **Anna K. DENNIS** (daughter of **John DENNIS** and **Grace UNKNOWN**), who was born on 7 April 1891 in Pen Argyl. She died on 15 May 1971 in Phillipsburg, Warren County, New Jersey, and was buried in Fairview Cemetery.[234] Clarence M. HOWELL and Anna K. DENNIS had the following children:

+2187 i. **Raymond C. HOWELL**.
2188 ii. **Mildred HOWELL** was born on 23 August 1913 in Pen Argyl. She died on 4 June 1978 in Wilson, Northampton County, and was buried in Memorial Shrine Cemetery, Northampton County. She was a registered nurse. She married **Paul R. YOUNG**.

1653. **William L. HOWELL** was born on 19 June 1894 in West Bangor, Pennsylvania. He died in Septemeber 1962 in Pen Argyl, Northampton County, and was buried in Fairview Cemetery, Pen Argyl. He married **Flossie PARSONS** (daughter of **Samuel PARSONS** and **Henrietta UNKNOWN**), who was born on 16 March 1895 in West Bangor. She died in August 1971 in Bethlehem, Northampton, County, and was buried in Fairview Cemetery.[235] William L. HOWELL and Flossie PARSONS had one child:

2189 i. **Turner L. HOWELL** was born in 1916 in Pen Argyl. He died on 8 April 1977 in Bethlehem, and was buried in Fairview Cemetery, Pen Argyl. He had been a personnel director and business administrator for the city of Bethlehem, and later, administrative officer for the Lehigh County Authority. He was a member of Rosemount Lutheran Church.[236] He married **Claire M. ALBERT** (daughter of **Earl ALBERT** and **Mame HARDING)** who was born in 1920 and died on 25 September 1990. She was buried in Pen Argyl.

---

[234]Obituary, Easton (PA) Ezpress, 17 May 1971.
[235]Obituary, Easton (PA) Express, August 1971.
[236]Obituary, Easton (PA) Express),9 April 1977.

was an office manager for Bethlehem Steel Corp.[237]

1656. **Louis Eilenberger HOWELL** was born on 17 March 1885 in New York City. He died on 31 January 1977 in Ft. Pierce, St. Lucie County, Florida, and was buried in Millcrest Memorial Gardens, Ft. Pierce. His social security records have him as Louis Howell, but he is burial records say Marshall HOWELL. He married (1) **Caroline Gertrude ZIMMERMAN**, who was born in 1893, died in 1979, and was buried in Woodlawn Cemetery, Bronx, New York. They had one child:

+2190 i. **Robert Louis James HOWELL**.

Louis married (2) **Olive BARSS**, who was born on 10 August 1895. She died on 30 August 1977, and was buried in Hillcrest Cemetery, Fort Pierce.

1657. **Emma EILENBERGER** was born in November 1886., and died on 5 February 1968. She married **Emil RUMPF**. Their children were:

2191 i. **Emil RUMPF**.
2192 ii. **Ruth RUMPF**.
2193 iii. **Theresa RUMPF**.

1658. **John E. EILENBERGER** was born on 3 December 1889; he died on 6 December 1978, and was buried in Kensico Cemetery, Valhalla, New York. He married **Amelia KRYGER**, who was born on 18 November 1888 in Denmark. She died on 8 January 1919 in Bronx, New York, and was buried in Woodlawn Cemetery, Bronx. John married (2) **Ruth VANDERHOF.** Their children were:

2194 i. **John E. EILENBERGER** was born on 22 July 1920, died on 6 February 1921, and was buried in Woodlawn Cemetery, Bronx.
2195 ii. **Edwin EILENBERGER**.
2196 iii. **James EILENBERGER**.
2197 iv. **Paul EILENBERGER**.
2198 v. **John EILENBERGER**.

1659. **Louisa "Minnie" EILENBERGER** was born on 25 April 1891 in New York City. She died on 11 July 1971. She married **John Frank LYONS** on 30 August 1911. He was born on 16 October 1882 in Newark, New Jersey, and died on 3 August 1955, Both were buried in George Washington Park, Paramus, NJ. They had these children:

2199 i. **Agnes Louise LYONS** was born on 22 May 1912 and died on 15 November 1993 in Ridgefield, New Jersey. She married **Wilfred STONER**.
2200 ii. **John Ellsworth LYONS** was born on 4 May 1914, and

---

[237]Obituary, The Morning Call, 26 Sept. 1990, p. 9.

died on 15 November 1993 in Ridgefield, New Jersey. She married **Wilfred STONER**.

2200 ii. **John Ellsworth LYONS** was born on 4 May 1914, and died on 29 February 1968. He married **Adele SCHULTZ**.

2201 iii. **Ruth Watkins LYONS** was born on 13 March 1916. She married **Harry STAHL**.

2202 iv. **Florence Viola LYONS** was born on 8 January 1920 and died on 5 July 1981. She married **John TAMBURRO**.

2203 v. **Franklyn Leslie LYONS** was born on 16 November 1922.

2204 vi. **William Stewart LYONS** was born on 17 September 1924. He married **Ruth KUHLMAN**.

2205 vii. **Robert Bradley LYONS** was born on 26 July 1926. He married **Rita DIMMICK**.

2206 viii. **Walter Collier LYONS** was born on 14 March 1928. He married **Joan FLANNIGAN**.

2207 ix. **Betty Anne LYONS** was born on 13 March 1931. She married George **BRUNNER**.

2208 x. **Richard LYONS** died at 8 days.

2209 xi. **Joan LYONS** died at 8 months.

1661. **Edward Osmund EILENBERGER** was born on 24 October 1897 in New York City, NY. He died on 21 October 1945 in New York City, NY. He married **Daisy GARTEY**. Their children were:

2210 i. **Anna EILENBERGER**. Anna burned to death.

2211 ii. **Daisy EILENBERGER**.

2212 iii. **Edward EILENBERGER**.

1666. **Janet Olive HOWELL** was born on 25 January 1903. She died in January 1973, in Levittown, New York. She married **Hector MCDONALD**, who was born on 7 July 1900 and died in December 1976 in Levittown. Janet Olive HOWELL and Hector MCDONALD had the following children:

2213 i. **Florence Ann MCDONALD**.

2214 ii. **Elma MCDONALD**.

2215 iii. **Wallace MCDONALD**.

1667. **Milton Howard HOWELL** was born on 12 February 1904, and died on 14 September 1987 in Jamaica, Queens County, New York. He married **Jean UNKNOWN**. Milton and Jean had these children:

2216 i. **William Robert HOWELL**.

2217 ii. **Frederick HOWELL**.

2218 iii. **Jean HOWELL**.

2219 iv. **Milton HOWELL**.
2220 v. **Raymond HOWELL**.
2221 vi. **Patricia HOWELL**.
2222 vii. **Elizabeth HOWELL**.
2223 viii. **Margaret HOWELL**.
2224 ix. **Frances HOWELL**.
2225 x. **Nancy HOWELL**.
2226 xi. **Richard HOWELL**.
2227 xii. **Jerard HOWELL**.
2228 xiii. **Robert HOWELL**.
2229 xiv. **Thomas HOWELL**.
2230 xv. **David HOWELL** died at 6 months.

1668. **Euphemia Perle HOWELL** was born on 11 October 1905. She died on 14 January 1974 in Sag Harbor, New York. She was married to **George GEDDIE**, who was born on 24 January 1895 and died in Sag Harbor in January 1975. Euphemia Perle HOWELL and George GEDDIE had the following children:

2231 i. **Isabelle GEDDIE**.
2232 ii. **Charlotte GEDDIE**.
2233 iii. **George GEDDIE Jr**.
2234 iv. **Anne GEDDIE**.

1669. **Ruth Clarice HOWELL** was born on 7 February 1909. She died on 7 February 1962. She married **Edward FARMER**. Ruth Clarice HOWELL and Edward FARMER had the following children:

2235 i. **Virginia FARMER**.
2236 ii. **Ruth FARMER**.
2237 iii. **Audry FARMER**.
2238 iv. **Joan FARMER**.
2239 v. **Edwin FARMER**.
2240 vi. **Richard FARMER**.

1670. **Mildred HOWELL** was born on 24 April 1910. She was buried in Pinelawn Cemetery, Long Island, New York. Her husband, **Casper Grann LEWIS** was born on 23 October 1909. He died on 12 June 1974. Mildred HOWELL and Casper Grann LEWIS had the following children:

2241 i. **Ann LEWIS**.
2242 ii. **William David LEWIS**.
2243 iii. **Mildred Christina LEWIS**.
2244 iv. **Thomas Albert LEWIS**.
2245 v. **Robert Casper LEWIS**.
2246 vi. **Florence Amelia LEWIS**.

1672. **Marguerita Amelia HOWELL** was born on 9 August 1915. She married **Oscar HAUGEN**. Marguerita Amelia HOWELL and Oscar HAUGEN had the following children:

2247	i.	**Donald HAUGEN**.
2248	ii.	**Jon Christian HAUGEN**.
2249	iii.	**Albert HAUGEN**.
2250	iv.	**Phyllis HAUGEN**.
2251	v.	**Glen HAUGEN**.

1676. **Martha Jesse HOWELL** was born on 29 July 1896, and died on 17 October 1991 in Greenport, New York. She married **Gustav Eric ANDERSON**, who was born in 1897 in Sweden, and died on 19 November 1941 in a random shooting in Queens Village, NY. Martha and Gustav had these children:

+2252	i.	**Jean Virginia ANDERSON**.
+2253	ii.	**Robert Warren ANDERSON** .
+2254	iii.	**Winifred ANDERSON**.
2255	iv.	**Charles ANDERSON** died young.

1677. **Robert Marshall HOWELL** was born on 25 March 1903, and died on 28 December 1962, in Long Island. His wife was **Alma Olga MAASS**, who was born on 26 September 1908 in Brooklyn, and died on 22 December 1958. Robert Marshall HOWELL and Alma Olga MAASS had these children:

2256	i.	**Jeanette Ruth HOWELL** was born on 23 August 1927. She married **Robert POTTS** on 28 May 1948. He was born on 18 February 1925.
+2257	ii.	**Robert Marshall HOWELL Jr.**
2258	iii.	**Theodore Frederick HOWELL** was born on 25 July 1938. He married **Rebecca T. CAUCHI**.
2259	iv.	**Joyce Elaine HOWELL** was born on 25 June 1943. She married **Edward WORONTZOFF**.

1684. **Mary L. HOWELL** was born about 1916. She married Unknown APGAR. Mary L. HOWELL and Unknown APGAR had the following children:

2260	i.	**Janice APGAR**.
2261	ii.	**Frank APGAR**.
2262	iii.	**Fred APGAR**.
2263	iv.	**Richard APGAR**.
2264	v.	**Gregory APGAR**.
2265	vi.	**Keith APGAR**.
2266	vii.	**Dennis APGAR**.
2267	viii.	**Sherry APGAR**.
2268	ix.	**Terry APGAR**.
2269	x.	**Dwayne APGAR**.

1687. **Lavina HOWELL** married **Harry M. LOZIER**, who was born in 1920 in Buttzville, Warren County, New Jersey. He died in 1978 in Oxford, Warren County, and was buried in Pequest Union Cemetery, Great Meadows, NJ. He was a heavy equipment operator with Warren Paving Company. Harry served in the Army during World War II, was a member of the American Legion Post in Belvidere, New Jersey, and was a Methodist. Their children were:

2270 i. **Elaine LOZIER** lived in Dover, Delaware in 1978. She married **Unknown DAWSON**.

2271 ii. **Bonnie LOZIER** married **Unknown VOLL**, and they lived in Phillipsburg, Warren County, NJ in 1978.

1693. **George HOWELL** was born on 3 January 1930 in Belvidere, Warren County, New Jersey. He died on 7 November 1992 in Phillipsburg, Warren County, and was buried in Belvidere Cemetery, Belvidere. He was a chemical operator. He married **Ruth FORD**. They had one child:

2272 i. **George J. HOWELL**.

1697. **Walter R. HOWELL** was born on 1 April 1918 in Belvidere, Warren County, New Jersey. He died on 21 April 1999 in Phillipsburg, Warren County, NJ.[238] He served in the US Army during WWII, and was a molder in the steel foundry at Ingersoll-Rand Company in Phillipsburg for 30 years. He married **Constance M. COTUGNO** (daughter of **Cosmio COTUGNO** and **Nancy MARZULO**), who was born on 18 March 1918 in Phillipsburg. She died on 2 April 1992, and was buried in Fairmount Cemetery, Phillipsburg, Warren County. Walter and Constance had the following children:

2273 i. **Walter R. HOWELL Jr.**

2274 ii. **Dorothy HOWELL** married **Unknown KOHLER**. They live in Blakeslee, PA.

1698. **Helen EHLY** married **Robert NICKEL**, (son of **David NICKEL** and **Anna UEBERROTH**), who was born on 19 September 1916 in Phillipsburg, Warren County, NJ. Their children were:

2275 i. **Helen May NICKEL**.

2276 ii. **Robert NICKEL**.

2277 iii. **David L. NICKEL**.

1699. **Mary Catherine EHLY** was born on 22 December 1906 in Belvidere, Warren County, NJ. She died on 28 April 1976 in Easton, Northampton County,

---

[238]Obituary, Express-Times, Phillipsburg, NJ, 23 April 1999.

PA. She was married to **Albert YOUNG** on 12 March 1927. Albert YOUNG was born on 2 August 1906, and died in 1954. Their children were:

+2278 i. **Albert John "Jack" YOUNG.**
+2279 ii. **Ronald Allan YOUNG.**
+2280 iii. **Lois Alice YOUNG.**
+2281 iv. **Joan Elaine YOUNG.**
2282 v. **Donald Mitchell YOUNG** was born on 4 August 1940, and died on 25 June 1948.
2283 vi. **Carol YOUNG** was born on 10 December 1942. She married **Unknown FULMER.**
+2284 vii. **David L. YOUNG.**

1700. **Leo EHLY** married **May UNKNOWN**. Leo and May had one child:

2285 i. **Nicholas EHLY.**

1701. **Charles L. EHLY** was born in Phillipsburg, Warren County, NJ. He married **Betty CLICKNER**. Charles and Betty had the following children:

2286 i. **Betty Ann EHLY** was born on 28 July 1944.
+2287 ii. **Ann Marie EHLY.**
2288 iii. **Linda EHLY** was born on 7 August 1956.
2289 iv. **Leo Oscar EHLY** was born on 2 August 1966.

1705. **Elmer HOWELL** was married to **Carol DAVIS** (daughter of **Charles DAVIS**) on 11 September 1964 in Columbia, New Jersey. Carol DAVIS was born in Larksville, Luzerne County, Pennsylvania. Their children were:

2290 i. **Tina HOWELL** married **Unknown MCAULIFFE.** They lived in Williams Twp., Northampton County, PA.
2291 ii. **Richard HOWELL.**

1708. **Robert C. HOWELL** was born in 1924. He married **Irene M. TAUSCH** (daughter of **Frederick TAUSCH** and **Viola STECKEL**), who was born on 25 August 1929. She died on 29 December 1994, and was buried in Washington Cemetery, Warren County, NJ. Their children were:

2292 i. **Robert HOWELL.**
2293 ii. **Gary HOWELL.**
2294 iii. **Rick HOWELL.**

1709. **Rose TRIMMER** was born in 1923 in NJ. She married **John FOX**. Rose TRIMMER and John FOX had the following children:

2295 i. **Michael FOX.**
2296 ii. **Timothy FOX.**

1710. **Austin R. TRIMMER Jr.** was born on 11 February 1926 in Bridgeville, Warren County, New Jersey. He died on 23 March 1993 in Allentown, Northampton County, Pennsylvania, and was buried in Sts. Philip & James Cemetery, Greenwich, Warren County, New Jersey. He married **Ann ROHN**. Their children were:

2297	i.	**Kurt TRIMMER**.
2298	ii.	**Keith TRIMMER**.
2299	iii.	**Karen TRIMMER** married **Unknown FREY**.

1722. **Vida Igerna PRICE** was born on 26 May 1880 in Rutland, Humboldt County, Iowa. She married **Arthur MEYER**. Vida Igerna PRICE and Arthur MEYER had the following children:

+2300	i.	**Lorna MEYER**.
+2301	ii.	**Kenneth L. MEYER**.
2302	iii.	**Kelvin MEYER**.
2303	iv.	**Juanita J. MEYER**.
+2304	v.	**Robert K. MEYER**.

1726. **Malcolm Poyer PRICE** was born on 6 July 1895 in Carroll, Carroll County, Iowa. He died on 2 August 1975 in Waterloo, Black Hawk County, Iowa. He was married to **Mary Emily DAY** on 29 June 1921. Malcolm Poyer PRICE and Mary Emily DAY had the following children:

+2305	i.	**John Day PRICE**.
+2306	ii.	**Nancy Jane PRICE**.

1727. **Edna Mae PRICE** was born on 23 December 1889 in Everly, Clay County, Iowa. She died in November 1985, probably in Eureka, Lincoln County, Montana. She was married to **George GASAHL** on 31 July 1912. Edna Mae PRICE and George GASAHL had the following children:

+2307	i.	**Dorothy Edna GASAHL**.
+2308	ii.	**Lila Jeanette GASAHL**.
+2309	iii.	**Joyce Marie GASAHL**.

1728. **Ethel Daisy PRICE** was born on 22 February 1893 in Spirit Lake, Dickinson County, Iowa. She died on 27 November 1961 in Grants Pass, Josephine County, Oregon. She was married to **Percy Edward PLUID** on 25 December 1910 in Eureka, Lincoln County, Montana. Their children were:

2310	i.	**Charles Thomas PLUID** was born on 21 November 1911 in Eureka. He died on 25 August 1995, probably in Bonners Ferry, Boundary County, Idaho.
2311	ii.	**Keith Henderson PLUID** was born on 6 October 1914 in Eureka, and died in October 1986, probably in

Kalispell, Flathead County, MT.
2312 iii. **Karl Edward PLUID** was born on 6 October 1914 in Eureka, and died on 24 April 1937.
2313 iv. **Hannah Jean PLUID** was born on 6 January 1920 in Eureka.
+2314 v. **Lois Louise PLUID.**

1730. **Thomas Edward PRICE** was born on 2 July 1905 in Spirit Lake, Dickinson County, Iowa. He died on 19 February 1971 in Eureka, Lincoln County, Montana. He was married to **Alice Mary BEUTEL** on 16 September 1924 in Eureka. Thomas and Alice Mary had the following children:

2315 i. **Claudia Alice PRICE** was born on 12 May 1925 in Eureka. She married **Robert Francis HIGSON** on 25 July 1960 in Coeur d'Alene, Kootenai County, Idaho.
+2316 ii. **Thomas Henderson PRICE**
+2317 iii. **Phyllis Edith PRICE.**

1731. **Myrtle Veda PRICE** was born on 28 August 1891 in Ruthven, Palo Pinto County, Iowa. She died in Ft. Dodge, Webster County, IA. She was married to **E. J. LLOYD** in Spirit Lake, Dickinson County, Iowa. Myrtle Veda PRICE and E. J. LLOYD had the following children:

2318 i. **Elaine LLOYD** married **Unknown PERSON.**
2319 ii. **Jane LLOYD** married **David MARTENS.**

1732. **Mary Euphemia PRICE** was born on 20 August 1893 in Spirit Lake, Dickinson County, Iowa. She died on 16 May 1975, probably in Portland, Oregon. Mary was a doctor, who worked on a Navaho reservation. She was married to **Francis Leroy ROBERTS** in Spirit Lake. Mary Euphemia PRICE and Francis Leroy ROBERTS had the following children:

+2320 i. **Mary M. ROBERTS.**
+2321 ii. **Velma ROBERTS.**

1733. **Virginia Viola PRICE** was born on 17 June 1895 in Spirit Lake, Dickinson County, Iowa. She died on 8 May 1975 in Spirit Lake. She was married to **Walter Berkley BEDELL** on 13 August 1919 in Des Moines, Polk County, Iowa. Their children were:

+2322 i. **Berkley Warren BEDELL.**
+2323 ii. **Jack Harold BEDELL.**

1735. **Mary Elizabeth THOMAS** was born on 5 August 1891 in Spirit Lake, Dickinson County, Iowa. She died on 17 January 1965 in Long Beach, Los Angeles County, Clifornia. She was married to **William John CARPENTER** (son of **Aldus CARPENTER** and **Jane CHAPMAN**) on 26 April 1910 in Kalispell, Flathead County, Montana. Their children were:

+2324 i. **Violet Mildred CARPENTER**.
2325 ii. **William John CARPENTER** was born on 23 January 1918 in Eureka, Lincoln County, Montana. He died on 18 November 1933 in Wichita Falls, Wichita County, Texas.
+2326 iii. **Virginia May CARPENTER**.

1736. **Mabel Etta THOMAS** was born on 27 September 1893 in Spirit Lake, Dickinson County, Iowa. She died on 15 October 1991 in Montana. She was married to **Alvin Ole REIQUAM** on 8 November 1920. Mabel Etta THOMAS and Alvin Ole REIQUAM had the following children:

+2327 i. **Leslie Alvin REIQUAM**.
+2328 ii. **Eldon Thomas REIQUAM**.
+2329 iii. **Lila Anne REIQUAM**.
+2330 iv. **Howard Edward REIQUAM**.

1738. **Lettie Mae THOMAS** was born on 5 December 1897 in Spirit Lake, Dickinson County, Iowa. She died in 1933 in Los Angeles, Los Angeles County, CA. She married **Earl Clinton DEWOLF**. They had these children:

+2331 i. **Marion Faye DEWOLF**.
+2332 ii. **Phyllis Jean DEWOLF**.

1739. **Richard Morgan THOMAS** was born on 14 August 1904 in Spirit Lake, Dickinson County, Iowa. He died on 2 October 1943 in Bonners Ferry, Boundary County, Idaho. Richard owned the Thomas Chevrolet Company in Bonners Ferry. He was a member of the Elks lodge, the Masons, Lions and the Kootenai Valley Commercial Club. He was married to **Hazel Muriel SAWYER** on 15 May 1926 in Sandpoint, Bonner County, Idaho. Richard and Hazel had the following children:

2333 i. **Richard Allen THOMAS** was born on 20 March 1927 in Bonners Ferry. He died on 3 December 1962.
+2334 ii. **Donald Sawyer THOMAS**.

1740. **Arthur Edward THOMAS** was born on 18 December 1906 in Cherokee, Cherokee County, IA. He died in 1953 in Spokane, Spokane County, Washington. His wife was **Edith UNKNOWN**. Arthur and Edith had the following children:

2335 i. **Kathryn THOMAS** married **Unknown LITZENBERGER**.
2336 ii. **Patricia THOMAS** married **Unknown MCMAHON**.
2337 iii. **Edward THOMAS**.

1741. **Robert Charles THOMAS** was born on 27 November 1910 in Eureka, Lincoln County, Montana. He died in April 1967 in Spokane, Spokane County, Washington. He was married to **Alice DUNNING** on 20 November 1929 in Sandpoint, Bonner County, Idaho. Their children were:

2338 i. **Elaine THOMAS** married **Bruce BARRETT**.
2339 ii. **Bruce THOMAS**.
2340 iii. **Robert THOMAS**.

1742. **Louise Mildred THOMAS** was born on 3 September 1917. She was married to **Arthur Bruce DUNNING** in December 1945 in Spokane, Spokane County, Washington. Louise and Arthur Bruce DUNNING had one child:

2341 i. **Cheryl Louise DUNNING** was born on 4 October 1946. She married **John PRESTEK**.

1743. **Ethel May PRICE** was born on 7 March 1901 in West Pittston, Luzerne County, Pennsylvania[239]. She died in 1984 in Binghamton, NY. She was married to **Kenneth DEPUGH** about 1919. Ethel and Kenneth DEPUGH had one child:

2342 i. **Kenneth DEPUGH** was born about 1920 in Binghamton, NY.

1757. **Marion Ethel HOWELL** was born on 25 February 1922 in West Pittston, Luzerne County, Pennsylvania. She died on 7 December 1993 in New Milford, Susquehanna County, PA, and was buried on 9 December 1993 in New Milford. She was married to **Jack Robert PHETHEAN** (son of **Edward PHETHEAN** and **Hannah Mae EVANS**) on 11 February 1947 in West Pittston. Jack Robert PHETHEAN was born on 19 September 1918 in Avoca, Luzerne County. He died on 17 October 1980 in New Milford, and was buried there on 20 October 1980. Jack served in the US Army in WWII, and after the war ended, he worked for Jewel Tea for some time, then attended and graduated from Wilkes University in Wilkes Barre. He was a teacher in the Susquehanna School System, and within a few months of retirement, when he suffered a heart attack and died. Marion Ethel and Jack Robert PHETHEAN had these children:

+2343 i. **Pamela Gail PHETHEAN**.
+2344 ii. **Patricia Jane PHETHEAN**.
+2345 iii. **Phyllis Anne PHETHEAN**.
2346 iv. **John Robert PHETHEAN** was born on 9 March 1964 in New Milford, and died on 10 March 1964.

1764. **Sarah Virginia JONES** was born on 13 July 1922 in Elizabeth, New Jersey. She died on 6 July 1989 in Charlotte, North Carolina, and was buried in

---

239Birth records, West Pittston, PA Methodist Church 1872-1923. LDS Microfilm # 167296.

Sharon Memorial Park, Charlotte. Virginia was a psychology professor at Lock Haven University, Pa., retiring in 1984. She held bachelor's and master's degrees from Bucknell University. She was married (1) to **Earl HAEFELE** in February 1945 in West Pittston. She was divorced from Earl HAEFELE. Earl HAEFELE was born on 16 November 1920 in West Pittston. He died in September 1975 in Pennsylvania. Sarah Virginia JONES and Earl HAEFELE had one child:

2347 i. **Suzanne HAEFELE** was born on 20 November 1946 in West Pittston. She married (1) **Nathan KOENIGSBERG** in North Carolina, and they divorced. She married (2) **Richard WRAZEN** on 8 June 1991 in North Carolina. They also divorced. Suzanne had no children.

Virginia was married (2) to **William SMITH** about 1948. She was divorced from William SMITH. Sarah Virginia JONES and William SMITH had one child:

+2348 i. **Jeffrey William SMITH**.

Virginia married (3) **Donald EHALT**. Donald EHALT was born in April 1923 in Pennsylvania. He died in May 1978 in Lock Haven, Pennsylvania. Don was a bartender by trade. One of Virginia's letters indicated his father was ill in a hospital in Pittsburgh, so Don was probably from that area. There were no children of this marriage.

1765. **Helen Elizabeth JONES** was born on 30 January 1924 in Elizabeth, New Jersey. Helen was an elementary school teacher for many years, and moved to North Carolina upon retiring. She died on 24 September 1999, in Durham, North Carolina. Helen married (1) **Sam BRADLEY**, and they divorced. There were no children. She married (2) **Ray WADLOW** in Pennsylvania about 1950. He was born in Iowa on 5 February 1913, and died on 19 January 1999 in Arlington, Virginia. Helen Elizabeth JONES and Ray WADLOW had one child:

2349 i. **Kevin Charles WADLOW** was born on 13 May 1954. He is a graduate of Southern College, Lakeland, Florida. He married **Shelley Ann SIGO** on 28 December 1976. They are divorced.

1766. **Gladys Jane HOWELL** was born on 27 March 1930 in West Pittston, Luzerne County, Pennsylvania. She was married to **Thomas Harold DALE** on 25 October 1950 in West Pittston. He was the son of **Harold DALE** and **Violet ROSENCRANCE**, born on 27 July 1928 in West Pittston. He died there on 13 September 1989, and was buried on 16 September 1989 in Mountain View Cemetery, Harding, Luzerne County. Tom was the Chief of Police in West Pittston, and died of a heart attack at work. Tom had an Associate degree in Criminal Justice from Luzerne County Community College, and had served on the West Pittston police force for 31 years, as chief for 18 years. Their children are:

+2350 i. **Pamela Sue DALE**.

2351 ii. **Debra Lynn DALE** was born on 27 October 1957 in West Pittston. After her nurse's training, she chose to go to medical school, was accepted at Universidad Autonoma de Guadalajara in Mexico, received her degree, and interned in Bronx Lebanon and Albert Einstein Hospitals in New York City. She served her residency in internal medicine at New Rochelle, New York, Hospital. She married **Thomas WALEK**, M.D. in Tarrytown, New York on 11 June 1981. Both are practicing in Rhode Island.

1767. **Jane Louise WRIGLEY** was born on 28 May 1919 in Scranton, Lackawanna County, Pennylvania. She was married to **Harold George TRAHER** on 15 January 1942 in West Pittston, Luzerne County. Harold George TRAHER was born on 17 November 1919 in West Pittston. He died on 14 March 1987 in West Pittston, and was buried on 17 March 1987 in Mountain View Cemetery, Harding, Luzerne County. Harold was trained at the Glen Alden shops in West Pittston as a pattern maker. He joined the Navy after he and Jane were married, and was overseas for some time. After the war ended, he went into sales, and worked for several heavy equipment companies in the northeastern part of Pennsylvania. They lived in Williamsport for several years, and moved back to West Pittston when Nancy was small. Jane and Harold George TRAHER had one child:

+2352 i. **Nancy Jean TRAHER**.

1768. **Jeannette Ann JONES** was born on 16 June 1922 in West Pittston, Luzerne County, Pennsylvania. Jeannette is a graduate of Penn State University, worked at Armstrong Cork Company in Lancaster, PA, and served in the WAVES during WWII. After her discharge, she married **Edward PHETHEAN, Jr**. (son of **Edward PHETHEAN, Sr**. and **Hannah Mae EVANS**), on 8 June 1946 in West Pittston. Edward PHETHEAN, Jr. was born on 2 August 1920 in Avoca, Luzerne County, and died on 6 September 1997 in Leesburg, Lake County, Florida. He was buried on 15 September 1997 in National Cemetery, Bushnell, Sumter County, Florida. Ed worked for a Ford dealer in West Pittston after graduating from Wilkes University, and later for the US Internal Revenue Service as an Internal Inspector. Their children were:

+2353 i. **James PHETHEAN**.

+2354 ii. **Edward PHETHEAN**.

+2355 iii. **George Evans PHETHEAN**.

1769. **Harriet Elizabeth JONES** was born on 9 September 1923 in West Pittston, Luzerne County, Pennsylvania. Harriet worked in the accounting department of the Wyoming National Bank in Wilkes Barre. She was married to **Thomas Griffith DAVIES** (son of **Thomas DAVIES** and **Pearl GRIFFITH**) on 12

November 1943 in West Pittston. Thomas Griffith DAVIES was born on 24 November 1921 in Scranton, Lackawanna County, PA. He served in the Air Force during WWII. After the war, he worked for several bakeries in the Wilkes Barre area, and went to work for Liberty Mutual Insurance company in public relations. After retirement, he and Harriet moved to Mashpee, Massachusetts. Harriet Elizabeth JONES and Thomas Griffith DAVIES had the following children:

+2356 i. **Harriet Jean "Jay" DAVIES.**
+2357 ii. **Thomas William DAVIES.**
+2358 iii. **John Griffith DAVIES.**

1771. **Dolores PUGH** was born in West Pittston, Luzerne County, Pennsylvania. She married **Theodore TRUELOVE**. Dolores and Ted lived in her parents' house on Fremont Street in West Pittston, the same one in which Nancy and Kenny Heal now live. Dolores PUGH and Theodore TRUELOVE had the following children:

2359 i. **James TRUELOVE.**
2360 ii. **Martha TRUELOVE.**

1773. **Shirley PUGH** was born on 20 April 1918 in West Pittston, Luzerne County. She died in October 1977 in West Pittston. Shiirley married **Howard STRUBECK**, who was born on 19 December 1915 in PA. He died in November 1972 in West Pittston. Howard and his brother-in-law Ted TRUELOVE operated a Gulf gas station in West Pittston for several years. Shirley PUGH and Howard STRUBECK had one child:

2361 i. **Terry STRUBECK** is married, his wife's name is not known.

1784. **Harrison LeGrande GOODSPEED** was born on 23 August 1894 in Ann Arbor, Michigan. He died on 24 October 1973 in Northport, Leelanau County, Michigan. He married (1)**Dorothy Mercer RANKIN** on 14 February 1922 in Terre Haute, Indiana. She was born on 1 July 1897, and died on 25 April 1925 in Grand Rapids. They had two sons:

+ 2362 i. **Harrison LeGrande Peter GOODSPEED.**
2363 ii. **Walter GOODSPEED** was born in 1924 in Grand Rapids, and died there in 1925.

Harrison married (2) **Frances WARD** about 1926 in Grand Rapids. She was born on 23 October 1900. They had three children:

2364 iii. **Anne GOODSPEED** married (1) **Joseph MARTIN** and (2) **Al LEWIS.**
2365 iv. **Philip GOODSPEED** married **Jane UNKNOWN.**
2366 v. **Mary GOODSPEED** married **James "Jim" ALEXANDER.**

1789. **Ethel Fern HOWELL** was born on 13 October 1918 in Dallas Twp., Luzerne County, Pennsylvania. She was married to **George Lawrence ROGERS** on 31 December 1938 in Lehman Twp., Luzerne County. George Lawrence ROGERS was born on 1 October 1916. He died on 2 December 1986, and was buried in Memorial Shrine Cemetery, Carverton, Luzerne County. Their children are:

2367 i. **George Lawrence ROGERS Jr**. was born on 27 October 1939 in Luzerne County. He married **Wanda Fay GREEN**, who was born on 13 February 1942 and died on 2 August 1984.

+2368 ii. **Karen Fern ROGERS**.

2369 iii. **Thomas Vincent ROGERS** was born on 27 June 1944 in Luzerne County.

+2370 iv. **Jon Howell ROGERS**.

+2371 v. **Dianne Shirley ROGERS**.

1791. **Harry Morton HOWELL** was born on 23 October 1922 in Luzerne County, Pennsylvania. He married **Ruth ELSTON**, who was born on 31 May 1927. She died in April 1996. They had these children:

+2372 i. **Linda HOWELL**.

+2373 ii. **Nancy HOWELL**.

2374 iii. **James HOWELL** was born on 4 April 1959 in PA.

1792. **Shirley Ruth HOWELL** was born on 4 January 1926 in Luzerne County, Pennsylvania. She married **Benjamin ROOD**, who was born on 16 April 1926. Shirley and Benjamin ROOD had these children:

2375 i. **Benjamin Jackson ROOD Jr**. was born on 24 March 1958 in North Carolina. He married **Pamela DAVIS** on 12 October 1985.

2376 ii. **Richard ROOD** was born on 16 March 1966 in North Carolina. He married **Jami HAYNES** on 9 July 1988. She was born on 30 June 1970.

1793. **Harry Watson LEWIS** was born on 13 June 1928. He married **Roberta WING**, who was born on 13 May 1928. Harry Watson LEWIS and Roberta WING had the following children:

2377 i. **Deborah Jane LEWIS** was born on 5 August 1954. On 14 June 1980, she married **Mark Loriston STOCKWELL**, who was born on 31 October 1954.

2378 ii. **David Pritchard LEWIS** was born on 18 October 1956, and died on 4 February 1976.

+2379 iii. **Michael Jonathan LEWIS**.

1794. **Ethel Ruth LEWIS** was born on 19 July 1932. She married **Ambrose BREDBENNER Jr.**, who was born on 4 November 1929. Ethel Ruth and Ambrose BREDBENNER Jr. had these children:

+2380 i. **Melody Joy BREDBENNER**.
2381 ii. **Candice Dawn BREDBENNER** was born on 1 November 1955.
+2382 iii. **Tami Gay BREDBENNER**.

1796. **Edith Ann LEWIS** was born on 15 January 1934. She married **Bruce BATES**, who was born on 12 September 1925. Edith Ann LEWIS and Bruce BATES had one child:

2383 i. **Bruce BATES** was born on 16 March 1975.

1799. **Edna Pearl ROOT** was born on 7 June 1888 in Brooklyn Twp., Green Lake County, Wisconsin. She died on 18 April 1946 in Minneapolis, Hennepin County, Minnesota. She was married to **Perry Andrew (Andrea) OTIS** on 19 May 1909. Their children are:

2384 i. **Jessie OTIS** was married to **George ALBERT**.
2385 ii. **Edna Ruth OTIS** was born on 2 Mar 1912 in Minneapolis, Hennepin County. She married **Roscoe Cameron MCELDERRY** on 12 August 1933 in Minneapolis.
2386 iii. **Alfred OTIS** married **Grace UNKNOWN**.
2387 iv. **Ralph OTIS** married **Dora UNKNOWN**.
2388 v. **Evelyn OTIS**.
2389 vi. **Mildred OTIS** married **William OLSON**.

1800. **Leda Marie ROOT** was born on 20 January 1890 in Brooklyn Twp., Green Lake County, Wisconsin. She died on 5 August 1971 in Minneapolis, Minnesota. She was married to **Ray TORKELSON** on 3 December 1919 in Minneapolis, Hennepin County, Minnesota. Ray was born on 3 January 1889. Their son was:

2390 i. **Glenn TORKELSON**.

1802. **Ethel May ROOT** was born on 18 June 1894 in Brooklyn Twp., Green Lake County, Wisconsin. She died in 1957. She was married to **Walter A. NORDSTROM**. Their children were:

2391 i. **Wally NORDSTROM** was born in 1921.
2392 ii. **Frances June NORDSTROM** was married to **Joe PETRICK** in 1941.
2393 iii. **Doris NORDSTROM** was born in 1928.
2394 iv. **Arlene NORDSTROM** was born in 1929, and died in 1987. She married **William CHRISTENSON**.

1803. **Frances "Frank" George ROOT** was born on 18 February 1897 in Brooklyn Twp., Green Lake County, Wisconsin. He died on 16 November 1978, and was buried in Lorain Twp., Cemetery, Polk County, Wisconsin. He was married to **Stella Jeanette JOHNSON** on 5 April 1925. Stella was born on 24 February 1903 in Lorain Twp., and died on 13 September 1993 in Minneapolis, Minnesota. She was buried in Lorain Twp. Cemetery. Their children were:

2395 i. **Raymond Francis ROOT** was born on 4 January 1926 in Frederic, Polk County, WI. He married **Corrinne TJOMSLAND** on 3 July 1949.

2396 ii. **Joyce Stella ROOT** was born on 26 July 1927 in Lorain Twp. She married **Paul WEISER** on 28 July 1951.

2397 iii. **Merle Roger ROOT** was born on 2 August 1934 in Lorain Twp. He married **Dianne PALMER** on 10 May 1958.

1804. **Lin Howell ROOT** was born on 17 October 1899 in Brooklyn Twp., Green Lake County. He died on 14 December 1975 in Siren, Burnett County, Wisconsin. He married **Kathryne "Kitty" Agnes MCLAIN** (daughter of **Walter Isaac MCLAIN** and **Bedelia "Delia" Bridget SMITH**) on 24 September 1921 in Jamestown, Stutsman County, North Dakota. Their children were:

2398 i. **Margaret "Peggy" Ellen ROOT** was born on 24 February 1924 in St. Paul, Ramsey County, Minnesota. She died on 7 June 1997 in Amery, Polk County, Wisconsin. She married **Herbert William MARSCHALL** on 20 October 1941 in Cumberland, Barron County, Wisconsin.

+2399 ii. **Lin Howell ROOT**.

2400 iii. **Bonnie Jean "Root" BORTH** was born on 16 February 1938 in Frederic, Polk County, WI. She married **Eugene BEECROFT** on 4 September 1954 in Lorain Twp.

1805. **Mary Lucille ROOT** was born on 28 September 1901 in Brooklyn Twp., Green Lake County. She died in 1937, and was buried in Lorain Twp. Cemetery. She married **Vern L. CORTY**. Mary Lucille ROOT and Vern L. CORTY had two children:

2401 i. **Gloria CORTY** married **Lloyd BRUDVIG**.

2402 ii. **Lawrence "Larry" CORTY**.

1806. **Thelma CHESWORTH** was born in 1897 in Lackawanna County, Pennsylvania. She died in May 1982 in Hatboro, Bucks County, Pennsylvania. Her daughter said Thelma was adopted as a small child, but was never told of it until she was widowed. Thelma married **Edward SYLVANUS**, who died about 10 they married. Thelma CHESWORTH and Edward SYLVANUS had the following children:[240]

2403 i. **Edward SYLVANUS** was born in October 1929 in West Pittston.

2404 ii. **Elizabeth SYLVANUS** was born in 1933 in West Pittston.

1807. **Melvin H. VAN HORN** was born on 30 June 1885 in Columbia, Warren County, New Jersey. He died in Belvidere, Warren County, and was buried in Belvidere Cemetery. Melvin married (1) **Eva BARTHOLOMEW**, whose birth date is unknown. She died on 13 June 1948. Melvin H. VAN HORN and Eva BARTHOLOMEW had two children:

2405 i. **Mae VAN HORN** was born on 3 December 1908. She married **Raymond HESS**, who was born on 28 November 1900.

+2406 ii. **Harry (George) VAN HORN**.

After Eva's death, Melvin married (2) **Beatrice Winfrey RICKMAN**.

1809. **Hilton Laire BUTLER** was born on 8 March 1900 in Belvidere, Warren County, New Jersey. He died on 24 January 1985 in Toms River, NJ, of congestive heart failure. He was married to **Hannah Marion ALLEN** on 18 September 1926 in Belvidere. Hannah Marion ALLEN was born on 10 August 1903 in Belvidere. She died on 15 March 1986 in Toms River, NJ. Hilton Laire BUTLER and Hannah Marion ALLEN had two children:

+2407 i. **John William BUTLER**.

+2408 ii. **Barbara Allen BUTLER**.

1810. **Elma Hermione HATFIELD** was born on 17 October 1890. She died in June 1978 in Hastings-on-Hudson, New York. She was married to **Rudolph "Ralph" Werner RITTER** on 8 April 1916. Rudolph "Ralph" Werner RITTER was born on 22 March 1883 in St. Gaul, Switzerland. Elma Hermione HATFIELD and Rudolph "Ralph" Werner RITTER had one child:

+2409 i. **Eleanor Elizabeth RITTER**.

1811. **Ethel Winifred HATFIELD** was born on 30 April 1892 in Newburgh, New York. She died on 5 May 1979 in Pittsburgh, Allegheny, Pennsylvania. She was married to **George Edward ELBEL** on 20 June 1918 in New Rochelle, New York. George Edward ELBEL was born on 1 April 1888 in Pittsburgh, Allegheny, Pennsylvania. He died on 4 January 1984 in Pittsburgh. They had one child:

---

[240]Information contributed by Bette Glenn Cunningham, Longmeadow, Sarasota, FL. She is Elizabeth Sylvanus.

+2410 i. **Marjorie Elizabeth ELBEL.**

1812. **Vernon Leroy HATFIELD** was born on 14 May 1901 in Springfield Ohio. He died on 12 February 1979 in Emerson, New Jersey. He was married to **Ann Gertrude CLINTON** on 12 October 1946. Ann Gertrude CLINTON was born on 16 October 1914 in Jersey City, Hudson County, NJ. She died on 30 December 1988 in Davidsonville, Anne Arundel County, Maryland. They had one child:

+2411 i. **Peter Leroy HATFIELD.**

1813. **Helyn Elizabeth HATFIELD** was born on 17 November 1907 in Pittsburgh, Allegheny County, Pennsylvania. She died on 13 February 1987 in Portland, Multnomah County, Oregon. She was married to **John Edward WHITLOCK** on 18 August 1928 in Sheffield, Massachusetts. John Edward WHITLOCK was born on 5 August 1905 in Lenox, Massachusetts. He died on 24 May 1954 in Portland, Multnomah County. Helyn Elizabeth HATFIELD and John Edward WHITLOCK had one child:

2412 i. **William Melvin WHITLOCK.**

1816. **Louis BACON** married **Freda WENDT**. Louis BACON and Freda WENDT had these children:

2413 i. **Howard BACON.**
2414 ii. **Harold BACON.**
2415 iii. **Lawrence BACON.**
2416 iv. **Kenneth BACON.**
2417 v. **Donald BACON.**
2418 vi. **Louis BACON.**

1818. **Clayton FEAR** was married to **Una Vernette BACON**. Clayton FEAR and Una Vernette BACON had two children:

2419 i. **Ed Wyn FEAR.**
+2420 ii. **Janice Rochelle FEAR.**

1825. **Victor STEAD** was a teacher; he died in 1995 in Iowa. He was married to **Anna Katherine GRINDRA** in Iowa. Victor STEAD and Anna Katherine GRINDRA had the following children:

+2421 i. **Jerre Lee STEAD.**
+2422 ii. **Brian Earl STEAD.**
+2423 iii. **Jamie Joel STEAD.**

1826. **W. Vance STEAD** was born on 24 March 1922 in Hopkinton, Delaware County, Iowa. He was married to **Yola RODMAN** (daughter of **Harry**

RODMAN and **Iva REED**) on 25 November 1942 in Kirksville, Missouri. Yola RODMAN was born in 1923. Their children were:

+2424 i. **David Vance STEAD**.
2425 ii. **Margaret Jayne STEAD** was born on 19 June 1947 in Des Moines, Iowa. She married **John SLUSHER** on 13 December 1969 in Marion, Linn County, Iowa. John SLUSHER was born in 1944.
+2426 iii. **Thomas Lee STEAD**.
2427 iv. **Kathryn Suzanne STEAD** was born on 18 November 1957 in Monticello, Jones County, IA.

1827. **Gordon Frank STEAD** was born on 1 April 1925 in Hopkinton, Iowa. Gordon lives in Marion, Iowa. He was married to **Alma Lois HETFIELD** (daughter of **Benjamin HETFIELD** and **Alda OWENS**) on 24 August 1946. Alma Lois HETFIELD was born in 1923. Gordon Frank STEAD and Alma Lois HETFIELD had the following children:

2428 i. **Russell Lynn STEAD** was born on 30 August 1948.
2429 ii. **Benjamin Arthur STEAD** was born on 13 March 1950. He married **Jodi OVERLAND.**

1830. **Bernard Clark THOMPSON** was born on 20 July 1908 in Iowa. He died on 19 January 1967 in Cedar Rapids, Linn County,, Linn County,, Linn County,, Linn County,, Linn County,, Iowa, and was buried in Buck Creek Cemetery, Delaware County, Iowa. He was married to **Pauline Emma Henrietta OMMEN** on 23 October 1934 in Sandhill Evangelical Church, Langworthy, Iowa. Pauline Emma Henrietta OMMEN was born in 1911. She died in 1962. Bernard Clark THOMPSON and Pauline Emma Henrietta OMMEN had the following children:

2430 i. **Bernice Charity THOMPSON** was born in 1936.
2431 ii. **Leonard Clark THOMPSON** was born in 1937. He married **Margaret Ann "Marge" MCDONALD**, who was born in 1940.
+2432 iii. **Kathryn Eloise THOMPSON**.
+2433 iv. **Verna Marie THOMPSON**.

1832. **Maude Alberta THOMPSON** was born on 10 April 1913 in Iowa. She died on 15 June 1964 in San Francisco, California, after a long illness, and was buried in Olivet Cemetery, San Francisco. She was married to **Raymond SIEBELS** on 1 October 1937 in Monticello, Iowa. Alberta and her husband moved to San Francisco in 1942. He worked in the ship yards. Raymond married possibly twice more after Alberta's death. Raymond SIEBELS was born on 30 August 1902 in Minnesota. He died in 1996 in California. Maude Alberta THOMPSON and Raymond SIEBELS had the following children:

+2434 i. **Virginia Rae SIEBELS**.
+2435 ii. **Kristi Jean SIEBELS**.

2436 iii. **David August SIEBELS** was born on 20 March 1954.

1833. **Mildred Mae THOMPSON** was born on 13 February 1916 in Delhi, Delaware County, Iowa. She was married to **Maurice Corll THOMPSON** (son of **James THOMPSON** and **Urselena ARDUSER**) on 15 February 1933 in Galena, Jo Davis County, Illinois. Maurice Corll THOMPSON was born on 22 May 1913. He died on 13 April 1995 in Inglewood, Florida. He was buried in Oakwood Cemetery, Monticello, Iowa. Mildred Mae THOMPSON and Maurice Corll THOMPSON had one child:

+2437 i. **Blanche Marie THOMPSON**.

1834. **Vernon Bert THOMPSON** was born on 20 September 1920 in Buck Creek, Delaware County, Iowa. He died on 13 February 1985 in Hopkinton, Delaware County. Vernon served in the military in WWII, in the Pacific theater, receiving many medals and commendations, including the Bronze Star and the Purple Heart. His left arm was permanently damaged, and he underwent several operations to attempt repairs. He was married to **Evelyn Jean HUGGINS** (daughter of **Jess HUGGINS** and **Edna TOPPING**) on 25 June 1951 in Hopkinton, Delaware County, Iowa. Evelyn Jean HUGGINS was born in 1931. Vernon Bert THOMPSON and Evelyn Jean HUGGINS had the following children:

+2438 i. **Harold Vernon THOMPSON**.
+2439 ii. **Maxine Lorraine THOMPSON** was born on 11 November 1952.
+2440 iii. **Roger Lee THOMPSON**.
+2441 iv. **Lois Jane THOMPSON.**
2442 v. **Arlene Norma THOMPSON** was born on 30 July 1957, and died on 6 January 1958.
+2443 vi. **Deborah Ann "Debbie" THOMPSON**.
+2444 vii. **Norman Jay THOMPSON**.
+2445 viii. **Mary Elizabeth THOMPSON**.
+2446 ix. **Janice Janet THOMPSON**.
+2447 x. **Karen Kay THOMPSON.**
2448 xi. **Thomas Carl THOMPSON** was born on 23 September 1967 in Iowa. He married **Melody TAYLOR** in May 1992.
2449 xii. **Daniel Clair THOMPSON** was born on 21 January 1969.
2450 xiii. **James Donald THOMPSON** was born on 6 March 1974.

1836. **William John THOMPSON** was born on 8 May 1925 in Iowa. He died on 21 November 1990 in Cedar Rapids, Linn County,, Linn County,, Linn County,, Linn County,, Linn County,, Iowa. William John served in the Army during WWII, as a military policeman. After the war, he became a barber. He married (1) **Neva MILLARD**, who bore him no children; (2) **Carol Lee WALTON** (daughter of **Carl WALTON**) on 22 October 1947 in Iowa. Carol Lee WALTON was born in 1927. She died before 1995 in IA. William John THOMPSON and Carol Lee WALTON had the following children:

+2451 i. **Barbara Ann THOMPSON.**
+2452 ii. **Dennis Dee THOMPSON.**
+2453 iii. **Suzette Kay THOMPSON.**

He was married (3) to **Beulah Smith WILLIAMSON** on 29 November 1965 in Wadena, Minnesota. Beulah Smith WILLIAMSON was born in 1914.

1837. **Gertrude THOMPSON** was born on 28 August 1912 in Hopkinton, Delaware County, Iowa. She was married to **Paul GREEN** on 5 June 1935 in Hopkinton. Gertrude THOMPSON and Paul GREEN had the following children:

+2454 i. **Darwin GREEN.**
+2455 ii. **Merlyn GREEN.**
+2456 iii. **Sharon GREEN.**

1838. **Wayne "Buzzy" THOMPSON** was born on 3 May 1916 near Hopkinton, Delaware County, Iowa. He died on 3 March 1992 in Iowa. He was married (1) to **Wilma Ione SHEPPARD** (daughter of **John "Jack" SHEPPARD** and **Carrie DOWNS**) on 27 May 1936 in Hopkinton, Delaware County, Iowa. Wilma Ione SHEPPARD was born in 1917. She died in 1985. Wayne "Buzzy" THOMPSON and Wilma Ione SHEPPARD had the following children:

+2457 i. **Thelma THOMPSON.**
+2458 ii. **Marilyn THOMPSON.**

He was married (2) to **Pauline Lee SANDS** on 10 December 1987 in Manchester, Delaware County, Iowa.

1839. **Bernard THOMPSON** was born on 9 March 1920 in Hopkinton, Delaware County, Iowa. He died on 29 January 1997 in Manchester, Delaware County. He was married on 6 May 1950 to **Doris FLEMING**. Bernard THOMPSON and Doris FLEMING had the following children:

+2459 i. **Leslie Dean THOMPSON.**
+2460 ii. **Charlotte Kay THOMPSON.**
+2461 iii. **Regina Doris THOMPSON.**
2462 iv. **Corinne Louise THOMPSON** was born on 24 January 1959.
2463 v. **Danny THOMPSON.**

1840. **Glenn David THOMPSON** was born on 24 May 1929 in Hopkinton, Delaware County, Iowa. He died on 19 February 1991 in Iowa. He was married to **LaRue EHLERS** (daughter of **Henry EHLERS** and **Marie UNKNOWN**) in Hopkinton, Delaware County, Iowa. LaRue EHLERS was born in 1928. Glenn David THOMPSON and LaRue EHLERS had the following children:

+2464 i. **Susan THOMPSON**.
+2465 ii. **Linda Jean THOMPSON**.
+2466 iii. **Kris THOMPSON**.
2467 iv. **David Glenn THOMPSON** was born on 16 January 1957, and died on 19 February 1973.
2468 v. **Cory Allen THOMPSON** was born on 4 August 1969.

1842. **Richard Bruce CARTANO** was born on 3 July 1925 in Iowa. He married **Myrna Jean SIMPSON** (daughter of **Alexander SIMPSON** and **Phyllis HATCHER**), who was born in 1931. They live in Oakland, Alameda County, California. Richard Bruce CARTANO and Myrna Jean SIMPSON had the following children:

2469 i. **Jennifer Lynn CARTANO** was born on 16 February 1959.
+2470 ii. **Christopher Wilbur CARTANO**.
2471 iii. **Bruce CARTANO** died on 21 May 1982.

1843. **David CARTANO** was born on 6 April 1935 in Monticello, Jones County, Iowa. David teaches at the University of Miami, department of Sociology, in Coral Gables, Dade County, Florida. He was married to **Jo Ann COWAN** (daughter of **Elmer COWAN** and **Vila UNKNOWN**) on 30 May 1959 in Ankeny, Iowa. Jo Ann COWAN was born in 1938. David CARTANO and Jo Ann COWAN had the following children:

+2472 i. **Geoffrey David CARTANO**.
+2473 ii. **Ann Maria CARTANO**.

1845. **Betty THOMPSON** was born on 10 August 1923 in Hopkinton, Delaware County, Iowa. She was married to **Robert L. TIMMONS** (son of **Roy TIMMONS**) on 18 July 1944 in Lake City, Columbia County, Florida. Robert L. TIMMONS was born in 1923. Betty THOMPSON and Robert L. TIMMONS had the following children:

+2474 i. **Robert Michael TIMMONS**.
+2475 ii. **Richard Lee TIMMONS**.
+2476 iii. **Jo Ann TIMMONS.**

1846. **Jean K. THOMPSON** was born on 1 January 1926 in Hopkinton, Delaware County, Iowa. She died in 1995. She was married (1) to **Robert THESTHER** on 9 August 1947. Jean K. THOMPSON and Robert THESTHER had one child:

+2477 i. **Renee THESTHER**.

Jean was married (2) to **Joseph J. IMOEHL** on 13 June 1959 in Cedar Rapids, Linn County, Iowa. Joseph J. IMOEHL was born on 3 March 1920, and died on 17 October 1995 in Cedar Rapids, Linn County, Iowa.

1847. **Margaret "Peggy" THOMPSON** was born on 10 August 1927 in Hopkinton, Delaware County, Iowa. She was married (1) to **James M. CALLAHAN** on 28 December 1949 in Oak Park, Cook County, Illinois. James M. CALLAHAN died in 1977. Margaret "Peggy" and James M. CALLAHAN had the following children:

2478 i. **Patricia CALLAHAN** was born on 13 March 1951 in Oak Park, IL. She married **Donald TOW** on 5 November 1988 in Reno, Washoe County, Nevada.

+2479 ii. **Timothy J. CALLAHAN**.

2480 iii. **Kathryn Ann CALLAHAN** was born on 22 June 1959 in Burlingame, San Mateo County, California.

2481 iv. **Michael J. CALLAHAN** was born on 10 June 1961 in Cedar Rapids, Linn County, Iowa. Michael was apparently adopted by **Paul ORCUTT**, since he is known as **Michael ORCUTT**.

Margaret was married (2) to **Dr. Paul ORCUTT** on 13 June 1970 in Cedar Rapids, Linn County, Iowa. Dr. Paul ORCUTT was born in 1925.

1848. **Stephen William THOMPSON** was born on 11 September 1941 in Monticello, Jones County, Iowa. He died on 5 March 1997 in Toledo, Marion County, Iowa. He was married (1) to **Janice STEINMETZ** on 23 August 1964. Stephen William THOMPSON and Janice STEINMETZ had the following children:

2482 i. **Shawn Eric THOMPSON** was born on 14 March 1967. He died on 3 September 1978.

+2483 ii. **Aaron Todd THOMPSON**.

He was married (2) to **Joann SCHNEIDER** on 19 July 1975.

Stephen married (3) **Barbara TAFT** on 16 August 1985 in Toledo, Marion County, IA. Stephen William THOMPSON and Barbara TAFT had one child:

2484 i. **Unknown THOMPSON**.

1849. **Roger THOMPSON** was born on 21 September 1945. He was married to **Marge Ann MILLS** on 16 September 1970. Marge Ann MILLS was born in 1945. Roger THOMPSON and Marge Ann MILLS had the following children:

2485 i. **Matthew Allan THOMPSON** was born on 30 July 1973.

+2486 ii. **Julie Lynn THOMPSON**.

1850. **Barbara Ann HOWELL** was born on 1 March 1916 in Hood River, Hood River County, Oregon. She was married to **Leroy ELLIOTT** on 19 June 1939. Barbara and Leroy ELLIOTT had one child:

2487 i. **Monte ELLIOTT**.

1851. **Helen Virginia HOWELL** was born on 23 February 1922 in Hood River, Hood River County, Oregon. She was married to **William Howard PAASCH** on 6 August 1938. Helen and William Howard PAASCH had one child:

2488 i. **Phillip Howell PAASCH** was born on 31 December 1942.

1855. **Eila Maxine HOWELL** was born on 28 August 1919 in Hood River, Hood River County, Oregon. She was married to **Ronald Lad CARMICHAEL** (son of **David CARMICHAEL** and **Dorothy BULLARD**) on 23 December 1943 in Independence, Jackson County, Missouri. Eila Maxine HOWELL and Ronald Lad CARMICHAEL had the following children:

2489 i. **Ann Howell CARMICHAEL** was born on 26 February 1954 in Columbus, Franklin County, Ohio. She married (1) **Daryl W. MACK** on 11 January 1975. She married (2) **Charles S. WRIGHT** on 28 November 1982 in Kingsport, Hawkins County, Tennessee.

2490 ii. **Laurie Lucinda CARMICHAEL** was born on 20 April 1956. She married **James J. KNACKSTEDT** on 26 November 1983 in Salt Lake City, Utah.

1856. **Eileen Francis HOWELL** was born on 28 August 1919 in Hood River, Hood River County, Oregon. She died in September 1981 in Portland, Multnomah County, Oregon. She married **Melvin CHAPMAN**. Eileen Francis HOWELL and Melvin CHAPMAN had the following children:

2491 i. **Raymond CHAPMAN**.

2492 ii. **Larry CHAPMAN** married **Sylvia UNKNOWN**.

2493 iii. **Sally CHAPMAN**.

1857. **Harriet Elizabeth HOWELL** was born on 2 November 1922 in Hood River, Hood River County, Oregon. She married **Richard BABCOCK**. Harriet and Richard BABCOCK had the following children:

2494 i. **James BABCOCK**.

2495 ii. **Janet BABCOCK**.

1858. **Blanche La Rayne HOWELL** was born on 14 September 1924 in Hood River. She was married to **Calvin Norris WIRRICK** (son of **Harry WIRRICK** and **Thelma WEST**) on 31 August 1947 in Hood River. Blanche La Rayne HOWELL and Calvin Norris WIRRICK had the following children:

2496 i. **Judith Kay WIRRICK** was born on 21 October 1948. She married **Dale Edward LUFFMAN** on 22 August

August 1970 in Portland, Multnomah County, Oregon.

2497 ii. **David Allyn WIRRICK** was born on 2 February 1951. He married **Deborah Lea MUNDORFF** on 15 August 1975 in Portland.

1859. **Harry Lee HOWELL** was born on 9 August 1928 in Hood River, Hood River County, Oregon. He was married to **Sue Jane DEMPSEY** about 1950 in Independence, Jackson County, Missouri. Harry Lee HOWELL and Sue Jane DEMPSEY had the following children:

2498 i. **Harry Lee HOWELL.**

2499 ii. Deborah HOWELL.

2500 iii. **Yvonne HOWELL.**

2501 iv. **Kenneth HOWELL.**

1860. **Ira Miles EATON** was born on 10 July 1915 in North Bend, Coos County, Oregon. He was married to **Martha Elizabeth MCGINNIS** (daughter of **James MCGINNIS** and **Elsie MANN**) on 22 May 1942 in Portland, Multnomah County, Oregon. Ira and Martha Elizabeth had two children:

2502 i. **Linden Jean EATON** was born on 14 September 1950. She married **Richard HARRIS** on 17 June 1967 in Portland.

2503 ii **Laurel Susan EATON** was born on 28 April 1953. She married **Rod Josiah WODTAN** on 20 October 1977 in Vancouver, Clark County, Washington.

1861. **Glenn Alan EATON** was born on 15 July 1917 in Marshfield, Coos County, Oregon. He died on 8 February 1992 in Portland, Multnomah County, Oregon. He was married to **Jeannette Alice CHRISTIANSEN** in 1942. They had these children:

2504 i. **Lillian Alice EATON** was married (1) to **Glenn M. WARD**. She married (2) **Donald Lee KUSIEK** in 1992 in Cottage Grove, Lane County, Oregon.

2505 ii. **Glenn Alan EATON.**

1863. **Robert Lester EATON** was born on 31 January 1922 in Portland. He was married to **Phyllis Jean DANIELSON** on 10 October 1942 in Glendale, Los Angeles County, California. Robert Lester EATON and Phyllis Jean DANIELSON had the following children:

2506 i. **Robert Lester EATON Jr.** was born on 28 September 1945 in Portland. He married **Merlene BARKLEY** in April 1972 in Portland.

2507 ii. **Leonard Wayne EATON** was born on 29 December 1946 in Forest Grove, Washington County, Oregon.

He married **Jane LAUDIEN** in Portland.

2508 iii. **Cathy Jean EATON** was born on 13 March in Portland. She married **Wayne Melvin LOGEMAN** on 17 December 1977 in Portland.

1867. **Wanona Maxine KOONTZ** married **Donald STEWART**. Wanona Maxine KOONTZ and Donald STEWART have these children:

2509 i. **Wanona STEWART**.

2510 ii. **Wendy STEWART**.

1868. **Thelma Anita KOONTZ** was born on 12 November 1918. She was married to **Charles Robert STICHTER** (son of **George STICHTER** and **Shirley HARPERREE**) on 16 March 1940 in Glendale, Los Angeles County, CA. Their children are:

2511 i. **Charles Robert STICHTER** Jr. was born on 12 July 1942 in Pasadena, Los Angeles County, California. He married **Dael KIESLER** on 4 May 1969 in Albany, Albany County, New York.

2512 ii. **Patricia Louise STICHTER** was born on 10 March 1947 in Pasadena. She married (1) **Donald RUSSELL** in November 1973 in Reno, Washoe County, Nevada. She married (2) **Ronald Tipton ASBURY** in November 1979 in Denver, Arapahoe County, Colorado.

1869. **Frank Emmett KOONTZ** was born on 23 February 1923 in Los Angeles, Los Angeles County, California. He died on 28 November 1948 in Los Alamitos, Los Angeles County, California. He married (1) **Mary FARRELL**. Frank Emmett KOONTZ and Mary FARRELL had a child:

2513 i. **Lawrence Alan KOONTZ** was born on 2 June 1945 in Minneapolis, Hennepin County, Minnesota. He died on 24 August 1982 in Phoenix, Maricopa County, Arizona. He married **Linda UNKNOWN** on 14 February 1970.

Frank married (2) **Joyce Madeline ZENDA** in 1948. They had one child:

2514 i. **Frankie Lee KOONTZ** was born on 9 March 1949 in Torrance, Los Angeles County, California. She married **James Alan MURRAY** on 17 June 1970.

1872. **Dorothy Darlyne HOWELL** was born on 12 June 1926 in Hood River, Hood River County, Oregon. She was married (1) to **Vern LaGene REYNOLDS** (son of **Joseph REYNOLDS** and **Margaret BURT**). She was married (2) to **Donald Lent BOLTZEN** (son of **Henry BOLTZEN** and **Virginia LENT**) on 8

September 1946 in Byron, California. Dorothy and Donald Lent BOLTZEN had the following children:

2515 i. **Rock Howell BOLTZEN** was born on 15 November 1953. He married **Sandra Jean NASH**.

2516 ii. **January Darlyne BOLTZEN** was born on 9 June 1957.

1873. **Eva Mardell HOWELL** was born on 5 June 1932 in Tillamook, Tillamook County, Oregon. She was married to **Jesse John Marin ROMO** (son of **Refigio ROMO** and **Refugia MARIN**) on 23 May 1948 in Antioch, Contra Costa County, California. Eva and Jesse John Marin ROMO had the four sons:

2517 i. **Jesse Dennis ROMO** was born on 25 December 1948 in Antioch.

2518 ii. **Ricardo ROMO** was born on 6 October 1951 in Antioch.

2519 iii. **Gary Stephen ROMO** was born on 17 August 1953 in Antioch.

2520 iv. **Robert Michael ROMO** was born on 6 April 1955 in Antioch.

1874. **Elaine La Verne LARSON** was born on 8 January 1924 in Portland, Multnomah County, Oregon. She married (1) **Richard Leon MITCHELL** (son of **Lester MITCHELL** and **Pauline DORSON**) on 26 December 1945 in Portland. Elaine and Richard Leon MITCHELL had these children:

2521 i. **Mark Alan Mitchell BARBER** was born on 18 December 1947 in Portland. He died on 19 May 1997 in Tillamook, Tillamook County, Oregon. He married **Karen Marie HUGHES** on 11 July 1968 in Portland.

2522 ii. **Carol Lynn MITCHELL** was born on 14 August 1949 in Minneapolis, Hennepin County, Minnesota. She married **Leo Donald FENDER** on 16 August 1968 in Portland.

2523 iii. **Craig Richard Mitchell BARBER** was born on 3 October 1950 in Minneapolis.

Elaine married (2) **Walter Faver BARBER**. Elaine and Walter had these children:

2524 i. **Denise Ann BARBER** was born on 39 March 1957 in Portland. She married (1) **Steven Eugene SHORT** on 6 April 1979 in Portland. She married (2) **Steven Michael PRINCE** on 2 March 1985 in Portland.

2525 ii. **Lance Wayne BARBER** was born on 17 March 1959

in Portland. He married **Catherine Jane KIMBALL** on 2 October 1982 in Portland.

Elaine La Verne LARSON was married (3) to **Carl Axel LINNE** (son of **Carl LINNE** and **Lydia PALM**) on 7 June 1968 in Portland, Multnomah County, Oregon.

1876. **Donna Claire LARSON** was born on 1 August 1930 in Portland, Multnomah County, Oregon. She married **Frederick William GAULTER** (son of **William GAULTER** and **Blanche LUCKSINGER**) on 4 September 1948 in Liberty, Clay County, Missouri. Donna and Frederick had the following children:

2526 i. **Frederick Wayne GAULTER** was born on 16 June 1949 in Independence, Jackson County, Missouri. He married **Deborah Dorthea POSER** on 9 June 1975 in Chicago, Cook County, Illinoois

2527 ii. **Gregory Kent GAULTER** was born on 8 October 1950 in Independence. He married **Paula DOYLE** on 10 January 1973 in Independence.

2528 iii. **Janet Sue GAULTER** was born on 21 March 1952 in Independence. She married **Stanley Roger THRESHER** on 10 October 1970 in Independence.

2529 iv. **Gary Lee GAULTER** was born on 10 April 1954 in Independence. He married **Deborah Sue MCALLISTER** on 4 January 1975 there.

2530 v. **Steven Vance GAULTER** was born on 10 August 1955 in Independence, where he married **Jodi Lynn TUCKER** on 21 October 1977.

2531 vi. **Deanne Gae GAULTER** was born on 26 April 1960 in Independence. She married **Darrell Ray PORTER** on 29 November 1980 in Independence.

2532 vii. **Julie Ann GAULTER** was born on 6 September 1964 in Independence. She married **Timothy Russell LUTZ** on 3 August 1996 in Independence.

1877. **Wayne HOWELL** was born on 29 November 1930 in Portland, Multnomah County, Oregon. He was married (1) to **Greta MCCABE** in 1949. Their children were:

2533 i. **Alan Walter HOWELL** was born in 1949. He married **Kathleen WHITE**.

2534 ii. **Sally Jean HOWELL** married **David TETZLAFF**.

2535 iii. **Janet Mae HOWELL** was born on 17 December 1951. She married **Merwin EMERY** on 20 December 1986.

Wayne HOWELL was married (2) to **Betty KUSCH** on 16 August 1958.

1878. **Lois Lucille HOWELL** was born on 24 November 1935 in Portland, Multnomah County, Oregon. She was married to **Donald Verne KRUG** on 31 May 1952 in Portland. They had the following children:

2536 i. **Joanna Lois KRUG** was born on 14 January 1964.
2537 ii. **Janet Renee KRUG** was born on 31 October 1965 in Portland. She married **Terry Wayne FERGUSON**.

1879. **Victor Alan HOWELL** was born on 20 March 1940 in Portland, Multnomah County, Oregon. He was married to **Susan GAULT** in September 1961. Victor and Susan had the following children:

2538 i. **Robin Leslie HOWELL** was born on 10 May 1963. She married **Mark HAYS**.
2539 ii. **Victor Todd HOWELL** was born on 29 December 1969.

1886. **John Smith HOWELL** was born on 29 June 1888 in Sussex County, New Jersey. He died in 1955, and was buried in Beemerville Cemetery, Beemerville, Sussex County, New Jersey. John, usually called Smith, was the postmaster of Broadway, Sussex County, for 36 years. He had opened a store in Dover, New Jersey in partnership with Stephen Treadle while a young man, and later purchased a store in Broadway, which became the general store and post office for the town.

Smith was active with the Red Cross, served 2 terms on the Franklin Township Election Board, was a Mason, a member of Samaritan Lodge #98, of Sussex County, and belonged to the Methodist Church. He was married (1) to **Frances ARMSTRONG** (daughter of **Mary C. UNKNOWN**) on 11 November 1909. Frances ARMSTRONG was born in 1890 in Port Jervis, Orange County, New York. She died in October 1918, in the Influenza epidemic, and was buried in Beemerville Cemetery. John Smith HOWELL and Frances ARMSTRONG had one child:

+2540 i. **Robert Armstrong HOWELL**.

Smith was married (2) to **Sarah C. CLOUGH** on 15 December 1919 in New York City, New York. Sarah C. CLOUGH was born in 1892. She died in 1962, and was buried in Beemerville Cemetery. John Smith HOWELL and Sarah C. CLOUGH had one child:

+2541 i. **Morton S. HOWELL.**

1887. **Leon Judd HOWELL** was born on 17 February 1890. He died in May 1978, and was buried in Beemerville Cemetery. He married **Cora Jane CLARK**, who was born in 1891. She died in 1977, and was buried in Beemerville Cemetery. Leon Judd HOWELL and Cora Jane CLARK had these children:

+2542 i. **Earl HOWELL.**
2543 ii. **Leon Clark HOWELL** was born in 1918; he died in 1946, and was buried in Beemerville Cemetery.

1892. **Horace Beemer HOWELL** was born on 30 August 1900 in Dobbs Ferry, Westchester County, NY. He died on 9 April 1965 in Allentown, Lehigh County, Pennsylvania. He was buried on 12 April 1965 in Musconetcong Valley Cemetery, Hampton, New Jersey. Horace married **Janie G. FORSYTH** (daughter of **James FORSYTH** and **Ann ROBERTSON**), who was born on 3 August 1900 in Dobbs Ferry. She died in July 1984 in Phillipsburg, Warren County, NJ, and was buried in Musconetcong Valley Cemetery. Horace suffered a stroke about a year before his death, and seldom left his room. Horace and Bruce operated a contracting business prior to Horace's stroke. Horace and Janie had the following children:

+2544 i. **Anne HOWELL.**
2545 ii. **Bruce HOWELL** was born in 1927. He died on 9 April 1965 in Washington, Warren County, NJ, and was buried in Musconetcong Valley Cemetery. He had been a sergeant in the US Army during WWII.
2546 iii. **Lois HOWELL.**
+2547 iv. **Jean HOWELL.**
+2548 v. **Norma HOWELL.**
+2549 vi. **Evan HOWELL.**

1895. **Atchley HOWELL** was born on 4 September 1909 in Dobbs Ferry, Westchester County, New York. He died on 15 September 1981 in Oxford, Warren County, New Jersey, and was buried in Musconetcong Valley Cemetery. He was married to **Margaret A. DURYEA**, who was born in 1915. Atchley and Margaret had the following children:

+2550 i. **Arnold J. HOWELL.**
2551 ii. **Brenda HOWELL.**
2552 iii. **Lloyd HOWELL**
2553 iv. **Phillip HOWELL.**

1896. **Ruth HOWELL** was born on 15 June 1912 in NJ. She married **Carl K. MEICHSNER** (son of **Paul MEICHSNER** and **Marie MELLER**), who was born in Tallheim, Germany. Carl was a supervisor at the Warren County Residential Group Center of the New Jersey Department of Institutions and Agencies. He died on 20 April 1972 in Washington, Warren County, New Jersey. Ruth and Carl K. MEICHSNER had one child:

2554 i. **Bernice MEICHSNER** was married to **Unknown FRANKENFIELD.**

1899. **Ralph Lester HOWELL** was born on 13 January 1894. He died on 15 December 1966. He was a plumber. He lived in Camillus, Onondaga County,

New York. Ralph was part owner of the old Camillus Hardware company. He managed the plumbing and heating section. After he left the company, he had his own plumbing and heating business. On 4 April 1918, he was married to **Lucille Gertrude SHENK**, who was born on 21 March 1894. She died on 20 August 1976. Ralph Lester HOWELL and Lucille Gertrude SHENK had these children:

+2555 i. **Robert Shenk HOWELL.**
2556 ii. **Barbara Jean HOWELL** was born on 26 February 1922., and on 12 April 1952, she married **George Frederick SOLDAN**, who was born on 15 June 1918. They had no children.

1910. **Virginia HOWELL** was born in 1915 in Muskegon, Muskegon County, Mchigan. She died in 1982. She married **Richard CREAMER**, who was born in 1915 in Traverse City, Grand Traverse County, MI. He died in 1982 in Traverse City. Virginia HOWELL and Richard CREAMER had the following children:

2557 i. **Norman CREAMER** married **Kay COOPER**.
2558 ii. **David CREAMER** married **Bonnie KENTRIGH**.
2559 iii. **Thomas CREAMER** married **Judith CHILSON**.
2560 iv. **Kathleen CREAMER** married **John LOVELESS**.
2561 v. **Steven CREAMER**.

1911. **Dorothy HOWELL** was born on 20 February 1918 in Muskegon, Muskegon County, Mchigan. She died on 26 September 1993 in Amery, Wisconsin. She married **Arthur ERICKSON**. Dorothy HOWELL and Arthur ERICKSON had the following children:

2562 i. **Jackelyn ERICKSON** married twice, to **Charles MORK**, and **John COMPTON**, order not known.
2563 ii. **James ERICKSON** married **Patty MORGAN**.
2564 iii. **Richard ERICKSON** married **Pamela WESTED**.
2565 iv. **Randall ERICKSON** married **Mary BOURNE**.
2566 v. **Arthur ERICKSON** died in infancy.

1912. **Carl Clayton HOWELL** was born on 2 April 1921 in Muskegon, Muskegon County, Michigan. He married **Hazel GYEBNER**, who was born on 20 July 1925 in Michigan. She died in August 1983 in Muskegon. Carl Clayton HOWELL and Hazel GYEBNER had the following children:

+2567 i. **Carl Clayton. HOWELL Jr.**
+2568 ii. **John A. HOWELL**
2569 iii. **Timothy G. HOWELL** was born on 30 January 1953. He married (1) **Debbie THOMAS**, and (2) **Kathy SCHILLING**.
+2570 iv. **Laurie Kay HOWELL**.

1914. **Samuel David THOMPSON** was born in 1913. He married **Eleanore UNKNOWN**. Samuel David THOMPSON and Eleanore UNKNOWN had the following children:

2571 i. **Arnold THOMPSON**.
2572 ii. **Colleen THOMPSON**.

1915. **Robert John THOMPSON** was born in 1914. He died in 1968. He married **Inez Marion MATTSON**, who was born on 18 May 1917. She died in December 1974. Robert John THOMPSON and Inez Marion MATTSON had the following children:

2573 i. **Della Marie THOMPSON** was born in 1940. She married **Unknown LEHMAN.**
2574 ii. **George Robert THOMPSON** was born in 1942.
+2575 iii. **Robert John THOMPSON**.
2576 iv. **Gladys THOMPSON**.
2577 v. **Hazel THOMPSON**.
2578 vi. **Judy THOMPSON**.

1916. **Ervin THOMPSON** was born on 1 July 1916. He died in January 1978. He married **Selma Ruth BIEVER**, who was born in 1920, and died in 1982. Ervin and Selma Ruth had the following children:

2579 i. **James Michael THOMPSON** was born in 1937. He married **Kathleen Elizabeth COOK**.
2580 ii. **Carol Ann THOMPSON** was born in 1939. She married **Virgil Claire ASCHINGER**.
2581 iii. **Betty Lou THOMPSON** was born in 1944. She married **Fred Albin CHITKO**.
2582 iv. **Donna Rae THOMPSON** was born in 1946. She married **Anthony Paul MILLAN**.
2583 v. **Kim David THOMPSON** was born in 1951. He married **Debra Jean KRAWZE**.
2584 vi. **Donald Ervin THOMPSON** was born in 1954.

1917. **Julia Louise THOMPSON** was born on 31 May 1917. She died in April 1987 in New Berlin, Waukesha County, Wisconsin. She married **Norbert Theodore HAGENY**, who was born on 17 July 1912. He died in December 1983 in Rhinelander, Wisconsin. Julia Louise THOMPSON and Norbert Theodore HAGENY had the following children:

+2585 i. **Irene HAGENY**.
+2586 ii. **Mary Jean HAGENY**.
+2587 iii. **Norma Louise HAGENY**.
+2588 iv. **Judith Ann HAGENY**.
+2589 v. **Norbert John HAGENY**.

+2590 vi. **Nancy Lee HAGENY**.
+2591 vii. **Thomas Robert HAGENY**.
2592 viii. **James Leo HAGENY** was born in 1953. He married **Beth BLISS.**
+2593 ix. **Donna May HAGENY**.

1918. **Clarence Joseph THOMPSON** was born in 1918. He married **Marie Esther MILLER**, who was born in 1912. She died in 1987. Clarence Joseph THOMPSON and Marie Esther MILLER had these children:

+2594 i. **Cheryl Marie THOMPSON**.
+2595 ii. **Daryl Clarence THOMPSON**.

1919. **Marie Grace THOMPSON** was born in 1920. She died in 1987. She married **Stephen Paul ADLER**, who was born on 25 July 1908. He died in September 1987 in Milwaukee, Milwaukee County, Wisconsin. Marie Grace THOMPSON and Stephen Paul ADLER had the following children:

+2596 i. **Mary Ann ADLER**.
+2597 ii. **Stephen Irvin ADLER**.
+2598 iii. **Jill Julia ADLER**.
+2599 iv. **Jacqueline Agnes ADLER**.
2600 v. **Daniel Joseph ADLER** was born in 1946.
+2601 vi. **Colleen Diane ADLER**.
2602 vii. **Michael John ADLER** was born in 1954.

1920. **Florence Agnes THOMPSON** was born in 1922. She married (1) **Norman BISSONETTE**. Florence Agnes THOMPSON and Norman BISSONETTE had the following children:

2603 i. **Norman BISSONETTE**.
2604 ii. **Ronald BISSONETTE**.
2605 iii. **Allen BISSONETTE**.
2606 iv. **Gregory BISSONETTE**.
2607 v. **Brenda BISSONETTE**.
2608 vi. **Sandra BISSONETTE**.

Florence Agnes THOMPSON married (2) **Raymond SMITH**. He died in 1987.They had these children:

2609 i. **Jean SMITH.**
2610 ii. **Renee SMITH**.

1923. **Dorothy Margaret TROYER** was born on 4 October 1912 in Lac du Flambeau, Wisconsin. She was married to **Carl Nathaniel FURNESS** M.D. on 4 August 1935 in Valpariso, Indiana. Carl Nathaniel FURNESS M.D. was born on 9 October 1899 in Sullivan, Moultrie County, Illinois. He died on 16 February

1925. **Ruth Elizabeth TROYER** was born on 20 November 1919 in Ontonagon, Ontonagon County, Michigan. She married **Fred YOUNGQUIST** in 1939. They were divorced. Ruth and Fred YOUNGQUIST had the following children:

+2614	i.	**Sandra YOUNGQUIST**.
2615	ii.	**John YOUNGQUIST** was born in 1940 and died in 1980.
+2616	iii.	**Patti YOUNGQUIST**.
+2617	iv.	**Jay YOUNGQUIST.**
2618	v.	**Scott YOUNGQUIST** married **Judy KNIGHT.**
+2619	vi.	**Tina YOUNGQUIST.**

1926. **Donald Pierce TROYER** was born on 27 October 1918 in Pontiac, Oakland County, Michigan. He died on 24 May 1993 in Jackson, MI. He married **Carol Mae WALCOTT** on 9 December 1942 in Logansport, Cas County, Indiana. Carol Mae WALCOTT was born on 21 April 1921 in Ithaca, Gratiot County, Michigan. They had two children:

+2620	i.	**Bart Daniel TROYER.**
+2621	ii.	**Barbara Kathleen TROYER**.

1927. **Phyllis Ann TROYER** was born on 24 November 1923. She was married to **Earl Lloyd HUNT** on 9 November 1946 in Pontiac. Earl Lloyd HUNT was born on 10 September 1921 in Birmingham, Oakland County, MI. Phyllis Ann TROYER and Earl Lloyd HUNT had the following children:

+2622	i.	**Linda Ann HUNT**.
+2623	ii.	**Raymond Earl HUNT**.
2624	iii.	**Alice Jane HUNT** was born on 27 October 1952.

1928. **Alice Jane TROYER** was born on 27 October 1952. She was married to **Denny CHERRY** on 4 October 1974. Denny CHERRY was born on 22 November 1950. They had two children:

2625	i.	**Korynn Elaine CHERRY** was born on 21 September 1980.
2626	ii.	**Gwynn Michelle CHERRY** was born on 10 December 1987.

1929. **Jess Francis LAUNDRIE** was born on 19 May 1913 in Winchester, Vilas County, Wisconsin. He died on 18 September 1989 in Baraboo, Sauk County, Wisconsin.

He married **Ina PITTS** in Land O'Lakes, Vilas County, on 11 June 1939. Ina PITTS was born on 26 April 1914. Jess Francis LAUNDRIE and Ina PITTS had the following children:

+2627 i. **Ina (Jeanne) LAUNDRIE.**
+2628 ii. **Frank Henry LAUNDRIE.**
2629 iii. **Unknown LAUNDRIE** was born in 1947. He (or she) died in 1947.

1930. **Norene Lucille LAUNDRIE** was born on 28 February 1915 in Winchester, Wisconsin. She married (1) **Stanley HOY**, who was born on 17 February 1914, and died on 17 May 1988. Their children were:

+2630 i. **JoAnn HOY.**
+2631 ii. **Elsie Jane HOY.**
+2632 iii. **Judith Norene HOY.**

Norene was married (2) to **Ort BASTIAN**, who was born on 5 April 1911, and died in august 1983 in Hillsboro, Oregon.

1931. **Mary Odeal LAUNDRIE** was born on 17 December 1919 in Winchester. She died in March 1984 in Adams, Adams County, Wisconsin. She married **Edward HUNT**, who was born on 21 March 1912, and died in April 1984. Mary Odeal LAUNDRIE and Edward HUNT had the following children:

2633 i. **Richard Clark HUNT** was born on 26 August 1940.
2634 ii. **Thomas Edward HUNT** was born on 30 November 1943.
2635 iii. **Jay HUNT.**
2636 iv. **Robin HUNT.**

1933. **Jonah HOWELL** was born on 20 September 1899 in Hope, Warren County, New Jersey. He died on 3 August 1988 in Hope.[241] He was buried in Moravian Cemetery in Hope. Jonah had been employed by the maintenance department of the Jenny Jump State Park prior to his retirement. He was a member of St. John Methodist Church in Hope. He married **Ada D. ALLEN**, who was born in 1914, died on 17 September 1944 in Great Meadows, Warren County, NJ, and was buried in Moravian Cemetery. Jonah HOWELL and Ada D. ALLEN had one child:

+2637 i. **Robert A. HOWELL.**

1935. **Brevilla HOWELL** was born on 10 July 1906. She died on 15 September 1992. She married **Augustus W. LEIDA** (son of **Goodward LEIDA** and **Euphemia SWAYZE**). Augustus was born on 10 November 1896 in Oxford,

---

[241]Obituary, The Star-Gazette, (NJ), 11 August 1988.

Warren County, NJ, and died on 25 July 1970 in Hope, Warren County. He was a veteran of WWI, had worked for the New Jersey State Highways Department for 35 years, and served on the Hope Township School Board and as Tax Collector for the town. They had two children:

2638 i. **Donald LEIDA**.
2639 ii. **Nancy Ann LEIDA** married **Donald C. TREIBLE** on 27 September 1952 .[242]

1939. **Gladys L. HOWELL** was born about 1901 in Walnut Valley,Warren County, New Jersey. She died on 16 March 1956 of a heart attack, and was buried in Moravian Cemetery, Hope. She was a teller in the First National Bank in Hope at the time of her death. She was married to **Charles J. HILL** (son of **C. Walton HILL**) in May 1926. Charles J. HILL was born in 1903, and died on 3 May 1943. He was buried in Moravian Cemetery. Gladys L. HOWELL and Charles J. HILL had the following children:

+2640 i. **Dorothy V. HILL**.
2641 ii. **Barbara HILL**.

1940. **Grace Anna GIBBS** was married to **Mahlon JAYNE**. Their children were:

2642 i. **David Edward JAYNE**.
2643 ii. **Ruth Edith JAYNE**.

1941. **Josephine GIBBS** married **Oscar B. HAYES**. Josephine and Oscar had two children:

2644 i. **Alice B. HAYES**.
2645 ii. **John HAYES**.

1944. **Harry GIBBS** was married to **Edith B. UNKNOWN**. They had three children:

2646 i. **Caleb Q. GIBBS**.
2647 ii. **Kenneth Wesley GIBBS**.
2648 iii. **Lena Elizabeth GIBBS** .

1947. **Freda GIBBS** married **William VAN ARSDALE**. They lived in Port Morris, NJ. Freda GIBBS and William VAN ARSDALE had one child:

2649 i. **Gladys VAN ARSDALE**.

---

[242]Marriage notice, Washington (NJ) Star, 27 Sep 1952

1948. **Fannie GIBBS** married **Ross MILLER**. Fannie GIBBS and Ross MILLER had one child:

2650 i. **George MILLER**.

1985. **Margery HEMINGWAY** married **D. Chester TRUEX**. They lived in Newburgh, Orange County, New York. Their children were:

2651 i. **Spencer Linn TRUEX**.
2652 ii. **Richard Houston TRUEX**.

1987. **Mary Alice CONDIT** was born on 22 March 1947. She married **Efrain COSME**. They had two children:

2653 i. **Nellie Marie COSME**.
2654 ii. **Nilda Iris COSME**.

1988. **Alice SMEDES** married **Raymond LAPOINT**. They had two sons:

2655 i. **Raymond LAPOINT**.
2656 ii. **Michael LAPOINT**.

1994. **Richard Henry HOWELL** was born in 23 September 1909. He married **Lucile Caroline PERSBACKER** on 17 July 1949. Lucile was born on 1 April 1907. Richard died on 10 March 1971, after a heart attack. They had a daughter:

2657 i. **Betty Yvonne HOWELL**.

1999. **Dorothy Leone HOWELL** was born on 4 September 1913 in Brantford Twp., Brant County, Ontario. She died on 11 October 1979 in Brantford Twp., and was buried in St. George United Cemetery. She married **Lloyd Ormand GINGRICH**, who died in 1975 in Galt, Waterloo County, Ontario. He was buried in U.C. Cemetery, Carlisle, Ontario. Their son was:

2658 i. **Lloyd Herbert GINGRICH** was born on 19 August 1915.

2000. **Lloyd Herbert HOWELL** was born on 19 August 1915 in St. George, Brant County, Ontario. He was buried in Ayr Cemetery, N. Dumfries, Waterloo County, Ontario. He married **Evelyn Ruth HODGSON** (daughter of **John HODGSON** and **Agnes CLARK**), who was born on 15 September 1919 in Ayr, Waterloo County. She died on 3 February 1991 in Kitchener, Waterloo County, and was buried in Ayr Cemetery. Their children were:

+2659 i. **Ross Herbert HOWELL**.
+2660 ii. **William Lloyd HOWELL**.

2019. **Marion HOPKINS** was married to **Russell HENDERSON**. Marion HOPKINS and Russell HENDERSON had the following children:

2661 i. **Gerald HENDERSON**.
2662 ii. **Joyce HENDERSON**.

2026. **Laurie Alice PATTEN** was born in 1915. She died in 1996. She married **Benjamin F. GUYATT**, whoo was born in 1918. They had one child:

2663 i. **Diane Patten GUYATT** was born in 1943. She married **Peter A. J. MCDOUGALL**. They live in Quebec, Canada.

2041. **James Wilson HOWELL** was born on 27 August 1912 in S. Dumfries, Brant County, Ontario. He died on 22 April 1988 in Hamilton, Wentworth County, Ontario, and was buried in St. George United Cemetery. He raised Holstein cattle and 35 acres of apples. He was the third member of his family to serve as Warden of the county, having been elected in 1965. This honor has probably not been accorded to any other family in Brant County. He was married to **Mary Isabel ANDERSON** (daughter of **David ANDERSON** and **Margaret CARSWELL**) on 29 October 1932 in Galt, Waterloo County. Mary Isabel ANDERSON was born on 31 July 1912 in Galt. James and Mary Isabel had four children:

+2664 i. **William Bruce HOWELL**.
+2665 ii. **Margaret Ann HOWELL**.
+2666 iii. **Joyce Doreen HOWELL**.
+2667 iv. **Lynda Pauline HOWELL**.

2043. **John Arthur HOWELL** was born on 8 September 1920 in St. George, Brant County, Ontario. He died on 10 March 1965 in Brantford Twp., Brant County. He was married to **Mae Zoe MACLEOD** (daughter of **James Edmund MACLEOD** and **Ida May DRYSDALE**) on 2 December 1950 in Halifax, Nova Scotia. Mae Zoe MACLEOD was born on 15 September 1923 in Halifax. John Arthur HOWELL and Mae Zoe MACLEOD had one child:

+2668 i. **John Macleod HOWELL**.

2045. **William Morley BUCK** was born in Port Dover, Ontario on 25 November 1908. He married **Ruth MCGUIRE** on 5 November 1936 in New York City. They live in Delray Beach, FL, and have one child:.

2669 i. **Sally Lytton BUCK** was born on 19 November 1952 in Delray Beach, Palm Beach County, Florida.

2046. **John Harris BUCK** was born on 25 March 1912 in Port Dover. During WWII, he served with the Royal Canadian Air Force. He married **Annie Henrietta**

TATE on 26 September 1936 in Moose Jaw, Saskatchewan. She was born on 19 November 1912 in Moose Jaw. They have three children:

+2670 i. **Catherine Comer BUCK.**
2671 ii. **John Harris BUCK** was born on 17 July 1947 in Port Dover.
2672 iii. **Conrad BUCK** was born on 6 November 1949.

2047. **Edward Comer BUCK** was born on 1 June 1920 in Port Dover. He married (1) **Luana Murray DIXON** (daughter of a former Alabama governor). The marriage ended in divorce. They had three adopted children:

2673 i. **Edward Comer BUCK** was born on 19 August 1953 in Ft. Lauderdale, Broward County, Florida.
2674 ii. **Dixon BUCK** was born on 28 June 1955 in Ft. Lauderdale.
2675 iii. **Juliette BUCK** was born on 20 June 1957 in Florida.

Edward married (2) **Ada Marcelina GIL** on 11 June 1959 in Havana, Cuba. Ada was born on 16 January 1938 in Santa Clara, Cuba. They have two children:

2676 i. **Wendy BUCK** was born on 11 September 1960 in Ft. Lauderdale.
2677 ii. **Christopher Robin BUCK** was born on 18 July 1963 in Ft. Lauderdale.

2048. **James Orton BUCK** was born on 1 July 1913 in Bridgeport, Fairfield County, Connecticut. He married **Nancy Gulley FOSTER** in New York City on 19 April 1947. They have one child:

2678 i. **Clare Bowen BUCK** was born on 7 September 1950 in New York City.

2050. **Julian Randolph BUCK** was born on 9 February 1916 in Bridgeport. He married **Dorothy Evelyn RENFROE** on 4 April 1943. She was born on 14 March 1922 in Alabama. They have these children:

2679 i. **Julian Randolph BUCK** was born on 1 December 1946 in Montclair, Essex County, Nw Jersey.
2680 ii. **Karen BUCK** was born on 25 February 1948 in Dallas, Dallas County, Texas.
2681 iii. **Robert Treat BUCK** was born on 25 February 1957 in Dallas.

2052. **Orton Bertrum McLean HOWELL** was born on 5 January 1917 in Winnipeg, Manitoba. He was married to **Joan Louise Elizabeth WILEY** (daughter of **Charles WILEY** and **Ada Florence GIBBS**) on 30 July 1943 in

London, England. Joan Louise Elizabeth WILEY was born in 1924 in London, England. They had the following children:

+2682 i. **Wayne Orton Peter HOWELL**.
2683 ii. **Sandra Alice Joan HOWELL** was born on 5 October 1951 in Brighton, Sussex, England. She was married to **Michael Wells MILLARD** on 20 September 1975 in St. John's Church, Crawley, Sussex, England. Michael was born on 11 August 1947 in Manchester, Lancashire, England.

2054. **Leslie Weldon HOWELL** was born on 26 July 1933 in Dresden, Ontario. He was married to **Patricia Anne MOTT** (daughter of **Henry MOTT** and **Ida LEGUE**) on 6 November 1954 in Chatham, Ontario. Patricia Anne MOTT was born on 14 May 1934. Leslie and Patricia Anne had the following children:

2684 i. **Leslie Wayne HOWELL** was born on 22 September 1956 in Oshawa, Ontario. He married **Debra Elaine COSMAN** (daughter of **John COSMAN** and **Gertrude MORTON**) on 3 September 1978 in Oshawa. Debra was born on 30 December 1958 in Oshawa.
2685 ii. **Jeffrey Thomas HOWELL** was born on 1 March 1959 in Hamilton, Wentworth County, Ontario. He married **Sharon Lynn COSMAN** (daughter of **John COSMAN** and **Gertrude MORTON**) on 16 February 1990 in Oshawa. Sharon was born on 6 June 1961 in Oshawa.
2686 iii. **Jonathon Mark HOWELL** was born on 4 January 1963 in Oshawa, Ontario.

2055. **Maxwell Glen HOWELL** was born on 15 June 1937 in Dresden, Ontario. He was a Planning Director. He and Maxine are twins. He was married to **Ruth Anne HILBORN** (daughter of **Wesley HILBORN** and **Bessie WALDON**) on 28 August 1961 in Thedford, Lambton County, Ontario. Ruth Anne HILBORN was born on 20 August 1940 in Sarnia, Ontario. She was a Lab Technologist. Maxwell Glen HOWELL and Ruth Anne HILBORN had the following children:

2687 i. **Brian Wesley HOWELL** was born on 7 June 1962 in Chatham, Ontario.
2688 ii. **Sheila Anne HOWELL** was born on 28 May 1964 in Chatham, Ontario.

2056. **Maxine Lucille HOWELL** was born on 15 June 1937 in Dresden, Ontario. She was married to **James Samuel MCFADDEN** on 6 September 1958 in Chatham, Ontario. James Samuel MCFADDEN was born on 16 March 1936 in Chatham. Maxine and James Samuel MCFADDEN had these children:

2689 i. **Terri Lynn MCFADDEN** was born on 11 December 1959 in Chatham.
2690 ii. **Bradley J. MCFADDEN** was born on 7 March 1963 in Chatham.
2691 iii. **Kathren A. MCFADDEN** was born on 26 June 1964 in Chatham.

2057. **Muriel Grace HOWELL** was born on 26 September 1920 in Darlingford, Manitoba. She was married to **John Howard LAVERTY** on 1 August 1942 in Rogers Memorial Presbyterian Church, Toronto, Ontario. John Howard LAVERTY was born on 22 January 1916 in Rockwood, Ontario. Muriel Grace HOWELL and John Howard LAVERTY had the following children:

2692 i. **John Randall LAVERTY** was born on 17 January 1953 in Toronto, Ontario. He married **Cathy DESIVIAGE** on 15 September 1978.
+2693 ii. **Dale Ann LAVERTY**.

2058. **Jean Alva HOWELL** was born in 1921 in E. Kildonan, Manitoba. She was married to **John Wesley RUSK** on 24 October 1942 in Danforth United Church, Toronto. John Wesley RUSK was born on 6 June 1906 in Amabel Township, Allenford County, Ontario. He died on 17 January 1976, and was buried in Zion Cemetery, Amabel Twp. Jean and John Wesley RUSK had the following children:

+2694 i. **James Leslie RUSK**.
+2695 ii. **Robert John RUSK**.
2696 iii. **Morris RUSK** was born and died in Wiarton, Ontario.
+2697 iv. **Linda Suzanne RUSK**.
2698 v. **Donald Brock RUSK** was born on 14 September 1955 in Toronto. He married **Margaret Ann SENIOR** on 3 September 1978 in St. Andrew's Presbyterian Church in Owen Sound, Ontario.

2059. **Wayne Bertrum HOWELL** was born on 30 March 1923 in Beamsville, Ontario. He was married to **Dorothy Mary EDWARDS** (daughter of **William EDWARDS** and **Rosaline GENNING**) on 7 October 1944. Dorothy Mary EDWARDS was born on 10 February 1924. They had the following children:

+2699 i. **Ronald Wayne HOWELL**.
2700 ii. **Wendy Lynn HOWELL** was born on 4 December 1949 in London, Ontario. She married **Richard Wilton GREENE** on 22 August 1970.
2701 iii. **Sandra Lee HOWELL** was born on 19 August 1957 in Montreal, Quebec.

2063. **James Holmes SIMPSON** was born on 20 October 1923 in Teulon, Manitoba. He was married to **Elizabeth "Betty" BRYAN** on 27 August 1948 in

Thunder Bay, Ontario. Elizabeth "Betty" BRYAN was born on 17 November 1923. James and Elizabeth had these children:

+2702 i. **James Bryan SIMPSON**.
2703 ii. **Evan SIMPSON** was born on 25 March 1952. He married **Susan KEEGAN** in August 1976.

2064. **Patricia Ann SIMPSON** was born on 22 June 1930 in Winnipeg, Manitoba. She married **Glenn Franklin CLARK**, who was born on 27 March 1924 in Napanee, Ontario.They had these children:

+2704 i. **Laurie Jean CLARK**.
2705 ii. **Terry Glenn CLARK** was born on 1 May 1962 in Parry Sound, Ontario.
2706 iii. **Marnie Lynn CLARK** was born on 11 January 1969 in Perry Sound, Ontario.

2065. **Jean Elizabeth SIMPSON** was born on 19 March 1937 in Winnipeg, Manitoba, Canada. She and Janet are twins. She was married to **Leslie SKINNER** on 10 April 1965. Leslie SKINNER was born in Oak River, Manitoba. Jean Elizabeth SIMPSON and Leslie SKINNER had the following children:

2707 i. **Dana Lynn SKINNER** was born on 21 November 1965.
2708 ii. **Brent SKINNER** was born on 19 November 1966.
2709 iii. **Linda Jean SKINNER** was born on 26 November 1969.

2066. **Janet Elaine SIMPSON** was born on 19 March 1937 in Winnipeg, Manitoba. She was married to **Harold GUSTAFSON** on 19 July 1958. Janet Elaine and Harold GUSTAFSON had these children:

2710 i. **Cheryl Lynn GUSTAFSON** was born on 29 June 1960 in Winnipeg.
2711 ii. **Bruce GUSTAFSON** was born on 29 May 1962 in Winnipeg, Manitoba.
2712 iii. **Nancy Dawn GUSTAFSON** was born on 18 May 1964 in Winnipeg.

2067. **Helen Elizabeth DAVIDSON** was born on 1 March 1915 in Hamilton, Wentworth County, Ontario. She died on 16 July 1992 in Smiths Falls, Lanark County, Ontario, and was buried in Maple Vale Cemetery, Smiths Falls. She was married to **Arnold DUNHAM** in Cornwall, Ontario. Arnold DUNHAM was born in Smiths Falls, and died there on 26 December 1985. Helen Elizabeth DAVIDSON and Arnold DUNHAM had the following children:

2713 i. **Mary Margaret Elizabeth DUNHAM** married **Wilbert Paul FOURNIER**.

2714 ii. **Dorothy Diane DUNHAM** married **Donald FAIRFIELD**.

2715 iii. **Donald Lawrence DUNHAM** married **Betty UNKNOWN**.

2068. **Margaret Graham DAVIDSON** married **Joseph Robert EWING**. Margaret and Joseph Robert EWING had these children:

2716 i. **Carol Lynn EWING** married **William Thomas MCKELLAR**.

2717 ii. **Bruce Douglas EWING** married **Cynthia Mary BROWN**.

2069. **Dorothy Irene DAVIDSON** married **Evan Claude DUNCALFE**. They had two children:

2718 i. **David DUNCALFE** married (1) **Karen DOLAN**; (2) **Roma SENIUNAS**; and (3) **Barbara Leah BAGNALL**.

2719 ii. **Susan DUNCALFE** married (1) **Randy UNKNOWN**, and (2) **Alan BENDER**.

2070. **Jackson Graham DAVIDSON**. He married **Ruth Gladys ENGLAND** (daughter of **Walter ENGLAND** and **Mary RUTHERFORD**), who was born on 18 February 1929 in Burlington, Halton County, Ontario. She died on 25 September 1993 in Hamilton, Wentworth County, and was buried in Greenwood Cemetery, Burlington, Ontario. They had these children:

2720 i. **Jane Ellen DAVIDSON** married **Bruce Richard RICH**.

2721 ii. **Jackson Graham DAVIDSON** married **Crista Elizabeth CLINE**.

2083. **Fred PARKHILL** married **Margaret MCARTHUR**. They had these children:

2722 i. **Donald PARKHILL**.

2723 ii. **Kenneth PARKHILL**.

2724 iii. **Stanley PARKHILL**.

2725 iv. **Mary PARKHILL**.

2084. **Grace STEELE** was born in 1893. She died in 1931. She was married to **Lorne SLACK** in 1915. Grace STEELE and Lorne SLACK had one child:

2726 i. **Lorene STEELE** was born on 27 August 1922. She married **Unknown CULLEN**.

2085. **John Earlington "Jack" WALLEY** was born on 12 October 1912 in Birtle, Manitoba. He was married to **Alice EDMONSON** on 15 July 1936 in Brandon, Manitoba. Alice EDMONSON was born on 3 August 1911 in Birtle, Manitoba. John and Alice had two children:

+2727 i. **Valerie Ann WALLEY.**
+2728 ii. **William John WALLEY.**

2086. **Irene Marguarite WALLEY** was born on 18 June 1914 in Glenboro, Manitoba. She was married to **Edward Emmett DUFFY** on 6 February 1942 in Brandon, Manitoba. Edward Emmett DUFFY was born on 18 June 1918 in Vernon, British Columbia. He died on 8 January 1972 in Thunder Bay, Ontario. Irene Marguarite WALLEY and Edward Emmett DUFFY had the following children:

+2729 i. **Kathleen "Patricia" Anne DUFFY.**
2730 ii. **Ray Edward DUFFY** was born on 11 November 1946 in Birtle, Manitoba. He died on 13 November 1946 in Birtle.
+2731 iii. **Rae Marguarite DUFFY.**

2087. **Kathleen Maude WALLEY** was born on 19 September 1915 in Glenboro, Manitoba. She was married to **Thomas J. MATHEWS** on 9 April 1955 in Birtle, Manitoba. Thomas J. MATHEWS was born on 15 June 1915 in Utica, Oneida County, New York. Kathleen and Thomas J. MATHEWS had two children:

+2732 i. **Kathleen Marie MATHEWS.**
+2733 ii. **Laura Lee MATHEWS.**
2734 iii. **Marianne Jean MATHEWS** was born on 11 April 1952. She married **Thomas J. CHRISTMAN** on 19 August 1972.

2089. **Ernest Christie WALLEY** was born on 23 June 1925 in Birtle, Manitoba. He was married to **Maureen Jean NEWSHAM** on 29 July 1946 in Birtle, Manitoba. Maureen Jean NEWSHAM was born on 28 April 1922 in Birtle, Manitoba. Ernest and Maureen had two children:

+2735 i. **Donna Jean WALLEY.**
+2736 ii. **Betty Marie WALLEY.**

2090. **Marie Evelyn HAMES** was born on 11 December 1914 in Glenboro, Manitoba. She married Rev. **Fred J. DOUGLAS**, who was born in December 1914 in Glenboro, Manitoba. Marie Evelyn HAMES and Rev. Fred J. DOUGLAS had the following children:

+2737 i. **Peter Kenneth DOUGLAS.**
2738 ii. **Alice Marie DOUGLAS** was born on 15 August 1944 in Winnipeg, Manitoba. She died on 25 January

1945.

2739 iii. **David Hames DOUGLAS** was born on 7 September 1945 in Thunder Bay, Ontario.

2091. **Ellen Berta HAMES** was born on 26 March 1917 in Glenboro, Manitoba. She was married to **George Milne SHAND** on 5 August 1939 in Glenboro. George Milne SHAND was born on 1 November 1908 in Winnipeg, Manitoba. Ellen and George Milne SHAND had the following children:

+2740 i. **George Brian "Skip" SHAND**.
+2741 ii. **Terry Evelyn SHAND**.
+2742 iii. **Judy Elizabeth SHAND**.
2743 iv. **Bruce Hames SHAND** was born on 14 October 1951 in Marathon, Ontario.
+2744 v. **Lois Ellen SHAND**.

2092. **Elizabeth Jean HAMES** was born on 20 August 1921 in Glenboro, Manitoba. She was married to **Vernon Richard SCHMITT** on 6 July 1946 in Covington, Kenton County, Kentucky. Vernon Richard SCHMITT was born on 18 July 1909 in Columbus, Franklin County, Ohio. They had these children:

2745 i. **Helen Marie SCHMITT** was born on 3 February 1948 in Columbus. She married **Richard William MITCHELL** on 7 July 1979 in Denver, Arapahoe County, Colorado. He was born in June 1939 in Denver.
2746 ii. **Janet Louise SCHMITT** was born on 10 August 1951 in Columbus. She married **John William DOBSON** on 22 December 1973 in Albuquerque, Bernalilo County, New Mexico.
2747 iii. **Alice Carolyn SCHMITT** was born on 10 August 1955 in Columbus.

2095. **Cecil James MULHOLLAND** was born on 23 June 1926. He was married to **Jessie PATTON** on 12 November 1957 in Central Butte, Saskatchewan. Jessie PATTON was born on 3 November 1925 in Portavoe, County Down, Ireland. They had two children:

+2748 i. **Ellen Ivah MULHOLLAND**.
2749 ii. **Kenneth Cecil MULHOLLAND** was born on 14 July 1954 in Central Butte.

2096. **Marion Helen HOWELL** was born on 3 May 1921 in S. Dumfries, Brant County, Ontario. She married (1) **Martin RUSSELL**, on 20 March 1939. He was born in Holland Landing, Ontario. Marion Helen HOWELL and Martin RUSSELL had the following children:

2750 i. **Larry RUSSELL** was born on 9 April 1940 in St.

George, Brant County.

2751 ii. **David Richard RUSSELL** was born on 15 August 1941 in St. George.

2752 iii. **John Wayne RUSSELL** was born on 28 January 1944 in Prospect Hill, Ontario.

Helen married (2) **Charles Fish SKELTON**, about 1945.

2097. **Jack Philip HOWELL** was born on 1 December 1923 in S. Dumfries, Brant County, Ontario. Philip was an engineer who served 25 years in the Navy. He was married to **Vivian Elizabeth ROSS** on 27 March 1948 in St. Croix, Nova Scotia. Jack Philip HOWELL and Vivian ROSS had these children:

2753 i. **Barbara Jane HOWELL** was born on 6 June 1951 in Halifax, Nova Scotia.

2754 ii. **Joanne Elizabeth HOWELL** was born on 4 July 1953 in Halifax.

2755 iii. **David Ross HOWELL** was born on 25 November 1954 in Halifax.

2756 iv. **Peter Hunter HOWELL** was born on 26 April 1961 in Halifax.

2098. **William Herbert HOWELL** was born on 12 February 1925 in S. Dumfries, Brant County, Ontario. William grew up in the area of Hamilton, Ontario. He was married (1) to **Kathleen Marion HINDLE** (daughter of **Charles HINDLE** and **Kathleen HILL**) on 9 October 1954 in Toronto, York County, Ontario. William Herbert HOWELL and Kathleen Marion HINDLE had the following children:

2757 i. **Karen Louise HOWELL** was born on 28 November 1955 in Toronto. She is an accountant.

+2758 ii. **Allan Wayne HOWELL.**

2759 iii. **Dianne Kathleen HOWELL** was born on 8 December 1958 in Oshawa, Ontario. She is a travel consultant.

+2760 iv. **Arlene Patricia HOWELL.**

William married (2) **Kathleen Loreen THOMPSON** (daughter of **Stanley THOMPSON** and **Annie LANGLEY**) on 30 November 1987 in Florida.

2099. **Gordon Ker HOWELL** was born on 5 December 1926 in S. Dumfries, Brant County, Ontario. He was married to **Jean Mary THOMPSON** (daughter of **Edward THOMPSON** and **Verna VANSICKLE**) in Galt, Waterloo County, Ontario, on 30 May 1953. Jean THOMPSON was born in August 1928. Gordon Ker HOWELL and Jean THOMPSON had the following children:

2761 i. **Roger Norman HOWELL** was born on 6 November 1953.

2762 ii. **Gregory Edward HOWELL** was born on 13 December 1954.

2763 iii. **Deborah Anne HOWELL** was born on 8 August 1957.

2764 iv. **Brenda Lynn HOWELL** was born on 7 April 1959.

2765 v. **Glen William HOWELL** was born on 17 September 1963.

2100. **Jean Louise HOWELL** was born on 21 August 1929 in S. Dumfries, Brant County, Ontario. Jean owned a beauty shop on Main Street in Paris, Ontario. She married **Lloyd George RAMSEY** (son of George RAMSEY and **Ellen UNKNOWN**) on 13 August 1949 in St. George, Brant County. Jean Louise HOWELL and Lloyd RAMSEY had the following children:

2766 i. **Neil Lloyd RAMSEY** was born on 22 January 1950 in St. George.

2767 ii. **Robert George RAMSEY** was born on 9 March 1951 in St. George.

2768 iii. **Brian Malcolm RAMSEY** was born on 21 December 1952 in St. George. He married **Lois GURNEY** in 1972 in Bethel United Church, Paris, Ontario.

2101. **Kenneth Philip HOWELL** was born on 30 January 1940 in Galt, Waterloo, Ontario. He married (1) **Pauline BIDULKA** on 10 October 1964. They divorced in 1974. He married (2) **Marilyn DEFERD** (daughter of **Rudy DEFERD**) on 18 October 1974. They have one child:

2769 i. **Meredith Louise HOWELL** was born on 11 March 1977 in Kitchener, Waterloo County, Ontario.

2102. **Margaret Joyce HOWELL** was born on 14 September 1941 in Lynne, Ontario. She was married to **Joseph MCINTYRE** (son of **Alexander MCINTYRE** and **Jouita Christina MCKINNON**) on 16 July 1966. Joseph MCINTYRE was born on 27 June 1941 in Reserve Mines, Nova Scotia. Their children are:

2770 i. **Sandra Marie MCINTYRE** was born on 21 December 1968 in Brantford Twp., Brant County, Ontario. She and Sherri are twins.

2771 ii. **Sherri Anne MCINTYRE** was born on 21 December 1968 in Brantford Twp.

2772 iii. **Susan Elizabeth MCINTYRE** was born on 15 June 1970 in Brantford Twp.

2103. **Donald Howard HOWELL** was born on 15 February 1943 in Brantford Twp., Brant County. He is a Co-op manager. He married **Marie Louise KIEVELL** (daughter of **Edmund KIEVELL** and **Jean MINER**) on 4 September 1964 in Rock Chapel, Wentworth County. Marie Louise KIEVELL was born on 2

March 1944 in Hamilton, Wentworth County. She works at the Co-op. Their children are:

2773 i. **Kevin Edwin HOWELL** was born on 28 July 1965 in Hamilton.

2774 ii. **Mark William HOWELL** was born on 24 April 1969 in Brantford Twp.

2104. **Edwin Allen HOWELL** was born on 24 June 1945 in Brantford Twp., Brant County, Ontario. He is James' twin. He was married to **Penny GRISDALE** (daughter of **George GRISDALE** and **Jean STOTT**) on 23 June 1972 in Dundas, Ontario. Penny GRISDALE was born on 1 July 1945 in Hamilton, Wentworth County, Ontario. Edwin Allen HOWELL and Penny GRISDALE had one child:

2775 i. **Edwin Allan HOWELL** was born on 1 March 1971 in Brantford Twp.

2105. **James Edgar HOWELL** was born on 24 June 1945 in Brantford Twp., Brant County, Ontario. He is Edwin's twin. He was married to **Patricia MORLEY** on 9 January 1976 in Lynne, Ontario. James Edgar HOWELL and Patricia MORLEY had one child:

2776 i. **Margaret Jane HOWELL** was born on 9 October 1976 in Brantford Twp.

2107. **Mary Elizabeth HOWELL** was born on 25 April 1950 in Brantford Twp., Brant County, Ontario. She was married to **Ronald William MANNEN** (son of **William MANNEN** and **Isabelle WELTON**) on 27 June 1969 in St. George, Brant County. Ronald William MANNEN was born on 4 May 1943 in Copetown, Ontario. Mary Elizabeth and Ronald William MANNEN had these children:

2777 i. **Susan Lynn MANNEN** was born on 16 June 1971 in Brantford Twp.

2778 ii. **Daniel James MANNEN** was born on 19 July 1974 in Brantford Twp. He and Alan are twins.

2779 iii. **Alan Ronald MANNEN** was born on 19 July 1974 in Brantford Twp.

2108. **Glen Clifton LYONS** was born on 30 January 1932 in S. Dumfries, Brant County, Ontario. He was married (1) to **Dorothy Agnes SCOTLAND** on 2 September 1955 in St. George, Brant County, Ontario. They divorced in 1978. Dorothy Agnes SCOTLAND was born on 16 April 1932. Glen Clifton LYONS and Dorothy Agnes SCOTLAND had the following children:

2780 i. **Donna Marie LYONS** was born on 5 April 1957. She died on 16 December 1972, and was buried in St. Joseph's Cemetery, Brantford Twp.

+2781 ii. **Douglas Howard LYONS**.

2782 iii. **Katherine Patricia LYONS** was born on 5 July 1963. She died on 15 March 1985.

2783 iv. **Teressa Dorothy LYONS** was born on 16 August 1968. She died on 8 November 1968, and was buried in St. Joseph's Cemetery.

He was married (2) to **Nellie DZUBA** on 14 March 1979 in St. George, Brant County, Ontario. Nellie DZUBA was born on 2 October 1930 in Springfield, Manitoba.

2110. **Herbert Edward GERMAN** was born on 14 September 1937 in Brantford Twp., Brant County, Ontario. He was married (1)to **Phyllis Eleanor GREEN** (daughter of **H. Gordon GREEN** and **Joan WAIMAN**) on 22 June 1955 in Brantford Twp. Phyllis Eleanor GREEN was born on 29 November 1937. Herbert Edward GERMAN and Phyllis Eleanor GREEN had the following children:

+2784 i. **Carmen Bruce GERMAN**.

2785 ii. **Brian Herbert GERMAN** was born on 22 May 1959 in Brantford Twp.

+2786 iii. **Arlene Ann GERMAN**.

2787 iv. **Timothy GERMAN** was born on 2 June 1969.

He was married (2) to **Lynda Lee MCGLENISTER** on 15 June 1975 in Buffalo, Erie County, New York. Lynda Lee MCGLENISTER was born on 19 June 1942. They had one child:

2788 i. **Adam Wesley Frederick GERMAN** was born on 12 December 1980.

2111. **William Bruce GERMAN** was born on 21 January 1939 in Brantford Twp., Brant County, Ontario. He was married to **Joan HANSFORD** on 20 March 1965. Joan HANSFORD was born on 15 December 1937. William Bruce GERMAN and Joan HANSFORD had the following children:

2789 i. **Susan Iris GERMAN** was born on 9 September 1965. She married Kevin **Daniel KOTORYNSKI** on 20 May 1992 in Sidney, British Columbia. He was born on 22 May 1965.

2790 ii. **Paul William GERMAN** was born on 24 June 1969.

2112. **Raemond Fitzgerald GERMAN** was born on 30 November 1940 in S. Dumfries, Brant County, Ontario. He was married to **Don-nee Elizabeth SNIDER** (daughter of **Donald Leonard SNIDER** and **Elizabeth LYNCH**) on 13 August 1966 in Memorial Hall, University of Guelph. Don-nee Elizabeth SNIDER was born on 3 December 1940 in Brantford Twp., Brant County. Raemond Fitzgerald GERMAN and Don-nee Elizabeth SNIDER had the following children:

2791 i. **Donald Bradley Fitzgerald GERMAN** was born on 3

October 1970.

2792 ii. **Raechel Elizabeth Nan GERMAN** was born on 6 April 1972.

2113. **Katharine Jane MCCLURE** was born in 1943 in Brantford Twp., Brant County, Ontario. She was married to **Garry John THIELIN** on 2 October 1970 in Paris, Brant County. Garry John THIELIN was born on 3 October 1942 in Lethbridge, Alberta. Katharine and Garry had these children:

2793 i. **Barbara Jane THIELIN** was born on 6 May 1971 in Rapid City, Pennington County, South Dakota.

2794 ii. **Christine Marie THIELIN** was born on 13 December 1972 in Harrisburg, Saline County, Illinois.

2115. **Donald Morton MCCLURE** was born on 16 January 1949 in Brantford Twp., Brant County, Ontario. He was married to **Nancy Lynn WALLET** on 7 October 1978 in London, Ontario. Nancy Lynn WALLET was born on 2 August 1956 in London, Ontario. Donald and Nancy Lynn had two children:

2795 i. **Gavin John MCCLURE** was born on 11 August 1981 in London, Ontario.

2796 ii. **Daniel Thomas MCCLURE** was born on 29 October 1984 in London, Ontario.

2116. **John Herbert BUCHANAN** was born on 1 May 1935 in Brantford Twp., Brant County, Ontario. He was married to **Nancy Ann PRITCHARD** (daughter of **Andrew Lyle PRITCHARD** and **Agnes Mae HODGETTS**) on 7 October 1961 in Ottawa, Ontario. Nancy Ann PRITCHARD was born on 1 September 1936 in Nanaimo, British Columbia. John and Nancy had these children:

2797 i. **Heather Mae BUCHANAN** was born on 6 August 1964 in London, Ontario.

2798 ii. **James Andrew Bentley BUCHANAN** was born on 6 July 1966 in London, Ontario. He married **Linda Margaret WHITE** on 9 October 1983 in Aberfoyle, Ontario. She was born on 5 March 1959 in Regina, Saskatchewan.

2799 iii. **Jane Catherine BUCHANAN** was born on 9 May 1971 in Norwalk, Fairfield County, Connecticut.

2117. **Evelyn Mae BUCHANAN** was born on 20 March 1936 in Brantford Twp. She was married to **James Kenneth GOWMAN** (son of **Russell GOWMAN** and **Annie MCLEOD**) on 17 March 1956 in St. George, Brant County. James Kenneth GOWMAN was born on 10 June 1933 in Brantford Twp., Brant County. Their children were:

2800 i. **Mark James GOWMAN** was born on 1 May 1960 in London, Ontario, and died on 23 August 1960.

2801 ii. **Trent William GOWMAN** was born on 27 December 1961 in Kitchener, Waterloo County, Ontario, and died on 16 December 1963.

+2802 iii. **Richard James GOWMAN**.

2803 iv. **Susan Mae GOWMAN** was born on 13 July 1964 in Kitchener. She married **David REIBEL** on 11 February 1989 in Kitchener. He was born on 13 January 1963.

2804 v. **David Ronald GOWMAN** was born on 16 December 1966 in North York, Ontario.

2118. **Richard Bentley BUCHANAN** was born on 1 October 1940 in Brantford Twp., Brant County, Ontario. He was married (1) to **Susan Elizabeth DUNN** (daughter of **Geoffrey A. DUNN**) on 7 May 1966 in West Vancouver, British Columbia. Susan Elizabeth DUNN was born on 17 April 1943. Richard Bentley BUCHANAN and Susan Elizabeth DUNN had the following children:

2805 i. **Sarah Elizabeth BUCHANAN** was born on 13 July 1969 in North Vancouver, British Columbia.

2806 ii. **Jonathan Michael BUCHANAN** was born on 22 March 1974 in North Vancouver.

He was married (2) to **Esther KERR** on 11 August 1980 in North Vancouver, British Columbia. Esther KERR was born on 7 July 1942.

2127. **Cyrus George SHAVER** was born on 21 December 1898 in Kaleida, Manitoba. He died on 1 July 1960 in Dugald, Manitoba. He was married to **Norine Helen DASHER** on 4 June 1927 in Melvindale, Ecorse Twp., Michigan. Norine Helen DASHER was born on 5 March 1908 in Melvindale. Cyrus George SHAVER and Norine Helen DASHER had the following children:

2807 i. **George Wesley SHAVER** was born on 24 March 1928 in Melvindale. He married **Irene Louise IVES** on 20 May 1950.

+2808 ii. **Allen Lesley SHAVER**.

2809 iii. **Joanne Delores SHAVER** was born on 10 April 1932 in Winnipeg. She died on 8 January 1983 in Dugald, Manitoba. She married **Albert Byron COOK** on 5 August 1949.

2810 iv. **Ronald Arthur SHAVER** was born on 19 August 1933 in Winnipeg, and died on 9 August 1982 in Dugald, Manitoba.

2811 v. **Shirley Eileen SHAVER** was born on 29 December 1936 in Winnipeg. She married **Gordon SWANE** on 24 July 1954.

2130. **Margaret Kathleen MULLOY** was born on 7 May 1921. She was married to **John Harold ENGLISH** on 1 May 1946. John Harold ENGLISH was born on

1 September 1920 in Harwick Township, Ontario. Margaret Kathleen MULLOY and John Harold ENGLISH had these children:

+2812 i. **Robert John ENGLISH**.
+2813 ii. **Leslie Margaret ENGLISH**.
+2814 iii. **Mary Kathleen ENGLISH**.

2133. **Alta Doreen CRAMER** was born in 1925. She married **Lowell SHOUP**. They had a daughter:

+2815 i. **Debra Colleen SHOUP**.

2146. **Donald Horace MITCHELL** was born on 6 February 1934 in Detroit, Wayne County, Mchigan. He was married to **Joan Edith BITTEKOEFER** on 2 December 1961. Their children are:

2816 i. **Jon Erik MITCHELL** was born on 6 February 1963.
2817 ii. **Kerin Leslie MITCHELL** was born on 14 August 1966.

2147. **Charles Theodore MITCHELL** was born on 22 May 1936 in Detroit, Wayne County, Michigan. He was married to **Janet Ruth REUTER** on 4 October 1958. Janet Ruth REUTER was born on 22 November 1938. Charles Theodore MITCHELL and Janet Ruth REUTER had the following children:

+2818 i. **Kenneth Charles MITCHELL**.
2819 ii. **Douglas Alan MITCHELL** was born on 5 November 1963.
+2820 iii. **Cheryl Ruth MITCHELL**.

NINTH GENERATION

2148. **Ruth Elizabeth HOWELL** was born on 12 April 1917. She died on 11 May 1939, and was buried in Arndt's Cemetery, Easton, Northampton County, Pennsylvania. She was married to **Philip T. CHAMBERLAIN** on 2 October 1934. Ruth and Philip were divorced. They had one child:

2821 i. **Marilyn Yvonne CHAMBERLAIN** was born on 9 June 1935, and died on 13 June 1935.

2150. **Lawrence H. LAUBACH** was born on 25 February 1927 in Phillipsburg, Warren County, New Jersey. He died on 4 November 1992 in Southbridge, Massachusetts, and was buried in Calvary Cemetery, Harmony, Warren County. Lawrence served as a PFC in the Army during World War II. He was married to **Mary C. COMPTON** in June 1959. They had these children:

2822 i. **R. Gerald LAUBACH**.
2823 ii. **Rebecca LAUBACH** married **Unknown FILLEBRON**.

2151. **Kenneth M. LAUBACH** was born on 10 February 1928 in Phillipsburg, Warren County, New Jersey. He died on 8 December 1997 in Stewartsville, Warren County, and was buried in St. Mary's Cemetery, Alpha, Warren County. He was a truck driver. He married (1) **Barbara BURGSTRESSER**. They were divorced. Kenneth M. LAUBACH and Barbara BURGSTRESSER had one child:

+2824 i. **Kenneth LAUBACH**.

Kenneth M. LAUBACH married (2) **Patricia Ann MCNAMEE**. They had the following children:

+2825 i. **John LAUBACH**.
2826 ii. **Trisha Katherine LAUBACH** was born on 12 October 1968. She married **John Joseph FLECK III** on 29 July 1995.
+2827 iii. **Clayton Robert LAUBACH**.

2152. **Meryl "Bobbie" LAUBACH** married **Clark RICE**. Their children are:

+2828 i. **Clark RICE Jr.**
2829 ii. **Abby RICE.**
2830 iii. **Mark RICE**.

2153. **Harriet LAUBACH** married **James KOCH**. Harriet and James had these children:

+2831 i. **Terri KOCH**.
2832 ii. **Tonilynn KOCH**.

2833 iii. **James KOCH**.
2834 iv. **Pamela KOCH**.
+2735 v. **Patty KOCH**.
+2836 vi. **Kenneth KOCH**.
+2837 vii. **Steven KOCH**.

2154. **Mark R. "Mickey" LAUBACH** married **Dorothy UNKNOWN**. Their children were:

+2838 i. **Mark LAUBACH**.
2839 ii. **Crystal LAUBACH**.

2155. **William M. LAUBACH** married **Dorothy ALLSHOUSE**. Their children are:

+2840 i. **Eric LAUBACH**.
2841 ii. **Leslie LAUBACH** married **John WYCKOFF**.
2842 iii. **Mark LAUBACH**.

2157. **Robert L. HOWELL** was born in 1924. He married (1) and was divorced from **Helen BERGER**. Robert L. HOWELL and Helen BERGER had three children:

+2843 i. **Robert L. HOWELL Jr**.
+2844 ii. **Donald HOWELL**.
+2845 iii. **Paula HOWELL**.

Robert married (2) **Laura A. HOFFMAN**, who was born in 1919 in Franklin Twp., Warren County, NJ. She died in 1994 in Washington, Warren County, and was buried in Musconetcong Valley Cemetery, Hampton, Warren County, NJ.

2158. **Walter HOWELL** married **Renetta UNKNOWN**. They had four children:

2846 i. **Sharon HOWELL**.
2847 ii. **Faith HOWELL**.
2848 iii. **Richard HOWELL**.
2849 iv. **Kimberly HOWELL**.

2159. **Mary Lou HOWELL** was born on 3 November 1942 in Easton, Northampton County, Pennsylvania. She was married (1) to **Edward G. WEAN**, who was born on 23 June 1942. She was divorced from Edward G. WEAN. Mary Lou HOWELL and Edward G. WEAN had these children:

+2850 i. **Edward WEAN**.
+2851 ii. **Andrea Lynn WEAN**.
2852 iii. **John WEAN** was born on 22 October 1969 in Phillipsburg, Warren County, New Jersey.
2853 iv. **Trisha WEAN** was born on 21 November 1970 in

Phillipsburg.

Mary Lou was married (2) to **Wayne TITUS** on 25 November 1980.

2160. **Andrea Lee HOWELL** was born on 17 February 1953 in Phillipsburg, Warren County, New Jersey. She was married to **Rodney STECKEL** on 4 December 1976 in Williams Twp., Northampton County, Pennsylvania. Rodney STECKEL was born on 30 June 1942. She was divorced from Rodney STECKEL. Their children are:

2854 i. **Jared Reed STECKEL** was born on 19 June 1982 in Easton, Northampton County.
2855 ii. **Kori Leigh STECKEL** was born on 27 March 1986 in Easton.

2161. **Melody Ann HOWELL** was born on 9 November 1955 in Phillipsburg, Warren County, New Jersey. She is a secretary. She was married to **Gary SNYDER** (son of **Thomas SNYDER** and **Bessie TESTA**) on 13 March 1976 in Sts. Philip & James Church, Greenwich, Warren County. Gary SNYDER, born on 6 October 1956 in Phillipsburg, is a roofer. Melody Ann and Gary have these children:

2856 i. **Matthew Thomas SNYDER** was born on 25 June 1984 in Phillipsburg.
2857 ii. **Kaitlyn SNYDER** was born on 12 June 1986 in Phillipsburg.
2858 iii. **Haylee Ryann SNYDER** was born on 16 March 1988 in Phillipsburg.
2859 iv. **Shayne Michael SNYDER** was born on 1 December 1989 in Phillipsburg.

2163. **Phyllis Jean HOWELL** was born on 21 June 1959 in Phillipsburg, Warren County, New Jersey. She is a secretary. She was married to **William Lawrence VERNON** on 5 April 1986 in Lopatcong, Warren County. William Lawrence VERNON was born on 23 June 1956 in Phillipsburg. He is a truck driver. Phyllis Jean HOWELL and William Lawrence VERNON have a child:

2860 i. **Brittany Lee VERNON** was born on 13 August 1988 in Phillipsburg.

2166. **Michele Ann HOWELL** was born on 18 February 1970 in Phillipsburg, Warren County, New Jersey. She is a customer service agent. She was married to **Michael Anthony DI SORA** on 27 October 1990 in St. Anthony's Church, Easton, Northampton County, PA. Michael Anthony DI SORA was born on 21 September 1967 in Easton. He is a shipping supervisor. Michele Ann HOWELL and Michael Anthony DI SORA had these children:

2861 i. **Taylor Alexis DI SORA** was born on 23 August 1992 in Easton.

2862 ii. **Evan Howell DI SORA** was born on 26 April 1995 in Easton.

2168. **Harold Walter RUSSELL Jr**. was born on 7 July 1945 in Easton, Northampton County, Pennsylvania. He was married to **Beverly Ann TRINKLEY** (daughter of **Robert TRINKLEY** and **Delores HIGHLAND**) on 11 May 1968 in Easton. Beverly Ann TRINKLEY was born on 5 July 1947 in Easton. They have a child:

2863 i. **Courtney Lynn RUSSELL** was born on 7 March 1975 in Easton.

2169. **Gary RUSSELL** was born on 2 June 1952 in Easton, Northampton County, Pennsylvania. He was married to **Deborah Lee KIRCHGASSNER** (daughter of **Joseph KIRCHGASSNER** and **Shirley YOST**) on 23 June 1973 in Easton. Deborah Lee KIRCHGASSNER was born on 26 May 1953. Their children are:

2864 i. **Gary Jason RUSSELL** was born on 17 April 1975 in Easton.

2865 ii. **Torie Anne RUSSELL** was born on 20 May 1977 in Easton.

2866 iii. **Amber Lee RUSSELL** was born on 26 October 1985 in Seoul, Korea. Amber was adopted by the Russell's, on 28 January 1986.

2170. **William Fraley RUSSELL** was born on 20 February 1957 in Easton, Northampton County, Pennsylvania. He was married to **Sylvia Ann MILLER** on 12 June 1982. Sylvia Ann MILLER was born on 15 September 1962 in Buffalo, Erie County, New York. William and Sylvia Ann had these children:

2867 i. **Joshua Michael RUSSELL** was born on 25 May 1987 in Tampa, Hillsborough County, Florida.

2868 ii. **Daniel Robert RUSSELL** was born on 8 February 1992 in Tampa.

2171. **Donald BALABAN Jr**. was born on 30 November 1958 in Easton, Northampton County, Pennsylvania. He married **Debbie UNKNOWN**, who was born on 24 February 1960. Donald and Debbie have a son:

2869 i. **Dallas BALABAN** was born on 22 July 1990 in Tampa.

2171. **Helen "Honeygirl" BALABAN** was born on 17 November 1960 in Tampa, Hillsborugh County, Florida. She married **Paul GLENNON**, who was born on 16 June 1958 in Malden, Massachusetts. They had these children:

2870 i. **Nicole GLENNON** was born on 29 November 1990 in Tampa.

2871 ii. **Brittney GLENNON** was born on 31 May 1995 in Tampa.

2176. **Robert John HOWELL** was born on 21 July 1938. He died on 20 December 1983 in Phillipsburg, Warren County, New Jersey and was buried in Stewartsville Cemetery, Stewartsville, NJ. He was a roofer. He married **Dawn SEIBERT** on 2 July 1960. Their children are:

2872 i. **Penny Alberta HOWELL** was born on 27 May 1961 in Warren County, NJ. She married **James P. BURKE** on 21 June 1982 in Warren County.

2873 ii. **John R. HOWELL.**

2177. **Doris Marie HOWELL** was born on 2 June 1941. She was married to **Jack HAGGERTY** on 1 October 1960. Doris and Jack HAGGERTY had these children:

2874 i. **Jeffrey Gordon HAGGERTY** was born on 1 October 1961.

2187. **Raymond C. HOWELL** was born on 26 February 1911, in Pen Argyl, Northampton County, Pennsylvania. He died on 10 January 1995 in Easton, Norhtampton County, and was buried in Union Cemetery, Belfast, Northampton County. He was a plant manager. He married **Arlene K. BROWN** (daughter of **James BROWN** and **Katherine RUFF**), in November 1931. Arlene was born on 20 September 1911 in Pen Argyl. She died on 8 June 1993 in Phillipsburg, Warren County, New Jersey, and was buried in Union Cemetery, Belfast, Northampton County. She was a cloth examiner.[243] Their children were:

+2875 i. **Charmaine J. HOWELL.**

2876 ii. **Keith R. HOWELL.**

2190. **Robert Louis James HOWELL** was born on 29 September 1917. He was married to **Dorothy Ann CONNELLY** on 31 December 1939. Dorothy Ann CONNELLY was born on 8 February 1920. Their children were:

2877 i. **Robert HOWELL** was born on 18 March 1943. He died on 8 August 1968.

2878 ii. **Donald HOWELL** was born on 24 June 1946. He married **Eileen ORSULAK**, who was born on 24 February 1943.

2879 iii. **Marianne HOWELL** was born on 1 May 1951. She married **Scott MACDONALD**, who was born on 24 November 1950.

2880 iv. **Joan HOWELL** was born on 28 January 1953. She

---

[243]Obituary, Easton (PA) Express, 10 June 1993.

married **Edgar CRAMER**, who was born on 12 February 1946.

2252. **Jean Virginia ANDERSON** was born on 1 November 1921 in New York City. She married **Herbert PODEYN** on 4 December 1942. Herbert was born on 8 June 1919 in Elmhurst, Queens, NY, and died in 1982. Their children were:

2881 i. **Debra Jean PODEYN** was born on 24 September 1954 in New York City. She married **Glenn MORRIS.**

2882 ii. **Jill Kirsten PODEYN** was born on 31 March 1958 in East Meadow, NY. She married **Scott LURTON**.

2883 iii. **Eric Herbert PODEYN** was born on 28 June 1964 in Bayshore, NY. He married **Francesca PAQUI**.

2253. **Robert Warren ANDERSON** was born on 22 August 1923 in Brooklyn, New York. He died on 10 October 1974 in Burlington, Vermont. He married **Dorothy PASETTI**, who was born on 2 June 1923. They had these children:

2884 i. **Robert ANDERSON Jr.** was born on 15 January 1951 in Flushing, New York.

2885 ii. **Edmund Scott ANDERSON** was born on 29 October 1955 in Wallingford, New Haven County, Connecticut.

2886 iii. **Eric Douglas ANDERSON** was born on 1 October 1962 in Wallingford.

2887 iv. **Thomas ANDERSON** was born on 20 September 1964 in Wallingford.

2888 v. **Karen ANDERSON** was born in 1966.

2889 vi. **Unknown ANDERSON**, Karen's twin died at birth.

2254. **Winifred ANDERSON** was born on 29 December 1924. She was married in March 1945 to **Marcus HEPBURN**, who was born on 19 March 1923 and died on 6 January 1963 in Titusville, Brevard County, Florida. Their children are:

+2890 i. **Barbara Lee HEPBURN**.

2891 ii. **Marcus HEPBURN Jr.**

2892 iii. **Patricia Ann HEPBURN**.

2893 iv. **Dennis Robert HEPBURN**.

2894 v. **James Bryan HEPBURN**.

2257. **Robert Marshall HOWELL Jr.** was born on 11 June 1934. He was married (1) to **Joan N. PUKNAT** on 2 September 1961. They were divorced. She was born on 17 November 1933. Their children were:

2895 i. **Suzanne Doris HOWELL** was born on 18 January

1964.

2896 ii. **Robert Jason HOWELL** was born on 6 August 1966.

Robert Marshall HOWELL shares his life with **Anne Catherine TIRACCHIA**, who was born on 20 July 1939.

2278. **Albert John "Jack" YOUNG** was born on 2 November 1927. He was married to **Bernice SMITH.** Albert John YOUNG and Bernice SMITH had the following children:

+2897 i. **Robert Alan YOUNG**.
+2898 ii. **Bonnie YOUNG**.
2899 iii. **Brian YOUNG** was born on 10 August 1963.
2900 iv. **Barry YOUNG** was born on 10 November 1965 in NJ.

2279. **Ronald Allan YOUNG** married (1) **Barbara MOYER**. They had one child:

2901 i. **Unknown YOUNG** was born in 1958.

Ronald Allan YOUNG married (2) **Barbara REDINGTON**. They had the following children:

2902 i. **Ronald YOUNG Jr**. was born on 9 June 1962.
2903 ii. **Darlene YOUNG** was born on 14 May 1964.
2904 iii. **Deborah YOUNG** was born on 9 December 1965.
2905 iv. **Cheryl YOUNG** was born on 7 March 1969.

2280. **Lois Alice YOUNG** was born on 13 August 1929. She married **John L. BLACK**(son of **John L. BLACK SR.** and **Lelia HAFLER**), who was born in Durham, Bucks County, Pennsylvania in 1925. John died on 14 November 1992. Lois and John had these children:

2906 i. **John L. BLACK** was born on 2 December 1948.
2907 ii. **Lynn Marie BLACK** was born on 6 October, and died on 16 November 1951.
2908 iii. **Mitchell BLACK** was born on 24 July 1953.
+2909 iv. **Lisa BLACK**.
2910 v. **Lori Ann BLACK** was born on 21 April 1960. She married **Unknown DEPAIN**.

2281. **Joan Elaine YOUNG** was born on 13 July 1932. She married **Philip R. JONES**. Their children are:

2911 i. **Philip R. JONES** was born on 18 May 1952.
2912 ii. **Troyann JONES** was born on 24 August 1957.

2284. **David L. YOUNG** was born on 22 January 1946. He died on 13 December 1968 in Phillipsburg, Warren County, New Jersey, and was buried in Northampton Memorial Shrine Cemetery, Palmer, Pennsylvania. He was married to **Linda Louise MANNING** in First Presbyterian Church, Bloomsbury, NJ. David L. YOUNG and Linda Louise MANNING had the following children:

2913 i. **Stacy YOUNG**.
2914 ii. **Lynn YOUNG**.

2287. **Ann Marie EHLY** was born on 30 October 1952. She married and divorced **Patrick LILLY**. Patrick LILLY was born on 20 February 1956 in Easton, Northampton County, PA. He was born on 20 February 1956 in Easton. Ann Marie and Patrick had one child:

2915 i. **Paul Brian LILLY** was born on 28 December 1971 in Phillipsburg, Warren County, New Jersey.

2300. **Lorna MEYER** married **Don MCQUATTERS**. Their children are:

+2916 i. **Pat MCQUATTERS**.
2917 ii. **Mike MCQUATTERS**.

2301. **Kenneth L. MEYER** was married to **UNKNOWN**. They have one child:

2918 i. **Ruth E. MEYER**.

2304. **Robert K. MEYER** married **UNKNOWN**. They have one child:

2919 i. **Robin Jo MEYER**.

2305. **John Day PRICE** married **UNKNOWN**. They have one child:

2920 i. **Kevin Jerome PRICE**.

2306. **Nancy Jane PRICE** was born on 16 March 1925 in Sioux Falls, Minnehaha County, South Dakota. She was married to **Howard John THOMPSON** on 2 May 1945 in Cedar Falls, Black Hawk County, Iowa. Nancy Jane PRICE and Howard John THOMPSON had the following children:

2921 i. **Catherine Rose THOMPSON** was born on 12 March 1955 in Iowa City, Johnson County, Iowa. She married **David GLESSNER** on 17 February 1993 in Cedar Falls.
2922 ii. **John Howard THOMPSON** was born on 12 March 1955 in Iowa City. He married **Charlotte GILLIKIN** on 22 December 1988 in Kissimmee, Osceola County, Florida.
2923 iii. **David Malcolm THOMPSON** was born on 17 August

1957 in Waterloo, Black Hawk County, Iowa.

2307. **Dorothy Edna GASAHL** was born on 11 March 1915. She was married to **Russell Garret SWABY** on 29 May 1939 in Eureka, Lincoln County, Montana. Their children were:

+2924 i. **James Archie SWABY**.
+2925 ii. **Lila Mae SWABY**.
+2926 iii. **Elaine Joyce SWABY**.
2927 iv. **Gordon George SWABY** was born on 1 July 1947 in Great Falls, Cascade County, Montana. He married **Barbara Emily SIENKBEIL** on 16 June 1973 in Great Falls.

2308. **Lila Jeanette GASAHL** was born on 16 April 1917. She was married to **Jess Willard BOLEN** on 17 August 1942 in Waycross, Ware County, Georgia. Lila and Jess BOLEN had the following children:

2928 i. **Kathleen Marie BOLEN** was born on 25 August 1946 in Whitefish, Flathead County, Montana. She married **John WHITTAKER** on 22 September 1970 in Long Beach, Los Angeles County, California.
2929 ii. **Rebecca May BOLEN** was born on 15 December 1950 in Whitefish. She married **Randall HERZBERG** on 8 November 1973 in Eureka, Lincoln County, Montana.

2309. **Joyce Marie GASAHL** was born on 17 August 1926 in Eureka, Lincoln County, Montana. She was married (1) to **Charles ZIELINSKI** on 11 February 1945 in Oglesby, LaSalle County, Illinois. Joyce Marie GASAHL and Charles ZIELINSKI had the following children:

+2930 i. **Joann ZIELINSKI**.
+2931 ii. **Edna Marie ZIELINSKI**.
+2932 iii. **Connie Sue ZIELINSKI**.

Joyce was married (2) to **Densil HAYES** on 4 September 1977 in Streator, LaSalle County, Illinois.

2314. **Lois Louise PLUID** was born on 24 April 1927 in Eureka, Lincoln County, Montana. She was married to **Charles Howard FRANKLIN** on 17 August 1946 in Kalispell, Flathead County, Montana. They had these children:

2933 i. **Gary Keith FRANKLIN** was born on 21 July 1947 in Eureka. He married **Bess Evelyn LAIRD** on 12 December 1976 in Kalispell.
2934 ii. **Terry Lee FRANKLIN** was born on 16 June 1950 in Kalispell. He married **Valerie Jo SMITH** on 2

June 1976 in Kalispell.

2935 iii. **John Howard FRANKLIN** was born on 4 April 1955 in Kalispell. He married **Debra Kay RASK** on 21 August 1976 in Evergreen, Jefferson County, MT.

2936 iv. **Karla Jean FRANKLIN** was born on 30 August 1959 in Whitefish, Flathead County, MT.

Lois married (2) **Martin Oliver SHAND** on 4 June 1966 in Bonners Ferry, Boundary County, Idaho.

2316. **Thomas Henderson PRICE** was born on 16 July 1926 in Eureka, Lincoln County, Montana. He married (1) **Helen Ruth SHENEFELT** on 8 June 1946 in Kalispell, Flathead County, Montana. Thomas Henderson PRICE and Helen Ruth SHENEFELT had the following children:

+2937 i. **Thomas Edward (PRICE) DELONG**.

He was married (2) to **Helen Ruth ALAVANA** on 30 May 1949 in Eureka, Lincoln County, MT. Thomas Henderson PRICE and Helen Ruth ALAVANA had the following children:

2938 i. **Barry Jay PRICE** was born on 3 October 1965.

He was married (3) to **Norma Jane SWENSON** on 24 June 1967 in Bonners Ferry, Boundary County, Idaho. Thomas Henderson PRICE and Norma Jane SWENSON had a child:

2939 i. **Thomas Henderson PRICE** was born on 2 May 1970 in Kalispell, Flathead County, Montana.

2317. **Phyllis Edith PRICE** was born on 13 November 1928 in Eureka, Lincoln County, Montana. She married (1) **Gene Leonard CAMPBELL**. Phyllis and Gene Leonard CAMPBELL had one child:

+2940 i. **Leonard Gene (CAMPBELL) (THOMPSON) NELSON**.

Phyllis was married (2) to **Richard Darwin THOMPSON** on 4 May 1953 in Great Falls, Cascade County, Montana. Phyllis Edith PRICE and Richard Darwin THOMPSON had the following children:

2941 i. **Tanya Lee (THOMPSON) NELSON** was born on 11 March 1954 in Great Falls. She married **Richard Arthur CARLSON** on 31 December 1975.

2942 ii. **Vicky Jo (THOMPSON) NELSON** was born on 13 October 1956 in Great Falls.

Phyllis was married (3) to **Walter Garth NELSON** on 21 December 1963 in Coeur d'Alene, Kootenai County, Idaho. Phyllis Edith PRICE and Walter Garth NELSON had the following children:

2943 i. **Walter Garth NELSON** was born on 8 February 1965 in Kalispell, Flathead County, Montana.

2320. **Mary M. ROBERTS** married **Jack W. MUSGROVE**. Their child is:

2944 i. **Jean W. MUSGROVE** was born in 1943.

2321. **Velma ROBERTS** married **Unknown STEVENS**. Their child is:

2945 i. **Marilyn STEVENS** was born in 1946.

2322. **Berkley Warren BEDELL** was born on 5 March 1921 in Spirit Lake, Dickinson County, Iowa. He was married to **Elinor Margaret HEALY** on 29 August 1943 in Minneapolis, Hennepin County, Minnesota. Berkley Warren BEDELL and Elinor Margaret HEALY had the following children:

+2946 i. **Kenneth Berkley BEDELL**.
2947 ii. **Thomas Walter BEDELL** was born on 25 January 1950 in Spirit Lake.
2948 iii. **Joanne Marie BEDELL** was born on 5 October 1952 in Spirit Lake. She married **Michael W. QUINN** on 3 July 1976 in Spirit Lake.

2323. **Jack Harold BEDELL** was born on 19 December 1923 in Spirit Lake, Dickinson County, Iowa. He was married to **Marcia Ann DOWDEN** on 29 May 1943 in Minneapolis, Hennepin County, Minnesota. Jack Harold BEDELL and Marcia Ann DOWDEN had the following children:

+2949 i. **Nadine Lyn BEDELL**.
+2950 ii. **David William BEDELL**.
+2951 iii. **Richard Charles BEDELL**.

2324. **Violet Mildred CARPENTER** was born on 6 December 1911 in Eureka, Lincoln County, Montana. She died on 21 December 1996 in Long Beach, Los Angeles County, California.. She was married to **William Gregory COLLINS** (son of **Horace COLLINS** and **Mattie PAGE**) on 25 March 1931 in Lawton, Comanche County, Oklahoma. Violet and William Gregory COLLINS had the following children:

+2952 i. **Muriel Elizabeth COLLINS**.
+2953 ii. **Maryevelyn COLLINS**.
+2954 iii. **Kathleen Elaine COLLINS**.

2326. **Virginia May CARPENTER** was born on 16 July 1920 in Clayton, Union County, New Mexico. She died on 24 November 1964 in Long Beach, Los Angeles County, California. She was married (1) to Lloyd Robert **HERSHEY** in Riverside, Riverside County, California. Their children are:

+2955 i. **Janet HERSHEY**.
2956 ii. **William Robert HERSHEY** was born on 26 December 1953 in Long Beach. He died on 2 May 1998.

Virginia married (2) **Jess H. STANBROUGH Jr**. Jess was a prisoner of war in WWII.

2327. **Leslie Alvin REIQUAM** was born on 18 August 1921 in Great Falls, Cascade County, Montana. He died on 11 December 1990. He was married to **DeLora Louise DAVIS** on 4 December 1945 in Boise, Ada County, Idaho. Leslie Alvin REIQUAM and DeLora Louise DAVIS had the following children:

2957 i. **Barbara Lyn REIQUAM** was born on 20 August 1946 in Chula Vista, San Diego County, California. She married **David Thomas EAVENSON** on 23 August 1969 in Boise, Ada County, Idaho.
2958 ii. **Leslie Jean REIQUAM** was born on 27 December 1951 in Boise. She married (1) **Jim BLACK**, and (2) **Gordon Edward RIEGER**.

2328. **Eldon Thomas REIQUAM** was born on 28 December 1922 in Great Falls, Cascade County, Montana. He died on 20 November 1995 in Washington. He was married to **Dorothy Lena RIPLEY** on 24 August 1947 in Chinook, Blaine County, Montana. Eldon and Dorothy had the following children:

2959 i. **Sandra Gail REIQUAM** was born on 22 November 1948 in Denver, Arapahoe County, Colorado.
2960 ii. **Thomas Denny REIQUAM** was born on 19 December 1951 in Bismarck, Burleigh County, North Dakota. He died on 29 May 1970.
2961 iii. **Scott Evan REIQUAM** was born on 9 October 1959 in Seattle, King County, Washington.

2329. **Lila Anne REIQUAM** was born on 31 August 1924 in Choteau, Teton County, Montana. She was married to **Ralph Winten HVIDSTEN** on 15 June 1947 in Choteau, Teton County, Montana. Lila Anne REIQUAM and Ralph Winten HVIDSTEN had the following children:

2962 i. **Janet Elaine HVIDSTEN** was born on 24 February 1949 in Crookston, Polk County, Minnesota.
2963 ii. **Thomas Alvin HVIDSTEN** was born on 7 March 1950 in Crookston.
+2964 iii. **Douglas Ralph HVIDSTEN** was born on 9 July 1951 in

Crookston. He married **Kaye Marie GRYSKIEWICZ** on 11 June 1971 in Stephen, Marshall County, Minnesota.

2965 iv. **Daniel Edward HVIDSTEN** was born on 23 July 1953 in Crookston. He married **Pamela Mary KOSTRYEWSKI** on 26 October 1974 in Grand Forks, Grand Forks County, North Dakota.

2966 v. **William Erie HVIDSTEN** was born on 21 August 1956 in Grand Forks.

2330. **Howard Edward REIQUAM** was born on 7 March 1931 in Conrad, Pondera County, Montana. He died on 24 February 1994 in Chicago, Cook County, Illinois. He married **Sarah Catherine "Sally" GILTNER** on 21 September 1957 in Sheffield, Bureau County, Illinois. They had these children:

2967 i. **Abbie Teresa REIQUAM** was born on 30 May 1958 in Chicago.

2968 ii. **Peter REIQUAM** was born on 7 May 1959 in Seattle, King County, Washington.

2969 iii. **Jennie Helen REIQUAM** was born on 12 July 1960 in Seattle.

2331. **Marion Faye DEWOLF** was born on 13 June 1922 in Bonners Ferry, Boundary County, Idaho. She was married to **Wayne Allen ASHLEY** on 4 July 1942 in Chico, Butte County, California. Marion Faye DEWOLF and Wayne Allen ASHLEY had the following children:

+2970 i. **David DeWolf ASHLEY**.

+2971 ii. **Faye Ellen ASHLEY**.

2972 iii. **Mary Ann ASHLEY** was born on 28 December 1953 in Denver, Arapahoe County, Colorado.

2973 iv. **Elizabeth Jane ASHLEY** was born on 12 August 1956.

2332. **Phyllis Jean DEWOLF** was born on 3 March 1924 in Bonners Ferry, Boundary County, Idaho. She was married (1) to **James Albin WATTS** on 4 March 1944 in San Jose, Santa Clara County, Caligornia. Phyllis Jean DEWOLF and James Albin WATTS had the following children:

+2974 i. **Peggy Jean WATTS**.

2975 ii. **James Allen WATTS** was born on 18 January 1948 in Bridgeport, Wise County, Texas.

2976 iii. **John Clinton WATTS** was born on 15 February 1949 in Bridgeport.

Phyllis was married (2) to **Duane Dale BLAKE** on 2 November 1972 in Denver, Arapahoe County, Colorado.

2334. **Donald Sawyer THOMAS** was born on 28 May 1931 in Bonners Ferry, Boundary County, Idaho. He married **Lorna Rae BYERS** on 10 June 1950 in

Coeur d'Alene, Kootenai County, Idaho. Donald Sawyer THOMAS and Lorna Rae BYERS had the following children:

2977 i. **Debra Louise THOMAS** was born on 27 June 1952 in Spokane, Spokane County, WA.

2978 ii. **Vicki Lynn THOMAS** was born on 31 January 1954 in Spokane.

2979 iii. **Doreen Kay THOMAS** was born on 7 June 1956 in Spokane, and married **Richard Francis BURNELL** on 2 August 1975 in Spokane.

2343. **Pamela Gail PHETHEAN** was born on 5 September 1948 in North Carolina. She was married to **Richard BAGNALL** on 27 December 1969 in New Milford, Susquehanna County, Pennsylvania. Richard BAGNALL was born on 19 September 1949. Richard is a teacher in the schools in Susquehanna, and a football coach. Pamela Gail PHETHEAN and Richard BAGNALL had the following children:

2980 i. **Jennifer BAGNALL** was born on 9 March 1971 in NC. She married **Michael DROUGHT** in Susquehanna in June 1999.

2344. **Patricia Jane PHETHEAN** was born on 18 March 1954 in West Pittston, Luzerne County, Pennsylvania. She was married to **Ronald SULLIVAN** on 28 November 1981 in New Milford, Susquehanna County, Pennsylvania. Ronald SULLIVAN was born on 15 December 1951. Patricia and Ronald have a son:

2981 i. **John William SULLIVAN** was born on 22 September 1983 in New Milford.

2345. **Phyllis Anne PHETHEAN** was born on 23 November 1957 in West Pittston, Luzerne County, Pennsylvania. She was married to **Lloyd SHELDON** on 8 June 1974 in New Milford, Susquehanna County, PA. Lloyd SHELDON was born on 8 April 1954. Phyllis and Lloyd SHELDON had the following children:

2982 i. **Sarah SHELDON** was born on 20 September 1975 in New Milford.

2983 ii. **Samuel SHELDON** was born on 15 September 1977 in New Milford.

2984 iii. **Catherine SHELDON** was born on 1 September 1978 in New Milford.

2348. **Jeffrey William SMITH** was born about 1948 in Pennsylvania. Jeff was an insurance agent in the Harrisburg, Dauphin County, Pennsylvania area for several years, and moved to North Carolina after Suzanne married Nat KOENIGSBERG. He was married to **Sue KODAD** about 1972 in PA. They are divorced. Jeffrey and Sue had the following children:

2985 i. **Jeffrey William SMITH II** was born on 17 January 1977 in Harrisburg, Dauphin County, PA.

2986 ii. **Siri SMITH** was born on 25 March 1980 in Harrisburg.

2350. **Pamela Sue DALE** was born on 25 May 1956 in West Pittston, Luzerne County, Pennsylvania. Pam is a nurse, has a Bachelor of Science degree in Nursing from Wilkes College, Wilkes Barre, Luzerne County. She was married to **Anthony John PIAZZA** on 1 August 1981 in West Pittston. Anthony John PIAZZA was born on 16 November 1955. Pamela and Anthony PIAZZA have these children:

2987 i. **Kimberly Ann PIAZZA** was born on 19 April 1985 in Pittston, Luzerne County, Pennsylvania.

2988 ii. **Kristen Marie PIAZZA** was born on 3 October 1988 in Pittston.

2352. **Nancy Jean TRAHER** was born on 18 March 1949 in Scranton, Lackawanna County, Pennsylvania. Nancy is secretary to the minister at the West Pittston Methodist Church. She is a graduate of Keystone Junior College, in Factoryville, PA. She was married to **Kenneth HEAL** on 3 June 1972 in West Pittston. Kenneth HEAL was born on 2 November 1950 in West Pittston. Kenny is a teacher in the Wyoming Area Schools. Nancy Jean and Kenneth HEAL have two sons:

2989 i. **Eric HEAL** was born on 24 August 1974 in West Pittston

2990 ii. **Bryan HEAL** was born on 11 November 1979 in West Pittston.

2353. **James PHETHEAN** was born on 8 May 1948 in Pittston, Luzerne, PA. Jim is a graduate of Wilkes University. He was married to **Theresa Marie KOPPINGER** (daughter of **Matthew Francis KOPPINGER** and **Marjorie Ellen MCCARTY**) on 28 November 1987 in Tampa, Hillsborough County, FL. Terri was born on 11 April 1961 in Dearborn, Wayne County, MI. They have have a son:

2991 i. **James Edward PHETHEAN** was born on 24 June 1998 in Tampa.

2354. **Edward PHETHEAN III** was born on 14 April 1954 in Kingston, Luzerne Coounty, Pennsylvania. Ted is an electronics technician. He was married to **Debra HERRON** (daughter of **Sidney HERRON** and **Lorraine BLATTEAU**) on 28 April 1979 in Croydon, Bucks County, Pennsylvania. Debra HERRON was born on 19 December 1955 in Philadelphia, Philadelphia County, PA. Their children are:

2992 i. **Edward PHETHEAN IV** was born on 24 August 1980

in Bristol, Bucks County, Pennsylvania.

2993 ii. **John William PHETHEAN** was born on 4 November 1988 in Bristol.

2994 iii. **Matthew Lucas PHETHEAN** was born on 27 September 1991 in Bristol.

2995 iv. **Zachary Lewis PHETHEAN** was born on 14 October 1994 in Bristol.

2355. **George Evans PHETHEAN** was born on 23 September 1957 in Bristol, Bucks County, Pennsylvania. He married **Vickie Jane STORY** (daughter of **Richard STORY** and **Johnnie May ZEIGLER**) on 25 January 1987 in Hawthorne, Marion County, Florida. Vickie Jane STORY was born on 6 January 1957 in Ft. Lauderdale, Broward County, Florida. George and Vickie have three children:

2996 i. **Amy Anastasia PHETHEAN** was born on 9 June 1987 in Eustis, Lake County, Florida.

2997 ii. **Dylan Thomas PHETHEAN** was born on 23 August 1991 in Eustis.

2998 iii. **Margaret Noel PHETHEAN** was born on 7 December 1993 in Eustis.

2356. **Harriet Jean "Jay" DAVIES** was born on 29 September 1945 in West Pittston, Luzerne County, Pennsylvania. She died on 14 January 1994, of melanoma, in Pleasant Prairie, Wisconsin.[244] She was buried in May 1994 in West Pittston Cemetery, Luzerne County, PA. Harriet was known in the family as Jay. She was a graduate of Boston University in Journalism. She was married (1) to **Paul GOUGH** in June 1968 in Sudbury, Massachusetts. She was divorced from Paul GOUGH. Paul GOUGH was born on 22 October 1945. Jay and Paul had a son:

2999 i. **Paul J. GOUGH** was born on 2 October 1968 in Connecticut. He married (1) **Cheryl LUCAS** on 31 March 1991 in Southbury, CT. They were divorced in 1996. He married (2) **Michelle LAGRAVE** on 24 May 1997 in Livermore, Maine.

Jay was married (2) to **Brent SHELTON** (son of **Unknown SHELTON** and **Unknown GLASCOE**) in 1982 in Hartford, Fairfield County, Connecticut. Brent SHELTON was born on 3 October 1949. Brent is a civilian employee of the U.S. Navy. Harriet Jean "Jay" DAVIES and Brent SHELTON had one child:

3000 i. **Julie SHELTON** was born on 21 May 1983 in Coronado, California. [245]

---

[244]Personal knowledge of Jeannette J. Phethean, her aunt.
[245]ibid.

2357. **Thomas William "Bill" DAVIES** was born on 5 April 1948 in West Pittston, Luzerne County, Pennsylvania. Bill was married to **Sally Jo PUNCHES** (daughter of **Richard Gene PUNCHES** and **Marilyn HAND**) on 13 September 1981 in Indianapolis, Marion County, Indiana. Sally Jo PUNCHES was born in Lincoln, Lancaster County, Nebraska. Their children are:

3001 i. **Sarah Elizabeth DAVIES** was born on 13 October 1988 in Dallas, Texas.

3002 ii. **Thomas Richard DAVIES** was born on 26 February 1991 in Dallas.

2358. **John Griffith DAVIES** was born on 20 November 1952 in West Pittston, Luzerne County, Pennsylvania. He was married to **Catherine Lorraine McCarthy PATCH** in 1975 in Boston, Massachusetts. Catherine Lorraine McCarthy PATCH was born on 16 August 1946 in Boston, Massachusetts. Their son is:

3003 i. **Steven Clifford DAVIES** was born on 24 may 1972 in Boston, MA. He married (1) Crystal VALENTINE on 14 May 1994 in Arizona, while both were in the Air Force. Steven and Crystal were divorced. There were no children. Steven married (2) **Carrie Marie STEPHENS** (daughter of Mr. & Mrs. **Robert STEPHENS**) on 24 May 1999 in Gilbert, Arizona.

2362. **Harrison LeGrande Peter GOODSPEED** was born on 22 April 1923 in Grand Rapids, Michigan. He married **Marilou POHL** on 2 December 1944. Marilou was born on 23 August 1925. They have four children:

3004 i. **Marfy Mary Frances GOODSPEED** was born on 22 September 1945. She married **Richard Alan "Dick" ZIMMER** on 27 December 1965 in Grand Rapids.

3005 ii. **Dorothy Rankin GOODSPEED** was born on 9 August 1947. She married **Ivan MILLER**.

3006 iii. **Harrison LeGrande Peter GOODSPEED III** was born in 1950.

3007 iv. **Barrett Michael GOODSPEED** was born on 29 September 1952. He married **Donna MANDRIOTA**.

2368. **Karen Fern ROGERS** was born on 19 February 1943 in Luzerne County, Pennsylvania. She married **Albert Emerson PERREGO**, who was born on 16 December 1936 in Dallas Twp., Luzerne County. He died on 21 September 1993. Karen and Albert Emerson PERREGO had the following children:

+3008 i. **Barbara Jean PERREGO**.

+3009 ii. **Bonnie Elizabeth PERREGO.**
3010 iii. **Alan Emerson PERREGO** was born on 4 September 1971 in Luzerne County.

2370. **Jon Howell ROGERS** was born on 8 October 1946 in Luzerne County, Pennsylvania. He was married to **Roberta BOYLE** in September 1969. Roberta BOYLE was born on 3 November 1947. Jon Howell ROGERS and Roberta BOYLE had the following children:

3011 i. **Lori Ann ROGERS** was born in 1970.
3012 ii. **Jon Michael ROGERS** was born in 1972.

2371. **Dianne Shirley ROGERS** was born on 19 December 1949 in Luzerne County, Pennsylvania. She was married to **Lawrence Lee RALSTON** on 4 May 1970. Lawrence Lee RALSTON was born in 1949. Dianne Shirley ROGERS and Lawrence Lee RALSTON had the following children:

+3013 i. **Stephen RALSTON.**
3014 ii. **Melissa RALSTON** was born in 1976.
3015 iii. **Cherie RALSTON** was born in 1978.
3016 iv. **Kenneth RALSTON** was born in 1981.

2372. **Linda HOWELL** married **Vincent CASTELLI**. Linda HOWELL and Vincent CASTELLI had these children:

3017 i. **Lauren CASTELLI** was born on 24 January 1978.
3018 ii. **Gina M. CASTELLI** was born on 1 March 1980.

2373. **Nancy HOWELL** was born on 17 December 1954 in Pennsylvania. She was married to **Ralph IDE** on 5 October 1973. Ralph IDE was born on 24 April 1953. Nancy and Ralph IDE had the following children:

3019 i. **Nathan IDE** was born on 18 July 1980.
3020 ii. **Sarah Elizabeth IDE** was born on 5 February 1984.
3021 iii. **Kaitlyn IDE** was born on 10 January 1989.

2379. **Michael Jonathan LEWIS** was born on 10 October 1958. He was married to **Susan Lorrain PERRIN** on 24 May 1986. Susan Lorrain PERRIN was born on 12 December 1962. Michael and Susan had the following children:

3022 i. **Elizabeth Grace LEWIS** was born on 23 March 1989.

2380. **Melody Joy BREDBENNER** was born on 18 May 1953. She was married to **Jeffrey SCHLOSS**, who was born on 19 September 1949. Melody and Jeffrey SCHLOSS had the following children:

3023 i. **Nathanael SCHLOSS** was born on 2 May 1981.
3024 ii. **Micah SCHLOSS** was born on 21 November 1983.

3025 iii. **Gabriel SCHLOSS**.

2382. **Tami Gay BREDBENNER** was married to **WAYNE COHWELL**. They have one child:

3026 i. **Travis Clinton COHWELL**.

2399. **Lin Howell ROOT** was born on 10 June 1925 in St. Paul, Ramsey County, Minnesota. He is a veteran of WWII, a construction worker and a farmer. He was married to **Elnora Jeanette COOAN** on 8 October 1948 in St. Paul. Elnora Jeanette COOAN was born on 7 September 1928 in Washburn County, Wisconsin. Lin Howell ROOT and Elnora Jeanette COOAN had the following children:

3027 i. **Kathy Lynn ROOT** was born on 19 August 1950 in Siren, Burnett County, Wisconsin. She married **Terry Richard ARMSTRONG** on 27 February 1971 in Concord, Contra Costa County, California.

3028 ii. **Mary Ellen ROOT** was born on 24 February 1952 in Frederic, Polk County, Wisconsin. She married **Charles "Chuck" Allen ENGDAHL** on 29 October 1977 in Frederic.

+3029 iii. **Lin Howell ROOT**.

3030 iv. **Diana Jean ROOT** was born on 1 June 1955 in Frederic. She married **Scott Raymond WOODS** on 8 September 1973 in Frederic.

3031 v. **Cindy Ann ROOT** was born on 28 March 1957 in Frederic. She married (1) **Ronald Lee RITCHEY** on 10 June 1978 in Frederic. She married (2) **Lewis BYERLY**.

3032 vi. **Terry Lee ROOT** was born on 10 March 1959 in Frederic. He married Gayle **Kathleen HAZELTINE** on 27 February 1982 in Frederic.

3033 vii. **Kevin Jay ROOT** was born on 18 July 1960 in Frederic.

3034 viii. **Larry Lin ROOT** was born on 25 December 1951 in Frederic. He married **Lynn Renae GOODRIE** on 10 August 1990 in Balsam Lake, Polk County, WI.

2406. **Harry (George) VAN HORN** was born on 27 September 1910 in White Twp. Warren County, New Jersey. He died on 14 February 1984 in Phillipsburg, Warren County. He married **Nellie F. HOFF**, who was born on 3 June 1911. She died in 1982. Their children are:

3035 i. **Eva VAN HORN** was born on 7 August 1931. She married **Donald ALLEN**, who was born on 23 November 1933.

3036 ii. **Harry VAN HORN** was born on 29 April 1934. He married **Elizabeth WALTZ**, who was born on 30

November 1932.

3037 iii. **Charles VAN HORN** was born on 9 April 1939.

3038 iv. **Robert F. VAN HORN** was born on 29 January 1941. He married **Clara FILBURN**, who was born on 30 April 1940.

3039 v. **Frances VAN HORN** was born on 1 December 1945. She married **Charles LAUER**, who was born on 20 January 1948.

2407. **John William BUTLER** was born on 4 June 1928 in Belvidere, Warren County, New Jersey. He was married to **Phyllis Irene VAN FOSSEN** on 5 April 1959. Phyllis Irene VAN FOSSEN was born on 26 May 1937 in Crimora, Virginia. Their children are:

+3040 i. **Theresa Lynn BUTLER**.

3041 ii. **David Allen BUTLER** was born on 18 November 1960 in Waynesboro, Virginia.

2408. **Barbara Allen BUTLER** was born on 26 November 1930. She was married to **Stewart WASHBURN** on 23 August 1953 in Belvidere, Warren County, NJ. Stewart WASHBURN was born on 4 September 1924 in Salem, Massachusetts. Barbara and Stewart WASHBURN had the following children:

3042 i. **Kerry Jean WASHBURN** was born on 29 August 1956 in Bridgeport, Connecticut. She married **Robert WOODSON** on 18 September 1987 in Austin, Texas.

+3043 ii. **Jay William WASHBURN**.

2409. **Eleanor Elizabeth RITTER** was born on 10 July 1919. She died on 12 June 1994 in Gainesville, Georgia, of Lou Gehrig's disease. She married **Donald Max GRIEB**, who was born on 4 August 1916, probably in New York. He died on 17 June 1989 in Columbia, South Carolina. Their children were:

3044 i. **Donna L. GRIEB** married **James LEE**.

3045 ii. **Gary GRIEB**.

3046 iii. **Paul Michael GRIEB**.

2410. **Marjorie Elizabeth ELBEL** was married to **William John PAXTON**. They had one child:

+3047 i. **William George PAXTON**.

2411. **Peter Leroy HATFIELD** married **Nancy Elizabeth CARDELLICHIO**. They had two children:

3048 i. **Brett HATFIELD**.

3049 ii. **Todd Vincent HATFIELD**.

2420. **Janice Rochelle FEAR** married **Zane NAIBERT**. Janice and Zane NAIBERT had two children:

3050 i. **Unknown male NAIBERT**.
3051 ii. **Stacy NAIBERT**.

2421. **Jerre Lee STEAD** was born on 8 January 1942 in Maquoteka, Iowa. Jerre retired at 55, but found he wasn't happy staying at home, so is working for a California company, commuting between that state and Arizona each week. He was married to **Mary Joy KLOPPENBURG**. Their children are:

+3052 i. **Joel Anthony STEAD**.
+3053 ii. **Jay Arthur STEAD**.

2422. **Brian Earl STEAD** was born on 24 January 1949 in Clinton, Iowa. He married **Saundra RICH**, who was born on 9 August 1950. Brian Earl STEAD and Saundra RICH had the following children:

3054 i. **Abby Catherine STEAD** was born on 28 August 1978 in Sumner, Iowa.
3055 ii. **Aaron STEAD** was born on 8 February 1980 in Sumner.

2423. **Jamie Joel STEAD** was born on 25 March 1953 in Maquoteka, Iowa. Jamie and his wife are divorced. He has been teaching music in Humboldt, Iowa schools, but in 1997, he took a leave of absence, and has been living in Arizona. Jamie Joel STEAD and **UNKNOWN** had the following children:

3056 i. **Jason Jamie STEAD** was born on 19 January 1979 in Humboldt, Iowa.
3057 ii. **Scott David STEAD** was born on 8 April 1981 in Humboldt, Iowa.

2424. **David Vance STEAD** was born on 5 July 1943 in Monticello, Jones County, Iowa. He was married to **Cathy Ilene FRICK** on 17 June 1967. Cathy Ilene FRICK was born in 1946. Their children are:

3058 i. **Tracy Lynn STEAD** was born in 1970.
3059 ii. **Kelly Christine STEAD** was born in 1973.

2426. **Thomas Lee STEAD** was born on 11 September 1950 in Ames, Iowa. He was married to **Mary Ann KEITH** on 25 May 1973 in Rockwell City, Iowa. Mary Ann KEITH was born in 1950. Thomas Lee STEAD and Mary Ann KEITH had the following children:

3060 i. **Ryan Thomas STEAD** was born in 1976.
3061 ii. **Karyn Patricia STEAD** was born in 1978.

2432. **Kathryn Eloise THOMPSON** was born on 13 May 1939 in Iowa. She was married to **Henry John ZYLSTRA** on 18 December 1965. Henry John ZYLSTRA was born in 1940. Kathryn Eloise THOMPSON and Henry John ZYLSTRA had the following children:

3062 i. **Eric John ZYLSTRA** was born in 1970.
3063 ii. **David Jay ZYLSTRA** was born in 1972.

2433. **Verna Marie THOMPSON** was born on 3 April 1943. She was married to **Ronald Guy CARTANO**. Ronald Guy CARTANO was born in 1937. He died in 1976. Their children are:

3064 i. **Denise Raylene CARTANO** was born in 1972.
3065 ii. **Mark Allen CARTANO** was born in 1976.

2434. **Virginia Rae SIEBELS** was born on 26 March 1945 in CA.. She was married to **Steven ELLIOTT** on 11 September 1971. Virginia and Steven ELLIOTT had the following children:

3066 i. **Patricia Lee ELLIOTT** was born on 13 December 1973. She married **Michael Christopher KOKER**, who was born in 1969.
3067 ii. **Kathryn Rae ELLIOTT** was born on 23 June 1975. She married Todd **Frederick LINDLEY**, who was born in 1974.
3068 iii. **Jeffrey Steven ELLIOTT** was born on 27 September 1978.

2435. **Kristi Jean SIEBELS** was born on 15 September 1951 in California. She married **Karl AIELLO**, and they have two children:

3069 i. **Brook Ray AIELLO** was born in August 1981.
3070 ii. **Joseph Karl AIELLO** was born in December 1982.

2437. **Blanche Marie THOMPSON** was born on 10 August 1933 in Hopkinton, Union Twp., Delaware County, Iowa. She was married to **Dorrance Leo DONOVAN** on 12 February 1953 in Cedar Rapids, Linn County, Iowa. Dorrance Leo DONOVAN was born on 13 May 1931. Dorrance is known as "Doc". Blanche Marie THOMPSON and Dorrance Leo DONOVAN had a daughter:

+3071 i. **Pamela Kay DONOVAN**.

2438. **Harold Vernon THOMPSON** was born on 17 November 1951 in Iowa. He was married to **Barbara Jane SULLIVAN** on 16 June 1973 in Waterloo, Iowa. Their children are:

+3072 i. **Sherry Lynn THOMPSON**.
3073 ii. **Brian Harold THOMPSON**.

2439. **Maxine Lorraine THOMPSON** was born on 11 November 1952 in Iowa. She was married to **Gary BEEMAN** on 16 October 1970 in Manchester, Delaware County, IA. Gary BEEMAN was born in 1948. Maxine Lorraine THOMPSON and Gary BEEMAN had the following children:

+3074	i.	**Carrie Ann BEEMAN**.
3075	ii.	**Gary Lee BEEMAN** was born in 1975.
3076	iii.	**Shawn Jessdale BEEMAN** was born in 1977.

2440. **Roger Lee THOMPSON** was born on 12 November 1954 in Iowa. He was married to **Donna SAVERBY** on 12 May 1973. He was divorced from Donna SAVERBY. Donna SAVERBY was born in 1956. Roger Lee THOMPSON and Donna SAVERBY had a son:

+3077	i.	**Jerry Lee THOMPSON**.

2441. **Lois Jane THOMPSON** was born on 23 April 1956 in Iowa. She was married to **Don C. BROYLES** on 10 October 1992. Lois Jane THOMPSON and Don C. BROYLES had a son:

3078	i.	**Jeffrey Arthur BROYLES** was born in 1993.

2443. **Deborah Ann "Debbie" THOMPSON** was born on 26 August 1958 in Iowa. She was married (1)) to **Jim DEMOHT**. Deborah was married (2) to **Jim PECK** on 1 December 1976. Deborah and Jim PECK had a daughter:

+3079	i.	**Heather Ann PECK**.
3080	ii.	**Jason James PECK** was born in 1978.
3081	iii.	**Jessica Sarah PECK** was born in 1982.

2444. **Norman Jay THOMPSON** was born on 5 April 1961. He was married (1) to **Ann FRITZGERALD** on 17 October 1983. Norman Jay THOMPSON and Ann FRITZGERALD had the following children:

3082	i.	**Jacqualan Ann THOMPSON** was born in 1982.
3083	ii.	**Stephney Jean THOMPSON** was born in 1984.

He was married (2) to **Carolyn UNKNOWN** on 20 June 1995.

2445. **Mary Elizabeth THOMPSON** was born on 7 November 1962 in Iowa. She was married to **Lee Leroy SPROSTON** in May 1982. Mary Elizabeth and Lee Leroy SPROSTON had these children:

3084	i.	**Jennifer Lee SPROSTON** was born in 1979.
3085	ii.	**Heidi Mae SPROSTON** was born in 1981.
3086	iii.	**Stephanie Jean SPROSTON** was born in 1984.
3087	iv.	**Joshua LeRoy SPROSTON** was born in 1984.

2446. **Janice Janet THOMPSON** was born on 5 February 1964 in Iowa. She was married to **Raymond BOGE** on 4 May 1985. Janice Janet THOMPSON and Raymond BOGE had the following children:

3088 i. **Timothy Ray BOGE** was born in 1986.
3089 ii. **Jamie Alan BOGE** was born in 1988.
3090 iii. **Jeremy Evan BOGE** was born in 1990.
3091 iv. **Tosha Marie BOGE** was born in 1993.

2447. **Karen Kay THOMPSON** was born on 20 April 1966 in Iowa. She was married to **Carl John OLMSTEAD** in August 1992. Karen and Carl John OLMSTEAD had the following children:

3092 i. **Jessy Lee OLMSTEAD** was born in 1987.
3093 ii. **Brett John OLMSTEAD** was born in 1989.
3094 iii. **Dustin Vernon Walter OLMSTEAD** was born in 1991.

2451. **Barbara Ann THOMPSON** was born on 18 September 1948. She was married to **Tom BRISLAWN** on 6 September 1969. Barbara Ann and Tom BRISLAWN had a son:

3095 i. **Tommy Joe BRISLAWN** was born in 1970.

2452. **Dennis Dee THOMPSON** was born on 24 July 1951. He was married to **Wendy FREEMAN** on 6 June 1970. Dennis and Wendy had one child:

3096 i. **Misty Lynn THOMPSON** was born in 1970.

2453. **Suzette Kay THOMPSON** was born on 6 December 1952 in Iowa. She was married to **Chester SHERRETS** on 28 February 1978. Chester SHERRETS was born in 1924. He died in 1985. Suzette and Chester SHERRETS had a child:

3097 i. **Chester John SHERRETS** was born in 1978.

2454. **Darwin GREEN** was born on 31 May 1941 in Independence, Iowa. He was married to **Betty Lee BACON** on 5 June 1960 in Hopkinton, Delaware County, Iowa. Betty Lee BACON was born in 1942. Darwin GREEN and Betty Lee BACON had the following children:

+3098 i. **Todd GREEN**.
+3099 ii. **Darin GREEN**.
+3100 iii. **Brian GREEN**.

2455. **Merlyn GREEN** was born on 16 January 1945 in Monticello, Jones County, Iowa. He was married to **Barbara VESEY** on 17 July 1965 in Delhi, Delaware County, IA. Barbara VESEY was born in 1947. Merlyn GREEN and Barbara VESEY had the following children:

+3101 i. **Mark GREEN**.
3102 ii. **Bruce GREEN** was born in 1968.
3103 iii. **Valerie GREEN** was born in 1973.

2456. **Sharon GREEN** was born on 25 May 1948 in Monticello, Jones County, Iowa. She was married to **Robert PORTER** on 18 December 1966 in Hopkinton, Delaware County, IA. Robert PORTER was born in 1947. Sharon GREEN and Robert PORTER had the following children:

3104 i. **Brendon PORTER** was born in 1970. He married **Michelle UNKNOWN**.
3105 ii. **Shelby PORTER** was born in 1984.

2457. **Thelma THOMPSON** was born on 13 April 1937 in Iowa. She was married (1) to **Russell JONES** on 25 June 1954 in Hopkinton, Delaware County, IA. Russell JONES was born in 1936. He died in 1996. Thelma THOMPSON and Russell JONES had the following children:

3106 i. **Timothy Dean JONES** was born in 1955.
3107 ii. **Michael Scott JONES** was born in 1957.
+3108 iii. **Patrick Charles JONES**.
3109 iv. **Cynthia Ann JONES** was born in 1960.

Thelma was married (2) to **Richard JACOBS** on 14 February 1989.

2458. **Marilyn THOMPSON** was born on 9 January 1939 in Hopkinton, Delaware County, Iowa. She was married to **Merlin LANG** on 14 October 1956. Merlin LANG was born in 1934. Their children are:

+3110 i. **Gary Wayne LANG**.
+3111 ii. **Ricky Lee LANG**.
+3112 iii. **Scott Allen LANG**.

2459. **Leslie Dean THOMPSON** was born on 3 December 1950 in Monticello, Jones County, Iowa. He was married to **Jan BEAN** on 10 August 1974 in Iowa Falls, Iowa. Their children are:

3113 i. **Kristy Lynn THOMPSON** was born in 1976. She married **Jerry STULER**.
3114 ii. **Royce Elliot THOMPSON** was born in 1978.
3115 iii. **Lillian Erin THOMPSON** was born in 1981.

2460. **Charlotte Kay THOMPSON** was born on 3 April 1952 in Monticello, Jones County, Iowa. She was married to **John NACHTMAN** on 9 October 1976. They had these children:

3116 i. **Cheryl Ann NACHTMAN** was born in 1977.
3117 ii. **Sara Kay NACHTMAN** was born in 1970.

3118 iii. **Ann Marie NACHTMAN** was born in 1981.
3119 iv. **Rebecca Jo NACHTMAN** was born in 1984.

2461. **Regina Doris THOMPSON** was born on 17 February 1957. She was married to **Larry GOLDSMITH** on 16 April 1977. Regina and Larry GOLDSMITH had the following children:

3120 i. **Chad Allen GOLDSMITH** was born in 1977.
3121 ii. **Bradley Lawrence GOLDSMITH** was born in 1978.
3122 iii. **Craig Anthony GOLDSMITH** was born in 1982.
3123 iv. **Karl David GOLDSMITH** was born in 1983.
3124 v. **Kurt Douglas GOLDSMITH** was born in 1984.

2464. **Susan THOMPSON** was born on 30 January 1951. She died on 4 January 1987. She married **Jim MANN**. Susan THOMPSON and Jim MANN had the following children:

3125 i. **Heather MANN**.
3126 ii. **David MANN**.

2465. **Linda Jean THOMPSON** was born on 24 January 1955. She married **Don SWANSON**. Linda Jean THOMPSON and Don SWANSON had the following children:

3127 i. **Emily SWANSON**.
3128 ii. **Leah SWANSON**.

2466. **Kris THOMPSON** was born on 6 January 1956. She married **Tom KRAMER**. Kris THOMPSON and Tom KRAMER had the following children:

3129 i. **Tim KRAMER**.
3130 ii. **Beth KRAMER**.
3131 iii. **Brian KRAMER**.
3132 iv. **Unknown KRAMER**.

2470. **Christopher Wilbur CARTANO** was born on 22 February 1961. He married **Cindy CASTALDO**. Christopher Wilbur CARTANO and Cindy CASTALDO had the following children:

3133 i. **Corinne Nicole CARTANO** was born in 1992.
3134 ii. **Calvin Alexander CARTANO** was born in 1994.

2472. **Geoffrey David CARTANO** was born on 27 November 1961 in Columbus, Franklin County, Ohio. He was married to **Elizabeth WHELAN** on 21 May 1994. They have a son:

3135 i. **Corey Alexander CARTANO**.

2473. **Ann Maria CARTANO** was born on 7 September 1963 in Bogota, Colombia. She was married to **William WEINER** on 27 June 1984 in Appleton, Outagamie County, WI. Their children are:

3136	i.	**Brittany Rachel WEINER.**
3137	ii.	**Tristan Hannah WEINER.**
3138	iii.	**Caina Jo WEINER.**

2474. **Robert Michael TIMMONS** was born on 9 June 1946 in Cedar Rapids, Linn County, Iowa. He was married to **Mary Stamats HEDGIS** on 25 June 1985 in Cedar Rapids. Their children are:

3139	i.	**Brohn Michael TIMMONS.**
3140	ii.	**Kyle Gentry TIMMONS.**
3141	iii.	**Andrew Howell TIMMONS.**
3142	iv.	**David Dunreath TIMMONS.**
3143	v.	**Sally Hedgis TIMMONS.**

2475. **Richard Lee TIMMONS** was born on 23 July 1949 in Cedar Rapids, Linn County, Iowa. He was married to **Colleen LYNESS** on 27 November 1971 in Ryan, Delaware County, Iowa. They have a son:

3144	i.	**Robert Travis TIMMONS.**

2476. **Jo Ann TIMMONS** was born on 5 November 1951 in Marshalltown, Iowa. She was married to **Steven MONTAGUE** on 4 October 1975 in Cedar Rapids, Linn County, Iowa. Their children are:

3145	i.	**B. J. MONTAGUE.**
3146	ii.	**Leigh Rae MONTAGUE.**

2477. **Renee THESTHER** was born on 30 December 1951 in Cedar Rapids, Linn County, Iowa. She was married to **Rick WEETER** on 17 October 1981 in Cedar Rapids, Linn County, Iowa. Their children are:

3147	i.	**Shane Christian WEETER** was born in 1983.
3148	ii.	**Stacy Renee WEETER** was born in 1985.

2479. **Timothy J. CALLAHAN** was born on 24 September 1952 in Minneapolis, Hennepin County, Minnesota. He was married to **UNKNOWN** on 22 September 1975 in CA. They had two children:

3149	i.	**James W. CALLAHAN** was born in 1977.
3150	ii.	**David Paul CALLAHAN** was born in 1982.

2483. **Aaron Todd THOMPSON** was born on 6 January 1970. Aaron lives in Virginia. He married **Amy REYNOLDS**, who was born in 1976. Aaron and Amy REYNOLDS have a son:

3151 i. **Shawn Robert THOMPSON** was born in 1995.

2486. **Julie Lynn THOMPSON** was born on 3 August 1977. Julie has two children:

3152 i. **Michael John Hunter THOMPSON** was born in 1993.

3153 ii. **Elizabeth Mari Hunter THOMPSON** was born in 1996.

2540. **Robert Armstrong HOWELL** was a farmer in Asbury, New Jersey. He married **Martha DOSCHER** in 1934 in New Jersey. Robert Armstrong HOWELL and Martha DOSCHER had one child:

3154 i. **Sarah Frances HOWELL** was born in 1937.

2541. **Morton S. HOWELL** was born on 17 February 1921. He died on 5 May 1955. He was buried in Beemerville Cemetery, Beemerville, NJ. Morton committed suicide because of his experiences in WWII. He married **Lois DAVIDSON**, who was born in New York City. They had two children:

3155 i. **Andrew HOWELL.**

3156 ii. **Judd HOWELL.**

2542. **Earl HOWELL** married **Janet RUNYON**. They were divorced. They had had these children:[246]

+3157 i. **Nancy Joan Howell STRUBLE.**

+3158 ii. **Barbara Jane Howell STRUBLE.**

Janet Runyon married (2) **Harold STRUBLE**, who adopted the girls.

2544. **Anne HOWELL** was born on 15 January 1926, in Washington, Warren County, New Jersey. She married, on 2 June 1948, **Joseph E. FRITTS** (son of **A. Earl FRITTS** and **Ruth GERARD**), who was born on 3 October 1925 in Washington.. He died on 6 January 1995 in Flemington, Hunterdon County, NJ, and was buried in Musconetcong Valley Cemetery, Hampton, NJ. He was a truck driver. Their children, all born in Phillipsburg, Warren County, are:

3159 i. **Janie FRITTS** was born on 13 April 1949. She died in 1949.

+3160 ii. **Stephen John FRITTS.**

3161 iii. **Joseph "Jody" H. FRITTS** was born on 8 July 1952. He married **Cindy CALL** on 3 August 1977.

---

[246]Information on this family contributed by Alfred M. Compton, 3100 North Rd., Box 1, Naples FL 34104.

+3162 iv. **Kenneth Allan FRITTS.**
+3163 v. **Rosalyn FRITTS.**
+3164 vi. **David Charles FRITTS.**
3165 vii. **Melissa Kate FRITTS** was born on 2 April 1961.

2547. **Jean HOWELL** was born on 20 August 1929, and died on 7 March 1994. She married **Thomas SIMONS**, and in 1984, they lived in Washington, Warren County, New Jersey. Jean and Thomas SIMONS had these children:

3166 i. **James SIMONS.**
3167 ii. **Bertrand Thurston SIMONS.**

2548. **Norma HOWELL** was born on 2 November 1930. She married **John Bordleman CLINE** on 18 June 1952. John was born on 23 May 1931 in Franklin Township, Warren County, New Jersey. Their children are:

3168 i. **John Bordleman CLINE** was born on 25 March 1953 in Broadway, Warren County.
3169 ii. **Robert Whitfield CLINE** was born on 27 January 1954 in Washington, Warren County.
3170 iii. **Howard Bruce CLINE** was born on 5 July 1955 in Arlington, Massachusetts.
3171 iv. **Janie Alexandria CLINE** was born on 14 January 1957 in York, Pennsylvania.
3172 v. **Norma Ellen CLINE** was born on 25 October 1959 in Pittsfield, Massachusetts.
3173 vi. **Andrew Hunt CLINE** was born on 29 January 1962 in Pittsfield, Massachusetts.

2549. **Evan HOWELL** was born on 30 March 1937. He lived in Washington, Warren County, New Jersey. He married **Irene Ann MELROY** (daughter of **Nathan Ford MELROY** and **Alma HOFFMAN**), who was born on 2 May 1937. Evan HOWELL and Irene Ann MELROY had the following children:

3174 i. **Evan Bruce HOWELL** was born on 20 December 1958.
3175 ii. **Richard Charles HOWELL** was born on 24 January 1961.

2550. **Arnold J. HOWELL** was a Realtor. He married (1) **Mary Ellen STOVER**. They had one son:

+3176 i. **Arnold J. HOWELL Jr.**

Arnold married (2) **Mary Jane NYOGER**. Arnold and Mary Jane had the following children:

3177 i. **Brandon HOWELL.**

2555. **Robert Shenk HOWELL** was born on 24 November 1919. He served in the US Army during WWII. and worked on several railroads on Syracuse, New York and the surrounding area. The family lived in Camillus, Onondaga County, New York, but moved to Skaneatles Falls, NY in 1960. He married **Shirley June BUTTON**, who was born on 26 June 1920. Robert and Shirley had the following children:

+3179 i. **Wayne Phillip HOWELL.**
3180 ii. **Arlie Lynn HOWELL** was born on 10 October 1947. He married **Linda Beth WEIMAN**, who was born on 1 November 1951. Arlie served in the US Navy, and later worked at Fay's Drug Company as a Distribution Center manager.
+3181 iii. **Dana Kurt HOWELL.**
+3182 iv. **Milan Gene HOWELL.**

2567. **Carl Clayton HOWELL Jr.** was born on 15 September 1944 in Muskegon, Muskegon County, Michigan. He married (1) **Sue BROWN**. Their children are:

3183 i. **Carl Clayton HOWELL IV** was born in 1966.
+3184 ii. **Tara HOWELL** was born in 1967.
3185 iii. **Trina HOWELL** was born in 1969.

Carl married (2) **Judy STUBBLEFIELD.**

2568. **John A. HOWELL** was born on 22 February 1949 in Muskegon, Muskegon County, Michigan. He married **Marcella KING**. John died on 20 January 1984 in Muskegon. John and Marcella had these children:

3186 i. **Sharron HOWELL** was born in 1972.
3187 ii. **Trisha HOWELL** was born in 1978.

2570. **Laurie Kay HOWELL** was born on 27 February 1957 in Muskegon, Muskegon County, Michigan. She married **William VELKER**, who was born in 1955. Laurie and William VELKER had these children:

3188 i. **Nathan Howell VELKER** was born on 7 January 1984.
3189 ii. **Elizabeth Susan VELKER** was born on 15 January 1988.

2575. **Robert John THOMPSON** was born in 1944. He married **June Dolores HICKS**, who was born in 1944. Robert John THOMPSON and June Dolores HICKS had the following children:

+3190 i. **Jeffrey Ronald THOMPSON.**

+3191	ii.	**Robert Forest THOMPSON**.
+3192	iii.	**Richard Scott THOMPSON**.
+3193	iv.	**Daniel Paul THOMPSON**.
3194	v.	**Tara Lee THOMPSON** was born in 1975.
3195	vi.	**Darren Lee THOMPSON** was born and died in 1975.
3196	vii.	**Bradley Lee THOMPSON** was born and died in 1975.

2585. **Irene HAGENY** was born in 1937. She married **Lawrence W. RAPPLEY**. They had these children:

3197	i.	**Lawrence RAPPLEY** was born in 1958.
3198	ii.	**James RAPPLEY** was born in 1959.
3199	iii.	**Julie RAPPLEY** was born in 1961.
3200	iv.	**Sandy RAPPLEY** was born in 1962.
3201	v.	**Joseph RAPPLEY** was born in 1964.
3202	vi.	**Katrina RAPPLEY** was born in 1971.

2586. **Mary Jean HAGENY** was born in 1938. She married **Duane D. FREUND**. Their children are:

3203	i.	**Daniel FREUND**.
3204	ii.	**Carolee FREUND**.
3205	iii.	**Katie FREUND**.
3206	iv.	**Timothy FREUND**.
3207	v.	**Holly FREUND**.

2587. **Norma Louise HAGENY** married **William J. REIMER**. Norma and William J. REIMER had these children:

3208	i.	**Cindy REIMER**.
3209	ii.	**Patty REIMER**.
3210	iii.	**Robert REIMER**.
3211	iv.	**Nancy REIMER**.
3212	v.	**David REIMER**.

2588. **Judith Ann HAGENY** was born in 1944. She married **Gerald A. WINCHELL**. Their children are:

3213	i.	**Thomas WINCHELL**.
3214	ii.	**Mary WINCHELL**.

2589. **Norbert John HAGENY** was born in 1945. He married **Jane Marie FOUST**. Their children are:

3215	i.	**Todd HAGENY**.
3216	ii.	**Amy HAGENY**.
3217	iii.	**Jesse HAGENY**.

3218 iv. **Ryan HAGENY**.
3219 v. **Luke HAGENY**.

2590. **Nancy Lee HAGENY** was born in 1946. She married **Michael G. HOBBS**. They had these children:

3220 i. **Cheryl HOBBS**.
3221 ii. **Kathy HOBBS**.
3222 iii. **Paula HOBBS**.
3223 iv. **Jody HOBBS**.
3224 v. **Paul HOBBS**.
3225 vi. **Mary HOBBS**.

2591. **Thomas Robert HAGENY** was born in 1948. He married **Sharon Marie ELLIS**. They have one child:

3226 i. **Tara HAGENY** was born in 1976.

2592. **Donna May HAGENY** was born in 1954. She married **Larry COLBURN**. They have two children:

3227 i. **Misty COLBURN**.
3228 ii. **Kimberly COLBURN**.

2594. **Cheryl Marie THOMPSON** was born in 1946. She married **Donald L. LAWTON**, and they have three children:

3229 i. **Kevin Avery LAWTON** was born in 1965.
3230 ii. **Darin Lee LAWTON** was born in 1968.
3231 iii. **Corey Earl LAWTON** was born in 1969.

2595. **Daryl Clarence THOMPSON** was born in 1951. He married **Jacqueline HUFF**. They had three children:

3232 i. **Unnamed male THOMPSON** was born and died in 1977.
3233 ii. **Joseph Dale THOMPSON** was born in 1979.
3234 iii. **Travis Lee THOMPSON** was born in 1979.

2596. **Mary Ann ADLER** was born on 24 July 1941. She died on 30 September 1990. She married **McClellan Larry GRINOLDS**, who was born in 1936. Their children are:

3235 i. **Shannon Marie GRINOLDS** was born in 1967.
3236 ii. **Nicole Ann GRINOLDS** was born in 1969.

2597. **Stephen Irvin ADLER** was born in 1942. He married (1) **Cleopatra ERNST**, who was born in 1942. Stephen Irvin ADLER and Cleopatra ERNST had the following children:

3237 i. **Stephen Thomas ADLER** was born in 1962.
3238 ii. **Paul ADLER** was born in 1964.
+3239 iii. **Christine Marie ADLER.**

Stephen Irvin ADLER married (2) **Valerie RAMSDELL**. They had the following children:

3240 i. **Nathan Stephen ADLER** was born in 1976.
+3241 ii. **Adam Stephen ADLER.**
3242 iii. **Marie Irene ADLER** was born in 1979.

2598. **Jill Julia ADLER** was born in 1943. She married **Patrick Lester Geary JONES**, who was born in 1948. He died in 1993. Jill and Patrick Lester Geary JONES had one child:

+3243 i. **Patrick Lester JONES.**

2599. **Jacqueline Agnes ADLER** was born in 1943. She married **James Benjamin RUDOLPH**, who was born in 1943. Jacqueline and James Benjamin RUDOLPH had the following children:

3244 i. **Jennifer Lynn RUDOLPH** was born on 26 March 1963. She married **Stephen Wiley SCOTT**.
3245 ii. **Daniel Jon RUDOLPH** was born in 1966.
3246 iii. **Mark James RUDOLPH** was born in 1968.
3247 iv. **Joel David RUDOLPH** was born in 1971.

2601. **Colleen Diane ADLER** was born in 1948. She married **Michael Edward SCHNEIDER**, who was born in 1948. Colleen Diane ADLER and Michael Edward SCHNEIDER had the following children:

3248 i. **Sonja Marie SCHNEIDER** was born in 1972. She died in 1977.
3249 ii. **Christian Michael SCHNEIDER** was born in 1973.
+3250 iii. **Stacey Lyn SCHNEIDER.**
3251 iv. **Carrie Ann SCHNEIDER** was born in 1977.
3252 v. **Catherine Marie SCHNEIDER** was born in 1979.
3253 vi. **Karen Leigh SCHNEIDER** was born in 1986.

2611. **Carol Jean FURNESS** was born on 3 May 1939 in Chicago, Cook County, IL. She was married to **Ruel Thomas BLAGG** on 31 December 1960. Carol and Ruel Thomas BLAGG had these children:

3254 i. **Thomas BLAGG** was born on 16 March 1962. He

lived in Orly, France.

3255 ii. **Carla BLAGG** was born on 30 September 1967. She died on 4 January 1988, and was buried in Sierra Vista, Arizona.

2612. **Marilyn FURNESS** was born on 25 July 1941 in Chicago, Cook County, IllinooisL. She was married to **John E. MORGAN** on 19 January 1963 in Chicago. John E. MORGAN was born on 10 January 1910. Marilyn FURNESS and John E. MORGAN had the following children:

+3256 i. **Diane Elizabeth MORGAN**.

3257 ii. **David John MORGAN** was born on 26 March 1963. He married **Tracie GILBREATH.**

2613. **Bette Ann FURNESS** was born on 1 July 1943. She was married to **George Joseph SKERTICH** on 10 April 1965. Bette Ann FURNESS and George Joseph SKERTICH had the following children:

3258 i. **George Joseph SKERTICH III** was born on 11 November 1967.

3259 ii. **Nancy Lee SKERTICH** was born on 4 August 1969.

2614. **Sandra YOUNGQUIST** was born on 1 March 1939. She married **UNKNOWN**. They had a son:

3260 i. **Jerry UNKNOWN** was born on 14 December 1957.

2616. **Patti YOUNGQUIST** married **Jim SIEGELE**. Patti and Jim SIEGELE had these children:

3261 i. **Michael SIEGELE**.

3262 ii. **Terry SIEGELE**.

3263 iii. **Kelly SIEGELE**.

2617. **Jay YOUNGQUIST** died in August 1983. He was married to **UNKNOWN.** Their daughter is:

3264 i. **Amy YOUNGQUIST** was born on 12 June 1983.

2619. **Tina YOUNGQUIST** was married (1) to **Unknown SLIZEWSKI**. They had two children:

3265 i. **Clint SLIZEWSKI** was born on 14 May 1979.

3266 ii. **Lance SLIZEWSKI** was born on 9 September 1984.

Tina was married (2) to **Dale OESTREICH** on 1 November 1969.

2620. **Bart Daniel TROYER** was born on 26 January 1948 in Lansing, Michigan. He married and divorced (1) **Barbara LUFF**. He was married (2) to **Nancy Cheryl THEIS** on 12 March 1976. Nancy Cheryl THEIS was born on 18 May 1947. Bert Daniel TROYER and Nancy Cheryl THEIS had the following children:

3267 i. **Brooke Walcott TROYER** was born on 17 January 1977.

3268 ii. **Grant Pierce TROYER** was born in 31 May 1980.

2621. **Barbara Kathleen TROYER** was born on 30 April 1954 in Bad Axe, Michigan. She was married to **Thomas DEPOUW** on 4 March 1978. Barbara and Thomas DEPOUW had the following children:

3269 i. **Michael DEPOUW** was born on 3 July 1981.

3270 ii. **Stephanie DEPOUW** was born on 12 March 1983.

2622. **Linda Ann HUNT** was born on 21 December 1947 in Pontiac, Oakland Coounty, Michigan. She married (1) **Angus Stewart MACIVOR III.** Linda and Angus Stewart MACIVOR III had a daughter:

3271 i. **Heather Lynn MACIVOR** was born on 6 June 1972. She married **Will FOLSON** on 9 September 1995. Will FOLSON was born on 3 July 1971.

Linda was married (2) to **William BRADEN** on 18 June 1993. William BRADEN was born on 12 March 1942.

2623. **Raymond Earl HUNT** was born on 27 November 1950 in Pontiac, MI. He was married (1) to **Patricia BUTLER**. They were divorced. He was married (2) to **Janet FELKINS** on 5 February 1977. Janet FELKINS was born on 9 December 1952. Their children were:

3272 i. **Ashley LuAnn HUNT** was born on 30 October 1985.

3273 ii. **Whitney Nicole HUNT** was born on 14 April 1989.

2627. **Ina (Jeanne) LAUNDRIE** was born on 28 May 1942. She married **David John Hofer FUGINA**, who was born on 5 March 1941. He was an Attorney. Their children are:

3274 i. **Eric Michael FUGINA** was born on 30 April 1968.

3275 ii. **Mark Scott FUGINA** was born on 31 May 1970.

2628. **Frank Henry LAUNDRIE** was born on 11 September 1943. He married (1) **Susan MUSON**, who was born in 1944. Frank Henry LAUNDRIE and Susan MUSON had a son:

3276 i. **Jonathan Scott LAUNDRIE** was born on 27 April 1971.

3277 i. **Heather Ann LAUNDRIE** was born on 29 March 1979.
3278 ii. **Heidi Beth LAUNDRIE** was born on 17 May 1981.

2630. **JoAnn HOY** was born on 21 March 1941. She married **Gordon Michael FORD**. Their children are:

3279 i. **Nancy FORD**.
3280 ii. **Unknown male FORD**.

2631. **Elsie Jane HOY** was born on 24 November 1943. She married **John Howard BIGELOW**. Their son is:

3281 i. **John BIGELOW Jr.**

2632. **Judith Norene HOY** was born on 30 January 1946. She married **Jeffrey Howard BLACK**. They had these children:

3282 i. **Peter BLACK**.
3283 ii. **Andrew BLACK**.

2637. **Robert A. HOWELL** was married to **Julia KOVATCH** (daughter of **Louis KOVATCH** and **Elizabeth VAS**) in June 1971. Julia KOVATCH was born on 12 June 1940 in Brainards, Harmony, Warren County, New Jersey. She died on 14 December 1994 in Hale Hospital, Haverhill, Massachusetts, and was buried in St. Mary's Cemetery, Alpha, Warren County, New Jersey. Their children were:

3284 i. **Rebecca A. HOWELL** died 16 January at 22 months in Hale Hospital, Haverhill, Massachusetts.
3285 ii. **Matthew R. HOWELL** was living in New Ipswich, New Hampshire in 1994.
3286 iii. **Daniel C. HOWELL** was living in North Andover, Massachusetts in 1994.

2640. **Dorothy V. HILL** was born in 1931 in New Jersey, and she died there in 1990. She was buried in Moravian Cemetery, Hope, NJ. She married **Leon C. KITCHEN**, who was born on 17 May 1928 in Columbia, New Jersey. He died on 14 December 1997 in Newton, Sussex County, NJ, and was buried in Moravian Cemetery, Hope. Dorothy V. HILL and Leon C. KITCHEN had the following children:

3287 i. **Michael KITCHEN** lived in Blairstown, New Jersey in 1997.
3288 ii. **Bonnie KITCHEN** married Unknown EAMIGH.
3289 iii. **Jodi KITCHEN** married Unknown GEBHART.

2659. **Ross Herbert HOWELL** was born on 16 December 1941 in Galt, Waterloo County, Ontario. He was a truck driver. He was married to **Dianne Elizabeth QUAIL** (daughter of **Edward James QUAIL** and **Anne Isabel SLATER**) on 27 November 1965 in St. James Anglican Church, Guelph, Ontario. Dianne Elizabeth QUAIL was born on 6 November 1943 in Guelph, Wellington County, Ontario. She was an RNA (Registered Nurse Assistant).Their children were:

3290 i. **Bradley Slater HOWELL** was born on 11 December 1965 in Guelph.

3291 ii. **Edward James HOWELL** was born on 19 September 1969 in Guelph.

3292 iii. **Laura Patricia HOWELL** was born on 26 February 1972.

2660. **William Lloyd HOWELL** was born on 6 May 1944 in Brantford Twp., Brant County, Ontario. He was married to **Sandra Christeen HOWLING** (daughter of **Eben Dewert HOWLING** and **Irene May SPIES**) on 13 August 1966 in New Dundee, Ontario. Sandra Christeen HOWLING was born on 19 September 1946 in Floradale, Waterloo County, Ontario. They had these children:

3293 i. **Cathy Lynn HOWELL** was born on 25 April 1970 in Galt, Waterloo County, Ontario.

3294 ii. **Richard William HOWELL** was born on 29 October 1972 in Kitchener, Waterloo County, Ontario.

2664. **William Bruce HOWELL** was born on 8 October 1936 in Brantford Twp., Brant County, Ontario. He died on 30 December 1985 in S. Dumfries, Brant County, and was buried in St. George United Cemetery. William was killed when a corn crib collapsed on him. He was married to **Elizabeth Lou JACKSON** (daughter of **Chester Morgan JACKSON** and **Sheelaugh Norris COURT**) on 19 July 1958 in St. George, Brant County. Elizabeth Lou JACKSON was born on 24 October 1936 in Orangeville, Ontario. She was buried in St. George United Cemetery. William Bruce HOWELL and Elizabeth Lou JACKSON had the following children:

3295 i. **James Morgan HOWELL** was born on 20 May 1959 in Brantford Twp.

3296 ii. **Kenneth Douglas HOWELL** was born and died on 22 May 1963 in Brantford Twp. He was buried in St. George United Cemetery.

3297 iii. **Elizabeth Susan HOWELL** was born on 17 May 1964 in Brantford Twp.

3298 iv. **Patricia Louise HOWELL** was born on 3 June 1969 in Brantford Twp.

2665. **Margaret Ann HOWELL** was born on 25 February 1942 in Brantford Twp., Brant County, Ontario. She was married to **Ross Edwin FAIR** on 6 August

1966 in St. George, Brant County. Ross Edwin FAIR was born on 20 September 1934 in Brantford Twp. Their children were:

3299 i. **Kevin Ross FAIR** was born on 7 March 1958 in Brantford Twp.

3300 ii. **Karl Robert FAIR** was born on 1 April 1959 in Brantford Twp.

3301 iii. **Leanne Elizabeth FAIR** was born on 17 February 1969 in Brantford Twp.

3302 iv. **Heather Joyce FAIR** was born on 8 March 1975 in Brantford Twp.

2666. **Joyce Doreen HOWELL** was born on 2 July 1943 in Brantford Twp., Brant County, Ontario. She was married to **Earl George MONKHOUSE** on 27 August 1963 in St. George, Brant County. Earl George MONKHOUSE was born on 8 August 1941 in Brantford Twp. Their children are:

3303 i. **Diane Christine MONKHOUSE** was born on 4 September 1964 in Brantford Twp.

3304 ii. **David Edward MONKHOUSE** was born on 19 July 1966 in Brantford Twp.

2667. **Lynda Pauline HOWELL** was born on 26 January 1947 in Brantford Twp. She married **Rodger Alexander Murray LYSTER**, who was born on 30 January 1947. Lynda and Rodger had these children:

3305 i. **Rebecca Christine LYSTER** was born on 12 June 1972 in Brantford Twp.

3306 ii. **Richard Alexander LYSTER** was born on 11 May 1974 in Hawkesbury, Ontario.

2668. **John Macleod HOWELL** was born on 23 January 1957 in Brantford Twp., Brant County, Ontario. He was married to **Babette WARKIEWICZ** on 6 April 1987 in St. George, Brant County. She was born on 17 September 1957 in Korschbroich, Germany. Their son is:

3307 i. **John Alexander HOWELL** was born on 20 September 1993 in Toronto, Ontario.

2670. **Catherine Comer BUCK** was born on 9 February 1942 in Moose Jaw, Saskatchewan. She married **Donald Charles Rogers BROOKS** on 1 December 1960 in Dillon, South Carolina. He was born on 29 January 1941 in Brantford, Ontario. They have two children:

3308 i. **Dean Andrews BROOKS** was born on 23 November 1961 in London, Ontario.

3309 ii. **James Donald Comer BROOKS** was born on 17 March 1964 in Brantford, Ontario.

2682. **Wayne Orton Peter HOWELL** was born on 14 December 1948 in Hamilton, Wentworth, Ontario. He was married to **Kim LEMINDEN** (daughter of **George LEMINDEN** and **Patricia UNKNOWN**) in February 1972 in Horsham, England. Kim LEMINDEN was born on 31 January 1954 in London, England. She died on 17 November 1978 in Crawley, Sussex County, England, in an automobile accident. Wayne Orton Peter HOWELL and Kim LEMINDEN had a son:

3310 i. **Benjamin HOWELL** was born on 21 March 1976.

2693. **Dale Ann LAVERTY** was born on 27 April 1955 in Toronto, Ontario. She was married to **Alfred Randy WOOD** on 25 January 1980 in Toronto. Alfred Randy WOOD was born on 28 August 1954 in Toronto. Dale Ann LAVERTY and Alfred Randy WOOD had a daughter:

3311 i. **Jennifer Kristine WOOD** was born on 4 November 1973 in Toronto.

2694. **James Leslie RUSK** was born on 23 July 1943 in Toronto, Ontario. He was married to **Susan Irene JONES** on 21 August 1971 in Central United Church, Windsor, Ontario. Susan Irene JONES was born on 12 June 1950 in Windsor. Their children are:

3312 i. **James Jeffrey RUSK** was born on 30 September 1973.

3313 ii. **Colleen Ellen RUSK** was born on 4 January 1976.

3314 iii. **Katharine Elizabeth RUSK** was born on 4 February 1980.

2695. **Robert John RUSK** was born on 7 August 1944 in Wiarton, Ontario. He was a Sergeant in the Metro Toronto Police. He was married to **Joanne Marie PEARSON** on 19 September 1964 in the Baptist Church, Owen Sound, Ontario. Robert and Joanne had the following children:

3315 i. **Robert James RUSK** was born on 18 March 1965 in Toronto, Ontario.

3316 ii. **Ronald Arthur RUSK** was born on 12 October 1966 in New York.

3317 iii. **Denise Marie RUSK** was born on 22 January 1974 in New York.

2697. **Linda Suzanne RUSK** was born on 19 March 1950 in Wiarton, Ontario. She was married to **Munro Willard MORRIS** on 10 May 1973 in Barrie, Ontario. Munro Willard MORRIS was born on 27 June 1951 in Owen Sound, Ontario. Linda and Munro Willard MORRIS had these children:

3318 i. **Melanie Dawn MORRIS** was born on 15 October 1974 in Kingston, Ontario.

3319 ii. **Amanda Blythe MORRIS** was born on 4 April 1978.

3320 iii. **Sean Willard MORRIS** was born on 8 March 1979.

2699. **Ronald Wayne HOWELL** was born on 30 October 1945 in Toronto, Ontario. He married **Joy Diane HUGGETT** (daughter of **Jack HUGGETT** and **Jean COOPER**) on 23 August 1969 in Gravenhurst, Ontario. Joy was born on 26 January 1948 in Toronto. They have one child:

3321 i. **Andrea Candice HOWELL** was born on 10 March 1976 in Barrie, Ontario.

2702. **James Bryan SIMPSON** was born on 9 May 1950 in Thunder Bay, Ontario. He was married to **Janice Barbara ROSS** on 14 September 1974. They have a son:

3322 i. **James Ian SIMPSON** was born on 29 December 1979 in Geraldton, Ontario.

2704. **Laurie Jean CLARK** was born on 14 September 1958 in Parry Sound, Ontario. She married **Glenn WALKER**. Laurie Jean CLARK and Glenn WALKER had a son:

3323 i. **Jeremy Glenn WALKER** was born on 7 October 1989 in Parry Sound.

2727. **Valerie Ann WALLEY** was born on 9 July 1937 in Birtle, Manitoba. She was married to **Dale Elmer ADAMS** on 9 July 1958. Dale was born on 24 February 1932 in Alamont, Manitoba. They have these children:

3324 i. **Timothy John ADAMS** was born on 6 October 1959.
3325 ii. **Leah Louise ADAMS** was born on 25 May 1968.

2728. **William John WALLEY** was born in 1939 in Birtle, Manitoba. He was married to **Judith MCLEAN** on 2 September 1966. Judith was born on 3 November 1942 in Birtle. Their children are:

3326 i. **Lisa Michelle WALLEY** was born on 7 February 1964 in Saskatoon, Saskatchewan.
3327 ii. **John Francis WALLEY** was born on 22 May 1969 in Grand Forks, North Dakota.

2729. **Kathleen "Patricia" Anne DUFFY** was born on 29 September 1943 in Birtle, Manitoba. She was married to **Kenneth Wayne SMITH** on 22 June 1963 in Portage, La Prairie, Manitoba. Kenneth Wayne SMITH was born in Portage on 26 August 1940. They had the following children:

3328 i. **Leanne Denise SMITH** was born on 23 September 1963.
3329 ii. **Jason Douglas SMITH** was born on 15 October 1966.

3330 iii. **Kyle Bradford SMITH** was born on 19 May 1969.

2731. **Rae Marguarite DUFFY** was born on 27 February 1949 in Minnedosa, Manitoba. She was married to **Martin SCHIMMEL** on 8 July 1967 in Winnipeg, Manitoba. Martin was born on 28 November 1943 in Ede, Holland. Rae Marguarite DUFFY and Martin SCHIMMEL had these children:

3331 i. **Pamela Maria SCHIMMEL** was born on 18 February 1968.
3332 ii. **Meredith Rae SCHIMMEL** was born on 12 March 1971.
3333 iii. **Lita Marlene SCHIMMEL** was born on 26 August 1975.

2732. **Kathleen Marie MATHEWS** was born on 15 June 1945 in Birtle, Manitoba. She was married to **Richard A. MARRAZZO** on 15 May 1965. Richard A. MARRAZZO was born on 1 January 1943 in Salem, New York. Kathleen Marie MATHEWS and Richard A. MARRAZZO had these children:

3334 i. **Michele MARRAZZO** was born on 21 February 1966 in Glens Falls, New York.
3335 ii. **Adrienne L. MARRAZZO** was born on 28 May 1968 in Murray, Kentucky.
3336 iii. **Marc A. MARRAZZO** was born on 28 April 1969 in Murray, Kentucky.
3337 iv. **Lori Ann MARRAZZO** was born on 26 July 1971 in Utica, New York.

2733. **Laura Lee MATHEWS** was born on 6 January 1948 in Utica, New York. She was married to **John A. BUSH** on 26 January 1969 in Oswego, New York. Laura and John have these children:

3338 i. **Jeffrey BUSH** was born on 23 August 1969.
3339 ii. **Brian BUSH** was born on 10 January 1973.
3340 iii. **Michael BUSH** was born on 11 October 1975.

2735. **Donna Jean WALLEY** was born on 8 August 1947 in Russell, Manitoba. She was married to **Garth Alexander SARARAS** on 29 June 1970 in Birtle, Manitoba. Garth was born on 15 February 1943 in Miniota, Manitoba. Their children are:

3341 i. **Kirby Dawn SARARAS** was born on 1 January 1975.
3342 ii. **Stacey Lee SARARAS** was born on 10 May 1977.

2736. **Betty Marie WALLEY** was born on 26 November 1950 in Birtle, Manitoba. She was married to **Barry Marie DAVIDSON** on 3 September 1971 in Birtle. Barry Marie DAVIDSON was born on 27 August 1949 in Birtle. Betty Marie WALLEY and Barry Marie DAVIDSON had the following children:

3343 i. **Jordin James DAVIDSON** was born on 2 April 1976 in Flin Flon, Manitoba.

3344 ii. **Jayson Walley DAVIDSON** was born on 12 April 1978 in Flin Flon.

2737. **Peter Kenneth DOUGLAS** was born on 30 July 1943 in Winnipeg, Manitoba. He was married to **Elsie Catherine AITCHISON** on 27 December 1966 in Winnipeg. Elsie was born on 11 June 1945 in The Pas, Manitoba. Their children are:

3345 i. **Scott Robert DOUGLAS** was born on 24 January 1969 in Rainy River, Ontario.

3346 ii. **Andrew David DOUGLAS** was born on 6 January 1973 in Winnipeg.

2740. **George Brian "Skip" SHAND** was born on 6 April 1941 in Winnipeg, Manitoba. He was married to **Patricia Margaret MARTIN** on 22 March 1963 in Winnipeg. Patricia Margaret MARTIN was born on 29 November 1942 in Winnipeg. Their children are:

3347 i. **Alison Frances SHAND** was born on 17 May 1970 in Toronto, Ontario.

3348 ii. **Fiona Margaret SHAND** was born on 1 October 1978.

2741. **Terry Evelyn SHAND** was born on 17 June 1943 in Dryden, Ontario. She was married to **Michael Henry BARRETT** on 22 March 1963 in Thunder Bay, Ontario. Michael Henry BARRETT was born on 28 January 1938 in Port Dover, Ontario. Terry and Michael Henry BARRETT had these children:

3349 i. **Kimberly Shaun BARRETT** was born on 29 May 1964 in Marathon, Ontario.

3350 ii. **Scott Gregory BARRETT** was born on 8 May 1967 in North Bay, Ontario.

2742. **Judy Elizabeth SHAND** was born on 31 August 1946 in Dryden, Ontario. She was married to **Donald David HARBARENKO** on 6 March 1965 in Winnipeg, Manitoba. He was born on 20 April 1937 in Glendon, Alberta. Judy and Donald David HARBARENKO had the following children:

3351 i. **David "Cameron" HARBARENKO** was born on 8 January 1966 in Vancouver, British Columbia.

3352 ii. **Kerry Donald HARBARENKO** was born on 22 December 1967 in Vancouver.

3353 iii. **Leslie Ellen HARBARENKO** was born on 16 February 1973 in Richmond, British Columbia.

3354 iv. **Colin Shand HARBARENKO** was born on 15 June 1976 in Vancouver.

2744. **Lois Ellen SHAND** was born on 4 July 1953 in Marathon, Ontario. She married **Craig Albert FAULKNER** on 16 July 1976 in Dryden, Ontario. He was born on 25 June 1949 in Kenora, Ontario. Lois Ellen SHAND and Craig Albert FAULKNER had the following children:

3355 i. **Joanne Elaine FAULKNER** was born on 6 March 1973 in Dryden, Ontario.
3356 ii. **Laura Lois FAULKNER** was born on 18 September 1978 in Kenora, Ontario.

2748. **Ellen Ivah MULHOLLAND** was born on 17 October 1951 in Central Butte, Saskatchewan. She was married to **James Robert LAYBOURNE** on 16 April 1977. He was born on 25 May 1953 in Central Butte, Saskatchewan. He was an Elevator Agent and a farmer. Ellen and James had one child:

3357 i. **Nicole Dawn LAYBOURNE** was born on 10 March 1979 in Central Butte.

2759. **Allan Wayne HOWELL** was born on 15 February 1957. He was a building supply salesman. He was married to **Victoria Gaye MILLER** (daughter of **Bruce MILLER** and **Amy WILLES**) on 16 August 1980 in Sonya, Ontario. Allan and Victoria had the following children:

3358 i. **Jennifer Lyn HOWELL** was born on 26 August 1981 in Sonya, Ontario.
3359 ii. **Rachel Anne HOWELL** was born on 8 March 1984.
3360 iii. **Robin Sarah HOWELL** was born on 27 December 1985.
3361 iv. **Jessica Lisa HOWELL** was born on 23 May 1988.
3362 v. **Kelsie Amy Kathleen HOWELL** was born on 14 August 1992 in Pleasant Point, Ontario.

2760. **Arlene Patricia HOWELL** was born on 19 September 1960 in Oshawa, Ontario County, Ontario. She was married to **Reginald David LYON** (son of **Reginald LYON** and **Margaret MASON**) on 15 September 1991 in Markham, Ontario. They have two children:

3363 i. **Jacob Tyler David LYON** was born on 2 September 1993.
3364 ii. **Gemma Kathleen Margaret LYON** was born on 12 December 1995.

2781. **Douglas Howard LYONS** was born on 4 December 1958. He was married to **Sherry Lee MCCORMICK** on 17 May 1986 in Brantford Twp., Brant County, Ontario. They have a son:

3365 i. **Cody Douglas LYONS** was born on 14 May 1991 in Brantford Twp.

2784. **Carmen Bruce GERMAN** was born on 25 November 1956 in Brantford Twp., Brant County, Ontario. He married **Pamela Margaret LONGLEY** on 20 December 1985 in Paris, Brant County. She was born on 20 September 1957 in Kingston, Ontario. Their children were:

3366 i. **Brandon Thomas GERMAN** was born on 8 January 1976 in Brantford Twp.

3367 ii. **Benjamin Jeremiah GERMAN** was born on 8 May 1981 in Edmonton, Alberta.

3368 iii. **Jacquelyn Lorraine GERMAN** was born on 20 June 1988 in Brantford Twp.

2786. **Arlene Ann GERMAN** was born on 24 May 1962 in Brantford Twp., Brant County, Ontario. She married **John PAUL** on 28 December 1985. He was born on 23 February 1962. Arlene and John PAUL have the following children:

3369 i. **Danielle Ann PAUL** was born on 5 March 1985.

3370 ii. **Tanis Hilary Lynn PAUL** was born on 1 January 1989.

2802. **Richard James GOWMAN** was born on 12 November 1962 in Kitchener, Waterloo County, Ontario. He married **Shelly Lynn TEET** on 30 May 1987 in Preston, Waterloo County. She was born on 6 January 1967 in Galt, Waterloo County, Ontario. Richard and Shelly have one child:

3371 i. **Calvin Kenneth James GOWMAN** was born on 31 October 1994 in Kitchener.

2809. **Allen Lesley SHAVER** was born on 25 June 1929 in Winnipeg, Manitoba. He was married to **Ruth Eileen SCHWARTZ** on 21 June 1952 in Winnipeg. Ruth Eileen SCHWARTZ was born on 3 December 1934 in Winnipeg. Their children are:

3372 i. **Norine Leslie SHAVER** was born on 12 December 1953 in Winnipeg. She married **Robert HANCOCK** on 6 October 1984.

3373 ii. **Darrel Allen SHAVER** was born on 19 December 1954 He married **Wendy Maureen DICKSON** on 22 May 1976.

3374 iii. **Terrence Ronald SHAVER** was born on 19 December 1955 in Winnipeg. He married (1) **Bernadine Ivy BURGESS** on 16 May 1980. He married (2) **Mary Elizabeth LAMONT** on 25 March 1989.

3375 iv. **Daniel Arthur SHAVER** was born on 13 October 1957.

3376 v. **Timothy Robert SHAVER** was born on 7 July 1959 in Winnipeg. He married **Laura Janet WILCOX** on 13 July 1991.

3377 vi. **Nancy Lynn SHAVER** was born on 2 March 1961 in

Winnipeg. She married **Robin John LYTLE** on 27 December 1984.

3378 vii. **David Wesley SHAVER** was born on 15 November 1963 in Winnipeg. He married **Lisa Nicole PINKNEY** on 2 June 1990.

3379 viii. **Christine Marie SHAVER** was born on 22 Mary 1968 in Winnipeg. She married **Colin John CRELLIN** on 20 May 1989.

2812. **Robert John ENGLISH** was born on 15 April 1947 in Chatham, Ontario. He was married to **Susan Elaine MCNEIL** in 1969 in London, Ontario. He was divorced from Susan Elaine MCNEIL in 1979. Susan Elaine MCNEIL was born on 14 May 1949 in Chatham, Ontario. Their children are:

3380 i. **Andrew Tyler ENGLISH** was born on 9 January 1971 in Chatham.

3381 ii. **Amanda Susan ENGLISH** was born on 3 September 1973 in Chatham.

2813. **Leslie Margaret ENGLISH** was born on 13 August 1949 in Chatham, Ontario. She was married to **Brian Douglas JENKINS** on 8 August 1973 in Chatham. He was born on 17 October 1948. Leslie Margaret ENGLISH and Brian Douglas JENKINS had the following children:

3382 i. **Mason Jonathon JENKINS** was born on 13 March 1977 in Chatham

3383 ii. **Jennifer Ann JENKINS** was born on 15 May 1979 in Chatham.

2814. **Mary Kathleen ENGLISH** was born on 5 July 1957 in Chatham, Ontario. She was married to **Daniel John ANDREWS** on 28 December 1974 in Chatham. Daniel John ANDREWS was born in April 1951. Mary Kathleen ENGLISH and Daniel John ANDREWS had a daughter:

3384 i. **Kathleen Denise ANDREWS** was born on 16 January 1979 in Leamington, Ontario.

2815. **Debra Colleen SHOUP** was born in 1957 in Canada. She was married to **Steven REYNEN** in 1981 in Canada. Debra Colleen SHOUP and Steven REYNEN had the following children:

3385 i. **Scott REYNEN** was born in 1982 in Alberta, Canada.

3386 ii. **Stephanie REYNEN** was born in 1987 in Alberta.

3387 iii. **Randy REYNEN** was born in 1989 in Alberta.

2818. **Kenneth Charles MITCHELL** was born on 12 January 1962. He was married to **Arnell Kay EISENMANN** on 5 April 1984. Their children are:

3388 i. **Ryan Kenneth MITCHELL** was born on 17 January 1987.

3389 ii. **Torrey Clinton MITCHELL** was born on 22 June 1989.

3390 iii. **Samantha Darlene MITCHELL** was born on 17 December 1991.

2820. **Cheryl Ruth MITCHELL** was born on 3 September 1968. She was married to **Christopher COWELL** on 22 July 1994. Cheryl Ruth MITCHELL and Christopher COWELL have a son:

3391 i. **Lucas Victor COWELL** was born on 11 January 1997.

TENTH GENERATION

2824. **Kenneth LAUBACH** was born on 8 September 1950 in Phillipsburg, Warren County, NJ. He married **Melissa DEBOER**. Kenneth LAUBACH and Melissa DEBOER had the following children:

3392 i. **Barbara Ann LAUBACH** was born in April 1976.
3393 ii. **Kenneth Eric LAUBACH**.
3394 iii. **Katie Beth LAUBACH**.

2825. **John LAUBACH** was born on 16 April 1966. He married **Susan SWISHER**. They have three children:

3395 i. **Jessica LAUBACH** was born in August 1987.
3396 ii. **Amanda LAUBACH** was born in December 1991.
3397 iii. **Emma LAUBACH** was born in December 1991.

2827. **Clayton Robert LAUBACH** was born on 6 September 1975. He married **Carrie WALTERS.** Their child is:

3398 i. **Clayton Robert LAUBACH Jr**. was born on 3 March 1995.

2828. **Clark RICE Jr.** married **Nancy UNKNOWN**. They have these children:

3399 i. **Amy RICE.**
3400 ii. **Karina RICE**.

2831. **Terri KOCH** married **John NIEMAN**. Terri and John NIEMAN had the following children:

3401 i. **Krista NIEMAN**.
3402 ii. **John NIEMAN**.

2834. **Pamela KOCH** married (1) **Unknown PONCE**. Their children are:

3403 i. **Jill PONCE**.
3404 ii. **Cassie PONCE**.

Pamela married (2) **David RODENBAUGH**.

2835. **Patty KOCH** married **John CONSENTINO**. Patty and John had the following children:

3405 i. **Jason CONSENTINO**.
3406 ii. **James CONSENTINO**.
3407 iii. **John CONSENTINO**.

2836. **Kenneth KOCH** married **Debra DEPALMA**. They had these children:

3408 i. **Jeremiah KOCH** was born about 1989.
3409 ii. **Hannah Ruth KOCH** was born on 2 October 1997 in Bethlehem, Northampton County, PA.

2837. **Steven KOCH** married (1) **UNKNOWN**. They had two children:

3410 i. **Noah KOCH**.
3411 ii. **Stephanie KOCH**.

Steven married (2) **Terry UNKNOWN**. Steven and Terry have one child:

+3412 i. **Steven KOCH Jr**.

2838. **Mark LAUBACH** married **UNKNOWN**. They have these children:

3413 i. **Steven LAUBACH**.
3414 ii. **Unknown LAUBACH**.

2840. **Eric LAUBACH** married **Leah MINORICS**. Their children are:

3415 i. **Tyler LAUBACH**.
3416 ii. **Zachary LAUBACH**.

2841. **Leslie LAUBACH** married **John WYCKOFF**. They have two children:

3417 i. **Noelle WYCKOFF** was born in 1993 in Belvidere, Warren County, NJ.
3418 ii. **Olivia Marie WYCKOFF** was born on 1 June 1999 in Belvidere.

2843. **Robert L. HOWELL Jr**. married **Roberta Linda JOHNSON**. They had the following children:

3419 i. **Robert L. HOWELL III.**
3420 ii. **Michael HOWELL**.
+3421 iii. **Mark HOWELL** .

2844. **Donald HOWELL** married (1) **Martha KELSO**, and they divorced. Their son is:

3422 i. **Donald HOWELL Jr**.

Donald married (2) **Jackie UNKNOWN**, and they divorced. They had one child:

3423 i. **Randy HOWELL**.

Donald married (3) **Barbara FITO**, and they divorced. They had one child:

3424 i. **Tracy HOWELL**.

Donald married (4) and divorced **Virginia HILL**.

2845. **Paula HOWELL** married **Charles RUSH**. They were divorced. They had these children:

3425 i. **Jodi RUSH** married **Unknown PONATOWSKI**.
+3426 ii. **Tracy RUSH**.

2850. **Edward WEAN** was born on 31 August 1963 in Phillipsburg, Warren County, NJ. He was married (1) to **Kimberly KETTENBERGH** about 1988 in Easton, Northampton County, PA. They were divorced. Their children were:

3427 i. **Joshua WEAN** was born on 7 January 1989 in Easton.
3428 ii. **Ryan WEAN** was born on 19 April 1990 in Easton.

He was married (2) to **Chrisann MACDOUGAL**. Edward WEAN and Chrisann MACDOUGAL had these children:

3429 i. **Alyssa WEAN** was born on 10 May 1994.
3430 ii. **Nicole Arlene WEAN** was born on 31 March 1998 in Bethlehem, Northampton County, PA.

2851. **Andrea Lynn WEAN** was born on 13 August 1964 in Phillipsburg, Warren County, NJ. Andrea was married to **David WOOLF**. She was divorced from David WOOLF. Andrea Lynn WEAN and **William TERSIGNI** have a daughter:

3431 i. **Amanda Lynn TERSIGNI** was born on 29 July 1997 in Palmer Twp., Northampton County, PA. [247]

2875. **Charmaine J. HOWELL** married **Robert E. FLOREY** on 31 July 1954. Robert was born in Tatamy, PA in 1934. He died in an automobile accident in Texas on 27 July 1998. Charmaine and Robert E. FLOREY had one child:

+3432 i. **Lori FLOREY**.

2890. **Barbara Lee HEPBURN** was born on 22 October 1945 in Jamaica, New York. She married **Kenneth FISHER,** who was born on 23 October 1944 in Van Lear, Kentucky. They have a child:

---

[247]Birth announcement, Easton Express, August 1997.

2897. **Robert Alan YOUNG** was born on 10 July 1953. He married **Karen Ruth MEYER** in Phillipsburg, Warren County, NJ. They have a daughter:

3434 i. **Unknown YOUNG** was born on 23 June 1989.

2898. **Bonnie YOUNG** was born on 14 June 1957 in NJ. She was married to **John TODD** on 11 October 1975 in the Methodist Church in Bloomsbury, NJ. Bonnie YOUNG and John TODD had these children:

3435 i. **Michael John TODD** was born on 8 March 1976 in NJ.
3436 ii. **Kelly Jo TODD** was born on 19 March 1979 in NJ.

2909. **Lisa BLACK** was born on 11 October 1954. Lisa has one child:

3437 i. **Kristin BLACK** was born on 3 August 1975.

2916. **Pat MCQUATTERS** married **Richard GUGGE**. Their children were:

3438 i. **Tracy GUGGE**.
3439 ii. **Tricia GUGGE**.

2924. **James Archie SWABY** was born on 14 June, year not known. He was married to **Mary Ann PETERSON** on 22 December 1971 in Great Falls, Cascade County, MT. Their son is::

3440 i. **Matthew James SWABY** was born on 25 June 1977 in Corvallis, Benton County, Oregon.

2925. **Lila Mae SWABY** was born on 7 June 1940 in Hardin, Big Horn County, Montana. She was married (1) to **Harold Douglas SUNGREN** on 23 November 1958 in Great Falls, Cascade County, MT. Lila and Harold had these children:

3441 i. **Tami Marie SUNGREN** was born on 5 November 1959 in Great Falls.
3442 ii. **Keith Douglas SUNGREN** was born on 11 November 1961 in Chester, Liberty County, Montana.
3443 iii. **Paul Scott SUNGREN** was born on 3 April 1963 in Shelby, Toole County, Montana.

Lila Mae was married (2) to **Stanley Lynn MCCARTER** on 7 August 1971 in Bonners Ferry, Boundary County, Idaho. Lila Mae SWABY and Stanley Lynn MCCARTER had a daughter:

3444 i. **Stacy Jean MCCARTER** was born on 7 April 1972 in Shelby, Toole County, Montana.

2926. **Elaine Joyce SWABY** was born on 9 January 1943 in Great Falls, Cascade County, MT. She was married to **Daniel Eugene MEYER** on 17 June 1961 in Great Falls. Elaine and Daniel Eugene MEYER had the following children:

3445 i. **Richard Daniel MEYER** was born on 27 September 1963 in Great Falls.

3446 ii. **Scott Dean MEYER** was born on 5 September 1968 in Yakima, Yakima County, Washington.

2930. **Joann ZIELINSKI** was born on 18 October 1946 in Oglesby, LaSalle County, Illinois. She was married (1) to **Dale Patrick PREISER** on 31 October 1946 in Peru, La Salle County, IL. Joann and Dale PREISER had these children:

3447 i. **Michael Scott PREISER** was born on 1 January 1966 in La Salle, LaSalle County, IL.

3448 ii. **Dale Thomas PREISER** was born on 10 March 1967 in La Salle.

Joann was married (2) to **Dan LIVESAY** on 4 March 1972 in Rockton, Winnebago County, IL.

2931. **Edna Marie ZIELINSKI** was born on 3 April 1948 in LaSalle. She was married to **John Jay OLSON** on 2 July 1968 in Parris Island, Beaufort County, South Carolina. They have a son:

3449 i. **William John OLSON** was born on 3 April 1971 in Parris Island.

2932. **Connie Sue ZIELINSKI** was born on 26 November 1952 in Oglesby, LaSalle County, IL. She was married to **Mark David KUDULA** on 8 April in Peru, La Salle County, IL. Connie Sue and Mark David KUDULA had a daughter:

3450 i. **Necole Alissa KUDULA** was born on 10 August 1976 in La Salle.

2937. **Thomas Edward (PRICE) DELONG** was born on 10 March 1947 in Whitefish, Flathead County, Montana. He was married to **Jillian Eleanor SPENSLIEY** in Paris, France. Thomas and Jillian had a son:

3451 i. **Jonathan Paul DELONG** was born in San Diego, San Diego County, California.

2940. **Leonard Gene (CAMPBELL) (THOMPSON) NELSON** was born on 13 November 1945 in Pittston, Luzerne County, Pennsylvania. He was married to **Pesenta Mercy FAGAL** on 16 August 1971 in Yap District, Caroline Islands, Pacific Ocean. Leonard Gene (CAMPBELL) (THOMPSON) NELSON and Pesenta Mercy FAGAL had the following children:

3452 i. **Peggy Ann NELSON** was born on 20 November 1971 in Kalispell, Flathead County, Montana.
3453 ii. **Evelyn NELSON** was born on 23 April 1973 in Yap District, Caroline Islands, Pacific Ocean.
3454 iii. **Bret Leonard NELSON** was born on 20 July 1976 in Kalispell, Flathead County, MT.

2946. **Kenneth Berkley BEDELL** was born on 16 October 1947 in Spirit Lake, Dickinson County, Iowa. He was married to **Kathryn Ann HALE** on 20 June 1970 in Portland, Middlesex County, Connecticut. Their children are:

3455 i. **Charity Lyn BEDELL** was born on 8 May 1974 in Ithaca, Tompkins County, New York.
3456 ii. **Sarah Grace BEDELL** was born on 29 March 1977 in Mbabane, Swaziland, Africa.

2949. **Nadine Lyn BEDELL** was born on 29 March 1947 in Iowa City, Johnson County, IA. She was married to **James Richard SCHUCHERT** on 17 June 1967 in Spirit Lake, Dickinson County, IA. Nadine and James had these children:

3457 i. **Todd James SCHUCHERT** was born on 30 September 1968 in Spirit Lake.
3458 ii. **Chad Christopher SCHUCHERT** was born on 22 January 1973 in St. Joseph, Buchanan County, Missouri.

2950. **David William BEDELL** was born on 25 May 1950 in Iowa City, Johnson County, IA. He was married to **Kristi COOK** on 23 August 1969 in Spirit Lake, Dickinson County, IA. David and Kristi had the following children:

3459 i. **Clayton David BEDELL** was born on 1 October 1973 in Memphis, Shelby County, Tennessee.
3460 ii. **Aaron Richard BEDELL** was born on 5 January 1976 in Camp Springs, Prince Georges County, Maryland.

2951. **Richard Charles BEDELL** was born on 25 May 1950 in Iowa City, Johnson County, IA. He was married to **Kathleen GROLLMAN** on 20 December 1972 in Spirit Lake, Dickinson County, IA. Richard Charles BEDELL and Kathleen GROLLMAN had the following children:

3461 i. **Wade Richard BEDELL** was born on 5 October 1973 in Memphis, Shelby County, Tennessee.
3462 ii. **Courtney Kathleen BEDELL** was born on 12 February 1976 in Maitland, Orange County, Florida.

2952. **Muriel Elizabeth COLLINS** was born on 23 July 1932 in Wichita Falls, Wichita County, Texas. She was married to **Ray Douglas DAVIS** (son of **Ray**

DAVIS and **Portia CHAMBERS**) on 13 December 1953 in Long Beach, Los Angeles County, California. Muriel and Ray had these children:

3463 i. **Michael Paul DAVIS** was born on 15 October 1954 in Long Beach. He married **Julianna Rochelle MARTY** on 7 September 1974 in Long Beach.

3464 ii. **Matthew Douglas DAVIS** was born on 1 May 1959 in Long Beach. He married **Becky Marie OLERUD** on 10 September 1978 in Indio, Riverside County, CA.

2953. **Maryevelyn COLLINS** was born on 26 September 1934 in Wichita Falls, Wichita County, Texas. She was married to **Frank HARRIS** on 24 June 1956 in Long Beach, Los Angeles County, CA. Their children are:

3465 i. **David Gregory HARRIS** was born on 1 September 1958 in Harbor City, Los Angeles County, CA. He married (1) **Lisa Michele DETTIS** on 13 July 1983 in Rancho Palo Verdes, Los Angeles County, CA. David married (2)**Anne Louise BEATTY** on 23 June 1991 in Fairfax, Marin County, CA.

3466 ii. **William Leroy HARRIS** was born on 3 August 1960 in Harbor City. He married **Nancy Patricia COULSON** on 27 August 1994 on Anaheim, Los Angeles County, CA.

3467 iii. **Steven Glen HARRIS** was born on 30 April 1963 in Harbor City. He married **Rita UNKNOWN** in Avalon, Los Angeles County, CA.

2954. **Kathleen Elaine COLLINS** was born on 3 April 1947 in Long Beach, Los Angeles County, CA. She was married (1) to **William Dean STINNETT** on 21 October 1966 in Long Beach. Kathleen Elaine COLLINS and William Dean STINNETT had the following children:

3468 i. **Jennifer Alaine (STINNETT) AYRES** was born on 15 January 1972 in Long Beach. She married **Daniel Harvey PENNER** on 18 November 1995 in Cypress, Orange County, CA.

3469 ii. **Mark Aaron (STINNETT) AYRES** was born on 21 February 1975 in Bellflower, Los Angeles County.

Kathleen was married (2) to **Michael David AYRES** on 15 November 1980 in Long Beach. Kathleen Elaine COLLINS and Michael David AYRES had a son:

3470 i. **Samuel David AYRES** was born on 8 February 1983 in CA.

2955. **Janet HERSHEY** was born on 2 September 1952 in Long Beach, Los Angeles County, CA. She was married to **Marty DUBOIS** in 1975. Janet HERSHEY and Marty DUBOIS had a daughter:

3471 i. **Jessica DUBOIS** was born in July 1983.

2970. **David DeWolf ASHLEY** was born on 22 May 1943 in McCook, Red Willow County, Nebraska. He was married to **Pauline PELLINERI** on 31 August 1967. They had the following children:

3472 i. **Jamie Faye ASHLEY** was born on 11 May 1968.
3473 ii. **Davida Maryann ASHLEY** was born on 19 August 1970.
3474 iii. **Shari Elizabeth ASHLEY** was born on 19 October 1971.

2971. **Faye Ellen ASHLEY** was born on 1 November 1948 in San Jose, Santa Clara County, CA. She was married to **Dennis James BOYDSTUN** on 25 March 1967. They had one child:

3475 i. **Amber Ellen BOYDSTUN** was born on 9 February 1977 in Boulder, Boulder County, CO.

2974. **Peggy Jean WATTS** was born on 17 April 1946 in Dallas, Dallas County, Texas. She was married to **Thomas Gerald GRAY** on 6 February 1965 in Denver, Arapahoe County, Colorado. Their children are:

3476 i. **Paula Jean GRAY** was born on 3 February 1966 in Ft. Collins, Larimer County, CO.
3477 ii. **Donna Jane GRAY** was born on 18 June 1967 in Des Moines, Polk County, Iowa.
3578 iii. **Thomas Gerald GRAY** was born on 15 January 1969 in Des Moines.

3008. **Barbara Jean PERREGO** was born on 1 August 1963 in Wilkes Barre, Luzerne County, Pennsylvania. She was married to **Charles Herbert CRANE** on 28 July 1984. Charles Herbert CRANE was born on 29 December 1962. Their children are:

3479 i. **Renee Anne CRANE** was born on 21 July 1985 in Kingston, Luzerne County.
3480 ii. **Amanda Jean CRANE** was born on 3 August 1987 in Kingston.
3481 iii. **Charles Eugene CRANE II** was born on 31 October 1988 in Kingston.
3482 iv. **Nathan Emerson CRANE** was born on 28 April 1992 in Kingston.
3483 v. **Quentin Rogers CRANE** was born on 6 April 1995 in

Kingston.

3009. **Bonnie Elizabeth PERREGO** was born on 12 August 1966 in New York. She married **William FELKER** who was born on 20 December. Bonnie and William FELKER had these children:

3484 i. **Jacob Aaron FELKER** was born on 17 April 1995 in Luzerne County, Pennsylvania.

3485 ii. **Paige Elizabeth FELKER** was born on 27 June 1997 in Kingston.

3013. **Stephen RALSTON** was born in 1971. He married **Tina UNKNOWN**, and they had a son:

3486 i. **Christopher RALSTON** was born in 1995.

3029. **Lin Howell ROOT** was born on 1 July 1953 in Frederic, Polk County, Wisconsin. He was married to **Alice Mae SCHMIDT** on 17 July 1976 in Frederic, Polk County. Lin and Alice Mae had a son:

3487 i. **Lin Howell ROOT** was born in 1980.

3040. **Theresa Lynn BUTLER** was born on 26 December 1959 in Waynesboro, Virginia. She was married to **Michael Anthony BUDA** on 12 March 1988 in Pacific Grove, California. Michael Anthony BUDA was born on 4 December 1952. Theresa Lynn BUTLER and Michael Anthony BUDA had the following children:

3488 i. **Andriana Van Fossen BUDA** was born on 12 November 1989.

3489 ii. **Michaela Razzano BUDA** was born on 27 February 1992.

3490 iii. **Nathaniel Cale BUDA** was born on 11 February 1995.

3043. **Jay William WASHBURN** was born on 21 February 1960 in Bridgeport, Connecticut. He was married(1) to **Robyn DIBELLA** in 1980 in Fairfield, CT. They are divorced. They had these children:

3491 i. **Darryl Anne WASHBURN** was born on 12 January 1981.

3492 ii. **Jillian Christine WASHBURN** was born on 4 December 1982.

Jay was married (2) to **Cindy DIONIS** on 5 October 1991 in Bridgeport, CT.

3047. **William George PAXTON** married **Karen Teresa SNEIDER**. Their children are:

3493 i. **Martha Elizabeth PAXTON**.
3494 ii. **Thomas William PAXTON**.

3052. **Joel Anthony STEAD** was born on 28 June 1962 in Iowa City, IA. He was married to **Michele Elizabeth BYFIELD** on 30 August 1986. Michele was born on 27 February 1963. Their children are:

3495 i. **Sydney Elizabeth STEAD** was born on 22 August 1991 in Santa Cruz, Colorado.
3496 ii. **Madeline Michelene STEAD** was born on 26 March 1993 in Santa Cruz, CO.

3053. **Jay Arthur STEAD** was born on 11 December 1963 in Iowa City, IA. He was married to **Robyn DAVID** on 3 July 1993. Robyn was born on 19 December 1968 in Wellington, New Zealand. They had a child:

3497 i. **Samuel Bryden STEAD** was born on 28 March 1997 in Dayton, OH.

3071. **Pamela Kay DONOVAN** was born on 10 July 1962. She was married to **Kurt BERENS** in 1991. Pamela is a physician in Texas. Kay DONOVAN and Kurt BERENS had these children:

3498 i. **Donovan Patrick BERENS** was born in November 1992.
3499 ii. **Pauline Margaret BERENS** was born in March 1994 in Dallas, Texas.
3500 iii. **Dylan Luke BERENS** was born in 1997 in Dallas, TX.

3072. **Sherry Lynn THOMPSON** was born in 1974. Sherry Lynn THOMPSON had one child:

3501 i. **Sierra Lynn DEGROTTE** was born in 1997.

3074. **Carrie Ann BEEMAN** was born in 1972. Carrie has one child:

3502 i. **Crissy Loraine HINES** was born in 1995.

3077. **Jerry Lee THOMPSON** was born in 1973. He married **Bonnie DOMEYER**. Their children are:

3503 i. **Thomas Lee THOMPSON** was born in 1994.

3079. **Heather Ann PECK** was born in 1977. Heather Ann PECK has one child:

3504 i. **Rebecka Ann PECK** was born in 1994.

3098. **Todd GREEN** was born in 1961. He married **Tara YATES** who was born in 1965. Todd GREEN and Tara YATES had the following children:

3505 i. **Natalie GREEN** was born in 1990.
3506 ii. **Lauren GREEN** was born in 1994.

3099. **Darin GREEN** was born in 1965. He married **Kelly YOUNG**. Their children are:

3507 i. **Kyle GREEN** was born in 1994.
3508 ii. **Chase GREEN** was born in 1997.

3100. **Brian GREEN** was born in 1968. He married **Amy LEVENS** who was born in 1965. Brian GREEN and Amy LEVENS have a son:

3509 i. **Gavin GREEN** was born in 1997.

3101. **Mark GREEN** was born in 1966. He married **Carmen LERMINI**. Their daughter is:

3510 i. **Rachel GREEN** was born in 1995.

3108. **Patrick Charles JONES** was born in 1959. He married **Sheena LEIGH**, and they have a son:

3511 i. **Casey Wayne JONES** was born in 1989.

3110. **Gary Wayne LANG** married **Linda Kay STEGER**. Gary and Linda had children:

3512 i. **Melissa Sue LANG** was born in 1983.
3513 ii. **Melanie Marie LANG** was born in 1986.

3111. **Ricky Lee LANG** was born in 1959. He married **Diane Kay SCHNEITER**. Their children are:

3514 i. **Kyle John LANG** was born in 1981.
3515 ii. **Brian Michael LANG** was born and died in 1983.
3516 iii. **Craig Allen LANG** was born in 1985.
3517 iv. **Kelsey Kay LANG** was born in 1994.

3112. **Scott Allen LANG** was born in 1965. He married **Junella Jo ALDEN**. They have a daughter:

3518 i. **Brittany Lynn LANG** was born in 1992.

3157. **Nancy Joan Howell STRUBLE** married **Albert Martin COMPTON**. They had these children:

3519 i. **Scott Allen COMPTON** married **Terry Elizabeth EZELL**.
3520 ii. **Laine David COMPTON** married **Candace Faith BOOTH**.
3521 iii. **Rondi Lynne COMPTON** married **Brian CAPPS**.

3158. **Barbara Jane Howell STRUBLE** married **Norman RICHARDS**. Their children are:

3522 i. **Terry Sue RICHARDS**.
3523 ii. **Mickey RICHARDS**.
3524 iii. **Billy Jo Shelley Elizabeth RICHARDS** married **Lawrence HATCH**.
3525 iv. **Jamie RICHARDS**.

3160. **Stephen John FRITTS** was born on 3 November 1950 in Phillipsburg, Warren County, New Jersey. He married **Shelly STAUFFER** on 1 September 1973. They have three daughters:

3526 i. **Courtney FRITTS** was born on 15 November 1978.
3527 ii. **Erin FRITTS** was born on 16 September 1981.
3528 iii. **Casey FRITTS** was born on 7 March 1984.

3162. **Kenneth Allan FRITTS** was born on 18 September 1953 in Phillipsburg. He married **Gwen WHEDON** on 16 July 1977. These are their children:

3529 i. **Elena FRITTS** was born on 21 July 1979.
3530 ii. **Rosa FRITTS** was born on 22 June 1980.
3531 iii. **Jacob FRITTS** was born on 29 August 1981.
3532 iv. **Lindsay FRITTS** was born in April 1991.

3163. **Rosalyn FRITTS** was born on 27 June 1955 in Phillipsburg. She married **Douglas DASHINE** on 5 March 1988. They had one child:

3533 i. **Brian Joseph FRITTS** was born on 12 March 1982.

3164. **David Charles FRITTS** was born on 25 October 1958. He married **Debra MEYERS** on 24 July 1981. They have these children:

3534 i. **Bruce FRITTS** was born on 24 June 1981.
3535 ii. **Tiffany FRITTS** was born on 23 June 1983.
3536 iii. **Alan FRITTS** was born n on 17 April 1985.

3176. **Arnold J. HOWELL Jr**. married **Patricia MOUNT**. Arnold and Patricia had these children:

3537 i. **Derek HOWELL** was born in 1987 in Washington,

Warren County, NJ.

3538 ii. **Morgan HOWELL** was born in 1992 in Washington.

3539 iii. **Blaire Kathleen HOWELL** was born on 11 August 1997 in Phillipsburg, Warren County, NJ.

3179. **Wayne Phillip HOWELL** was born on 3 October 1942. He worked for the New York Department of Public Works for several years, and then for Fay's Drug Company in the distribution center. He married **Bonnie Christine WRIGHT** who was born on 4 June 1947. Their children are:

3540 i. **Todd Jeffrey HOWELL** was born on 1 October 1968.

3541 ii. **Eric Matthew HOWELL** was born on 15 July 1973.

3181. **Dana Kurt HOWELL** was born on 14 November 1951. Dana worked in the parts department of a motorcycle shop. He married **Susan MAJORS** on 1 August 1981. Dana and Susan had two children:

3542 i. **Maranda June HOWELL** was born on 12 march 1982.

3543 ii. **Kory Robert HOWELL** was born on 22 July 1983.

3182. **Milan Gene HOWELL** was born on 10 July 1955. Milan worked at a wire mill. On 30 June 1979, he married **Robin Lee BEGGS** who was born on 9 July 1958. They have two children:

3544 i. **Heidi Lynn HOWELL** was born on 9 June 1980.

3545 ii. **Heather Lynn HOWELL** was born on 28 February 1984.

3184. **Tara HOWELL** was born in 1967. Tara has one child:

3546 i. **Chantel HOWELL** was born in 1987.

3190. **Jeffrey Ronald THOMPSON** was born in 1966. He married **Gail MYHOUSESKY**. Jeffrey Ronald THOMPSON and Gail MYHOUSESKY had the following children:

3547 i. **Elona Mae THOMPSON** was born in 1988.

3548 ii. **Mikala Renae THOMPSON** was born in 1992.

3191. **Robert Forest THOMPSON** was born in 1968. He married **Rhonda POWELL**. Robert Forest THOMPSON and Rhonda POWELL had the following children:

3549 i. **Robert James THOMPSON** was born in 1986.D

3550 ii. **Crystal Rachel THOMPSON** was born in 1987.

3192. **Richard Scott THOMPSON** was born in 1972. HE married **Shelley LITZ**. Richard Scott THOMPSON and Shelley LITZ have a daughter:

3551 i. **Aerial Jean THOMPSON** was born in 1992.

3193. **Daniel Paul THOMPSON** was born in 1974. He married **Jody WALLACE**. Daniel Paul THOMPSON and Jody WALLACE have a son:

3552 i. **Chad Daniel THOMPSON** was born in 1991.

3239. **Christine Marie ADLER** was born in 1966. She married **Brian HOLLIDAY**. Christine Marie ADLER and Brian HOLLIDAY have a son:

3553 i. **Nathan Douglas HOLLIDAY** was born in 1991.

3241. **Adam Stephen ADLER** was born in 1978. Adam's wife's name is not known. Adam Stephen ADLER and **UNKNOWN** have a son:

3554 i. **Corey Matthew ADLER** was born in 1993.

3243. **Patrick Lester JONES** was born in 1968. His wife, **Lisa ZIMMERMAN** was born in 1974. Patrick Lester JONES and Lisa ZIMMERMAN have a son:

3555 i. **Christopher Stephen JONES** was born in 1992.

3250. **Stacey Lyn SCHNEIDER** was born in 1975. Her husband, **Leon PEDHAM** was born in 1976. Stacey and Leon PEDHAM have a son:

3556 i. **Tory Benjamin Garret PEDHAM** was born in 1993.

3256. **Diane Elizabeth MORGAN** was born on 17 July 1963. She was married to **Samuel Allen BLYTHE** on 24 August 1985. Samuel Allen BLYTHE was born on 9 September 1959. Diane and Samuel BLYTHE had the following children:

3557 i. **Casey BLYTHE** was born on 16 May 1989.
3558 ii. **Samuel BLYTHE** was born on 1 October 1992.

ELEVENTH GENERATION

3412. **Steven KOCH Jr**. married **UNKNOWN**. Steven KOCH Jr. and UNKNOWN had the following children:

3559 i. **Noah KOCH**.
3560 ii. **Stephanie KOCH**.

3421. **Mark HOWELL** married **Cherry BERCAW** (daughter of **William BERCAW** and **Adele UNKNOWN**) on 29 March 1997.[248] They have a daughter:

3561 i. **Allison Marie HOWELL** was born on 11 December 1998 in Phillipsburg, NJ.[249]

3424. **Tracy RUSH** married **Steven GALASSO**. Tracy RUSH and Steven GALASSO had the following children:

3562 i. **Tyler GALASSO** was born in 1994.
3563 ii. **Travis GALASSO** was born on 30 September 1996 in Bethlehem, Northampton, County, PA.

3432. **Lori FLOREY** married **Unknown FEHNEL**. They live in Belfast, PA. They have one son.

3564 i. **Unknown FEHNEL**.

---

[248]Marriage announcement, Easton (PA) Express, 3 April 1997.
[249]Birth notice Easton Easton (PA) Express, 11 Dec 1998.

INDEX

www.ingramcontent.com/pod-product-compliance
Lightning Source LLC
Chambersburg PA
CBHW071635270326
41928CB00010B/1933
9780788414596